W9-CEF-902

Leningrad

Also by Michael Jones

The King's Mother
Bosworth 1485 – Psychology of a Battle
Agincourt 1415 – A Battlefield Guide
Stalingrad: How The Red Army Triumphed

Leningrad

State of Siege

MICHAEL JONES

A Member of the Perseus Books Group
New York

First published in the United States in 2008 by Basic Books,
A Member of the Perseus Books Group
Published in Great Britain in 2008 by John Murray

Books published by Basic Books are available at special discounts for bulk purchases in the United States by corporations, institutions, and other organizations. For more information, please contact the Special Markets Department at the Perseus Books Group, 2300 Chestnut Street, Suite 200, Philadelphia, PA 19103, or call (800) 810-4145, ext. 5000, or e-mail special.markets@perseusbooks.com.

A CIP catalog record for this book is available from the Library of Congress
ISBN-13: 978-0-465-01153-7
LCCN: 2008921305

British Hardback ISBN: 978-0-7165-6922-7
British Paperback ISBN: 978-0-7165-6932-6
10 9 8 7 6 5 4 3 2 1

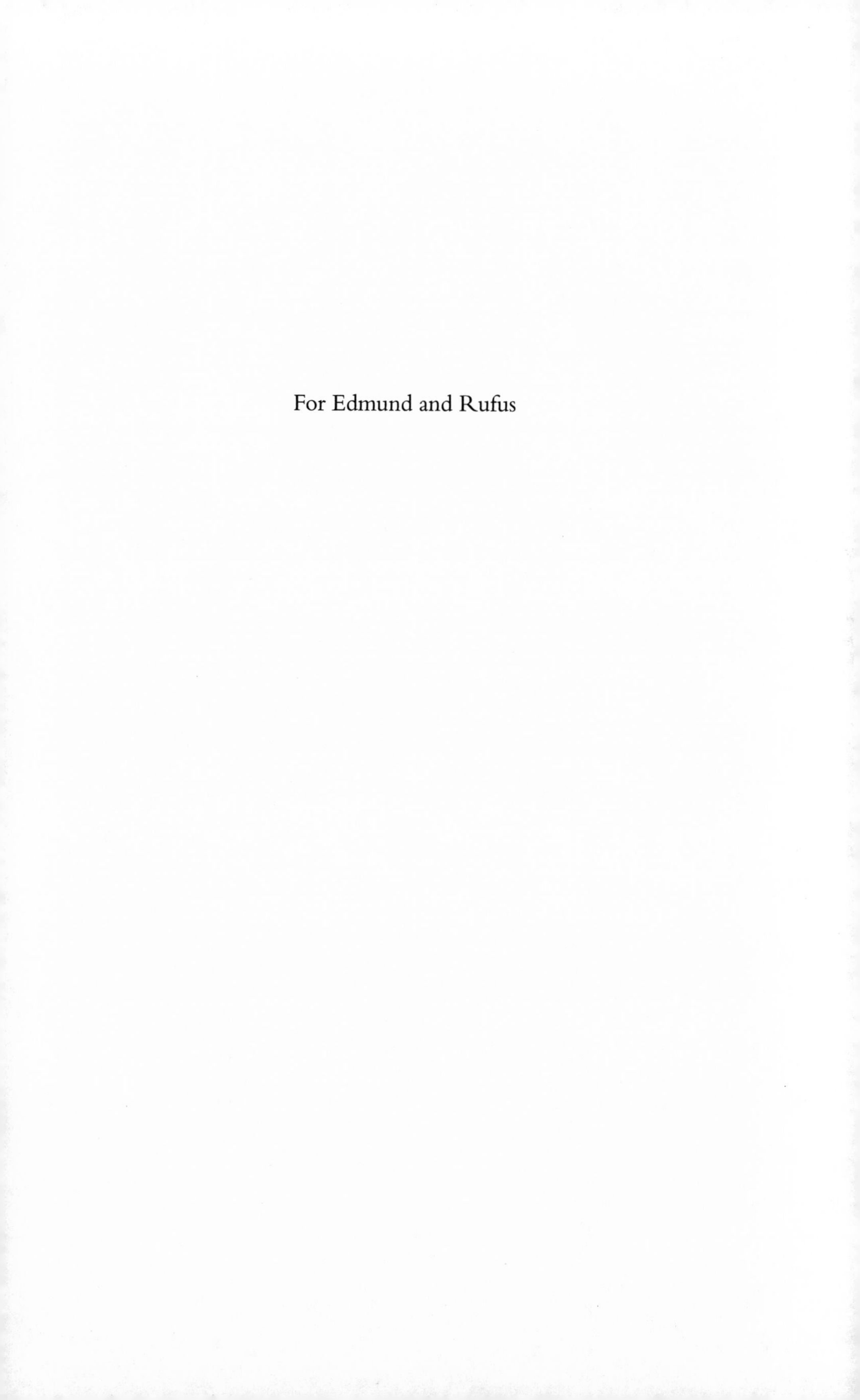

For Edmund and Rufus

Contents

List of Illustrations

Acknowledgements: I am profoundly grateful to Elena Martilla, who allowed me unlimited use of her siege drawings (1, 4–7, 10–13, 16, 18–19, 23, 29) and to the Director of the Museum of the Blockade, St Petersburg, for permission to reproduce the photographs (2–3, 8-9, 14–15, 17, 20–22, 24–28, 30–34). The curator of the museum's archive kindly found the photographs of the performance of Shostakovich's Seventh. The photo of the Piskaryov Cemetery (35) was taken by me.

List of Maps

Preface

In early September 1941 Hitler's armies cut the last roads leading into besieged Leningrad (now St Petersburg) and, in the words of the poet Olga Berggolts, 'the noose of the blockade tightened around the city's throat'. There followed the most horrific siege in history.

This book grew out of my work as a battlefield guide on the Second World War's Eastern Front. I am grateful to Midas and Holts Battlefield Tours, who helped set up the Siege of Leningrad tour, and to Oleg Alexandrov, of our associated Russian travel company, who first facilitated meetings with Red Army veterans of the fighting. I want to take my readers on a journey, allowing them to experience the exceptional power of this story – its sheer horror, but also its capacity to inspire and move us.

My understanding of the siege is informed not by official Soviet records of the people's valour but by actual accounts of those trapped in the city. I am deeply grateful to three veterans who have been a constant source of encouragement and support: Svetlana Magaeva, who generously gave me access to her psychological profiles of siege survivors; artist Elena Martilla, who allowed me to use her remarkable collection of sketches – drawn during the blockade – and Irina Skripachyova, head of the St Petersburg Siege Veterans' Association, who arranged countless meetings for me. All have enormously enhanced this work.

I use an interview process that I employed with Red Army veterans in my previous book on the battle of Stalingrad, building up a rapport and then working together to establish the psychological contours of the story. I am deeply grateful to the siege survivors who have shared their experiences with me and who have pointed me towards diaries – published and unpublished – that are honest about the horror descending on the city. Their many contributions are acknowledged in the endnotes. A particularly moving meeting was with survivors of the Lychkovo train massacre on their first ever reunion, in March 2007.

Others have perished, and can speak to us only through their personal papers. I owe another debt of thanks to the director of the Blockade Museum for allowing me access to its many siege diaries and letters. Olga Prut, who oversees the Museum 'The Muses Were Not Silent', dedicated to cultural life during the siege, and especially the performance of Shostakovich's Seventh, and musicologist Professor Andrei Krukov, have kindly given me additional material.

I also draw on accounts already published. The siege diaries of Vera Inber, Elena Kochina and Elena Skrjabina exist in translation, as does the groundbreaking compilation by Ales Adamovich and Daniil Granin, *A Book of the Blockade*. Cynthia Simmons and Nina Perlina have also brought out an important collection of siege experiences. More is available in Russian, and fresh material is emerging all the time – the most recent, from the Centre for Oral History at the European University of St Petersburg, came out in 2006. And I have greatly benefited from the major research on the siege undertaken by Richard Bidlack and Nikita Lomagin.

Lena Yakovleva undertook translation and interpretation work in Moscow, and Anna Artiushina did the same in St Petersburg, as well as locating many valuable references for me. Caroline Walton made a number of additional translations and kindly provided me with extracts from Alexander Boldyrev's diary. David M. Glantz and Albert Axell have also helped me with a number of specific points. In general I have followed sources' transliterations from Cyrillic script, although on occasions I have standardised spellings of forenames and word endings.

I am grateful to David Glantz for background material on the city map of Leningrad, and to Svetlana Magaeva and Albert Pleysier for help with the maps of the siege lines and the 'Road of Life'. The German advance is drawn from information in Leon Goure's *The Siege of Leningrad*; the dispositions in Operation Spark are from

Robert F. Baumann's 'Operation Spark: breaking through the siege of Leningrad', in *Combined Arms in Battle since 1939*, ed. Roger J. Spillar (Fort Leavenworth, 1992).

I owe a particular debt of gratitude to my agent, Charlie Viney, and to Roland Philipps and Rowan Yapp at John Murray, for their encouragement and support as this work developed. The first three chapters of the book are thematic, and look at the period leading up to the siege of Leningrad from the point of view of the advancing Germans, the Soviet authorities defending the city and finally the ordinary civilians. The subsequent chapters follow a roughly chronological sequence. Their focal point is the three-month period from mid-December 1941 to mid-March 1942 when conditions within Leningrad were at their worst.

In 1969 Harrison Salisbury brought out a book on the siege. Much new material has emerged since, and a complete retelling has now become possible. I am a military historian with a strong interest in battle psychology and the vital role of morale: what motivates people to fight on in the most desperate of circumstances. I look at German strategy and Russian tactics, but concentrate more on the inner battlefield of the psyche. The suffering of Leningrad's civilian population and the resilience of many of the survivors move me deeply. Leningraders withstood the siege at extraordinary cost. I want to give readers a fresh understanding of what they endured, and how they emerged victorious.

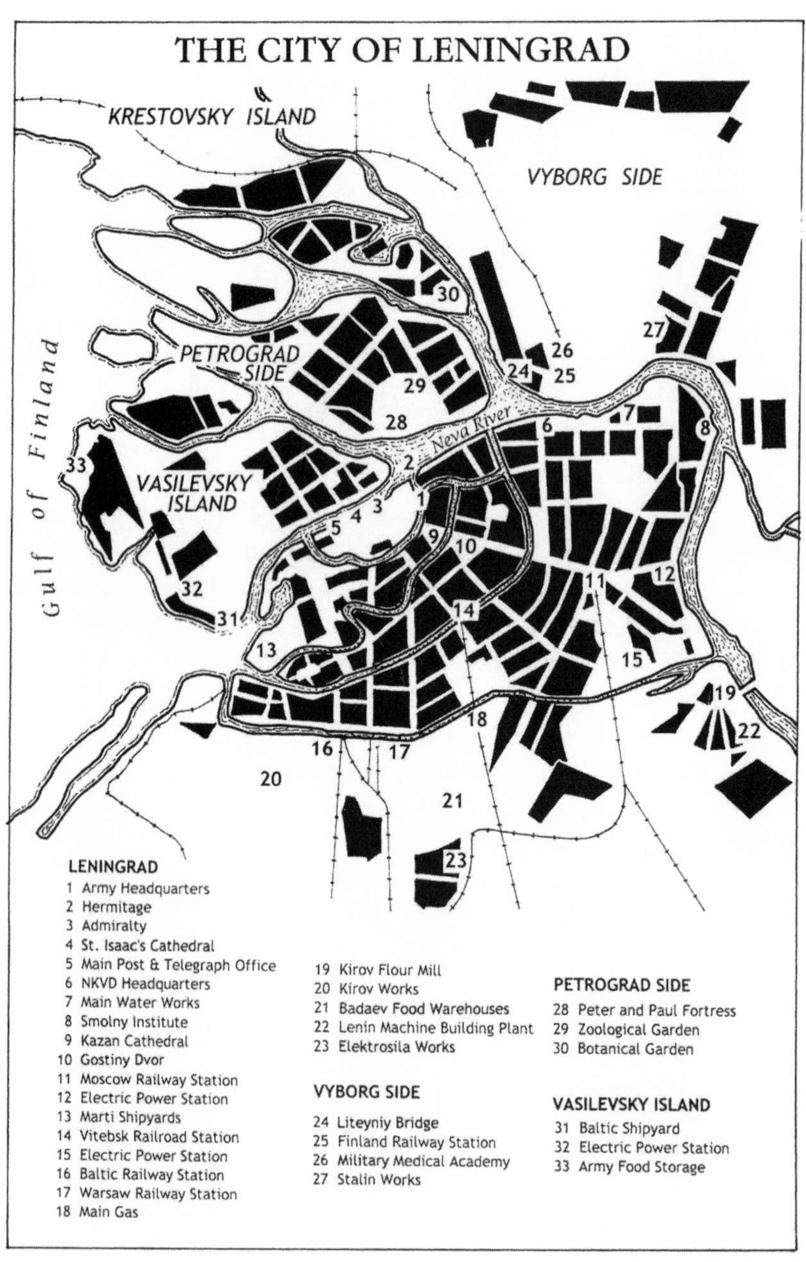
THE CITY OF LENINGRAD
KRESTOVSKY ISLAND
VYBORG SIDE
PETROGRAD SIDE
VASILEVSKY ISLAND
Gulf of Finland
Neva River
LENINGRAD
1 Army Headquarters
2 Hermitage
3 Admiralty
4 St. Isaac's Cathedral
5 Main Post & Telegraph Office
6 NKVD Headquarters
7 Main Water Works
8 Smolny Institute
9 Kazan Cathedral
10 Gostiny Dvor
11 Moscow Railway Station
12 Electric Power Station
13 Marti Shipyards
14 Vitebsk Railroad Station
15 Electric Power Station
16 Baltic Railway Station
17 Warsaw Railway Station
18 Main Gas
19 Kirov Flour Mill
20 Kirov Works
21 Badaev Food Warehouses
22 Lenin Machine Building Plant
23 Elektrosila Works
VYBORG SIDE
24 Liteyniy Bridge
25 Finland Railway Station
26 Military Medical Academy
27 Stalin Works
PETROGRAD SIDE
28 Peter and Paul Fortress
29 Zoological Garden
30 Botanical Garden
VASILEVSKY ISLAND
31 Baltic Shipyard
32 Electric Power Station
33 Army Food Storage

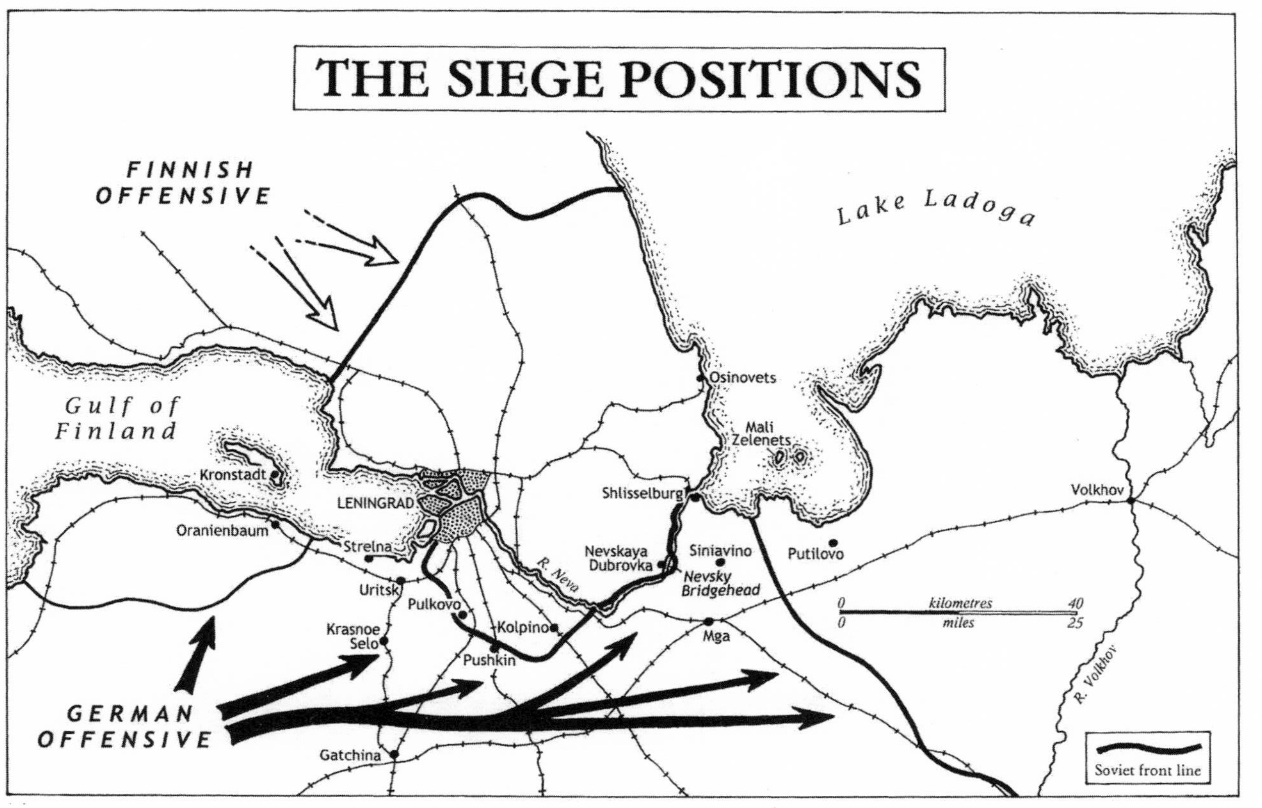
THE SIEGE POSITIONS
FINNISH OFFENSIVE
Lake Ladoga
Gulf of Finland
Osinovets
Mali Zelenets
Kronstadt
LENINGRAD
Oranienbaum
Strelna
Shlisselburg
Volkhov
Nevskaya Dubrovka
Siniavino
Nevsky Bridgehead
Putilovo
R. Neva
Uritsk
Pulkovo
Krasnoe Selo
Kolpino
Pushkin
Mga
0 kilometres 40
0 miles 25
R. Volkhov
GERMAN OFFENSIVE
Gatchina
Soviet front line

Timeline

The siege of Leningrad – popularly known as the 900 days – lasted 872 days, from 8 September 1941, when the Germans first blockaded the city, to 27 January 1944, when their armies were finally repulsed from Leningrad. Here are some of the key dates.

22 June 1941: Germany invades the Soviet Union.

26 June: Manstein's LVI Panzer Corps seizes the Dvina bridges.

8 July: Hoepner's Fourth Panzer Group breaches the Stalin Line at Pskov.

11 July: Marshal Kliment Voroshilov is appointed commander of the North-Western Front and takes over Leningrad's defence.

14 July: Reinhardt's Panzers establish a bridgehead on the far side of the Luga river, 'opening the gates to Leningrad'.

15–16 August: Manstein turns the Soviet position at Lake Ilmen, allowing a German advance on Leningrad from the south-east.

18 August: The Lychkovo train massacre: the Luftwaffe bombs a trainload of Leningrad children being evacuated from the city.

8 September: The Germans capture Shlisselburg, blockading Leningrad, and commencing an 872-day siege. The Badaev food warehouses are destroyed by incendiary bombs.

11 September: Voroshilov is dismissed by Stalin, and replaced by General Georgi Zhukov.

20 September: Zhukov sends Soviet forces across Neva river to establish the Nevsky bridgehead.

22 September: Hitler states: 'All offers of surrender from Leningrad must be rejected, as the problem of housing and feeding the people cannot and should not be solved by us. In this struggle for survival, we have no interest in keeping even a proportion of the city's population alive.'

5 October: Zhukov ordered back to Moscow. Andrei Zhdanov is left in overall charge of Leningrad's defence.

8 November: The Germans capture Tikhvin, severing the last rail route bringing supplies to the city, via Lake Ladoga. Hitler announces triumphantly: 'Leningrad is doomed to die of famine.'

22 November: First convoy of lorries brings in supplies across Lake Ladoga's 'Road of Life'.

10 December: The Red Army recaptures Tikhvin.

1 January 1942: Leningrad now has only a two-day supply of food in its reserve, and no supplementary fats or protein.

8 January: First hospital opens for the treatment of starvation.

25 January: Last working hydroelectric power station closes, leaving Leningrad without running water, heat or electricity.

27 January: Food supply and distribution breaks down within the city.

31 January: Leningrad's registry office records 96,694 deaths this month; many more go unreported.

18 February: First reports of a dysentery outbreak in Leningrad.

28 February: 192,766 deaths reported for January and February. The unofficial figure is believed to exceed 20,000 a day.

27 March: All able-bodied citizens clean the city's streets and courtyards.

1 April: Lieutenant-General Leonid Govorov takes command of Leningrad Front.

5 April: On 700th Anniversary of Alexander Nevsky's victory over the Teutonic Knights, the Germans launch an air attack on the Baltic Fleet.

15 April: Tram services resume along three routes into the city.

27 April: The last Soviet defenders on the Nevsky bridgehead are overrun by the Germans.

18 June: A fuel pipeline is laid across Lake Ladoga, bringing petrol into Leningrad.

9 August: Performance of Shostakovich's Seventh Symphony at Leningrad's Philharmonic Hall.

4 September: Manstein has to divert forces intended for a fresh assault on the city and fight a battle of attrition south of Lake Ladoga.

18 January 1943: Operation Spark breaks German blockade.

6 February: First trainload of provisions reaches Leningrad along the overland route.

21 September: Army Group North prepares a fall-back position – the Panther Line – 150 miles west of Leningrad.

15 January 1944: Soviet assault against remaining German siege positions. The soldiers form up under their colours and make the oath: 'We swear vengeance for the agony of Leningrad!'

27 January: Govorov's offensive secures the complete liberation of Leningrad – ending the 872-day siege.

Bread Rations

The rationing system used by the city authorities during the siege of Leningrad was divided into three categories: the first was for blue-collar workers, who received the largest amount of food, the second was for white-collar workers, the third for their dependants, who received the smallest. This system reflected the priorities of the Soviet state – it was designed to maximise industrial output, and it provided minimal protection for the most vulnerable within the city. Many homeless refugees who arrived in Leningrad from the Baltic States or the surrounding countryside were unable to secure any ration cards at all. As the siege worsened, and supplies of flour diminished, the bread was increasingly adulterated with other substances, including sawdust and wood shavings.

These statistics tell a grim story – but it is not the full one. Towards the end of January 1942, several days after an increase in the bread ration was announced, there was a complete collapse in the food-distribution system and ordinary people were unable to obtain any food at all for about a week. Temperatures had dropped to below −30 degrees Celsius, and there was no longer any electricity, heating, light or water in the city. This catastrophe – which dramatically accelerated the death rate, and led to parts of Leningrad falling under the control of gangsters and cannibals – was subsequently suppressed in Soviet histories of the siege.

The lowest allowance – 125 grams – is the equivalent of three slices from a medium-sized loaf. Such a portion would ideally provide about 250 calories, but bread in besieged Leningrad – increasingly adulterated – contained far less. A man needs approximately 2,500 calories of food a day to sustain body weight and health, a woman 2,000, and a child 1,000 plus 100 for each year of life.

Leningrad bread rations – in grams:

	Factory workers	**Office workers**	**Dependants**
18 July 1941	800	600	400
2 September 1941	600	400	300
11 September 1941	500	300	250
1 October 1941	400	200	200
13 November 1941	300	150	150
20 November 1941	250	125	125
25 December 1941	350	200	200
24 January 1942	400	300	250
11 February 1942	500	400	300
22 February 1942	600	500	400

Figures reproduced courtesy of the Museum of the Blockade, St Petersburg.

Introduction

WALKING THROUGH THE streets of St Petersburg one is overwhelmed by colour. This city of islands – the Venice of the North – is radiant with every hue. My eyes feast on the jewel-coloured buildings, the burnished golden domes, the rich amber stonework. Anyone experiencing St Petersburg feels profoundly in touch with the glories of its past. It is almost impossible to imagine a grey life being lived here. This is where Pushkin created his greatest poems, where Dostoevsky wrote *The Brothers Karamazov* and where Andrei Voronikhin – once a serf – built the cathedral of the Kazan Icon of the Mother of God. All the richness of Russian artistic life finds expression in this place.

This was the birthplace of the Bolshevik Revolution – an ideology which replaced inherited power and privilege with a belief in the supremacy of the people – and its tsarist nomenclature mutated to Leningrad. I am intrigued that Bolshevism was born in the place where the creative soul of the Russian people most fully expressed itself. The battleship *Aurora*, which signalled the storming of the Winter Palace, is still maintained here as a memorial to that epoch-defining moment.

The city was always far more than just a community of artists. From its very inception, on 16 May 1703, when Peter the Great is said to have snatched a halberd from one of his soldiers, cut two strips of turf, and declared, 'Here there shall be a town,' it has had to struggle for its existence. Conditions were dire as a workforce recruited from prisoners of war and volunteers from the far reaches of the Russian Empire struggled against starvation, cold, disease and exhaustion to erect the wooden fortress in the marshes that was to evolve into a great city. But at no point in its turbulent history has it come closer to utter destruction than under the onslaught of Nazi Germany during the Second World War.

I am walking along the Liteyniy Prospect in central St Petersburg, one of the oldest streets in the city, running due north to the River Neva, and now a bustling shopping district. I turn off into Solyanoy Pereulok, a quieter residential area, looking for the distinctive shape of the twin anti-aircraft cannon which flank the entrance to a remarkable museum, devoted to the 'blockade', the three-year siege of Bolshevik Leningrad during the Second World War. Visiting the Blockade Museum is a profoundly moving experience. I go first to its centrepiece – a reconstruction of how a typical Leningrad apartment looked during the siege. The windows are boarded up and the walls blackened with smoke. There are few pieces of furniture – most have been burned as fuel on the tiny stove. This was an absolute struggle for survival. The trams stopped running, the power had given out, food was dwindling away. Day after dreadful day, people retreated into themselves and, through three abysmally cold Russian winters, tried to stay alive.

The museum has more than 35,000 exhibits, including personal belongings of the defenders of the city, army newspapers, diaries, soldiers' letters from the front, photographs, weapons and decorations. But there is one item I return to, again and again. It is a drawing by a nine-year-old boy, made in January 1942. He had sketched a loaf of bread and written underneath it: 'Starvation – how hungry I am!' Within months he was dead, along with countless thousands of others, victims of the most terrible siege in history.

This suffering was no accident. The German armies besieging Leningrad were deliberately starving the city's inhabitants. Much denial of this stark fact still remains, and it came to a head in 2004 with the opening of a cemetery on the sixtieth anniversary of the lifting of the blockade, for Wehrmacht soldiers who had died during the siege. Photographer Michael Stephan, who spoke with many of the German veterans returning to the site, stated bluntly: 'I have a problem with this big cemetery and some of those who come here to remember their fallen comrades, with their banners and medals, claiming that they were unaware of civilian deaths. Many still speak of themselves as victims. I ask them, "Victims of what – Hitler? You were soldiers. You cannot be unaware of the fact that you were encircling a really big city. You must have seen it. You can't be blind." '

At the Nuremberg tribunal in 1946 a German prisoner of war testified that the besieging army punctiliously shelled Leningrad in the morning from 8.00 to 9.00, then from 11.00 to 12.00, in the afternoon from 5.00 to 6.00, and in the evening from 8.00 to 10.00. 'This way', he said, 'the shelling would kill as many people as possible, destroy factories and vital buildings, and most importantly, attempt to destroy the morale of the Leningraders.' Alongside this onslaught, famine was a weapon of conscious choice.

This vibrant, cultured city of more than two and a half million people was facing a calculated assault. Its very right to exist was at stake. Siege survivor Lidiya Lifanova has not thrown away a piece of food for over sixty years, stating simply that 'For me, bread is priceless.' By the winter of 1941 many Leningraders' daily ration of bread was a mere 125 grams. This was adulterated with cottonseed, flax cake and mouldy grain. The Blockade Museum demonstrates these pitifully small rations, together with the scales used to measure them.

Vladimir Moroz remembers the pain of climbing up stairs in a state of emaciation: 'It was like a bad dream – where you can't move despite repeated, desperate attempts.' In the struggle against famine people were to face horrors we would now find unimaginable. Starvation tore apart families, tore apart the very fabric of life. One account in the Blockade Museum by a siege survivor is chilling: 'I watched my mother and father die. I knew perfectly well they were starving. But I wanted their bread more than I wanted them to stay alive. And they knew that. That's what I remember about the blockade: the feeling that you wanted your parents to die because you wanted their bread.'

The Blockade Museum exhibits some of the diaries of those who survived the siege. Many more are kept in its archives. I am drawn to the story of Vera Lyudyno. Lyudyno was seventeen when the siege began. She had been born with slightly deformed joints and was in a cast due to surgery performed on her legs, so was unable to retreat to the air-raid shelter when the warnings sounded, and had to stay above ground. Her father remained to comfort and reassure her. They would play chess, and when she became too frightened he would gently remind her, 'Your move.'

Vera Lyudyno could do nothing but stare out of the window of her apartment and describe what she subsequently recorded in her diary: 'I wrote honestly about the frightful hunger, constant bombardments, the frozen bodies of dead people.' Her account reflects not just the city's heroic struggle, but a darker story also – the story of the inability of the Soviet state to protect its citizens and the cruelty the siege sometimes brought out in its victims. 'It was a time that revealed the worst and the best qualities of people, most of whom already lived by one instinct – to eat.' One of her neighbours, an opera singer, devoured his entire monthly ration of seven ounces of meat all at once so that no one would steal it. Another neighbour wore a bag on her chest where she kept her bread portion, fearing her daughter or grandchildren might tear it from her. 'That woman died later with the bag still on her chest.'

There was widespread looting and cannibalism. Children in her building disappeared, only for their clothes and bones to be found later in the apartment of a violinist neighbour. The violinist's five-year-old son also disappeared. Lyudyno's family resorted to cooking gelatine from leather belts, or glue flavoured with bay leaves: 'When you ate it your stomach felt like it was on fire and you got very thirsty. But the trick was not to drink anything, to preserve the feeling of satiety.'

Lyudyno's mother lost her ration card when she left the city to help build the defences. Party officials confiscated it. 'My mama told me that many people were dying there from hunger, because they had almost no food. But someone in authority really wanted to hide that fact, so the bodies of these people were put in carts, propped up as if they were sitting, and then driven off somewhere.' These were unwelcome truths to the Soviet authorities, and within a month of the 900-day siege being lifted, on 27 January 1944, Lyudyno had been arrested and her diary confiscated as anti-state propaganda. Within a few years, the original Museum of the Defence of Leningrad suffered a similar fate. It had put on its first exhibition in 1944 and the building was officially opened in 1946. But the starkness of what it contained was deemed too painful and it was closed within three years, its contents dispersed, its director imprisoned. It was not until 1989 that the Blockade Museum was eventually founded.

State censorship was rigorous and arbitrary. Official policy never allowed the release of any photograph of war-torn Leningrad that showed more than three dead people. When Harrison Salisbury's book on the siege was published in 1969, on the twenty-fifth anniversary of its ending, *Pravda* brought out a full-page attack, charging Salisbury with besmirching the heroism of Leningrad and demeaning the Communist Party's role in the city's defence.

What Salisbury fought to establish is now openly acknowledged. But what Leningrad endured was far more horrifying than he described. In 2002 secret police records were released. They reveal that during the siege at least 300 people were executed for cannibalism and over 1,400 imprisoned for it. In the early days of the blockade, morale was often desperately low. New research shows that in the winter of 1941 law and order began to break down and parts of the city fell under the control of gangsters and cannibals. Leningrad was teetering on the very edge of the abyss, but, remarkably, that collapse did not happen. It was not merely the Red Army that saved Leningrad from utter ruin. This book will tell the story of this city's survival, and what made that possible – how the people of Leningrad found the resources within themselves to endure and to survive.

For, while some of the city's inhabitants disintegrated under the strain, others fought to preserve their human values. In the midst of horror, as the siege survivor Irina Skripachyova described it, 'helping others was crucial to survival'. People moved in with relatives and friends, supporting each other. 'Sharing became our way of life,' Skripachyova said, 'and helping others, keeping busy, working, taking responsibility, gave strength to people.' She emphasised the importance of morale and motivation, even in the most desperate of circumstances. Daniil Granin, who spent many years interviewing siege survivors, also said: 'Morale was one of the major characteristics of the heroic battle for Leningrad, not patriotism, but rather the perseverance of the intellect, the protest against the humiliation of hunger, against the dehumanisation. Those who saved others were saved themselves. Art and culture helped.'

How was it possible to keep a sense of human values during this mind-numbing catastrophe? Dmitry Likhachev, who maintained his scientific research during the siege – more as an act of faith than anything else – wrote movingly: 'The human brain was the last to go. When limbs stopped moving and the fingers could no longer do up buttons, and there was no strength left to close the mouth, the skin grew darker and stuck to the teeth, the brain continued working. People wrote diaries, philosophical treatises and demonstrated unbelievable tenacity.'

Faced with unimaginable suffering, extraordinary inner resources also came to life. Nine-year-old Klara Taubert was one of the few survivors of the Lychkovo massacre of 18 August 1941 – when the Luftwaffe deliberately bombed a trainload of children who were being evacuated from Leningrad. She made the journey back into the city in a state of total shock, and when she arrived at the family home – her face blackened, barefoot and in rags – she was so dishevelled that at first no one recognised her. But that autumn everything changed. As the city's food supplies diminished Klara found that she loved helping people, and she began to thrive on this sense of responsibility. During the winter of 1941–2, as starvation took hold, and the bodies of neighbours were found lying in the passageway, Taubert's family locked their last, emergency supply of bread in a small cupboard and gave Klara the key. They told her that they trusted her strength of character. 'That trust sustained me,' Taubert said proudly, 'and gave me a supreme sense of self-belief.'

The Blockade Museum testifies to that tenacity and shows how people managed to survive against such brutal odds. All around the main hall are clustered exhibits on artistic life during the siege. Despite the lack of resources, several theatres and concert halls continued to function throughout. Even in the winter of 1941–2, when temperatures plummeted to −40 degrees Celsius, Leningrad's starving inhabitants managed to attend exhibitions and concerts. Radio Leningrad was the lifeline that held people together and through it they shared their culture and encouraged one another. The sound recording of the poet Anna Akhmatova, speaking to her fellow citizens in September 1941, is preserved and it catches the mood of defiance. Akhmatova had heard the 'dragon's shriek' of falling bombs, as with a gas mask over her shoulder she guarded roofs, made sandbags and wrote verses. She spoke quietly: 'The Germans want to destroy our city – the city of Peter, the city of Pushkin, of Dostoevsky and Alexander Blok, the city of great culture and achievement. This city is part of my life. In Leningrad I became a poet. I, like all of you, live with one unconquerable belief – that Leningrad will never be fascist.'

The greatest symbol of this defiance was an extraordinary orchestral concert. On 9 August 1942 the besieged city put on a performance of Shostakovich's Seventh Symphony. Another museum, at School No. 235 in St Petersburg's suburbs, is dedicated to it. A huge bronze of Shostakovich – along with the famous poster announcing the concert – dominates the museum anteroom. We see sketches of the orchestra on display, visual records of this remarkable event: battered music-stands, torn sheet music and some of the original instruments. The outsize concert outfit of the emaciated conductor, Karl Eliasberg, is exhibited. Wasting away through hunger, he conducted the orchestra with his dinner jacket hanging from him like a shroud.

The symbolic importance of this concert was enormous. Composer Dmitry Shostakovich had stayed in Leningrad and begun work on his Seventh Symphony during the first month of the blockade. Later, Stalin insisted that he be evacuated, but Shostakovich dedicated the finished symphony to his native city. In March 1942 the musical score was flown into besieged Leningrad by special military plane.

Trombonist Viktor Orlovsky is one of the two surviving musicians who performed at the Leningrad premiere of the Seventh Symphony on 9 August 1942. 'Being an artist during the siege was both an overwhelming and heartbreaking experience,' Orlovsky recalls. 'The halls were always packed, which I thought was extraordinary.' The Radio Committee Orchestra held its first rehearsal on 30 March 1942. It lasted a mere twenty minutes, with Eliasberg so feeble that he had to be driven in on a sledge. The orchestra had been re-formed with one powerful idea in mind – to give a sense of dignity and worth to starving Leningraders living without electricity or heat. The Germans had boasted that they would capture the city on 9 August and hold a victory celebration at Leningrad's Astoria Hotel. The date for the Seventh Symphony's premiere was thus deliberately chosen.

Orlovsky vividly remembers the atmosphere of the concert: 'People were all dressed up and some had even had their hair done. It felt like a victory. At the end, our conductor, Eliasberg, received one bouquet of flowers from a teenage girl. She turned to the orchestra and said simply, "My family did this because life has to go on as normal – whatever happens around us." '

It was this unconquerable spirit which saved Leningrad. Many years after the war Karl Eliasberg was approached by a group of German tourists, who said that they had come to the city especially to see him. They had been in the besieging army outside the city, so close that they were able to intercept Leningrad's radio signals, and hear the broadcast of Shostakovich's Seventh. Now these veterans said: 'It had a slow but powerful effect on us. The realisation began to dawn that we would never take Leningrad. But something else started to happen. We began to see that there was something stronger than starvation, fear and death – the will to stay human.'

Before leaving St Petersburg for the first time, I travelled to the city's northern suburbs, to visit the Piskaryov Memorial Cemetery.

At the nadir of the siege, in the winter of 1941–2, the mass burials had begun here. Nobody had the strength to dig the frozen ground, so sappers blasted pits into which the mass of unidentified bodies was tipped. Over half a million were buried like this. With wood desperately needed for heating Leningraders' frozen apartments, few could afford coffins. After the war, it was decided to transform the site into a memorial to the siege. The inscription on the entrance gate declares: 'To the victims of the blockade. Your heroic deed will rest eternal in the hearts of generations to come.' As I walked down the cemetery's main central avenue I saw a succession of low grassy mounds. There were 186 in all, with each marked by a granite slab, simply recording the year of burial of those lying beneath it. Then, by the memorial fence, overlooking a small lake, I found a stunning image: a burial urn and a sprig. The urn represents the city's grief; the sprig is a symbol of life that continues.

To my Western eyes, the lack of crosses in the cemetery is disconcerting. The sheer enormity of this place creates a sense of remoteness – the suffering and the courage of ordinary civilians is somehow lost in the vastness which, for all its solemnity, is not on a human scale. By using the scattered fragments of Leningraders' war diaries and personal reminiscences I want to bring humanity back into this extraordinary story and allow these lost voices to speak again.

The terrible siege of Leningrad was not all heroic deeds and selfless actions. People were driven to ugly extremes, and in such desperation not every citizen behaved as a hero of the revolution should. When the human fullness of the story is lost – the struggle, the failures, the horror – a vital dimension of the experience is lost with it. Real courage lies not in unthinking heroism, but in the very act of overcoming fear and despair.

After the war the poet Olga Berggolts visited this vast cemetery. Somewhere under one of those immense monuments her own husband lay buried. She herself had endured the entire blockade, but was shaken by the mile-long avenue with its markers and laconic inscriptions: '1941', '1942', '1943', '1944'. So many nameless victims, she reflected. Later her words were to be carved on the granite memorial in the cemetery:

> Know you who gaze upon these stones,
> None is forgotten, and nothing is forgotten!

1

'An Almost Scientific Method'

The German Advance

IT HAD BEEN a quiet night shift for signals operator Mikhail Neishtadt at the Leningrad Military District HQ. Then suddenly, just before 4.00 a.m. on 22 June 1941, the telegraph machine came to life. It was Red Army HQ – Leningrad's military commander was 'wanted urgently for consultation'. Neishtadt was nonplussed. Something was clearly up – but what? The commander wasn't even in the city that night, so he decided to put a call through to his chief of staff.

The staff officer thoroughly resented being woken up and arrived at HQ forty minutes later in a foul mood. 'This had better be important,' he snarled. A second telegram had arrived and Neishtadt passed it to him. Its single, stark sentence read: 'German troops have crossed the borders of the Soviet Union.' Operation Barbarossa – Hitler's invasion of Russia – had begun.

'It was like a nightmare,' Neishtadt said, 'and we all desperately wanted to wake up from it, and find everything normal again.' Nobody could quite believe that Germany had launched an attack. The two countries had agreed a peace treaty, after all, and Hitler was fighting a war against Britain in the west. At 5.20 a.m. Marshal Timoshenko, the Soviet Union's defence minister, came on to the line. 'Prepare our troops for war – but do not engage,' Timoshenko said carefully. Then, struggling to master his emotions, he repeated several times, 'We must not be provocative. Under no circumstances must our troops retaliate.'

Hearing these words, Neishtadt felt a chill pass through his body. 'Our supreme command could not comprehend what was happening,' he admitted.

> Still reeling in shock, they decided that our army – which was under a devastating attack – should nevertheless not respond. With hindsight, such a reaction was clearly nonsensical, but we were imagining that the war would somehow just go away. My shift was supposed to finish at 8.00 a.m., but the city authorities kept us locked in the building until midday. In those first, terrible hours, they didn't want anyone to know about the German invasion – they hoped against hope that it might be some kind of misunderstanding, that it all might still be rectified.

It soon became clear, however, that this was not some little misunderstanding on the border, but a colossal assault involving three million German troops and thousands of tanks and planes, advancing along an 1,800-mile front running from the Baltic to the Black Sea. 'A cascade of explosions reverberated around us,' Wehrmacht infantryman Wilhelm Lubbeck remembered. 'Our artillery unleashed a short but devastating bombardment of the enemy's positions, and the flashes of light from the explosions lit the entire eastern horizon. Then, as dawn broke, a ceaseless droning echoed in the sky above us. Wave after wave of planes were appearing – Heinkels and Junkers, Stukas and Messerschmitts – all flying east.' Then Lubbeck heard something different. A deep, powerful rumbling shook the ground around him. Hundreds of tank engines were revving up. The Panzers were on the move.

Orders had reached Wilhelm Lubbeck's unit just a few days earlier announcing that 'the invasion of Russia was at hand'. The men were assembled in East Prussia close to the little town of Tilsit, where the Emperor Napoleon of France and Tsar Alexander of Russia had conducted their abortive peace negotiations a century and a half earlier. The apparently cordial discussions had availed nothing: in 1812 Napoleon had launched a massive invasion. Now another was commencing on the same gigantic scale. 'Preparations in the previous few weeks had suggested an attack against the Soviet Union might be imminent,' German infantryman Walter Stoll recalled, 'but we could hardly believe it when it happened.' A vast chain of events was being set in motion.

It was a moment the Führer had long awaited. At 3.00 a.m. on 22 June, an hour before the attack began, his order of the day was read to the troops:

> Soldiers of the Eastern Front, weighed down for many months by grave anxieties, compelled to keep silent, I can at last speak openly to you. At this moment, a military build-up is taking place which has no equal in world history . . . You are going into action in order to save the whole of European civilisation and culture. German soldiers, you are about to join battle – a hard and crucial battle. The destiny of Europe, the future of the German Reich, the existence of our nation, now lies in your hands alone.

The invasion had been kept secret from those on the front line, but Hitler had been planning it for many months. Just before the Second World War Germany and the Soviet Union had signed a non-aggression treaty, an alliance of expediency allowing them together to carry out the brutal partition of Poland before Hitler turned his attention to the war in western Europe. But in the autumn of 1939, shortly after the treaty was signed, the Führer's adjutant, Nicolaus von Below, remembered the German dictator saying that the war in the west was only a brief diversion, 'so that he would not be stabbed in the back when he launched his decisive confrontation with Bolshevism'.

In July 1940 Hitler began informing chosen army leaders of these plans. He instructed a small team, headed by General Friedrich Paulus, to work out how the invasion might be conducted and then report back to him. That summer the Führer ordered a large military complex to be built in the forests of eastern Prussia, near the town of Rastenburg. It masqueraded as a chemical plant, but in fact it was a sprawling warren of offices, bunkers and conference rooms. Hitler had already chosen its name – the Wolf's Lair. It would be the headquarters of his predatory war in the east.

At the beginning of December 1940 Paulus' team presented their findings, and preparations gathered momentum. On 18 December the Führer signed a directive for his secret operation, which was intended 'to crush the Soviet Union in a rapid campaign'. It was given a grand codename, 'Barbarossa', deliberately recalling the twelfth-century German emperor who had launched a crusade against the Slavs. Hitler would now launch his own twentieth-century crusade against Bolshevism. The onslaught would commence on 22 June 1941, and Joseph Goebbels recorded one discussion about it with his leader. 'The Führer estimates the operation will take four months,' Goebbels wrote confidently. 'I reckon fewer. Bolshevism will collapse like a pack of cards.'

Hitler had long detested this rival ideology. When he wrote *Mein Kampf* he expounded on his unique sense of mission, to lead Germany from misery to greatness through creating a racially pure Aryan community. To safeguard this community, his long-term goal was to destroy Soviet communism and create *Lebensraum*, living space, for the German people by conquering Slav lands in the east. In *Mein Kampf* Bolshevism was portrayed as part of an international Jewish conspiracy, allied to a primitive Slavic culture that Hitler both despised and feared. He believed that war against Russia was an absolute necessity for the survival of the German people.

This deeply felt conviction, and the hateful prejudice which accompanied it, always underlay the Führer's foreign policy. A treaty with the Soviet Union could only be a temporary measure, a ploy to buy him time, before the execution of his grand design. At a small conference at his Bavarian mountain retreat, the Berghof, on 22 August 1939 – the day his foreign minister Ribbentrop flew to Moscow to sign the non-aggression pact – Hitler reassured the party faithful. He spoke with consummate assurance. 'There is no time to lose,' he said to his assembled followers. 'War must come. This pact is only meant to stall for time. We must crush the Soviet Union.'

When Hitler briefed his army leaders some eighteen months later he was rather more circumspect. Nineteen-forty had been a year of glorious victories, but Britain had not yet been subdued, and the Führer was asking the Wehrmacht to fight a war on two fronts. Knowing that some at least would find this prospect unpalatable, he devised a military justification for Barbarossa, using a clever falsehood, that the Soviet Union itself was planning to break the treaty and attack Germany, and thus it was vital to forestall them. Those of the Führer's generals steeped in the Nazi ideology quickly grasped his real motives and enthusiastically embraced them. Foremost among them was Colonel-General Georg von Küchler, leader of the Wehrmacht's Eighteenth Army. On 25 April 1941 Küchler declared to his divisional commanders:

> We are separated from Russia, ideologically and racially, by a deep abyss. Russia is, if only by the mass of her territory, an Asian state. The Führer does not wish to palm off responsibility for Germany's existence to a later generation; he has decided to force the dispute with Russia before the year is out. If Germany wishes to live in peace for generations, safe from the threatening danger in the east, this cannot be a case of pushing Russia back a little – or even hundreds of kilometres – but the aim must be to annihilate European Russia, to dissolve the Russian state in Europe.

Sixty-year-old Küchler was a committed member of the Nazi Party and a fanatical hater of communism. An artillery officer in the First World War, he then fought for the volunteer Freikorps in the Baltic after the war had ended. These soldiers believed they had been entrusted with a sacred mission, to combat communism. Recognising a kindred spirit, Hitler promoted Küchler to army commander and then, at the outbreak of the Second World War, gave him a key role in his spreading offensive – in 1939 Küchler led German troops into Danzig, and in 1940 he headed the invasion of the Netherlands and Belgium. After the fall of Paris, he triumphantly reviewed the victorious Wehrmacht forces on the Champs Elysées.

Now, in 1941, as Hitler's attention turned east, Küchler and his Eighteenth Army were moved to Poland, to watch carefully over the Red Army forces on the other side of the partition line with the Soviet Union. Hilter instinctively sensed his commander's visceral hatred of the foe. On 6 June 1941 the notorious 'Commissar Order' was drawn up, asserting – once the invasion of Russia commenced – the army's right to shoot all Communist Party officials found in its path. Küchler enthusiastically supported the order. 'The political commissars', he stated robustly, 'are criminals. They are to be put before tribunals and sentenced to death. In a campaign in the east, these measures will save us German blood and we shall make headway faster.' The June 1941 issue of the Wehrmacht's army bulletin built up this hate propaganda for the troops:

> Anyone who has ever looked into the face of a Red Commissar knows what Bolsheviks are. There is no need here for theoretical reflections. It would be an insult to animals if one were to call the features of these – largely Jewish – tormentors of people, beasts. They are the embodiment of the infernal, of personified hatred of everything that is noble humanity. In the shape of these commissars, we witness the revolt of the subhuman against the noble blood.

In Barbarossa, Hitler envisioned a special role for Küchler and his Eighteenth Army. They would spearhead a German assault on Leningrad.

Leningrad would have been a target for any invasion force. The city – originally named St Petersburg after its founder, Peter the Great – was formed in 1703 in the crucible of Peter's great northern war with Sweden, a war bitterly fought for domination of the Baltic Sea. Peter wrested supremacy from this rival power, creating a mighty city on the mouth of the River Neva to maintain his hard-won access to the Baltic and give Russia a 'window to the west'. St Petersburg became a seat of imperial splendour – the capital of the Russian Empire and a symbol of its political, administrative and cultural vitality. Its imposing shipping and ordnance industries made it the country's most important military centre. In 1918 Russia's revolutionary Bolshevik regime – facing a dangerous civil war – transferred the capital to Moscow, but this great city on the Baltic Sea – renamed Leningrad in 1924 – remained home to the country's major armament factories and was the base of its powerful Baltic Fleet.

Hitler well understood Leningrad's economic and military significance. But he perceived the city primarily as a centre of political revolution and the birthplace of Bolshevism – the ideology he so loathed and detested. Lenin had founded his Union for the Struggle of the Working Class in St Petersburg in 1895 and had begun introducing Marxist socialism to the city's workers. The city became a hotbed of unrest against tsarist authority and in October 1917 was the focal point of the revolution that saw the Bolsheviks seize power in Russia. A year later, the Bolsheviks' military arm, the Red Guard – the future Red Army – was created within the city.

Leningrad was a major objective for Hitler. Operation Barbarossa envisaged a three-pronged assault on the Soviet Union. Army Group South would strike at the Ukraine, aiming for Kiev, the Donets industrial region and the Crimea. Army Group Centre would drive towards Minsk, Smolensk and then Moscow. Army Group North would fight its way through the Baltic region and capture Leningrad. Although these army groups would advance simultaneously, the offensive was nonetheless sequenced, and, crucially, the seizure of Leningrad was given strategic priority over the assault on the Soviet capital, Moscow. The Führer and the German high command fully understood the city's importance.

For Army Group North, Hitler chose his commanders carefully. Alongside Küchler's Eighteenth Army he placed the Sixteenth of General Ernst Busch. The fifty-seven-year-old Busch was, like Küchler, a fanatical Nazi, who had won a rapid series of promotions after Hitler came to power. He liked to remind his men of the Führer's vision, 'a National Socialist Greater Germany, united and strong in its belief and with an iron will for victory in its struggle for *Lebensraum*'. The struggle for living space would take place in the east, and at the start of Operation Barbarossa Busch declared to his soldiers: 'I am certain we shall not only defeat but destroy the enemy, and thereby create the preconditions for the total annihilation of the Bolshevik system.'

Shortly before he launched his invasion Hitler visited Army Group North's HQ, and stressed to its commanders and staff the crucial importance of their target. 'The fall of Leningrad will deprive the Soviet state of the symbol of its revolution,' he told them, 'a symbol which for the last twenty-four years has deeply sustained the Russian people. Reverses in battle will undermine the spirit of the Slavic race, but the loss of Leningrad will cause a complete and utter collapse.' He was well aware of the task facing these men. They had a considerable distance to cover and were opposed by Soviet forces dispersed over an immense area, from the recently occupied Baltic countries right back into the territory which had been the heartland of the old Russian Empire. Encirclement of the enemy would not be feasible in this vast landscape. Instead, having punched a hole in Soviet defences, Army Group North would have to keep pushing forward and maintain sufficient momentum to keep its adversary off balance. With this in mind, the Führer asked Field Marshal Ritter von Leeb to take overall command. In 1940 Leeb had broken France's much vaunted Maginot Line, the fortress line that was supposedly impregnable. Hitler now wanted him to do the same for the Stalin Line, the deep defensive system created by the Soviet dictator many miles behind the frontier. This string of well-constructed bunkers and strongpoints was the principal obstacle on the road to Leningrad.

Leeb was a veteran commander, sixty-five years old at the start of the Russian campaign. He had served in China during the Boxer rebellion, then as an artillery officer during the First World War, when he had been awarded the Bavarian military order of Max Josef for extreme valour. During the occupation of the Sudetenland in 1938 he had commanded the German Second Army and two years later, in July 1940, after his troops successfully breached France's Maginot Line, Hitler had promoted him to the rank of field marshal and awarded him the prestigious Knight's Cross. The Führer trusted Leeb's experience, believing that he could ably co-ordinate the northern offensive and execute the agreed strategy of fast forward movement. To assist him, and the two armies under his overall command – the Eighteenth and Sixteenth – he was also given a Panzer group. This consisted of three of the Wehrmacht's best tank divisions, with three motorised infantry divisions and the SS Totenkopf – Death's Head – Division in support.

Before reaching the Stalin Line, Leeb would be confronted with another, entirely natural barrier, the River Dvina, which marked the frontier between the Baltic States of Lithuania and Latvia. In the first, frenetic days of the war, it was vital to seize bridgeheads quickly across this major river, and not allow the devastated Red Army the chance to form up behind it. At Barbarossa's onset Leeb made a good decision. He split his Panzer forces, keeping back one tank corps to destroy the Soviet armour massed near the border that might threaten his advance, and unleashing the other in a race for the Dvina crossings. Motorised infantry commander Gustav Klinter was in one of the leading detachments: 'Heat, filth and clouds of dust were the characteristic snapshot of those days. We hardly saw any enemy apart from the occasional drive-by of prisoners. But the country had totally altered after we crossed the Reich border. Lithuania gave us a little taste of what we were to find in Russia: unkept sandy roads, intermittent settlements and ugly houses, which were more like huts.'

Here we first encounter the Germans' reflex distaste for their opponents and their 'primitive' way of life. Klinter's unit maintained their rapid momentum and were already sixty miles ahead of the main army group, the Panzers speeding towards the Dvina and the two vital bridges that spanned it, at Dvinsk, more than 180 miles east of the frontier. Klinter remembered closing in on the town:

> The air had that putrefying and pervasive burnt smell reminiscent of the battle zone and all nerves and senses began to detect the breath of war. Suddenly all heads switched to the right. The first dead of the Russian campaign lay before our eyes like a spectre – a Mongolian skull smashed in combat, a torn uniform and bare abdomen split by shell splinters. The column drew up and then accelerated ahead – the picture fell behind us. I sank back thoughtfully into my seat.

With Klinter racing towards the Dvina, Leeb's other armoured corps was about to pounce on the Red Army's tank force. Unwisely, the Soviet north-western command had massed all of its armour in one place, situated far too close to the frontier. German aerial reconnaissance quickly discovered its location, near the small Lithuanian town of Raseinai. Here were some of the Red Army's mightiest tanks, the KV-1s and KV-2s, monsters weighing forty-three and fifty-two tons respectively. A German tank man brought out the drama of the clash:

> The KV-1 and KV-2, which we first met here, were really something! Our company opened fire at about 800 yards, but it remained ineffective. We moved closer and closer to the enemy, who for his part continued to approach us unconcerned. Very soon we were facing each other at 50 to 100 yards. A fantastic exchange of fire took place without any visible German success. The Russian tanks continued to advance, and all armour-piercing shells simply bounced off them.

But, tellingly, the Germans triumphed at Raseinai in spite of such Soviet strength, and did so through sheer professionalism. They devised a way to counter their opponents, ensuring that all their units were working together and in touch through radio communication. The Panzers changed gear, reversed and carried out a close-combat slugging match with the Russians: 'Our tank regiment about-turned, and rumbled back with the KV-1s and KV-2s, roughly in line with them. We succeeded in immobilising some of them with shells at very close range – 30 to 60 yards.' The Germans then herded the Russian giants towards their own heavy artillery, whose barrels were brought down to the horizontal to fire point-blank at the advancing behemoths. Over 200 Soviet tanks were destroyed, with twenty-nine of the super-heavy KV-1s and KV-2s left gutted on the battlefield. The bulk of the Soviet armoured forces in the Baltic countries were annihilated and any threat to the German advance from the flanks removed.

The Dvina crossings were now within Leeb's grasp. Early on the morning of 26 June 1941, his 8th Panzer Division sped along the Kaunas–Leningrad motorway, its tank commanders propped up, field glasses at their eyes, as the tracks clanked and diesel engines roared. They had covered an astonishing distance of over 180 miles and were now approaching the outskirts of Dvinsk.

Three miles from the town the tanks suddenly ground to a halt and a strange column of four captured Soviet lorries overtook it, their drivers in Russian uniforms. This was a special unit of German military intelligence – its mission was to drive into the town, seize the bridges, prevent the Russians from blowing them up and hold on until the Panzers were able to join them.

The Russians remained completely unsuspecting. When the lorries reached the checkpoints the undercover drivers were asked by the sentries, 'Where are the Germans?' They received a cheery answer: 'Oh – a long way back!' They moved into the suburbs, threading their way past local traffic, but, as soon as the great road bridge across the Dvina appeared, the lorries accelerated hard and sped across. The first reached the other side; the second, challenged by a Russian soldier, opened up with its machine guns. A firefight broke out at the far end of the bridge. The moment gun flashes were seen above the town the waiting German tanks moved into action. Hatches were slammed down and the Panzers raced forward. At 8.00 a.m. Leeb received the signal: 'Surprise of Dvinsk and Dvina bridges successful. The road bridges are intact.' This was the type of warfare the Germans excelled in – *Blitzkrieg*, lightning war, constantly throwing the enemy off balance and keeping one step ahead of him. Their Army Group commander was jubilant: the Dvina bridgehead represented 'a stake in the heart of the enemy'.

Now Leeb could focus his attention on the Stalin Line, ahead of him. This long belt of fortifications had been constructed with considerable technical skill and, as his reconnaissance reports made clear, it was a formidable bulwark:

> It is a dangerous combination of concrete field works and natural obstacles, tank traps, mines, marshy belts around forts, artificial lakes enclosing defiles, cornfields cut according to the trajectory of machine-gun fire. Its whole extent, right up to the position of the defenders, is camouflaged with a consummate art. Along a front of 120 kilometres, a dozen barriers, proofed against shells and light bombs, have been constructed and sited in skilfully chosen fire positions.

The line had to be breached quickly and Leeb once again decided to entrust the mission to his Panzers. But, first, the infantry needed to catch up.

Wilhelm Lubbeck's 58th Division was heading the Eighteenth Army's march through northern Lithuania. 'We plodded countless miles through the stifling heat and thick clouds of dust,' Lubbeck recalled. 'We could hear the perpetual din of gunfire and explosions in the distance. In drainage ditches, and out in the fields that lined the road, hundreds of still warm, contorted bodies lay where they had fallen. The enemy tanks we passed were wrecked hulks, often still belching an oily black smoke.' The Red Army's troops and tanks had been caught in the open by German aircraft as they attempted to retreat. 'Such attacks were particularly devastating when our planes swept along roads crowded with Russian men and vehicles,' Lubbeck continued. 'They destroyed everything in their path.'

Seeing these casualties, he and his fellows thought about the meaning of this great war. The Baltic States had been occupied by the Soviet Union in 1940, and the evident relief of some of the population when Lubbeck's division arrived, and their calls of 'Liberator!', reinforced the men's sense of a just cause. 'I was fighting out of a belief that Soviet communism posed a grave threat to all of Europe and Western civilisation,' Lubbeck said. 'If we did not destroy the communist menace, it would destroy us.' He was aware of Nazi propaganda, which portrayed the Slavs as *Untermenschen*, subhumans, but he did not believe the soldiers around him embraced such extreme racial views. However, he added tellingly: 'For us, the Slavs were not a biologically inferior race of human beings; they were simply the ignorant inhabitants of an uncivilised and backward country.'

In truth, Lubbeck and his fellow fighters were being drawn into a struggle far darker and more complex than they could comprehend. On 25 June forward units of Ernst Busch's Sixteenth Army had entered the Lithuanian capital of Kaunas. Accompanying them were SS commandos from the newly formed Einsatzgruppe A, headed by Police General Walter Stahlecker. The *Einsatzgruppen* had been created shortly before the Russian invasion. Their name literally meant 'Task force', and they were officially designated as security detachments, safeguarding the movement of army supplies and policing newly conquered territory. Their unofficial purpose was to kill Jews, commissars and other 'undesirables'.

The forty-one-year-old Stahlecker was a well-educated Nazi and a long-standing police chief. He compiled a detailed private report setting out the activities of his group. On 25 June he personally led his detachment into Kaunas alongside regular troops of the Sixteenth Army. He wanted to start a massacre of the town's large Jewish population. 'Our security force was determined to solve the Jewish question with all means at its disposal, and as quickly as possible,' he stated. But his men decided to encourage Lithuanians to do the actual killing. 'At the beginning,' Stahlecker continued, 'it was preferable that our force kept in the background, since the harsh measures we were planning might upset some German circles of opinion.'

Stahlecker's commandos incited a group of Lithuanian partisans to start rounding up Jews. This action took place in broad daylight, in the streets and squares of a busy city, right under the nose of the Wehrmacht. On 26 June over a thousand Jews were herded together and then clubbed to death at the Lietukis Garage, less than 200 yards from Sixteenth Army's HQ. Large numbers of German soldiers stood by and watched. No one attempted to stop the killing.

Stahlecker had come to a private agreement with Sixteenth Army's commander, General Ernst Busch, who promised that his soldiers would not intervene in what were described as 'spontaneous self-cleansing actions'. The head of Einsatzgruppe A reported that more than 3,800 Jews were murdered in cold blood and then added: 'These self-cleansing operations went smoothly because the army authorities, *who had been informed beforehand* [italics added], showed understanding for this procedure.' A German ordnance sergeant from the 562nd Bakery Company later recalled: 'I saw these people being rounded up and then just had to look away, as they were clubbed to death right before our eyes. It was all so cruel and brutal. A great many German soldiers, as well as Lithuanians, stood there watching. They did not express either assent or disapproval – they just stood, totally indifferent.'

Decent Wehrmacht officers were outraged by what had happened. Franz von Roques, head of Army Group North's Rear Administration, personally inspected the sites and then, fearing that General Busch was complicit in the murder, appealed directly to Field Marshal von Leeb. Leeb became extremely defensive. After listening to Roques, he merely said that he had no influence over such measures, and all that one could do was to keep one's distance. In early July 1941 Hitler's chief adjutant, Colonel Rudolf Schmundt, visited Kaunas. When he heard of the massacre he said: 'Soldiers should not be burdened with these political questions – it is a matter of necessary cleaning-up operations.' The German army was well aware of the mass killing of Jews in Kaunas at the end of June 1941. By doing nothing to stop it, it offered *de facto* protection for the SS commandos and their accomplices. This case – in which the Wehrmacht willingly permitted mass murder – set a terrible precedent for later events, which would be played out on a much larger scale.

On 1 July Leeb visited Colonel-General Hoepner's Fourth Panzer Group. Morale was high. Leeb always liked to stress the importance of speed. 'Forward!' he would say. 'Don't stop for anything. Never let the enemy consolidate, once he has been thrown back.' Hoepner was an enthusiastic practitioner of Leeb's adage. A cavalryman in the First World War, the fifty-five-year-old general later became one of the first advocates of fast-moving armoured warfare, and had been given command of his own Panzer corps in 1938. Hoepner was originally critical of Hilter's aggressive foreign policy, but all that changed after the Führer's dramatic victory in France in 1940. He now approached the war in Russia with messianic zeal.

As his Panzers sped east, the commander of Fourth Panzer Group sent out an operational order to his troops. In it, Hoepner emphasised certain 'fundamental principles' for how future battles would be conducted. 'The war with Russia is a vital part of the German people's fight for existence,' he enjoined. 'It is the old fight of German against Slav, the defence of European culture against the Muscovite–Asiatic flood, and the repulse of Jewish Bolshevism.' He continued: 'This war must have as its goal the destruction of today's

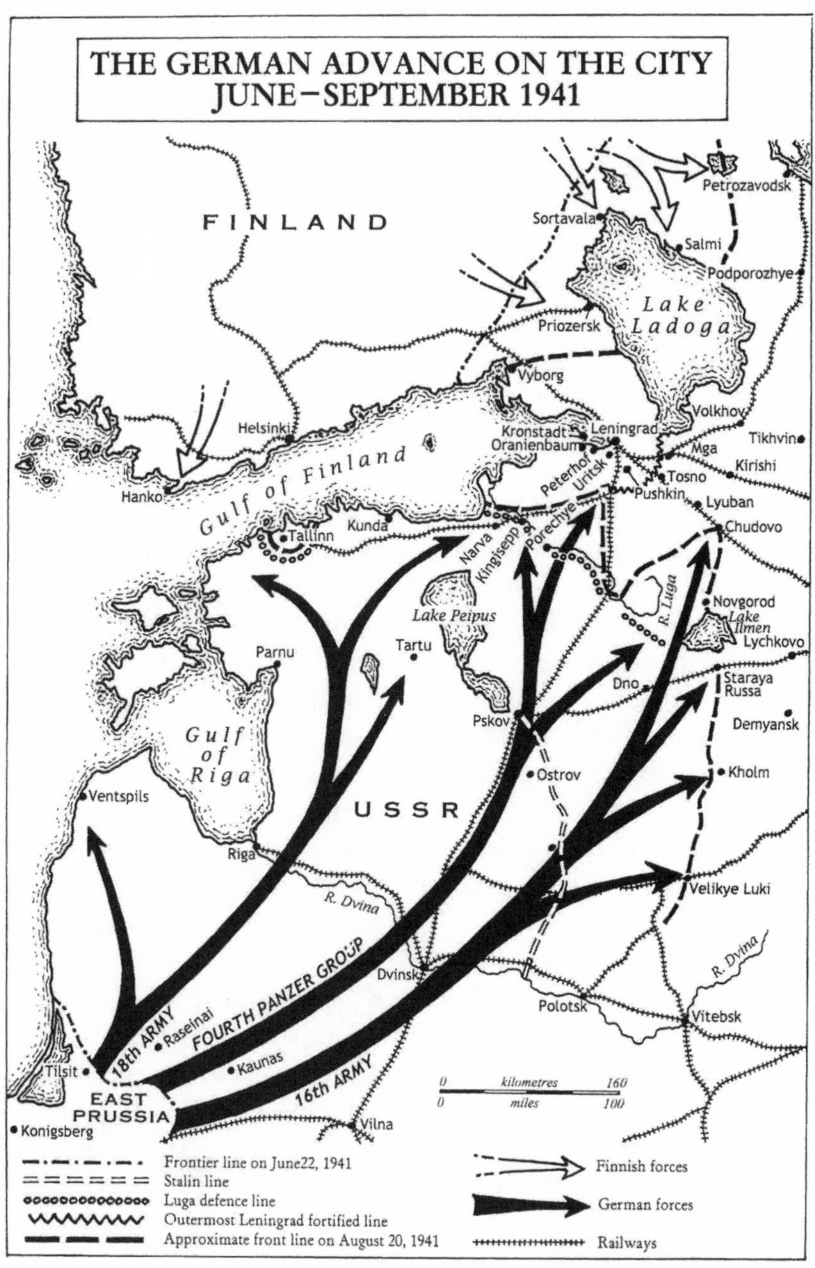

THE GERMAN ADVANCE ON THE CITY
JUNE–SEPTEMBER 1941
FINLAND
Sortavala
Petrozavodsk
Salmi
Podporozhye
Lake Ladoga
Priozersk
Vyborg
Helsinki
Hanko
Gulf of Finland
Kronstadt
Leningrad
Oranienbaum
Peterhof
Uritsk
Pushkin
Mga
Tosno
Volkhov
Tikhvin
Kirishi
Lyuban
Chudovo
Tallinn
Kunda
Narva
Kingisepp
Porechye
R. Luga
Novgorod
Lake Ilmen
Lychkovo
Lake Peipus
Tartu
Parnu
Dno
Staraya Russa
Demyansk
Pskov
Ostrov
Kholm
Gulf of Riga
Ventspils
USSR
Riga
Velikye Luki
R. Dvina
Dvinsk
Polotsk
Vitebsk
18th ARMY
Raseinai
FOURTH PANZER GROUP
Kaunas
16th ARMY
Tilsit
EAST PRUSSIA
Konigsberg
Vilna
0 kilometres 160
0 miles 100
Frontier line on June22, 1941
Stalin line
Luga defence line
Outermost Leningrad fortified line
Approximate front line on August 20, 1941
Finnish forces
German forces
Railways

Russia – and for this reason it must be conducted *with unheard-of harshness*. Every clash, from its conception to its execution, must be guided by an iron determination to annihilate the enemy completely and utterly. There is to be no mercy for the carriers of the current Russian–Bolshevik system.'

Hoepner's group was organised into two corps – the XLI and LVI – and an operational reserve. He had two highly able men serving under him. The fifty-four-year-old General Hans Reinhardt, commander of XLI Corps, was a dashing, enthusiastic leader who had gained renown in the Polish campaign in 1939 by breaching Warsaw's defences with his force of Panzers, for which he was awarded the Knight's Cross. Now Reinhardt wanted to gain the same honour against a far greater prize – the city of Leningrad.

General Erich von Manstein, fifty-three years old, commander of LVI Corps, was one of the most talented leaders in the Wehrmacht. In 1940, when Germany successfully invaded France, he had devised a radical plan of attack – Operation Sickle Cut – in which a massed force of Panzers had burst out of the Ardennes forest and then raced for the Meuse bridges, in order to outflank the surprised French armies to the north. For Barbarossa, Manstein had been wielding his sickle again – for his LVI Corps had covered 185 miles in a mere four days to seize the vital river crossings over the Dvina. The triumph had left him exultant. 'It is unlikely that I will ever again experience anything comparable to that impetuous dash,' he wrote. 'It was the fulfilment of every tank commander's dream.'

As Leeb, Hoepner, Reinhardt and Manstein met together there was a mood of excitement, for as the German commanders studied their maps a fresh opportunity was opening out before them. The bridgehead across the Dvina had been widened and fresh supplies had been brought up. Now another tank dash was beckoning – a leap of 155 miles, to capture the towns of Ostrov and Pskov and force open the Stalin Line.

On 2 July the Panzers raced forward. By 4 July Reinhardt had captured Ostrov; to the south of him Manstein had reached the old

Latvian–Russian border. The Red Army was unable to respond quickly enough to stop them. It sent reinforcements to Ostrov only to find it already in German hands. When more of its monster KV-2 tanks were committed, German field howitzers were in place to bombard them with concrete-piercing shells. Over 140 Soviet tanks were destroyed in this dramatic ambush, and on 8 July the Panzers pushed through the remaining Russian defences and captured Pskov, breaching the Stalin Line. Leeb sent out a euphoric communiqué to his troops: 'The enemy's attempts to construct a defensive front on the old Russian border have failed. We have broken through. Army Group North now attacks in the direction of Leningrad!'

Joseph Goebbels was with Hitler when news of Leeb's success reached the Wolf's Lair. 'No one now doubts that we shall be victorious in Russia,' he wrote in his diary. 'Of Bolshevism, nothing will be allowed to remain.' Then, deliberately using Leningrad's pre-revolutionary name, he added starkly: 'The Führer intends to have cities like Petersburg rubbed out.'

It seemed as if the Germans were running an exhilarating relay race. Hoepner now pushed his tanks forward in another audacious thrust. On 11 July Reinhardt's XLI Corps had moved up from Pskov, forcing its way through the difficult terrain east of Lake Peipus and seizing the town of Lyady and its bridge over the Narva. On the evening of the 13th Colonel Erhard Raus and his tank men were finishing their evening meal and taking a well-earned rest when General Reinhardt appeared. He chatted to the troops, and then told them that owing to the speed of their advance there was now a chance of breaking the Luga river line – the last major Soviet defence position before Leningrad – near Porechye. Everyone was exhausted. But, as Raus recalled, their commander's excitement was infectious: 'Reinhardt's rallying cry, "Let us open the gates to Leningrad!" kindled a flame in the heart of every soldier. All weariness was forgotten.' As dusk began to fall, the tank engines started to hum again.

Reinhardt's forces pushed on through the night. The following morning they gathered speed. There was one good road – with swamps on either side of it – and as the column accelerated Soviet planes appeared. The Russian pilots could not believe what they were seeing. They knew that Küchler's Eighteenth Army, further north-west, had stalled in the face of strong Red Army resistance at Narva. To the south, Manstein and the remainder of Fourth Panzer Group were held up by fierce fighting near Luga. Red Army divisions were in place on the far sides of the swamp. They simply did not understand how German forces could have got behind their position – surely these must be Soviet tanks, redeploying?

The planes flew off. Two hours later more appeared. They signalled, and then dropped leaflets on the German column, asking for their unit identification. The Panzers kept moving. More leaflets rained down. They now said: 'Identify yourselves or we will open fire!' The tanks accelerated through the clouds of swirling paper. The Soviet planes circled, and then flew off in bewilderment.

Late that night the leading tanks reached the bridges over the River Luga. The surprised Russian guards ran off in panic. At 10.00 p.m. a triumphant message was radioed through to Reinhardt: 'Bridgehead established – the gates to Leningrad are open!'

In their dramatic drive from Pskov to Porechye, on the far side of the Luga river, Reinhardt's Panzers had advanced another 120 miles. In just over three weeks of fighting they had covered nearly 500 miles, and were now less than seventy miles from Leningrad. But Soviet resistance was now stiffening, and the sheer speed of the German forces' progress meant that their position was becoming dangerously overstretched.

Difficult terrain now broke the force of Fourth Panzer Group's onslaught. Reinhardt's Panzers were holed up across the Luga, in need of reinforcement. But Küchler's Eighteenth Army was caught in the bottleneck of land north of Lake Peipus, struggling against a strongly defended Soviet position at Narva. To the south, Manstein's armoured column had entered a largely unmapped area of desolate swampland and was unable to come to Reinhardt's assistance. As it pushed through the wilderness lands between Opochka and Novgorod, it was strung out along the region's one major road, sixty miles from Reinhardt. In this increasingly bleak landscape of marshland and lakes, Manstein's Panzers outran their supply lines and were now receiving food, ammunition and fuel by air-drop.

The Russians now threw all their available forces at the Germans' exposed flank. They cut off 8th Panzer Division – the vanguard of Manstein's column – from the rest of the corps, exploiting the difficult terrain which denied the Panzers freedom of movement. Suddenly, the Germans were fighting for their lives. The operation report of one unit – the 3rd Motorised Infantry Division – revealed that in a single day they had repelled no fewer than seventeen infantry attacks and even their artillerymen were fighting in the front line. It was a drastic wake-up call for such technically trained officers – accustomed to conducting a highly mechanised war.

On 15 July the commander of one German battery, Lieutenant Alfred Hederich, found himself stuck in a remote forest clearing near Opochka. There was only one, poor-quality road, and impassable swamps lay to his right and left. To protect his men from surprise attack he had ordered the construction of wooden planks over the edge of the swamp, so that sentries could be stationed there. But somehow Russian infantry managed to infiltrate his position.

A series of massed infantry attacks began. German artillerymen were mown down before they could even get to their guns. Hederich crawled over and began firing; soon 10cm shells were exploding among the wave of attackers. The first enemy line collapsed on the edge of the clearing. But the Russians had now got their heavy machine guns into position and Hederich's gun shield was peppered with bullet marks. Then a dozen Soviet troops crawled within ten yards of his emplacement, leapt to their feet and charged. Hederich and his men seized whatever was at hand – spades, pistols and bayonets – and beat them off in a desperate hand-to-hand fight.

Four Russians were killed, with the rest disappearing into the scrub. The frantic struggle continued. Nearly all the Germans' ammunition had been expended, and tractor drivers and all other general services personnel were rushed into combat duty. Almost everybody had been wounded. The situation looked hopeless when by pure chance reinforcements arrived. A German motorcycle platoon had driven up the road and, seeing the carnage ahead of them, launched a surprise flanking attack. The Russians retreated. It was a most fortunate reprieve for Hederich's battered unit.

The bitter fighting in the swampland shook Manstein's force. Its advance had juddered to a halt in the area between the great lakes of Peipus and Ilmen, the historical Ingermannland, the boundary which had existed between the Teutonic Knights and the Russians in the Middle Ages. The Teutonic Knights had been ruthless colonisers with an abiding contempt for the people they had conquered. But the expansion of their military empire had been brought to a halt in this inhospitable landscape and ultimately they had been overwhelmed by the sheer number of their opponents. For a few harrowing days, the bruised combatants of the 8th Panzer Division must have wondered if history was about to repeat itself.

By bringing up reinforcements Manstein was able to fight his way through to his hard-pressed vanguard, and his skill retrieved the situation. But the Wehrmacht's high command realised that its strung-out army was in no position to attack Leningrad at this stage. Although Reinhardt held a vital bridgehead over the River Luga, he was unable to undertake any further advance, for his Panzer force had been reduced to little more than fifty operative tanks. Manstein's own tank strength had also been seriously weakened, and by the time he had rescued the 8th Panzers more than half of its vehicles were out of action. The fighting of mid-July convinced the Germans that they must strengthen their position, rather than continue to rush forward, and bring up vital reinforcements and supplies.

On 19 July Hitler brought out Directive 33, concerning 'The continuation of the war in the east'. He reviewed the triumphs of the last month, and paid tribute to Leeb's successes. 'A series of battles has culminated with the breach of the Stalin Line and a deep thrust undertaken by our Panzer forces,' he announced. But the Führer felt that this advantageous position now needed to be properly consolidated. 'The advance on Leningrad will only resume', he continued, 'when the Eighteenth Army has caught up with the Fourth Panzer Group and the [army group's] southern flank is adequately protected by the Sixteenth Army.'

'For the first time since the start of the campaign we are being confronted with stiff enemy opposition,' Wilhelm Lubbeck wrote that same day. The Eighteenth Army was colliding with Russian troops trying to retreat to Leningrad from the Baltic States. As combat grew tougher, some members of Army Group North were beginning to re-evaluate their Russian opponents. Max Simon, a captain in the SS Totenkopf Division accompanying Manstein's tank group, had been taken aback by the newfound determination of the enemy. The tenacity of their resistance in atrocious terrain struck him forcefully and he could not help but be impressed. He still sought to denigrate their performance, however, proclaiming to his men: 'the Russians are bandits, whipped into a frenzy by Bolshevik commissars and fanatical Red Army officers'. In despatches home Simon paid tribute to his Russian opponents, yet still attributed their resolve to the innate inferiority of the Slav: 'The native frugality of the Russian and Asiatic allows the restriction of the supply train of their combat troops to the minimum and also makes it possible to exploit the strength of the individual in a measure that seems unbelievable to the European.'

Here anti-communist rhetoric plainly gives way to the racist ideology which underlay the political justification for the German invasion: the Slavs are described as a race of inferior beings. It is their very savagery – insensitivity to weather conditions, uncivilised living and remarkable craftiness and guile – which renders them such impressive opponents: 'German officers, driving through a seemingly deserted village, would swear that there were neither troops nor inhabitants in the place but other troops following up would find themselves faced with a fortified position, defended by an infantry regiment, reinforced by all arms. The position had been so well camouflaged and the Soviet soldiers remained so still that the officers as they drove through had noticed nothing.' This 'animal cunning' was not to be underestimated, and Simon particularly warned against the dangers of getting enmeshed in a battle of attrition with a well-defended Russian foe:

> They blended themselves into the terrain and could dig themselves in in an amazingly short time. Their defensive positions were simple

> and effective. Machine guns were skilfully sited, and snipers, of whom there were forty or fifty to each company, were given the best positions. Trench mortars were available in all calibres and flame-throwers, often fitted with remote control, were used in conjunction with mortars so the attacking troops ran into a sea of flames. Well-concealed tanks stood by to take part in counter-attacks or were dug in at intervals. This was defence in depth – protected by wire entanglements and numerous minefields.

As the fighting intensified, German forces' behaviour towards their Russian opponents began to degenerate, and sometimes there were even indiscriminate shootings of unarmed prisoners. The flood of Nazi race propaganda was having an effect. In certain cases, the conduct of the soldiers actually harmed their own war effort. On 5 July the Sixteenth Army was forced to order that 'after the POWs have been organised into work battalions they should not be attacked and shot'. Less than two weeks later, the army's 12th Infantry Division had to repeat the injunction against the 'doing-in' of such prisoners. Real race hatred was emerging. Many captured Red Army soldiers were now being made to undertake long forced marches of hundreds of miles to camps situated far in the rear – thousands of them would die from hunger or exhaustion en route. On 31 July, the Sixteenth Army prohibited its divisional commanders from transporting prisoners in empty trains returning from the front, for fear of their 'contaminating and soiling the wagons'.

Police General Walter Stahlecker had organised the mass killings of Jews in Lithuania, Latvia and Estonia, but now that he was on Russian soil he wanted to expand what he called 'the fight against vermin'. On 17 July the remit of his Einsatzgruppe A was widened beyond Jews and commissars to include all important functionaries of the Soviet state, members of its regional governments and leading personalities of the business world and the Russian intelligentsia. Stahlecker was frustrated that, because of the distances involved, the poor quality of the Russian roads and shortages of vehicles and petrol, 'it would require the utmost effort to carry out these shootings'. But Hoepner's Fourth Panzer Group now came to his rescue. 'Co-operation between the armed forces and my *Einsatzgruppe* was generally good,' Stahlecker observed, 'but with the Fourth Panzer Group of Colonel-General Hoepner relations were particularly close and cordial.' Hoepner had warned that the war against Bolshevism would be conducted with 'unheard-of harshness'. When Reinhardt's troops secured the Luga bridgehead as a jumping-off point for an assault on Leningrad, Stahlecker's extermination squad was brought up to join them. 'When it was decided to bring German forces closer to Leningrad,' Stahlecker recalled,

> I was asked to expand the actions of Einsatzgruppe A in readiness for an entry into the city. Consequently, on 18 July 1941, I ordered Action Detachments 2 and 3, and the staff of my group, to move up to the Luga district, in order to prepare for these activities, and to be able to advance as early as possible into the suburbs of Leningrad, and then into the city itself. The movement of Einsatzgruppe A – which the army intended to use in Leningrad – was effected in agreement with Panzer Group Four *and as a result of their express wish* [italics added].

Stahlecker's report showed that in late July 1941 Hoepner was still hoping to attack and capture Leningrad. As part of his preparations, Einsatzgruppe A was asked to gather information on prominent members of the city and the extermination squads were then readied to go in with the army. In the meantime, Stahlecker noted, agreed 'cleansing work' was undertaken in consultation with Fourth Panzer Group, although such opportunities were limited, 'because all vehicles had been requisitioned for the expected advance into Leningrad'. One successful operation that did take place involved liquidating several hundred helpless inmates of a mental asylum – the army now required it as a barracks.

For those unhappy with such activities, General von Manstein had the following stern warning: 'The Jewish–Bolshevik system must be eradicated once and for all. It must never be allowed to intrude on our European sphere of influence again. German soldiers participating in this war are the bearers of an ethnic message.'

The Germans still believed that Leningrad lay within their grasp. They knew that the poor co-ordination between Russian infantry, tanks and air support would count strongly in their favour in the fighting for the city. Colonel Erhard Raus was struck by one engagement on the Luga bridgehead. The Soviet assault was well conceived, and initially advanced in a most threatening manner, with its tanks being supported by masses of infantry. The Germans quickly brought up flak guns, and a confused slugging match developed. In the chaos of the fast-moving fighting, Raus noticed that his opponents suddenly lost their way. The tanks became separated from the infantry, and then the infantry formations lost their cohesion. The enemy's lack of combat experience revealed itself in 'an irresolute rushing about in all directions'. The attack collapsed in utter failure.

The pause in the German advance had allowed the Soviets to bring up reinforcements. Raus was holding a small redoubt – ceaselessly battered by Soviet forces. But he never lost his confidence and self-belief. He believed that the Red Army's numbers were more than matched by the Wehrmacht's professional expertise.

The German Eighteenth Army was now pushing towards Reinhardt's Luga bridgehead, in readiness for an assault on Leningrad from the south-west. The Sixteenth Army was moving south, towards Lake Ilmen, to guard the flanks of this advance. The Russians doggedly continued to reinforce the remainder of the River Luga defence line with all the means at their disposal – constructing vast new earthworks and ditches and conscripting workers' militia to join the forces at the front.

On 8 August 1941 Reinhardt's Panzers were given the order to move forward. At 8.00 a.m. they started off from the Luga in pouring rain. Bad weather prevented effective air cover and two Soviet rifle divisions were in place to oppose them. The attack slowed – and rising casualties nearly led to its being called off altogether. At this point, Police General Stahlecker's Einsatzgruppe A 'teamed up with Fourth Panzer Group' and joined in the front-line fighting. Only on 14 August did they clear the ring of enemy fortifications and reach open ground. But Küchler's Eighteenth Army was coming up to join them, and Manstein's long-awaited tank force was also approaching. Then a worrying threat to the German position arrived from an entirely unexpected direction.

To take the pressure off Leningrad's defenders the Russians made a bold decision, launching a flank attack further south, at Demyansk, in the funnel of land between Lakes Ilmen and Selinger. A gap had appeared in the German line between Army Groups North and Centre, presenting an opportunity to disrupt the Wehrmacht's assault on Leningrad. The Russians seized it with all the forces available to them. Against three infantry divisions of the overstretched Sixteenth Army, which had laboriously fought its way into the transport centre of Staraya Russa, south of Lake Ilmen, they flung nine rifle divisions, one cavalry division and one armoured corps. The Russian plan was brutally simple: to overrun the Sixteenth Army's forces, then drive west, blocking the neck of land between Lakes Ilmen and Peipus and cut off the German armies advancing towards Leningrad.

On 15 August Manstein and his staff had spent the whole day moving north from Luga – a journey of 125 miles on frightful roads – to Lake Samro, just behind Reinhardt. They had nearly reached their long-anticipated attack position. Behind Manstein, negotiating the potholes and the patches of deep sand, came the massed motorcycle formations of the 3rd Motorised Infantry Division. Manstein's group was at last about to join with Reinhardt in a big push towards Leningrad.

By late evening Manstein and his officers, covered in dust, had finally reached Lake Samro. There was a glorious blood-red sunset behind the surrounding trees. Manstein had just ordered, 'On with your swimming trunks, gentlemen, and into the lake!' when a runner emerged from the communication van. 'A call from Panzer Group, Herr General.' Manstein frowned and the runner apologised. 'It's very urgent, Herr General. The Commander-in-Chief is on the line in person.' Manstein strode over to the field telephone. It was General Hoepner, the head of the entire Panzer Group: 'I've bad news, Manstein – our attack on Leningrad is off – a serious crisis has developed for Sixteenth Army on Lake Ilmen: you'll have to act as fire brigade. Halt your forces and turn about. You'll have to move south immediately.' Manstein was none too pleased and Hoepner immediately sensed it. 'Field Marshal von Leeb wouldn't stop our advance on Leningrad unless the situation was pretty serious,' he added. Manstein understood this, and responded, arriving on the following day at Dno – the Sixteenth Army Headquarters. This time the 160-mile journey had taken him thirteen hours.

Crucial moments during a military campaign can sometimes depend on apparently trivial events that impact strongly on a key commander. Great generalship depends on presence of mind, sharp focus and split-second decision-making. In Manstein's case it could have been just sheer annoyance that gave him the vital edge. He had spent innumerable hours bumping along Russia's ghastly dirt roads, and had then missed an eagerly anticipated swim. His blood was up.

What happened when he finally reached the Sixteenth Army was, even by his own standards, remarkable. While hard-pressed German troops were defending Lake Ilmen, Manstein drove round them – without pausing for rest – and slammed into the rear of the attacking Soviets. His fast motorised units created mayhem behind their lines and kept moving forward. The Russians began to panic. Then Manstein ordered his battered divisions on Lake Ilmen – outnumbered four to one – to go on the offensive and fling everything at the enemy. It was an extraordinary gamble, but proved to be absolutely correct. The entire Soviet army disintegrated. Manstein later wrote about the psychology of such a bold assault: 'I doubt if there is anything harder to learn than gauging the moment when a slackening of the enemy's resistance offers the attacker his decisive chance.' The German victory at Lake Ilmen fundamentally changed the strategic situation.

German victory had been snatched from the jaws of defeat. The Russians had lost a mass of manpower and equipment and a huge gap had been torn in their front. While they continued a resolute defence of the western approaches to Leningrad, flinging a series of obstacles in the path of Reinhardt's Panzers, another opportunity had now opened for the advancing Germans, to swing Manstein's tank force and the Sixteenth Army east, and make a second advance on Leningrad from this new direction, cutting all the city's remaining communication and supply routes. Rather than take Leningrad head on, with the enormous resource implications this held for their overtaxed force, they could instead isolate it from all help and support, and wait for it to fall.

On 18 August Goebbels visited Hitler at the Wolf's Lair, just as the Führer had learnt of Manstein's success. There was now a shift in his thinking. 'The Führer is not concerned with occupying particular cities,' Goebbels recorded. 'He wants to avoid casualties among our soldiers. Therefore he no longer intends to take Petersburg by force of arms, but rather to starve it into submission. Once it has been cut off, his plan is to bombard the city's means of supporting its population, using the Luftwaffe and artillery. Not much will be left of this place.' Then Goebbels made a most cruel aside. 'No doubt there will be a degree of chaos among its millions of inhabitants – but the Bolsheviks would not have it otherwise.' He concluded in a more matter-of-fact fashion. 'The first Luftwaffe attacks will hit Petersburg's water, power and gas stations.'

Manstein's Panzers and the Sixteenth Army were advancing rapidly. They had already captured Novgorod – the swastika hoisted over the golden dome of Russia's medieval capital – and were pushing on to the vital rail junction of Chudovo, which fell on 20 August to a surprise assault. Within a week German bombers were targeting Leningrad's last rail junction at Mga, and the town was captured on 30 August. On the western approaches to the city, Reinhardt's tanks were struggling forward against a mass of pillboxes, barbed wire and tank obstacles; to the east, German progress was astonishing. Their final target was the town of Shlisselburg on the banks of Lake Ladoga.

Shlisselburg was Leningrad's door to the east, where the River Neva meets Lake Ladoga. This was a place rich in history – for at the beginning of the eighteenth century Peter the Great had defeated the Swedes here, and its waterway joined with a series of canals linking Leningrad to the White Sea and the Arctic Ocean. The Soviets had utilised the lake and the lock gates of its canals for the generation of electricity. Shlisselburg held the key to Leningrad's communication system and the supply of power to its industries.

At 6.45 a.m. on 8 September German assault groups moved into position around the town. Reconnaissance patrols reported its eastern edge held by weak enemy forces – clearly the Russians did not expect an attack from this direction. It was a unique opportunity, and at 7.00 a.m. the Germans attacked. Within forty minutes the German flag was being hoisted over Shlisselburg's church steeple.

After signing the non-aggression pact with Germany, the Soviet Union had expanded its influence in the Baltic, taking over the states of Lithuania, Latvia and Estonia, fighting a war with Finland, and in its aftermath annexing Finnish territory. Now Stalin's expansionist policies were coming back to haunt him. As the Germans advanced towards Leningrad, Finland declared war against the Soviet Union. By 8 September its soldiers had reached the old 1939 border between the two countries, recapturing lands between the Gulf of Finland and Lake Ladoga annexed by the Soviets in 1940. To the north of Leningrad, Finnish armies severed the city's supply and communication routes. With the loss of Shlisselburg, Leningrad had become an island – surrounded by troops and water. On 9 September Hans Jeschonnek, the Luftwaffe's chief of staff, noted in his diary: 'We hope to have achieved a tight encirclement of Leningrad within a week. Food already appears to be short there.'

Dr Werner Koeppen was liaison officer to Alfred Rosenberg, the Nazi Party's chief race theorist, the man who had first warned Hitler of the threat from Soviet Bolshevism, and who now – after the invasion of Russia – was Reich minister for the newly occupied territories in the east. Koeppen wrote gloatingly to his chief on 10 September:

> For three days now our 240mm guns have been firing into Leningrad. Luftwaffe bombing has already destroyed the largest waterworks. The Russians have only evacuated top-grade workers – and the population has been swollen by evacuees from the surrounding countryside. Already it is almost impossible to get bread, sugar or meat in the city. Leningrad is to be shut in – shot to pieces – and starved out.

By 15 September the Eighteenth Army was moving into position from the west, and finally closing the siege lines. As Wilhelm Lubbeck passed through the small town of Uritsk, close to the Gulf of Finland, he saw central Leningrad's high-rises and tall smokestacks, silhouetted against the horizon. Those entrenched on the

Pulkovo Heights, to the south-west of Leningrad, were treated to a panoramic view of the city, less than eight miles away, its golden cupolas and towers bathed in sunlight. It was tantalising and confusing for those officers and soldiers who were still expecting an all-out assault. But German infantryman Walter Broschei was a realist. Although unsure of the reason for not attacking the city below, he correctly guessed at it:

> In the middle of September we reached a chain of hills about five miles from the Gulf of Finland and ten miles south-west of Leningrad city centre. In the distance the city pulsed with life. It was bewildering – trains ran, chimneys smoked and busy maritime traffic ran on the Neva river. But we now had only 28 soldiers left from the 120 normally in the company and had now been gathered into so-called 'combat' battalions – totally unsuitable, in view of our reduced strength, to attack Leningrad.

Artillery observer Hans Mauermann also had few illusions about the outcome of further costly attacks on the city: 'Then suddenly it was halt – which was actually met with some satisfaction. Every day it had been attack, with all its uncertainties and not knowing what might happen. From the perspective of even further hardship this was very much welcome. The emotion swung between shame that we had not pulled it off to thanking God we did not have to go in there.'

On 16 September Hitler spoke frankly to Otto Abetz, the German ambassador to Vichy France: 'Petersburg – the poisonous nest from which, for so long, Asiatic venom has spewed forth into the Baltic – must vanish from the earth's surface. The city is already cut off. It only remains for us to bomb and bombard it, destroy its sources of water and power and then deny the population everything it needs to survive.'

That ghastly process had already commenced. Almost a week earlier, on 8 September – the day that Leningrad was first encircled by German troops – members of the Wehrmacht's Staff HQ held a meeting with Professor Ernst Ziegelmeyer, a leading expert from the Munich Institute of Nutrition. They requested his assistance, stating that the attack on Leningrad had become bogged down and they now wanted to blockade the city. They provided the scientist with a mass of data including Leningrad's population census, the amount of food stored in the city and expected winter temperatures in the region. In return, Ziegelmeyer was asked to make a series of calculations, to forecast what would happen to Leningrad once calorific intake fell and civilians were deprived of essential protein and fat. The questions were stark. How long would the blockade have to last, given existing rations, before people started dying? How would the process of dying develop, and how long would it take for the entire civilian population to die?

The following day the nutritionist reported back that within a month of maintaining a complete blockade of the city, an essential ration of 250 grams of bread per person would have to be introduced. It was physically impossible to live on such a ration for any extended period of time. So he recommended that the German army should maintain its blockade throughout the winter. Ziegelmeyer concluded briskly: 'It is not worth risking the lives of our troops. The Leningraders will die anyway. It is essential not to let a single person through our front line. The more of them that stay there, the sooner they will die, and then we will enter the city without trouble, without losing a single German soldier.' On 10 September Goebbels wrote in his diary: 'We shall not trouble ourselves with demanding Leningrad's capitulation. It can be destroyed *by an almost scientific method* [italics added].' This was the science of mass starvation, and the army was now left to work out the details.

In mid-September the German army's supreme command drew up a secret memorandum, exploring their options. 'Normal occupation' of Leningrad was rejected. They considered whether it might be acceptable to evacuate some children and old people, but they would 'let the remainder starve'. The favoured solution was to surround the entire city with an electrically charged wire fence, guarded with machine guns. But there remained a fear of 'epidemics spreading to our front' from the hapless populace. So it was proposed to order corps commanders to use artillery against any civilians trying to break out. Army command was unsure 'whether infantry would shoot at women and children trying to escape'. The 'proper solution' was then summarised as follows: 'Seal off Leningrad hermetically, then weaken it by terror and growing starvation. In the spring we shall occupy the town, remove the survivors into captivity in the interior of Russia and level Leningrad to the ground with high explosives.' General Alfred Jodl, the army chief of staff, personally approved the memorandum. He believed that it was 'morally justified' because of a risk that the Soviets might mine the city and the all-pervasive fear that German soldiers would be contaminated by Leningrad's population. There was, he warned, a 'serious danger of epidemics' if the city was occupied.

The uncompromising intentions of the German high command had begun to translate into military reality. They were articulated with the sort of bleak logic that might appeal to the self-preservation instincts of ordinary soldiers. Starving the inhabitants of Leningrad began to make tactical and operational sense. 'That Leningrad has been mined and will be defended to the last man has already been announced on Soviet radio,' stated Army Group North in its war diary in late September. 'Serious epidemics are anticipated. No German soldier need set foot in the place.'

Underpinning these statements lay the pitiless ideology of racial superiority. When asked about feeding Russian civilians in the occupied suburbs, the quartermaster of the German army, Eduard Wagner, had blandly remarked that there were shortages in the Reich and 'it is better our people have something and the Russians go hungry'. Twenty thousand factory workers in the German-held suburb of Pushkin were then abruptly deprived of food. The administrative order made clear that 'the provision of rations from army sources for the civilian population is out of the question'.

Some German soldiers were well aware what was going on – and accepted it. Infantry soldier Johannes Haferkampf put it bluntly: 'We had erected an impenetrable ring around Leningrad. All its inhabitants had been sentenced to death through hunger and disease. We did not think the Russians would be able to break through to the city or provide its people with provisions. The population was inevitably going to starve to death and that was the real intent of our higher command.'

Others began to struggle with their consciences. The commander of the 58th Infantry Division accepted that troops would have to fire upon any mass break-out, but felt that certain realities could not be ignored. His troops might initially obey orders, but he doubted whether 'they would retain their nerve and keep firing on women, children and harmless old men'. He was not the only one with misgivings. Everywhere civilians were being forcibly evacuated from the areas occupied by German soldiers encircling the city. Thousands were being moved along the Pskov road. They were mostly women, children and old men. Nobody knew where they were supposed to go. The Army Group North war diary admitted: 'Everybody had the impression that these people would sooner or later die from starvation. The scene had a particularly negative impact upon the German soldiers working along the same road.'

The die had now been cast. On 22 September, continuing contemptuously to use its pre-revolutionary name, Hitler issued an order entitled 'The future of the city of Petersburg'. His directive was issued to all generals, officers and soldiers on the northern front and its intentions could not have been clearer. Meeting with success everywhere, the war against Russia was at its high-water mark. In the south, nearly three-quarters of a million Soviet soldiers had been encircled at Kiev and German troops were racing unopposed through the Ukraine. The focus was now on a great offensive to smash the last Russian armies facing Army Group Centre, capture Moscow and finish the war. Hitler was jubilant, confidently believing that he could soon send Army Group North's Panzers to join the attack on Moscow. The blockade of Leningrad would be maintained by the infantry and the city pounded by heavy artillery, now within firing range. With Moscow in dire peril, the Soviets would be unable to help Leningrad. Hitler felt the city's utter vulnerability, and set out his plans for destroying it and starving its people to death:

> The Führer has decided to raze the city of Petersburg from the face of the earth. After the defeat of Soviet Russia there will not be the slightest reason for the future existence of this large city. It is proposed to blockade it closely and by means of artillery fire of all calibre and

> ceaseless bombardment from the air to raze it to the ground. If this creates a situation which produces calls for surrender, they will be refused. In this war, we are not interested in preserving even a part of the population of this large city.

When Hitler's soldiers received this statement of intent, its cruel logic seems to have reassured some on the ground. Artillery officer Rolf Dahm had earlier wondered why the advance on Leningrad had come to a halt. The arrival of the 'Führer Directive', as he called it, clarified things: 'Our command probably considered the problems we would have taking over a city of well over two million inhabitants that would have to be fed throughout the winter. Better to stay in front of the city and try and starve the inhabitants into submission.' Except that the inhabitants were not going to be starved into submission. They were going to be starved to death. An inexorable chain of events had been set in motion.

Hitler had spoken of 'ceaseless bombardment from the air'. On 8 September, the day that Shlisselburg fell and nutritionist Professor Ziegelmeyer met with army high command, the Germans launched their first major air attack on Leningrad. Their planes, which had massed at recently captured Estonian airfields, came over the city that evening, in two main waves. In the first, at 6.55 p.m., twenty-seven Junkers dropped over six thousand incendiary bombs. An hour later, the second wave delivered forty-eight high-explosive bombs of 500 to 1,000 pounds. They were aiming for one target – Leningrad's food warehouses.

The Badaev warehouses had been built by an old St Petersburg merchant just before the First World War. Entirely wooden, they had been put up in close proximity to each other – the gaps between the buildings were less than twenty-five feet – with the site covering several acres in the south-west quarter of the city. All the city's grain, meat, lard and butter was stored here. Astonishingly, the Leningrad authorities had not dispersed their food reserves. Now they all were to go up in a sea of flames. A tidal wave of two and a half thousand tons of molten sugar flooded into the Badaev's cellars. The smell of burning meat and the acrid stench of carbonised sugar filled the air.

Evgeny Moniushko was on fire duty that evening, manning the roof of a house on Griboiedov Street, near one of the city's canals. He had seen the occasional German aircraft before, but this was something entirely different:

> We had an excellent view of the southern horizon from our six-storey block. The heavy anti-aircraft fire began in the south. German aircraft appeared between the white puffs of explosions which covered the sky. Not single aeroplanes as before, but this time an entire formation of them – tens of aircraft from the look of it. They flew at low altitude – you could clearly see their engines, the shining disks of their spinning propellers, and the details on their tails. The aircraft dropped their bomb loads on the southern side of the city, and then proceeded north without changing direction, as if on parade. Where the bombs fell, a wall of smoke and dust appeared, rising higher and higher.

Moniushko began to realise there was something unusual about the blaze: 'The smoke didn't settle and didn't dissolve after the aeroplanes left; on the contrary, it grew thicker and thicker. When it started to get dark, the lower part of the smoke cloud was red coloured and became brighter as the darkness descended on the city. Finally, huge tongues of flame appeared between the dark silhouettes of the buildings.' The awful truth began to dawn: 'We learnt that the Badaev warehouses, which were filled with all our food reserves, were burning.'

In the days that followed, extracts from the diary of Leningrader Elena Skrjabina convey an inexorable and growing sense of menace:

> The Badaev warehouses are completely destroyed. All the supplies of the city were concentrated there. Isn't it strange that supplies were all kept just in that spot, a spot well known to the entire city? The Germans, of course, were well informed of this. The destruction of this storehouse threatens Leningrad with inevitable starvation. The whole city is steeped in clouds of smoke and the odour of burning ham and charred sugar.

Next day Skrjabina wrote: 'The destruction of the Badaev warehouses can already be felt. The daily ration has been lowered to 250 grams [for dependants]. Since there is almost nothing else besides this bread, the decrease is felt most strongly.' On 22 September, the very day of Hitler's directive about the fate of the city, Skrjabina looked into the future and feared the worst: 'We are approaching the greatest horror. It gets harder every day. The question of nourishment is the most important. Everyone is preoccupied with only one thought: where to get something edible so as not to starve to death. We have returned to prehistoric times. Life has been reduced to one thing – the hunt for food.'

2

'The Biggest Bag of Shit in the Army'

Attempts to Defend

WHILE GERMAN TROOPS were capturing Shlisselburg and sealing off Leningrad, the man entrusted with the defence of the region, Marshal Kliment Voroshilov, was desperately trying to conceal news of the town's fall from his master, Stalin. It was a double tragedy for Leningrad that as the great city faced the might of the advancing German Panzers, its defence had been entrusted to the incompetent Voroshilov, commander of the Soviet North-Western Front.

Voroshilov was a hero of the Russian Civil War and a fervent Bolshevik. He was also a loyal supporter of Stalin – and politically he could always be relied upon in an emergency. These qualities had allowed the ageing marshal to gain a place in the Soviet pantheon second only to Stalin himself. It was only years later that Nikita Khrushchev produced a blunter appraisal, succinctly describing him as 'the biggest bag of shit in the army'.

It was Voroshilov's woeful influence in the first vital months of the war that set in place the city's military disaster. As the Germans moved ever closer to Leningrad, Stalin was growing increasingly concerned. In July 1941 radio operator Mikhail Neishtadt was transferred to the city's Smolny Institute, the headquarters of Leningrad's civil and military administration. 'The calls from Moscow became more and more frequent,' Neishtadt remembered, 'and often Stalin was on the line in person. At first he called occasionally, and then more often. Finally, as the German threat hung menacingly over the city, it was day and night.' It was clear that something was seriously wrong, and that Stalin was losing confidence in Voroshilov's ability to organise Leningrad's defence properly.

In the Soviet era, Leningrad was not only the birthplace of the Bolshevik Revolution, but the centre of the country's heavy industry. 'Stalin knew the names – the family names – of the directors of all Leningrad's main factories,' Neishtadt recalled. 'His knowledge was extraordinary – he was paying attention to everything.' The Soviet dictator also knew that it would be a catastrophe if the Germans took the city. 'During the terrible summer of 1941,' Neishtadt continued, 'as our army kept retreating, Stalin began to say, more and more insistently: "Leningrad must never be given to the enemy!"'

There was a powerful historical echo behind this forceful declaration. Twenty-two years earlier, as the Bolsheviks had struggled to consolidate their power in the midst of a vicious civil war, the city had been under threat. In October 1919, the White Russian Army of General Nikolai Iudenich – another army motivated by a fanatical hatred of Bolshevism – had fought its way to the Pulkovo Heights above the city, the same high ground that the Germans were to reach in September 1941. At this earlier moment of crisis, Lenin – the driving force behind the Russian communist state – briefly lost heart, and prepared to give up the city. He simply did not believe that it could be defended.

Trotsky, the commander of the Red Army during the Civil War, refused to accept Lenin's decree. He understood that, however bleak the situation, it would be a body blow to Bolshevism if it lost the cradle of its revolution. He rallied the communist forces and beat back Iudenich. Stalin loathed Trotsky, but knew that he had made the right decision. In the early autumn of 1919 Lenin had panicked. In the early autumn of 1941, Stalin, his successor, would hold his nerve. Leningrad *would* be defended.

But Voroshilov – the man chosen by Stalin for this important task – simply wasn't up to the job. 'Stalin became more and more critical of his military decisions,' Neishtadt remembered. On one occasion, in increasing exasperation, he directly challenged the measures adopted by his hapless commander. Voroshilov was focusing on constructing one line of defence, along the Luga river, seventy miles from Leningrad. 'Stalin countermanded his instructions,' Neishtadt said. 'He insisted that Voroshilov create a system of defence in depth to protect the city.' But, although the Soviet dictator had lost faith in Voroshilov's military ability, he was strangely reluctant to remove the old warhorse from his post.

Stalin doubted Voroshilov's competence, but he knew that this Bolshevik diehard would remain absolutely loyal in a crisis. Loyalty was the key, for while the Soviet supremo recognised Leningrad's vital importance to the Soviet state, he was still deeply distrustful of the city. In the 1920s, as Stalin had manoeuvred his way to power, Leningrad's leaders had been suspicious of his designs, and the city had become a rival centre of influence within the Communist Party. Stalin never forgave – and he remembered this of Leningrad. On a more fundamental level, he also felt threatened by the city's tradition of free-thinking and its unique cultural identity. St Petersburg had been the home of the Russian intelligentsia. Leningrad carried that standard forward into the Bolshevik era.

In the late 1920s and 1930s, as Stalin created an increasingly totalitarian regime in the Soviet Union, he sought to impose a rigid conformity of thinking upon Leningrad. But he remained pathologically suspicious nonetheless. In August 1941, with the Germans rapidly approaching, the city authorities set up an additional defence committee to deal with their ever increasing workload. But they had not asked Stalin's permission to put this routine measure in place, and the Soviet dictator was incensed. However improbably, he imagined that the committee was a ruse, and that something far more sinister was going on behind his back – even that the city might be planning to negotiate with the Germans. The committee was promptly dissolved.

So Stalin kept Voroshilov in his post – however reluctantly – because he could always be relied upon. For a while, his instinctive distrust and fear of Leningrad overrode all other concerns. But in the critical days of early September 1941 Stalin's tolerance reached its breaking point. His commander's behaviour had become alarmingly erratic. On one occasion, on 11 September, Voroshilov suddenly turned up at the front line, waving a pistol and urging Russian soldiers into battle. He charged forward with them towards the German positions, but then ran out of breath and was left behind. The enemy remained completely unruffled, and after a sudden crescendo of artillery and machine-gun fire Voroshilov next encountered his men running back towards him at high speed. Leningraders were unimpressed by the marshal's heroics. Such was his mismanagement of the campaign, many now believed he was deliberately trying to get himself killed at the front rather than face the prospect of being recalled and shot on Stalin's orders.

The speed of the German advance into Russia in 1941 has created an aura of invincibility around its war machine. It seems inevitable now – as it must have done then – that the Wehrmacht's Panzers would race towards Leningrad that summer, and their Russian opponents – despite isolated instances of dogged courage and fanatical resistance – would largely be unable to stop them. But in reality there was nothing predetermined about the success of Hitler's forces. They might instead have been faced by a formidable Soviet commander, who not only understood the tactics of mechanised warfare but was able to anticipate them, and a well-trained and well-equipped army strong enough to counter their devastating *Blitzkrieg*. It was a tragedy for Leningrad, and for the Soviet Union as a whole, that this was not what came to pass.

Stalin's indulgence of Voroshilov was a symptom of a deeper malaise. In the decade before the outbreak of the Second World War there had been a struggle within the Soviet state between two factions. One sought to create a modern, professional Red Army; the other wished to impose a rigid political ideology on the armed forces, believing that communist faith rather than military hardware would be the reason for future Bolshevik success in battle. Kliment Voroshilov was the leading representative of the latter camp.

Before the war with Germany, Voroshilov's only military experience had been during the Russian Civil War, more than twenty years earlier. The son of a poor railway worker from southern Russia and a metalworker by trade, he rose to extraordinary fame when he successfully welded Bolshevik revolutionaries in the Ukraine into a fighting force. Voroshilov was utterly fearless in battle and his most lauded military action was to defend the city of

Tsaritsyn (later renamed Stalingrad) from the White Russian armies. It was during this turbulent time that he met and became friends with Joseph Stalin. But Voroshilov was never comfortable as an army leader.

The fight for Tsaritsyn in 1919 seems far removed from the battle for Leningrad in 1941, yet, frighteningly, both cities would be defended in a remarkably similar fashion. Sometimes history does repeat itself, and the two stories echo each other in a quite uncanny fashion. There was an ominous warning of the disaster that would later befall Leningrad when Trotsky remarked that Voroshilov's defence of Tsaritsyn combined the untamed spirit of guerrilla warfare with administrative chaos and anarchy. He was under no illusions over how this state of affairs had come about, writing to Lenin that in his opinion Voroshilov was at best capable of commanding no more than a regiment. At Tsaritsyn he was in charge of an army of 50,000 men; in 1941, on the North-Western Front, he was responsible for a series of armies totalling half a million soldiers. The omens for Leningrad's defence were hardly promising.

During the Civil War it had been difficult for anyone to ascertain what Voroshilov was up to. His compliant chief of staff seemed to spend most of the time in a drunken stupor, and although it was regular army practice to submit operational reports twice a day, Voroshilov's force failed to submit any operational reports whatsoever. To his fury, Stalin was to encounter similar difficulties when the Wehrmacht tightened its grip around Leningrad in 1941. He should not have been surprised, for the man in charge of the entire North-Western Front at this momentous time had already shown himself incapable of working within a regular army command system. This had been clear as early as 1919, when Voroshilov had refused to liaise with his front commander, and Trotsky explained why:

> Voroshilov was the man who most detested military professionals. 'The locksmith of Lugansk' – as he came to be called – was a hearty and impudent fellow, not overly intellectual but shrewd and unscrupulous. He could make neither head nor tail of military theory – but he was a gifted browbeater, and he had no compunction about using the

ideas of brighter subordinates and no false modesty about taking full credit for them.

At Tsaritsyn Voroshilov and Stalin had formed an unholy alliance – one which would prevail right up to the outbreak of the Second World War. Voroshilov spread the happy legend that together the two of them had rooted out dissident elements within the army and created true 'Red Bolshevism'. The irritating fact that they had completely ignored the instructions of the region's commander-in-chief was passed over, Voroshilov citing Stalin's cynical and self-serving justification: 'Our "military experts" are psychologically incapable of combating counter-revolution, being "staff" workers, who only know how to make sketches of field operations and draft plans . . . I shall correct these and many other shortcomings on the spot – even to the point of removing the officials and commanders who ruin matters – and shall continue to do so, in spite of formal difficulties, which I shall brush aside when necessary.'

This deep-seated animosity against military professionals would return to haunt both men in 1941, and during the first months of the war it spelt utter ruin for the country they were leading. A warning of this impending catastrophe was already present in 1919, when 'formal difficulties' associated with regular military procedure were 'brushed aside' in startlingly ruthless fashion. When the front commander sent some of his staff officers to Tsaritsyn to restore order, Stalin and Voroshilov arrested them, accused them of being counter-revolutionaries and confined them to a barge on the Volga river. Trotsky, the supreme commander, ordered their release, but when his telegram arrived Stalin wrote one word under it: 'Disregard'. The barge subsequently sank, without explanation – drowning all on board. Later, in private correspondence, Stalin and Voroshilov referred to the 'Tsaritsyn barge incident', and the necessity of disposing of 'unreliable military specialists' en masse, indicating that the two had decided together to get rid of the officers Trotsky wished to save.

Stalin and Voroshilov were thus complicit in a ruthless act of murder to serve their own political ends. Eighteen years later, in

1937, they would re-enact the same scenario on a much grander scale, supervising the purge of thousands of Red Army officers, many of whom were subsequently executed, because they were seen as a threat to Bolshevik power. These draconian measures weakened and demoralised the forces that were supposed to defend the country and encouraged many Wehrmacht generals to believe that a quick and easy victory against the Soviet Union was now a real possibility.

The Soviet system deliberately created its own mythology around past events. It chose to romanticise its triumphs during the Civil War, cloaking the fact that Voroshilov's defence of Tsaritsyn had been conducted in the most cavalier fashion. Having deliberately ignored the instructions of men with far greater military understanding and experience, Voroshilov had flung masses of poorly trained civilians into battle, insisting that the Red Army rely on more popular, 'partisan' activists. He was profligate in his use of soldiers and civilian recruits alike, only too happy to sacrifice them on the altar of the Bolshevik cause – a characteristic ruthlessness he shared with Stalin. This casual disregard for human life was the most chilling aspect of his defence of Leningrad in 1941.

In 1919, even Lenin had been worried. 'Voroshilov did without military experts and suffered 60,000 losses,' he noted in one memorandum. 'This is terrible . . . Comrade Voroshilov's trouble is that he doesn't want to jettison this old partisan way of thinking.' Voroshilov never would jettison it. As Stalin consolidated his power he promoted his friend to the post of commissar of the army and in the newly emerging Soviet Union Voroshilov enjoyed a massive personality cult, second only to the leader himself. His portrait was everywhere, songs were regularly composed in his honour and movies were even made about him. But he remained lazy and content to trade off these supposed glories from the past. His approach to the army he was meant to supervise was stagnant, creating a backwater in Soviet military thinking and ensuring Leningrad was defended in a fashion appropriate to a bygone revolutionary era twenty years earlier. Against the modern professional might of the German army the result was calamitous.

The tragedy for Leningrad was that things could have been so very different. The military commander of the city in the late 1920s and early 1930s was a man of an altogether different calibre – Mikhail Tukachevsky – an exceptionally gifted thinker and strategist. Tukachevsky was everything Voroshilov was not – intelligent, well educated and innovative. He was hard-working, and had a brilliant understanding of military affairs. One of the Red Army's leading generals, Marshal Koniev, later wrote in his memoirs: 'Of all our commanders in the 1930s, Tukachevsky, more than anyone else, deserved to be regarded as a modern military leader. If Tukachevsky had been managing the war with Germany in 1941 we would not have suffered such terrible reverses.' Under Tukachevsky, Leningrad had the most advanced armament factories in the Soviet Union and a coterie of leading military designers and thinkers. The city symbolised the possibility of fighting a modern, professional war.

Such a symbol could only be unsettling for someone whose entire martial philosophy was founded on unthinking Bolshevik dogma, and, unsurprisingly, Voroshilov and Tukachevsky detested each other. Lavrenti Beria, Stalin's dreaded chief of secret police (the NKVD), remarked that Voroshilov was pathologically jealous of any officer more intelligent than he was. In return, Tukachevsky loved to ridicule Voroshilov, telling stories that showed the marshal in a ridiculous light. Georgi Zhukov, one of the Soviet Union's most brilliant soldiers, witnessed one acerbic exchange at a meeting reviewing the Soviet Union's defence strategy. When Tukachevsky began his report Voroshilov interrupted with a particularly unhelpful suggestion. Tukachevsky responded in matter-of-fact fashion: 'Comrade People's Commissar, the commission cannot accept your amendment.' Voroshilov was taken aback. 'Why not?' he demanded. 'Because your amendments are incompetent, Comrade People's Commissar,' Tukachevsky continued serenely.

But Tukachevsky was a little too fond of putting people in their place. He had befriended the Leningrad composer Dmitry Shostakovich and once suggested that they both take a trip to the city's Hermitage Museum. Tukachevsky was travelling incognito, in civilian clothes, and at first they decided just to look at some of the paintings, then they tagged along with a guide. The guide in question was a young fellow – not particularly well educated – and after a while Tukachevsky began interrupting and correcting his commentary. His remarks were very much to the point, and soon everybody was listening to him, leaving the suddenly abandoned guide absolutely furious. 'Who is that?' he spat at Shostakovich. But when he learnt who it was his indignation was replaced by real fear. And Shostakovich knew the reason why: 'As commander of the military district, Tukachevsky had great power in Leningrad – if he had merely made the slightest complaint about the commentary, the guide would have been fired immediately.' Now things became quite farcical. The guide's angry manner vanished at once, replaced by eager, fawning adoration. 'He began thanking Tukachevsky for his priceless information,' Shostakovich recalled with wry amusement. 'Tukachevsky replied benignly, "Study, young man, study. It's never too late." As we headed towards the exit, Tukachevsky seemed very pleased with this adventure.'

However, Tukachevsky underestimated Voroshilov's political guile. Voroshilov, although completely subservient to Stalin, understood the Soviet leader's need for flattery and reassurance. In military matters he was out of his depth. But in the world of political intrigue he was a vindictive and dangerous opponent. The feud between Tukachevsky and Voroshilov came to have tragic consequences for Leningrad – and the country as a whole.

By the end of 1929, the Soviet state had launched its first five-year plan to expand industrial capability. A detailed plan for the defence industry should also have been drawn up, but Voroshilov had been unable to decide on one. Instead, a further group of military specialists were rounded up and subjected to a series of show trials. The main consequence of this action was to impede the development of vital aircraft and artillery technology.

From his Leningrad power-base Tukachevsky was lobbying for a modern army, but on 21 December 1929, on the occasion of Stalin's fiftieth birthday, Voroshilov brought out a clever piece of sycophancy: a short pamphlet entitled *Stalin and the Red Army*, eulogising Stalin's role as military leader. Since Voroshilov's main achievement as defence commissar was to purge the army of a number of former tsarist officers, whose military talents would be sorely missed, this was a remarkable stroke of opportunism. It reminded Stalin of their bond of friendship – brutally forged by the elimination of the officers at Tsaritsyn in 1919 – and the author's impeccable record of Bolshevik loyalty. Voroshilov felt threatened by Tukachevsky's military skill and hoped his pamphlet would safeguard his own position as defence chief. The pamphlet was widely publicised, and although it played havoc with Soviet history, the artful panegyric delighted Stalin.

Tukachevsky always looked forward in military affairs, anticipating that in the future the Soviet Union would face a mechanised war against a well-equipped European power; Voroshilov remained resolutely turned backwards, constantly refashioning the experiences of the Civil War into a sacred mantra, believing that once the Bolshevik faith was rekindled the Red Army would always prevail. Voroshilov's pamphlet portrayed his leader and friend as a one-man military fire brigade, rushing from place to place, shoring up the Bolshevik cause with true revolutionary ardour. Flattery was a shrewd option in the circumstances, for Voroshilov had been struggling with his defence work. He was at heart a cavalryman – who loved to ride and shoot – but hopelessly out of his depth with any modernisation plans for the army's artillery and tanks. In 1919 the Red Army had created a strong cavalry force, but the times were changing and Voroshilov was incapable of changing with them.

The frequent technical failures that bedevilled the modernisation programme – a result of Voroshilov's own incompetence – continued to be blamed on hapless 'military specialists', who, it was charged, were now orchestrating a plan to sabotage the entire defence industry. One engineer was arrested after Voroshilov claimed that 'a caste-like counter-revolutionary group of old specialists hinders the improvement of the artillery'. Similar groups were apparently sabotaging the steel production for machine guns, rifles and even specific weapons, such as the new 37mm gun. The Soviet foreign minister Viacheslav Molotov later commented: 'Much was expected of Voroshilov as commissar of defence. He wanted desperately to measure up, but he couldn't. He always lagged behind the times . . . he just didn't catch on to things.'

Meanwhile, Tukachevsky was using his time as chief of Leningrad's military district in a very different fashion, visiting the city's tank and munitions factories and gaining valuable experience in new weaponry. He was genuinely excited by these technological advances, and from this basis he proposed a wholesale rearmament of the Red Army. He saw a vital opportunity to accelerate the modernisation programme and thus strengthen the Soviet Union's capacity to defend its borders. Voroshilov opposed him – and canvassed Stalin's support. He sent the proposal to his leader with a spiteful covering note: 'Tukachevsky wants to be original and "radical". It's bad that there is a breed of people in the Red Army who take this "radicalism" at face value. I beg you to read both documents and give me your opinion.'

It is tempting to imagine that Stalin always had a clear blueprint for the Soviet Union's military development, but in this major arena he was at times genuinely uncertain how to proceed. While he shared Voroshilov's instinctive prejudice against military professionals, he also quickly grasped the vital importance of developing new technology. As a result, he was more open to the idea of creating a modern army than Voroshilov, but nevertheless suspicious of the scale of Tukachevsky's rearmament scheme, which he feared could be financially ruinous for the country. He commented to Voroshilov: 'The plan fulfils the view of purely military men, who often forget that the army forms part of the broader economic and cultural condition of the state.' But Voroshilov's triumph was not complete, as Stalin added an important caveat, making clear, despite his opposition to wholesale rearmament, that 'I respect Comrade Tukachevsky very much as an unusually competent comrade.' In contrast, while promoting Voroshilov to defence commissar as a reward for his political loyalty, Stalin recognised his limitations. Trotsky, now in exile, wrote perceptively:

> It is no secret that the old Bolshevik Voroshilov is a purely decorative figure. In Lenin's lifetime no one would have dreamt of electing him

> to the Central Committee. Although his personal courage in the Civil War is undeniable, he displays a complete lack of military and administrative ability and shows the outlook of a backwoodsman. Neither Stalin nor any other member of the Politburo has any illusions about his qualities as a military leader, and for this reason they make efforts to support him in office by giving him the assistance of far more able colleagues.

The future of the Red Army, and the capacity of the country as a whole to defend itself in a modern war, now hung on the rivalry between these two men and the opposing viewpoints they represented. Voroshilov was so desperately insecure about Tukachevsky that he drafted a triumphant letter to him, revealing his bitter animosity towards his rival. He began defensively, accusing Tukachevsky of spreading lies in alleging that he had neglected the need for new technical weapons and a strong army in general. This was, of course, the crux of the issue between them. Adopting a paternalistic tone, Voroshilov then suggested that Tukachevsky would be better employed drilling troops in the Leningrad military district rather than debating such larger matters: 'I wish that you would as soon as possible stop your very learned digression and concentrate all your knowledge and energy on practical work. This will bring immediate and concrete benefits to the cause, for which you and I have been appointed by the party, and this will better than anything else cure you of your incorrect and in my view politically harmful opinions.' Voroshilov made clear that he saw Tukachevsky as a divisive influence, who wished to create factions and splinter groups within the Red Army – and then, hiding behind Stalin's own criticism, concluded gloatingly: 'I send you his [Stalin's] appraisal of your "plan". It is obviously not flattering to you. But it is my deep conviction that his conclusion is correct.'

Voroshilov was unable to manage the army but he displayed an animal-like cunning in tenaciously clinging to power. He realised Tukachevsky's Achilles heel was his ambition – his rival had been likened in the Soviet press to a 'Red Napoleon', and Napoleon had of course used his military success to seize political power. Voroshilov played on this fear in his conversations with Stalin, accusing his rival of 'Red militarism', a dangerous phrase in the communist lexicon – implying that Tukachevsky was using rearmament as a smokescreen to build up an independent power-base in the army. In the letter drafted for Tukachevsky this same charge was repeated. But Voroshilov had to be sure of his ground.

When dramatic accusations surfaced against Tukachevsky – that he had become involved in a plot to bring down the Soviet government – Voroshilov did not know whether Stalin would believe them. So he held back, and did not despatch his carefully crafted letter to Tukachevsky. It remained a draft in his personal archive, with a note attached stating: 'Not sent'.

In August 1930, during a series of 'interrogations', two members of the Soviet military academy implicated Tukachevsky as leader of a right-wing conspiracy aiming to establish a military dictatorship. But Voroshilov was right to hesitate, for Stalin, well aware of his personal animosity towards Tukachevsky, was suspicious about the veracity of the information. The Soviet leader proceeded cautiously, making clear in a letter to a trusted Politburo ally: 'I don't know if Klim [Voroshilov] is informed. This would mean that Tukachevsky has been captured by an anti-Soviet group . . . Is this possible?' He added firmly, 'It is impossible to finish off this issue in the usual way (immediate arrest and so forth). We must ponder the matter carefully.' Following a through investigation, the charges were found to be groundless and in October 1930 Stalin was able to write to Molotov, his foreign secretary: 'As for Tukachevsky, he turned out to be 100 per cent clean. That is very good.' The Soviet leader now became interested in his plans for reforming the Red Army.

After careful discussion, some of Tukachevsky's plans were adopted and he was allowed to oversee production of a new range of tanks at Leningrad. On 7 May 1932 Stalin sent him a remarkable letter. Now he wrote, 'when some of the matters under discussion have become clearer for me, I must confess that my earlier judgment of you was too sharp'. He referred to Tukachevsky's modernising agenda approvingly, stressing the need for a 'growth of military transport technique, the development of the air force, the emergence of mechanised formations and a corresponding reorganisation of the army'. Stalin now expressed his full agreement with Tukachevsky: the old Bolshevik formula of attack en masse – the hallmark of Voroshilov's approach – was to be discarded in favour of the new vision of a modern professional army:

> It is not the number of divisions, but first of all their quality, and their supply with new equipment, that from now on will be the determining factor. I hope you will agree with me that a 6-million strong army, well equipped and organised in a new manner, will be fully satisfactory in order to defend the independence of our country, at all the frontiers, without exceptions. Such an army is also more or less within our capability.

If this policy had been properly enacted, with Tukachevsky at the helm, the German army would never have been able to reach Leningrad in the summer of 1941.

In his letter Stalin was even penitent. He recalled Tukachevsky's somewhat brisk attempts to free him from a certain 'conservatism of thinking' over tank production, and even managed a touch of rueful humour in his concluding remark: 'Don't scold me for the fact that I have started to correct my earlier shortcomings with a certain belatedness.'

Tukachevsky was now in the ascendant – and Voroshilov was forced to tag along, floundering under the new demands placed upon him. Stalin prodded him, frequently inquiring about the progress of the new defence industry programme. On one occasion Voroshilov complained that calculating the number of artillery rounds necessary in a phase of military expansion was 'extremely complicated'; on another, Tukachevsky noted with amusement that 'an attempt by our Defence Commissar to explain the principles of mobile warfare at an army meeting has sown complete disorder in the minds of the commanders there'.

Under Tukachevsky's guidance, the fighting capacity of the Red Army started to improve dramatically. In public, Voroshilov had little choice other than to praise Tukachevsky's modernising drive; in private he began to compile a dossier of information to deploy against his rival. Old prejudices die hard, and Voroshilov knew that, despite his conversion to a more modern military way of thinking, Stalin did not completely trust Tukachevsky, and as a result the political weathercock might well swing his way again. An opportunity was offered to Voroshilov through an extraordinary set of circumstances.

During the 1920s and early 1930s Germany and the Soviet Union engaged in a clandestine programme of military co-operation. Since the two nations were soon to become embroiled in one of the most ferocious and destructive wars in human history, this fact is quite astonishing. The programme was long kept secret by the Soviet government and the archival records, which show its full extent, have only recently become available.

Such military co-operation was of course directly prohibited by the Treaty of Versailles after the First World War, but both sides had much to gain from it. On the Soviet side, it provided access to Western industry and technology; on the German, it allowed military personnel to be trained and in particular to develop skills in fighter-aircraft flying and tank manoeuvre at secret Russian bases, far away from prying eyes. Germany had been deprived by the Versailles treaty of the right to have tanks, but from 1927 it ran a secret training base in the Soviet Union, codenamed 'Kama', at Kazan. German officers reached this tank school by going undercover, temporarily leaving their own army and travelling as civilians via Poland, on passports citing fictitious peacetime occupations. It is a considerable irony that one of the men trained here was Heinz Guderian, the architect of *Blitzkrieg* and one of Germany's most brilliant Panzer generals, who was later to unleash his tanks with deadly effect on the Soviet Union.

Voroshilov and Stalin would later deny any knowledge of these close contacts, but in reality they were kept well informed about them. On one occasion Voroshilov personally received a group of German military leaders – headed by Major-General Wilhelm Adam – when they were invited to visit the Soviet military academy in Moscow, and on 11 November 1931 he reported back to Stalin: 'I am sending you a record of my conversation with Adam. I will tell you about my impressions personally.' It was Tukachevsky who spent most time with the German delegation, a fact that would later be used against him, although he was privately already suspicious of German intentions towards Russia.

By 1933, with Hitler's rise to power and frequent attacks in the German press on the evils of communism, the relationship between the two countries was becoming strained. Voroshilov was under no illusions about the likelihood of maintaining a military partnership with the new Nazi regime. 'The German army is "friendly" with us, though in its heart hating us,' he said simply. He was also left under no illusions about Germany's rapidly developing armed might, receiving a report of 10 April 1933 which stated: 'It seems to us that in the field of motorisation, artillery weapons and communication facilities the Germans stand much higher than they reveal to us.' Real co-operation between the two powers was failing, and manipulation and deceit taking its place.

In the meantime, Voroshilov was carefully monitoring all Tukachevsky's activities. When the German generals were visiting the Soviet Union, and a return visit of Tukachevsky to Germany was proposed, an incautious remark was immediately noted. At a lunch reception, among a small group of military men, an informant reported, 'Comrade Tukachevsky repeatedly stressed that Germany, to extricate itself from the difficult political situation, should as soon as possible have an air fleet of 2,000 bombers.' When this document reached Voroshilov its incriminating potential was obvious, and three times, using a blue pencil, he heavily underscored these words.

In 1936 these tensions came to head. Tukachevsky and a group of fellow officers tried to get Voroshilov removed from his post of defence commissar on grounds of incompetence. Voroshilov retaliated by sending Stalin an intelligence intercept of the German Embassy's reports to Berlin on how Tukachevsky now displayed 'a big respect for the German army'. It was Voroshilov who won out.

The political atmosphere had changed. Wholesale purges were now commonplace within the country and Stalin was increasingly suspicious that an independent power-base did in fact exist within the Red Army. The Germans cleverly played on these fears, forging documents incriminating Tukachevsky in dealings with them, and then ensuring that they fell into the hands of Soviet intelligence. At the end of May 1937, Tukachevsky was arrested and tortured, a confession extracted, and he was then shot. A bloody purge of the Red Army followed, presided over by Stalin and Voroshilov, to root out thousands more 'plotters'. Lavrenti Beria, who took over the NKVD after Tukachevsky's death, later remarked to his son Sergo that he had never found any real proof that such a plot existed: 'Tukachevsky had done nothing against Stalin and the party, or at least nothing that would justify his arrest. His only offence was to attack that idiot Voroshilov.'

In the hot summer of 1941, with the Germans racing across Russia, Dmitry Shostakovich fondly recalled his friend Tukachevsky, believing things would have been very different if he was still in command of Leningrad at this perilous time:

> During the war I thought about Tukachevsky often. He had been called 'the Soviet Union's greatest military theoretician' and now we sorely lacked his clear mind. I thought of Tukachevsky when I dug trenches outside Leningrad in July 1941 . . . We were the Conservatoire group. The musicians looked pathetic and worked, I might add, very badly. One pianist came in a new suit. He delicately rolled up his trousers, revealing his spindly legs which were soon covered with mud to the thigh. Of course, everyone tried hard. So did I. But what kind of ditch-diggers were we? All of this should have been done before – much earlier and more professionally. It would have had more effect. The little that had been done earlier in terms of defence had been done under Tukachevsky.

Tukachevsky's arrest and execution had truly awful consequences. In November 1938 Voroshilov proudly announced that 'In the course of the purge of the Red Army in 1937–8, we have expelled more than 40,000 men.' Most of the expelled were shot. This was the fatal culmination of Voroshilov's loathing of military specialists, for the orders for the rooting out of supposed 'enemies of the people', former tsarist officers, 'Trotskyist double-dealers' and anyone considered ideologically dubious, were issued under a series of telegrams bearing his signature.

The head of the army was now launching a crazed assault on its entire officer corps, motivated by his own deep-seated prejudices and a desire to carry out Stalin's wishes and be worthy of his trust. Of the five marshals of the Soviet Union, three were shot; fifteen out of sixteen army commanders were eliminated; sixty out of sixty-seven corps commanders; 136 out of 169 divisional commanders. With things completely out of control, and the army virtually leaderless, Voroshilov was obliged on 3 January 1939 to issue order number 001, which read: 'Permission to arrest Red Army officers of senior, higher and middle ranks may only be given by me.'

Ordinary citizens of the Soviet Union were left totally bewildered by this state of affairs. One teenager described the effect of the military purges:

> We learnt the biographies of our army leaders by heart and then we were suddenly told that most of them were 'enemies of the people'. They didn't exactly tell us what they'd done, but simply affixed this label on them, and said that they were enemies who had contacts with foreign agents. Now, even 14- or 15-year-olds begin to wonder how these leaders, some of whom have been associated with Stalin for 20 years or more, suddenly become 'enemies of the people' and then become distrustful and suspicious. As a child I picked Voroshilov as my personal hero. Another boy chose Tukachevsky. All this boy's fantasies were destroyed. What should he think now, this boy, who believed so blindly before?

A veteran of the Soviet merchant marine explained that he began to lose faith in official propaganda around 1937: 'With Tukachevsky, I remember coming to school and someone was taking his portrait off the wall. Then all the boys were supposed to scratch out his picture from the text books and scribble derogatory phrases about him. It made me think – how could that happen, how could that be?'

The result of the wholesale purges was calamitous, as Nikita Khrushchev subsequently revealed: 'There is no question that we would have repelled the fascist invasion much more easily if the upper echelons of the Red Army command hadn't been wiped out. They had been men of considerable expertise and experience. Many of them had graduated from military academies and had gone through the Civil War. They were ready to discharge their soldierly duties for the sake of their country, but they never got the chance.' The modernising drive initiated by Tukachevsky ground to a halt.

With his rival removed, Voroshilov celebrated his success by busying himself in the studio of the Soviet painter Alexander Gerasimov. 'Gerasimov, a very talented artist, painted Voroshilov riding on horseback, Voroshilov skiing . . .' Molotov observed. 'Their association seemed to be one of mutual back-scratching.' He also developed an enthusiasm for the world of theatre, seeing himself as something of a connoisseur of opera. 'Voroshilov was much more interested in showing off his impressive military bearing at public celebrations than he was in supervising arms procurement and organising troop deployments,' Khrushchev declared. 'His negligence was criminal. His subordinates must have reported to him what things were like, but these reports rolled off him like water off a duck's back.'

Voroshilov's star role was in the 1938 film *If There Is War Tomorrow*, directed by Efim Dzigan. The hour-long feature set out to reassure the Soviet public that their army could easily deal with any attack by Hitler's regime. It showed fascist troops massing on Russia's borders, but although this sequence was menacing – with German soldiers climbing into their tanks and their planes roaring through the skies above them – Voroshilov then appeared in his best uniform, appealing to the peoples of the Soviet Union to repel the hated foe. His speech was a turning point, allowing Soviet troops to move quickly into battle and drive the Germans from their trenches and, keen horseman that he was, he ensured the film's biggest setpiece was a Red Army cavalry attack which vanquished the mechanised might of the Wehrmacht. Voroshilov had, after all, declared that the war was going to be fought on the aggressor's soil and it was going to be won there.

In March 1939 Voroshilov announced to the Communist Party Congress the complete defeat of the band of despicable traitors who had tried 'to destroy our army from within, to treacherously enfeeble it and to make its defeat certain in time of war'. He continued enthusiastically: 'This suppurating ulcer of treachery has been lanced. The Red Army has been rapidly and thoroughly purged of all this filth.' Then, to stormy and prolonged applause, he made a pledge to the nation: 'Our army stands as a watchful sentinel over our frontiers . . . ready at any moment to launch into battle against any enemy who dares to set foot on the sacred soil of the Soviet state . . . That enemy will be crushed and destroyed in short order . . . Our army is first class, better than any other army, an army that is technically well equipped and splendidly trained.' He concluded triumphantly: 'Comrades, our army is invincible!'

The 'invincibility' Voroshilov trumpeted was soon put to the test. In November 1939 the Soviet Union declared war on Finland. The Red Army was expected to win quickly and easily, but Molotov remembered an ominous moment before the war began. When the question of arming Russian soldiers with machine guns was raised Voroshilov rejected the measure. 'We do not have the industrial capacity to do this,' he stated blandly. Stalin was suspicious. 'How can you say that? Others have it – why not us?' Voroshilov suddenly became agitated: 'If we switch to submachine guns, where on earth will we find so many bullets? We'll never have enough!'

The war was to be fought from the Leningrad military district – and its preparations were organised by Voroshilov and the party boss there, Andrei Zhdanov. Voroshilov and Zhdanov made a strange contrast: Voroshilov, notoriously vain, was always immaculately kitted out whereas the portly Zhdanov, with his bloodshot, expressionless eyes, cared little about his appearance, looking as if he had never washed properly and leaving his shoulders covered with dandruff. He was known as 'the grey eminence'. Yet both men were diehard Bolshevik loyalists and enthusiastic executioners in the name of party ideology. The partnership of this Stalinist odd couple was played out to disastrous effect during the Soviet–Finnish war, and then – quite incredibly – reprised for the defence of Leningrad against the advancing Germans in 1941.

Zhdanov, realising that Stalin was suspicious of Leningrad – and fully understanding that the Soviet leader resented the city's independent outlook and way of thinking – presided over the political purges with the same frightening vigour that Voroshilov had demonstrated towards the army, rooting out imagined plots everywhere.

The suffering that Leningrad would endure during the German siege was presaged by two years of savage punishment meted out by its own leaders. During 1937–8 more than 30,000 Leningraders were arrested; some of these were executed, others deported to labour camps in Siberia and the Arctic. 'It was impossible to tell who would be killed next,' one survivor recalled. 'People died in delirium, confessing to a series of outrageous crimes – spying, sabotage, terrorism and wrecking. They vanished without a trace, and then their wives and children, entire families, disappeared as well.'

Zhdanov had the same gift as Voroshilov, a bloodhound's instinct for uncovering more and more imagined conspiracies. He even sent the NKVD into Leningrad's Hermitage Museum, discovering 'German spies' (in the Coin and Antiquities Department), 'Japanese spies' (in its Oriental Department) and 'class enemies' everywhere. One elderly curator – a long-time collector of antique arms and armour – was found guilty of 'storing weapons with the aim of using them in the organisation of an armed uprising'. In all, a dozen curators were shot as spies and a further fifty arrested and sentenced to terms of imprisonment in forced-labour camps.

Lyubov Shaporina described the atmosphere in Leningrad at the height of the purges in the summer of 1937: 'I am living in a communal nightmare. I keep getting the feeling that I am inside the Bryulov painting *The Last Days of Pompeii*. Columns are falling around me, one after another, there's no end to them; women run past me, fleeing with terror in their eyes.' On 10 October in the same year she spoke more directly about what was going on: 'The nausea rises in my throat when I hear how calmly people can say it: "He was shot, someone else was shot – shot, shot, shot." The word is ever present; it resonates through the air. People pronounce the words calmly, as though they were saying "He went to the theatre." The real meaning of the word doesn't reach our consciousness – all we hear is a sound.' The she continued revealingly:

> We don't have a mental image of those people actually dying under the bullets. You hear the names: Vitelko – a singer, who'd just recently performed in a competition; Natalia Sats – a theatre director; and many others. And there is the cruelty of exiling the wives of

> people who are arrested. People spread rumours that are so horrible you have to cover your ears: how they are sent out to the 'regions', in other words, into the bare desert. My friend Evgenia is living like a baby mouse, with a cat sitting right above her, waiting for just the right moment to finish her off [Evgenia's husband, the journalist Alexander Starchakov, had been arrested in November 1936]. Who will fall next, will it be you? And it's already so commonplace, you're not even scared any more . . .

The gifted Tukachevsky had worked closely with Leningrad's military establishment, and – suspicious of his legacy – Zhdanov singled it out for special attention. Towards the end of 1937, thousands of the city's best army and naval personnel were abruptly liquidated. One morning Shaporina woke early:

> It was about three in the morning, and I couldn't get back to sleep. There were no trams, it was completely quiet outside, except for an occasional car passing by. Suddenly I heard a burst of gunfire. And then another, ten minutes later. The shooting continued in bursts every ten or fifteen minutes until just after five. Then the trams started running and the street resumed its normal morning noise. I opened the window and listened, trying to figure out where the shots had been coming from. The Peter and Paul Fortress was near by, and this was the only place where they could be shooting. Were people being executed there? Between three and five in the morning it couldn't be a drill. Who were they shooting? And why?

Shaporina struggled to hold her night-time memory amid Leningrad's daytime bustle: 'Our consciousness is so deadened that sensations just slide across its hard, glossy surface, leaving no impression. To spend all night hearing living people, undoubtedly innocent people, being shot to death and not to lose your mind! And afterwards, to try and fall asleep and to go on sleeping, as though nothing had happened . . . How can you find the strength to live, if you let yourself think about what's going on around you?'

Arrests continued apace. On 15 January 1938 Shaporina noted another: 'Leva, our simple-minded theatre fan and prop man, was exiled to Chita. Straight into exile – without any form of investigation. At this rate, they might as well arrest the table or sofa.' Shaporina's friend Evgenia – the victim of the cat-and-mouse game – had also been arrested, a year after her husband, and she had now taken in the couple's children: 'Evgenia is in Tomsk – in a special prison camp. What threat could she pose to anyone, this unfortunate woman who raised her children in such a way that they didn't even utter a word of complaint when their father and then their mother were taken from them? They are still totally stunned. Little Mara said once, while reading *Pinocchio*: "How is it that Papa Carlo doesn't know how to find the country where all the happy people live? I thought everyone knew it's the USSR!"'

In early 1938 show trials took place to remove another mass of army leaders. Shaporina reflected on the accumulating weight of injustice and feared for her country:

> The great, great Dostoevsky! We now see, not in a dream, but right before our eyes, the herd of devils that entered into the swine: we see them as they never have been seen before. All through history people have struggled for power, have plotted revolutions but never have people worked so hard to destroy their own homeland . . . The really dangerous ones are Stalin and Voroshilov . . . It is unbearable to be living in the middle of it all. It's like walking around in a slaughter-house, with the air saturated with the smell of blood and carrion.

Everyday life in Leningrad was becoming more and more difficult. The purges had wiped out so many technical experts and experienced administrators that the city was falling into disrepair. In January 1939 Shaporina wrote: 'If you want to buy some manufactured product you have to spend all day in line for it. The factories are standing idle for lack of fuel. Yet the newspapers are in ecstasy about our happy and prosperous life and advances in worker discipline.'

Zhdanov, wishing to bask in Stalin's favour, now decided that the city was capable of organising the supply and logistics of the war against Finland. Even the NKVD boss Lavrenti Beria was left dumb-founded. His son Sergo remembered him saying: 'The stupid idea that this invasion could be carried out by the forces of the Leningrad Military District came from Zhdanov, and was endorsed by that "subtle strategist" Voroshilov.' Zhdanov assured Stalin that two to three weeks would be enough to subdue Finland. Stalin, remembering the strength of that country's Mannerheim Line – whose defences were linked to a series of lakes and rivers – was concerned that they might prove a formidable obstacle. 'No problem,' said Voroshilov happily. 'They'll all be frozen over.'

Mikhail Lukinov, an artilleryman with the 62nd Rifle Division, remembered the war's beginning in December 1939:

> Our soldiers arrived in Leningrad – the great city of Peter and Lenin, city of a revolution that shook the world, city of beautiful architectural ensembles, palaces and museums. But it couldn't be recognised now. It was a different Leningrad – a cold, harsh front line city, gloomy, dark and shrouded in snow. We unloaded at a freight station, our guns were pulled through the city in carts and horses, and trams with frost-covered windows carried us through the frozen streets to the northern suburbs.

Lukinov then said simply: 'We were told we had to make Leningrad safe and separate it from the dangerous Finnish border by creating a zone of Soviet land. But we couldn't understand the way in which the war was conducted: the failure to bomb the Finnish defences effectively, to use tanks properly or to employ airborne drops to outflank the enemy. Instead, they chose to throw our people straight in front of machine-gun and artillery emplacements.' After the initial Soviet offensive had bogged down, Admiral Nikolai Kuznetsov had indeed proposed a naval landing to the rear of the Finnish defences to turn the Mannerheim Line. Voroshilov vetoed the idea.

Voroshilov claimed that he had improved the efficiency of the Red Army through a series of much needed reforms. He had certainly instituted a startling career-advancement system in the wake of the purges: henceforth a commander's technical training and organisational abilities would be discounted in favour of his class background and participation in the ritual denunciation of colleagues. Captain Yanov, a tank battalion commander in the 138th Division, recalled how Voroshilov's new system worked in practice. The Red Army was supposed to launch an attack on a key Finnish defence position, at Hill 65, near Summa:

> At 6.00 a.m. on 17 December [1939] we were supposed to move to our jumping-off positions, but this presented us with incredible difficulties, for the roads were cluttered up with a whole variety of different units. We smashed our way through to the front line only to find a situation of total disorder. Another battalion of tanks had strayed into our area, and then another followed it. All these detachments were mixed up, and it was quite impossible to separate them and work out in what order they were supposed to carry out their duties. Then the regimental artillery arrived – hours late – and a line of infantry also forced their way into the scrum. It was a scene of indescribable chaos.

It was now midday, and the attack had been ordered for 12.30 p.m. Yanov went to find the commanding officer, but when he reached him the officer looked baffled.

> He stated, 'I do not know you – it is the 95th Tank Battalion that is supposed to be fighting with me'. I explained that according to the instructions of the corps commander my tank battalion was also supposed to be in the attack. He tried to sort things out, failed, and then sent me to his chief of staff, who was unable to make sense of things either. He simply waved the battle orders around – but these seemed to have been written thoughtlessly and hurriedly. I was sent on to the chief of communications to establish a link with the artillery, but nothing came of this as this fellow – both inexperienced and illiterate – was unable to use the radio transmitter properly, and kept crossing into the frequencies of completely different units. No communication with the artillery was ever established. Meanwhile, more and more people were crowding around the chief of staff seeking instructions. I just gave up – I could make no sense of what was going on – and I decided to await events.

As the Red Army moved forward, there was little reconnaissance of the enemy's positions and a woeful lack of overall strategic planning. In his reports to Stalin, Voroshilov characteristically tried to lay the blame on others – demanding courts martial and executions. 'I regard a radical purge of the corps, divisions and regiments as essential,' he exclaimed. But Red Army troops were running out of food, fuel and ammunition and suffering heavy casualties. 'We were not properly prepared for this war,' veteran Vasily Davidenko complained. 'Everything went wrong: I was a platoon leader and a forward observer for my regiment but when we reached the Mannerheim Line I didn't even have a map! We were forced to halt, allowing a Finnish reconnaissance plane to fly over and photograph our position and then direct an artillery strike against us. Unsurprisingly, our losses were very high.'

The first Soviet attack against the Mannerheim Line ended in costly failure, and in January 1940 an experienced military commander, Marshal Semyon Timoshenko, had to be brought in to retrieve the situation. The Red Army finally broke through and forced an end to the war in March 1940. To struggle so much against a small country like Finland was an embarrassing fiasco and Mikhail Lukinov remembered the hollow victory parade Voroshilov and Zhdanov organised in Leningrad:

> The regiments that had been deployed in the reserve, and had seen no fighting whatsoever, were brought back first and paraded through Leningrad like heroes, with celebratory banquets, gifts and greetings. And when the remnants of our own regiment entered the city – a real fighting unit which had finally broken the Mannerheim Line and carried all the hardships of war on its shoulders – the celebration was already over and everyone had gone home.

Scapegoats for the failure were quickly found – the hapless combatants who, through the incompetence of their superiors, had been surrounded and captured by the enemy. Now they would be accused of betraying their country. Lukinov encountered a most disturbing sight: 'At Leningrad's train station we saw freight cars, their windows entwined with barbed wire. They stood separately, on a different track, and guards – with their bayonets fixed – prevented anyone from getting close. But one railway worker whispered to me that inside were Russian soldiers who had been taken prisoner by the Finns.'

Voroshilov would later complain that he had been let down by poor intelligence-gathering, but the intelligence had been in place – it had simply not been consulted. After the war, Timoshenko remarked to Khrushchev: 'If only we had deployed our forces against the Finns in the way even a child could have figured out from looking at a map, things would have turned out differently.'

The only benefit to emerge from the Finnish war was that Stalin's eyes were finally opened to the truth about Voroshilov. Following this drastic display of his utter incompetence he was now summarily removed from his post of defence commissar. Stalin wrote scathingly: 'The war with Finland exposed the poor state and backwardness of the Defence Commissar's [Voroshilov's] leadership. The Red Army lacked mortars and machine guns, it had no proper inventory of aircraft and tanks, the troops had no proper winter clothing or food-supply bases. Great neglect was revealed in the development of artillery and aircraft and providing proper battle training . . . This all led to the war being drawn out and to unnecessary losses.'

The Soviet leader's frank appraisal was somewhat belated, but Voroshilov was now to be used only for political work, and kept out of military affairs. What happened next is hard to explain. Some fifteen months later – with the war against Germany just three weeks old – Stalin restored his old Tsaritsyn comrade to the front line. On 11 July 1941 Voroshilov was given command of the North-Western Front, with the responsibility of defending Leningrad. Two days later Zhdanov was named his second-in-command.

This strange decision echoed Stalin's earlier volte-face over Red Army reform, when after initially supporting Tukachevsky he changed his mind and backed Voroshilov instead. It strongly suggests that the Soviet leader was still disorientated, reeling from the shock of the surprise German attack. Whatever doubts he had about Voroshilov's military abilities, he knew that the old Bolshevik warhorse would support him at a time of crisis, and this loyalty was highly prized.

Stalin was worried about Leningrad's precarious position. Finland had joined the war as Germany's ally and was advancing on the city from the north. The Baltic States – only recently annexed by the Soviet Union – were already welcoming the Wehrmacht, and to the west of Leningrad Estonian forces were actively collaborating with the Germans and had already seized the southern part of the country. If Leningrad became politically isolated from the rest of the Soviet Union, Stalin feared that an opposition faction might seize control there and sue for a separate peace. Yet the appointment of Voroshilov was a blunder – one that would leave a catastrophic legacy for the city he was supposed to protect.

Radio operator Mikhail Neishtadt remembered his new commander's theatrical arrival at Leningrad's Smolny Institute on 11 July. 'It was just before midday when, with a sudden, ear-splitting bang, the door burst open and Marshal Voroshilov charged in, with Zhdanov running after him. The duty commander, Ilyichev, was so taken aback that he muddled up the two men's positions, announcing Voroshilov as secretary of Leningrad's Communist Party and Zhdanov as head of the army. Our staff listened in total bewilderment.' The cloud of confusion never really lifted.

When Voroshilov took charge in Leningrad he had on paper at least thirty divisions available for the defence of the region: some of these were fully manned, others still needed to be topped up with men and equipment. His priority should have been to create a system of defence in depth around the city, complete the training of the remainder of his force and then bring them into the battle lines. But, typically, Voroshilov neglected orthodox military thinking and instead concentrated all his resources on one line of defence, along the River Luga. The logic of his approach was to try and stop the German advance as far away from the city as possible. But by mobilising the population to build these defences and creating scratch volunteer forces to man them he was putting thousands of civilian lives at risk. He was offering Leningrad a one-trick pony, and once the Luga Line was outflanked from the south, the city no longer had any coherent system of defence.

Within a week, Voroshilov had despatched hundreds of thousands of people to work on the Luga Line, and militia units and workers' battalions were hastily formed up behind them. No proper system of defence in depth existed to support such grandiose dispositions. The real priority should have been to build up regular army formations. The front's chief of staff, Major-General Nikishev, later wrote: 'The difficulty of our situation lay in the fact that neither army nor divisional commanders had any real reserves. Every break in the line – even the smallest – had to be stopped up with scratch forces or units assembled any old how. To suppose that opposition to the German advance could be made by these militia units – which had only just formed up and were poorly organised – was completely unjustified.'

Voroshilov persisted nonetheless. Soviet soldiers watched in amazement as a mass of civilians from Leningrad suddenly appeared among them, sent out to work on the Luga defences. 'They were mostly women and teenagers,' one combatant remembered.

> There was little food for them or proper facilities, and no protection from the enemy. And the Germans were already within artillery range. They had an artillery spotter who was observing the area where they were digging through his binoculars. And then their shells fell – methodically, precisely. Our soldiers dashed from their dug-outs, grabbing youngsters and women, pulling them off the road and out of the line of fire. There is one image I will always remember. An incendiary shell landed on the road. A herd of cattle, frightened by the flaming asphalt, began a stampede, kicking up a huge cloud of dust. Then the terrified animals charged straight into a minefield.

Voroshilov's arrival was accompanied by a burst of defiant rhetoric. On 11 July 1941 a rousing proclamation was issued under his name and Zhdanov's: 'Comrades, Red Army men, commanders and political workers,' it began: 'Over the city of Lenin, the cradle of the Proletarian Revolution, looms the immediate danger of the invading enemy.' The decree demanded discipline from Leningrad's brave and honest defenders, before adding that anyone found leaving the front would go before a field tribunal and be shot, regardless of rank or responsibility. But over the next few days neither Voroshilov nor Zhdanov got a grip on the military situation. The diaries of ordinary Red Army soldiers – which were later captured by the Germans or confiscated by the NKVD – reveal the grim situation on the ground.

Military detachments were shuffled around aimlessly. Jacob Yushkevich's unit was sent out to meet the advancing forces of Germany's Army Group North in mid-July. He remembered driving through the streets of Leningrad with civilians dolefully following their passage, 'there is uncertainty in everyone's eyes, the citizens are concerned about us and we about ourselves'. They headed out of the city, and were then ordered to stop: 'They put us in lorries and suddenly propelled us in a completely different direction.' The men of his unit became separated and then tried to form up again, but they were now quite lost and in their confusion kept driving around each other. 'We have been moving for a few days now from place to place,' Yushkevich recorded. 'Sometimes we look for the rest of the battalion, and they on occasion look for us. During one such "manoeuvre" we covered a distance of 94 kilometres.'

Stephan Kuznetsov's unit arrived in Leningrad on 16 July 1941. The men were expecting to go quickly into action against the Germans. They were given uniforms of a marine battalion, but two days later new orders arrived, and these outfits were exchanged for regular army uniforms. Apparently they were now to form up as a reconnaissance unit. Their reconnaissance activities did not last long. On 20 July the bemused troops were told that there had been another change of plans and they would be joining the Baltic Fleet after all. But a day later these instructions were also countermanded. They were now to march to Peterhof and join a motorised battalion. When they reached Peterhof the motorised battalion had already left. On 23 July Kuznetsov and his fellows gathered around a field kitchen. They were exhausted – and thoroughly confused. No one had any idea where they were going or what they were supposed to do.

The mobilisation of these forces was totally disorganised. Stalin, alarmed by Voroshilov's actions, turned to a far more experienced commander – Lieutenant-General Vatutin – and ordered him to launch an armoured counter-attack against the flanks of the advancing Germans. Vatutin's forces responded with a desperate ferocity that briefly unnerved the Wehrmacht. It was a supreme irony that their heavy tanks – the KV-1s and KV-2s – whose production had been encouraged by Tukachevsky, had then been named after his arch-rival, the old cavalryman Kliment Voroshilov, who had done so much to hinder their progress.

But after two wasted weeks presiding over chaos Voroshilov now made a sudden, drastic intervention. Its content is little known, for the information was suppressed by the Soviet authorities for many years, but it was to have horrific consequences for Leningrad's civilian population.

Early in July 1941, the Soviet trade minister Anastas Mikoyan sent trainloads of grain and other foodstuffs westwards to the town of Pskov – a major armament and supply depot for the Red Army. But the Wehrmacht's Army Group North got there first, and rapidly seized the town. Mikoyan now took a crucial decision. On his own authority he diverted the massive convoy of food to Leningrad. Soviet cities were supplied by a strict quota system, but his justification was simple. He knew that Leningrad was already short of food (rationing had been introduced in the city on 18 July) and, concerned about the speed of the enemy's advance, felt it was only prudent to prepare for all eventualities, including a German siege of the city. As he saw it, additional food reserves for Leningrad – even if they exceeded a notional quota – would never be 'superfluous', but rather were absolutely necessary for the wellbeing of its citizens.

As the trainloads of vital provisions rolled towards Leningrad, Voroshilov heard of Mikoyan's decision and dramatically stepped in. He may have feared that these measures looked unnecessarily defeatist and that Stalin would disapprove of them. Whatever his justification, on his own authority as front commander he countermanded the order and halted the convoy south of Leningrad, at the rail junction of Novgorod. There it waited.

Voroshilov conferred with Zhdanov. Both men were afraid that receiving the food convoy might create a negative impression and, solely concerned with their own political survival, they determined not to allow it into Leningrad. Mikoyan was told that there was 'insufficient warehouse space' to receive the provisions. Food that could have saved the lives of hundreds of thousands of Leningraders was then transported elsewhere.

Early in August 1941 Red Army soldier Semyon Putyakov confided to his diary that 'administrative chaos' pervaded the Leningrad Front:

> Things are a total mess . . . We are constantly moved from place to place. All we do is make dug-outs – we receive no proper training: I haven't been instructed in any decent military skills. Finally our regiment has received a commanding lieutenant – Petrenko – but his orders leave even raw recruits totally exasperated. He lacks any real training or experience and only gets in the way. There was an article in the *Leningrad Pravda* extolling the virtues of our command system but I personally see only the most terrible mismanagement.

On 16 August, as Manstein's Panzers were routing Soviet forces at Lake Ilmen and preparing to outflank Voroshilov's defences, Putyakov wrote with a sense of foreboding: 'This is a war of technology – the side that wins will be technologically superior to the other. The Germans have advanced a greater distance in two months than they did in two years in the First World War. In contrast to us, they make particularly good use of intelligence and reconnaissance.'

Lieutenant Yushkevich's battalion, operating south of Leningrad, had now collided with Manstein's advancing forces. German aircraft flew overhead, spearheading the attack, and Yushkevich and his men were caught in their strafing fire. They ran across an open field into some nearby woods, but they had been spotted by the enemy and their position 'was raked with methodical persistence by bombs and machine-gun bullets'. Yushkevich heard a dreadful cry. Crawling towards the source of the screaming, he found one of his comrades dying in agony. The man's legs had been blasted away through the sheer force of a bomb explosion. 'That sight will always remain in my memory,' Yushkevich wrote in his diary. He rallied the survivors, and as evening fell rejoined his battalion. At dawn the air attacks started again.

Voroshilov was taken aback by the new and totally unexpected military threat from the south. On 20 August he ordered the creation of Home Guard battalions to defend Leningrad, deciding that these would include women volunteers and also teenagers, who as he saw it 'might be especially valuable for surveillance and communications work'. He admitted that there was now a serious shortage of weapons and ammunition but had a solution ready to combat the technological might of the enemy, announcing purposefully: 'The

Home Guard is to be armed with hunting guns, home-made explosives and sabres and daggers from Leningrad's museums.'

At the end of August Stalin, growing ever more concerned about the way the city was being defended, flew in a Politburo delegation on a fact-finding mission. Molotov recalled that there was no sign of Voroshilov when they reached the Leningrad Front HQ; he was eventually found racing around the front line, inspecting dug-outs. Alexei Kosygin, who held overall responsibility for supplies within the Soviet government, was candid: 'The city's administration had failed to understand the danger threatening Leningrad and did not seem to have concerned itself with such matters as the evacuation of civilians or industry.'

On 30 August Stephan Kuznetsov was working in Oranienbaum harbour – to the west of Leningrad, on the Gulf of Finland – and spoke with some of the refugees gathered there. Voroshilov, fearful of collaboration, was forcing thousands of civilians from towns and villages in the line of the German advance back into Leningrad. But he had not given any thought to how they would be fed. One refugee said to Kuznetsov: 'Our army is not allowing its citizens to stay behind and is forcibly moving everyone. But we cannot get bread. Everything is rationed in the city and we have not been issued with ration cards.' Kuznetsov was appalled. He wrote in his diary: 'This situation will lead to mass starvation.'

On 3 September Semyon Putyakov's unit was falling back towards the city. He noted glumly: 'Now we are at the gates of Leningrad and there is nowhere else to retreat to. Morale among our soldiers is terrible.' Lieutenant Yushkevich was equally explicit: 'Our soldiers are only issued with old rifles and we have pathetically few machine guns. We haven't any grenades either. There are no medics! This is not a military unit – we are simply cannon-fodder.' Germans were all around them and most of the battalion had already been killed – Yushkevich and the remnants of his company were 'being hunted through the woods like animals'. That night he wrote his last diary entry: 'Constant shooting – Panzers everywhere.' Wehrmacht soldiers, searching among the mounds of Soviet slain, recovered his notebook the following morning.

On 8 September the Germans captured Shlisselburg, sealing off Leningrad from the rest of the country. Stalin's patience finally snapped and he despatched a furious telegram to Voroshilov and Zhdanov: 'Your behaviour disturbs us . . . You informed us very chaotically about the loss of Shlisselburg. Will there be an end to these losses? Can one hope for some kind of improvement at the front? We insist that you now inform us two to three times a day of the situation and the measures you are taking.'

On the same day that Shlisselburg was seized the Germans had also bombed the Badaev food warehouses, and Lavrenti Beria later told his son Sergo: 'Voroshilov and Zhdanov had been instructed to disperse Leningrad's food reserve and build new storage sheds in different parts of the city. The army and NKVD had pressed for this to be done urgently. Through sheer incompetence, the work was delayed, and the wooden storehouses were burnt down by the Germans, dooming the city to famine.'

On 11 September Voroshilov returned from his pistol-waving expedition to the front line to be met by General Georgi Zhukov, who had flown into Leningrad on Stalin's orders to take command of the surrounded city. Voroshilov was abruptly dismissed from his post. Typically, Stalin now laid all the blame on the man he himself had put in command. Voroshilov was accused of 'serious mistakes made defending Leningrad'. His failure to grasp even the most elementary principles of modern warfare had at last become clear to his master: Voroshilov had 'neglected artillery defence' and instead had been 'distracted' by the creation of Home Guard battalions, 'which were poorly armed with shotguns, pikes and daggers'.

Almost any other Soviet commander demonstrating such staggering incompetence would have immediately faced the firing squad. Yet, remarkably, Voroshilov – although clearly in disgrace – was neither shot nor cashiered; instead, Stalin posted him far to the rear of the war effort where he could do less damage. Whether out of friendship or gratitude for his political loyalty, the Soviet leader could not dispense with him entirely. But their ghastly partnership as Red Army overseers – forged in an act of callous murder at Tsaritsyn in 1919 and cemented through the bloody purges of 1937–8 – was now over. Khrushchev recalled its extraordinary dissolution, shortly after Voroshilov's return to Moscow:

> I remember how, at his dacha, Stalin jumped up in a white-hot rage and started to berate Voroshilov. Voroshilov, seemingly unintimidated by this, also became incensed. He leapt up, turned red, and hurled Stalin's accusations back into his face. 'You have yourself to blame for all this!' he shouted. 'You're the one who annihilated the Old Guard of the army; you had our best generals killed!' Stalin rebuffed him, and at that, Voroshilov picked up a platter with a roast suckling pig on it and smashed it down on the table. It was the only time in my life I ever witnessed such an outburst.

On the evening of 11 September 1941, with Leningrad besieged by the enemy, Voroshilov shook hands with his staff before flying out of the stricken city. 'Farewell, comrades,' he said. 'They have called me to headquarters . . .' Voroshilov paused reflectively, then continued: 'Well, it has to be. This isn't the Civil War – we have to fight in another way.'

Leningrad's ordeal was only just beginning.

3

The Butcher's Hook

Ordinary Civilians' Experience

GERMANY DECLARED WAR on the Soviet Union on Sunday 22 June 1941. Leningraders retain vivid memories of what they were doing when the news was announced. Georgi Knyazev had been reading *Pravda* when a news item caught his eye. An archaeological team had travelled to Samarkand to open the tomb of the great medieval warrior Tamerlane, and the day before work had recommenced in the vault of the ancient Gur Amir palace. 'Today an exciting discovery has been made in the Mausoleum,' the paper announced. The team had been despatched from Leningrad to secure artefacts for a big new exhibition on the Mongol Empire being prepared at the city's Hermitage Museum. On Wednesday 18 June they had levered off the black-jade tomb slab; on Friday they had exhumed Tamerlane's body and measured his skeleton. Now *Pravda*'s morning edition carried a triumphant photo of the Leningrad archaeologist Mikhail Gerasimov holding aloft Tamerlane's skull.

Knyazev had been intrigued. He was director of the archive at Leningrad's Academy of Sciences, and was proud of the cultural tradition of his city and the drive to modernise the Soviet state. But he recalled reading how some local Uzbeks were opposed to the event. They had given a startling warning, reported by the Leningrad edition of *Pravda* with wry amusement: 'Popular legend, persisting to this day, holds that under this stone lies the source of terrible war.' Tamerlane had been a conqueror of monstrous cruelty. He laid waste nations with the speed of a whirlwind, leaving a trail of devastation and piles of skulls to mark the numbers of the fallen. But he had, after all, been dead for over 500 years. *Pravda* commented smoothly: 'Certain superstitious types believe spirits of the dead exercise power beyond the grave. They will no doubt make much of this exhumation.'

Georgi Knyazev finished reading his morning paper. Just after 11.00 a.m. the radio announced that Hitler had invaded Russia and later that day Knyazev had been moved to start a diary, beginning his first entry with the words: 'How everything on earth is repeated. In the fourteenth century Tamerlane conquered India, from the Indus to the Ganges, and also Persia and southern Russia. And now, far outdoing him, is the outrageous Hitler, who has brought so much suffering to other peoples, both the enslaved and humiliated and those who are fighting against his diabolical regime.' As he wrote, the scientist felt the intimations of real fear: blood throbbed in his head, and there was a strange sound 'like propellers whirring' resounding in his ears.

Elena Skrjabina remembered that beautiful June morning: 'Everything was as peaceful and calm as a still lake. The sun was shining and seemed to promise a perfect day.' She was preparing to take her eldest son and his best friend on a long-awaited trip to Peterhof in the Leningrad suburbs. The boys had never been there and were especially looking forward to seeing the palace's restored fountains. She flung open the bedroom windows letting in fresh morning air, feeling 'a wonderful sense of contentment and joy'. Outside the bedroom door she could hear the whisperings of their nanny, trying to restrain the youngest of their children, five-year-old Yura. Then her husband suddenly rang. He had heard worrying rumours and, greatly agitated, demanded that everyone be kept at home.

For many Leningraders, the declaration of war had an air of total unreality. It was the time of the summer White Nights, when daylight never leaves the city, and its inhabitants could stroll the streets and parks enjoying the glow of the midnight sun. Joseph Finkelstein was working at Leningrad's Research Institute as an engineer. He recalled that the night had been warm and bright. It was graduation time for many schools and he returned home late after a party. He remembered the girls in their long white evening dresses and high-heeled shoes, and how he had danced to the latest foxtrot melody 'Somewhere in Tahiti'. The next morning Finkelstein had gone out for a bite to eat, only to see a huge crowd gathered round a loudspeaker listening to the halting tones of the foreign minister Molotov declaring that 'German aircraft have bombed our cities. There is fierce fighting on our border.'

Despite this shocking news Leningrad initially retained its confidence and optimism. The war still seemed very far away. After all, people said to each other, hadn't Stalin declared, 'We will not yield an inch of our own land'? 'We sang patriotic songs,' Finkelstein recalled, 'with stirring refrains such as "We will destroy the enemy with one strong blow, We will suffer little bloodshed".' Nevertheless he felt he should be doing something, and on Monday morning he went to the recruiting office. He had received papers drafting him for July, but he wanted to take immediate action – his country was in danger. He joined a long queue:

> The atmosphere was noisy and chaotic, with many people cursing. Captains, majors and lieutenants were running from room to room. An orderly read my papers and yelled at me, 'Are you illiterate? It is clearly written when you need to be here. Do not disturb me – go home.' I answered, 'But the war has already started. I know German well – I can serve as an interpreter.' The orderly did not listen. 'Don't give me that crap! Get lost.'

Finkelstein's encounter with Soviet bureaucracy was alarmingly typical. The German attack was completely unexpected and there had been confusion at Leningrad's mobilisation centres. In the following few days the city remained quiet. Restaurants stayed open, the summer programmes of public entertainment continued and an initial buying spree tapered off when it was found that food supplies were still plentiful. Then, on 27 June, Leningrad's city council abruptly mobilised the population for defence work. According to a hurriedly passed decree all men between the ages of sixteen and fifty and women between sixteen and forty-five could be called up: the unemployed were to dig trenches for eight hours a day, the employed and students for three hours after work or classes. Managers of Leningrad's factories and apartment houses were told they must register everyone within twenty-four hours; failure to comply would lead to a hefty fine or imprisonment.

This was a first response to the rapidly approaching German threat. After the initial period of uncertain calm, Leningrad's administration had learnt to its consternation that Manstein's Panzers were already on the banks of the River Dvina, securing its bridging points. A mass of German tanks was now pointing like an arrow in the direction of their city. Clearly the war was not going to be contained in the frontier region, and the authorities swung from perplexed inaction to frenetic activity. Leningrad was now to be defended with a massive system of earthworks. It was imagined that these primitive obstacles would break the force of the German advance. The furthest ran along the Luga river, seventy miles west of the city; there were to be three smaller rings created around Leningrad's suburbs.

The city administration appealed to the patriotism of its population. Many wanted to do their bit and oppose the invader. Elena Kochina described the mood among her fellow workers, who were technical staff in one of Leningrad's laboratories: 'All of us dug anti-tank trenches around Leningrad today. I dug the earth with real pleasure – this was at last something practical! There were almost only women working in the trenches. Their kerchiefs flashed in the sun like coloured lights. It was as if there were a giant flower-bed girding the city.'

As alarm grew, the authorities approached their task with increasingly brutal determination but showed a poor grasp of practical organisation. Leningrad's civilians were to suffer real hardship in some of the outer construction work. On Voroshilov's arrival in the city, a fresh decree of 11 July had extended the period of forced labour, and the number who could be called up. One participant, a fifty-seven-year-old woman, recalled the oppressive conditions: 'we worked for 18 days without a break, 12 hours a day. The ground was as hard as a rock and most of the time we had to use a pick.'

On 11 July Elena Skrjabina confided in her diary, 'People are being sent away by the thousands to dig trenches,' but she was sceptical of the value of the exercise: 'No one is excused – young girls in sun-dresses and sandals, young boys in shorts and sport shirts. They are not even allowed to go home to change clothes. How much use can they really be? City kids don't know how to use a shovel, much less those heavy crowbars they must use to break up the dry, clay soil. The workers must sleep wherever they can, often under the open sky. As a result, many catch a chill and get sick, but absolutely no one is excused from duty.' She had witnessed the consequences of this: 'Young Tarnovskaya, who lives with us, is among the victims. I found her in bed with a high fever. Yesterday, when she returned from her place of work, it turned out that except for a light sundress, she had very little protective clothing. Apparently she will be ill for a long time.'

The external face of Leningrad had now begun to change. Familiar monuments were surrounded with sandbags. The famous equestrian statue of Peter the Great – the Bronze Horseman – disappeared under a mass of protective scaffolding. Industrial equipment was loaded up for evacuation. As the population helped dig the fortifications, Leningrad's very streets began to alter. Cross-shaped stickers appeared on windows – so that the glass wouldn't shatter in the event of a bombing raid. Lidiya Ginzburg remembered that, in the uncertainty of those early days, such mechanical activities had a soothing effect, distracting people from the awful foreboding of merely waiting. But she felt there was something poignant and strange about it too, reminiscent of a sparkling surgical ward, where there were as yet no wounded:

> Some people stuck the strips on in a rather intricate pattern. One way or another, the rows of windows with their paper stickers took on the form of ornament. From a distance on a sunny day it looked cheerful, recalling those decorative fretted scallops you see on the wooden huts of prosperous peasants. But everything changed if you looked closely. The yellowing of the paper, the blobs of paste, dirty newsprint showing through, the roughly trimmed edges – struck me as the symbolism of death and destruction, which had not yet had time to settle and attach itself.

This was action – but the true gravity of the situation had still not been properly understood by those running the city. Instead, the authorities anxiously tried to limit news of the enemy's advance. One of their first security measures was to confiscate all privately owned radio receivers, a step taken to deny people access to outside news. Instead the population was permitted to install cheap, small loudspeakers in their apartments, which were connected by wire to the local public address system, providing official Soviet news and propaganda. Posters, proclamations and leaflets were printed, bulletin boards set up, special newspapers circulated. These sources of news were unrestrained in their appeals to popular pride and patriotism, but much less forthcoming about the true situation at the front line. Official communiqués remained extremely vague about the formidable extent of the German advance.

On 8 July, Leeb's forces captured the strategically important town of Pskov, on the southern edge of Lake Peipus, halfway between the rivers Dvina and Luga. The Germans were moving forward with frightening speed. Still Leningrad's authorities downplayed the threat. Fighting 'in the direction of Pskov' was not reported until 12 July, and the town continued to be described as a 'battleground' until 24 July, when it had already been in German hands for sixteen days. Reinhardt's Panzers had now established their bridgehead across the River Luga. Subsequent communiqués ceased to refer to Pskov at all.

Although few people knew the exact extent of the military disasters, a strong sense began to emerge that something was really wrong. The greater the authorities' attempts to hide the truth, the more widespread became popular reliance on rumour and word-of-mouth information. One Leningrader wrote in his diary: 'from the veiled communiqués it is nevertheless absolutely clear that the Red Army is unable to stop the German offensive on any one of the defence lines'. People tended to interpret official news pessimistically, and assumed the worst. Descriptions of super-human deeds by individual Red Army soldiers or small units were a source of irritation. A sarcastic comment became popular: 'We are winning, but the Germans are advancing.'

In the uneasy days of early July, people were becoming frightened, but because of the news black-out the threat was glimpsed only from the corner of the eye. Leningrad's inhabitants found a different outlet for their growing concern: they began to fear that spies were in their midst. The authorities had always been nervous about enemy agents, and their propaganda had constantly warned the population to be on the look-out for them. In the weeks of the German advance, mass hysteria – spy mania – began to grow. People became increasingly suspicious of strangers. Guards were posted everywhere. Tram conductors stopped calling out street names 'in order to make it more difficult for spies to orientate themselves'. And there were numerous denunciations to the NKVD and militia. Unusual dress – too Western in style – a different accent, strange behaviour, was enough for many. Elena Kochina described an encounter with a suspicious Leningrader in early July:

> Spy mania, like an infectious disease, has struck everyone without exception. Yesterday, near the market, a little old woman dressed in a large mackintosh grabbed on to me. 'Did you see? A spy for sure!' she shouted, waving her short little arm after some man. 'He had trousers and a coat that were different colours.' I couldn't help but laugh. 'And a moustache that looked as though it had been pasted on.' Her close-set angry eyes bore into me. 'Excuse me . . .' I tore myself away. Before pushing off, she trailed me for several steps along the sidewalk. But, even to me, many people seem suspicious, the kind it would be worth keeping an eye on.

Recently released police records show little evidence of any actual agents being caught. But people were already noticing changes in themselves and others. On 5 July Elena Kochina recorded her first serious quarrel with her husband Dima. They were unsure whether to evacuate their young family or stay in the city: 'We argued. Offensive and unfair words flew back and forth between us. We were powerless to restrain them: they already lived their own, independent life in spite of us. This was our first quarrel. During his lunch break Dima came back home. "I can't work knowing that you're angry," he said, "let's make up." So we did. But something continued to stand between us. We were no longer who we had been before the quarrel, and no longer who we had been before the war.'

The growing sense of isolation was reinforced by an utter lack of charismatic leadership. In the early days of the Bolshevik Revolution such leadership had been close at hand. In October 1919, as the White Army of General Iudenich had approached the city, Red Army commander Leon Trotsky had come in person to rally the defenders. His impassioned speech transformed the mood of its people, inspiring them to defend the revolution. 'I make no secret of the fact that I have come here with a soul filled with alarm,' he told the assembled citizens. 'Perhaps no one else on earth has lived through what you have endured. But your city is the barometer for our Red Soviet Republic – its loss would be a catastrophe for all of Bolshevik Russia.' Trotsky concluded with a typical oratorical flourish: 'You are the torch of our Revolution, the iron rock upon which we will build the church of the future.'

'The inward rallying had begun,' one leading Bolshevik wrote. 'A new spirit began to rise within the workers' district.' Trotsky, always the superb revolutionary street tactician, recalled the moment the city's workers spontaneously turned to each other, exclaiming, 'We won't surrender, will we, comrades? No, we won't!' As Iudenich's forces prepared their assault, legions of enthused citizens transformed Leningrad into a labyrinthine fortress.

The situation in July 1941 could not have been more different. The administrators and placemen who now ran the city were entirely lacking in Trotsky's ardour. In the intervening years Leningrad had lost its popular leader, Sergei Kirov, assassinated in December 1934 – some said at the instigation of Stalin, who had feared him as a rival. A period of repression had followed. Kirov was replaced by Stalin's henchman Andrei Zhdanov – who was neither loved nor respected by Leningraders. Olga Grechina was a student at Leningrad State University when war broke out: 'No one talked about the city leaders; that theme was forbidden. There were always informers around. Of course, the people didn't like Zhdanov, because he was a "fat cat" – one of the worst we'd seen.' When Leningraders felt safe enough to speak their minds, the chain-smoking, overweight Zhdanov was most frequently called 'coward' or 'pig'.

Unlike Trotsky, Stalin did not travel to Leningrad and his belated radio address to the nation, on 3 July, scarcely roused the city's spirits. He commenced with the exhortation 'Brothers and sisters' – 'at least that was different,' recalled Joseph Finkelstein, 'he had never spoken to us like that before'. But the Soviet leader's appeal failed to gather momentum, and those who heard it were left unmoved. Georgi Knyazev noted that those who listened found the reception very bad and they couldn't make it out in many places. A passer-by told him: 'the accent was too pronounced and there were pauses, when you could hear the gurgling of water being poured into a glass'. What people could hear in between gulps sounded plaintive and apologetic. Stalin confessed that – for the time being at least – the Germans held the upper hand in man-power and weapons, as well as possessing the advantage of surprise. 'I wondered if he was going to announce his resignation,' one bemused listener remarked.

Stalin's savage political repression in Leningrad after the death of Kirov had already alienated many of its inhabitants from Bolshevism. In early July 1941 Elena Skrjabina found that her neighbour's husband had suddenly reappeared. He had languished in a prison camp for two years. His wife, who had fought to get the case reviewed, was initially overwhelmed with joy when he returned. But it did not last: 'A strained, strange relationship has grown up between them. He is fearful, crushed, jumpy, afraid to speak. In a whisper, she tells me what he endured. She says they beat him cruelly and often, demanding some sort of confession of his "crimes". He has a broken rib and is deaf in one ear.'

Far from creating unity of purpose as the Germans advanced, the nervous city authorities continued to make random, inexplicable arrests. On 8 July one of Skrjabina's co-workers disappeared: 'they came at night, searched, found nothing, confiscated nothing, but took her away anyway'. No one could offer any explanation for her sudden disappearance. Her brother had been drafted into the army and she was supporting an ageing mother, a tubercular sister and a three-year-old daughter. When Skrjabina visited, staying for half an hour, her own family wondered if she had been arrested too.

The callous relationship between the city's government and its citizens was well demonstrated in the decision to create a People's Army. Zhdanov wanted thousands of Leningraders to enlist in a citizen's militia as an emphatic response to Stalin's broadcast of 3 July. They would be volunteers, ready to defend their city 'to the last drop of blood'. Some zealous citizens, like Joseph Finkelstein, did step forward, moved by strong feelings of patriotism. Recruiting commissions then turned up at Leningrad's factories. They summoned individual employees and asked them if they 'wanted' to volunteer. They were warned that a refusal would be taken as sign of political disloyalty. One applicant was told, 'You are a Soviet man; you cannot refuse to volunteer'; another, in his late fifties with a weak heart, was reassured, 'Your state of health is of no significance – what is important is the very fact of volunteering and thereby displaying one's political attitude.'

Finkelstein remembered the emergence of this rag-tag fighting force: 'At the beginning of July the government began the creation of the Volunteer Army. Everybody could join this organisation – even those unfit for regular service. I was assigned to a newly forming People's Reserve Division. We were very short-staffed in junior officers and only had enough men to form a single regiment. We were temporarily sent to a school on Leningrad's Krestovsky Island. We shared it with student nurses ending their training. They say during war everything is forgiven – so you can imagine what was going on there.'

The city authorities tried harder. Those who still refused to volunteer were once more brought before the recruiting commission. 'Do you not wish to help your Motherland?' they were asked, in a threatening tone. Inducements were also offered: the families of volunteers would receive a larger allowance than those of regular draftees. Instructions were issued to the commissioners to recruit more widely, 'without considering too closely people's age or health'. People with weak hearts, arthritis and asthma soon found themselves shouldering rifles. Even the disabled were enlisted. Few people had any clear idea of what they were 'volunteering' for. Some were told they would serve in guard units within the city;

others that they would be called upon to fight only if the Germans entered Leningrad. Almost all expected to go through a lengthy period of training before being exposed to enemy fire.

By 12 July three divisions had been formed. They were desperately short of armaments and equipment. There were not enough rifles or uniforms, few light artillery pieces and scarcely any machine guns. The vast majority of volunteers had no training whatsoever and only a tiny fraction of their officers possessed any military experience. Not surprisingly, when they heard that Reinhardt's well-equipped Panzers had reached the Luga river on 15 July, there was panic.

A few regiments – including Finkelstein's – were retained for city defence, but Voroshilov and Zhdanov threw the rest into battle immediately. The authorities justified this by saying that 'although a people's division lacks necessary training and military experience, it makes up for this with its strong spirit'. The press published reports of volunteers learning soldiering quickly and performing heroically on the battlefield. But most of the People's Army was to be wiped out in a matter of days.

This senseless sacrifice was kept from ordinary civilians. Many had a strong sense of foreboding nonetheless. 'Workers at our Institute have joined the Volunteer Army and are heading for the front,' noted Elena Kochina. 'All day today we sewed knapsacks and collected them for the road leading to nowhere.' Georgi Knyazev also had his doubts: 'In the newspapers and on the radio appeals are made to the people to come to the defence of Leningrad. But things don't seem to have gone as they should with the People's Volunteers.' Yuri Ryabinkin, then a bright fifteen-year-old schoolboy, overheard some of his friends saying that they wanted to join the Volunteers, and wrote in his diary: 'Knowing a little about the insides of a rifle will not help you fight tanks.' Ryabinkin lived in the centre of the city, off the Nevsky Prospect, Leningrad's principal thoroughfare. From his vantage point, the young teenager saw the gap between official rhetoric and awful reality all too clearly:

> Every leader in the paper shouts out, 'We shall not surrender Leningrad! We shall defend it to the last!' But our army has not won

> any victories and there are not enough weapons. The militiamen in the streets and the People's Volunteers are armed with rifles of alarming vintage. The Germans roll forward with their tanks, and we are taught to fight them with a few grenades and bottles of incendiary fuel. That's how it is!

Georgi Knyazev was becoming conscious of the attitudes of those around him; while some remained positive, others were growing cynical or defeatist. He was worried. On 17 July he confided his fears to his diary. 'There are rumours going round that we are in extreme disarray. At a time like this, it's appalling. What is it that makes the Germans so frightening? It is their extraordinary degree of organisation, their precise, co-ordinated actions.'

Caught between an incompetent regime and a fearsome invader, Leningraders sensed that their lives were changing beyond all recognition. It is perhaps not surprising that Knyazev, an innately articulate and reflective man, should choose to keep a diary. But many others – ordinary people who would not undertake literary endeavours in calmer times – felt a strong wish to record what was happening, and the result is a rich variety of accounts of life in the city. Each diary relates an inner journey, and together they allow us to hear the real voice of Leningrad, which many of the diarists must have feared was about to be silenced by the enemy. Faina Prusova, a worker at the Petrovskaya Hospital, gave her son a thick exercise book and asked him to write down everything that happened to him and to other people. She too started to keep a war diary.

Yuri Ryabinkin, who had doubted the battle-worthiness of the city's volunteer force, was another energetic diarist. 'I was born in Leningrad on 2nd September 1925,' he wrote on the first page. 'I live with my mother, my sister and my aunt.' He added a little more about his family: 'My mother works at the regional committee of the building union. My aunt's a doctor and is now at the front. My sister is eight years old. Dad left us in 1933, married someone else and went to Karelia.' In the same year that Ryabinkin's father went away, his son had started school. He was now in the eighth grade. He enrolled in a Seafarers' Club over the summer, and loved it – his ambition was to join the navy – and was proud of the good marks he received for his studies. Amid this sunny confidence, some premonition had made Ryabinkin start a diary.

On 18 July 1941 food rationing was introduced in Leningrad, with cards required to purchase bread, butter and other products. The daily quota for bread was set at 800 grams for factory workers, 600 for office workers and 400 for dependants. The same day all city guides and street maps were withdrawn from use. The extraordinary art treasures of the Hermitage began to be loaded on to special trains. Its Picassos, Cézannes and Rembrandts were placed in protective crates. Georgi Knyazev felt Leningrad was losing part of its soul. Like many around him, he was becoming disillusioned by the policies of the city authorities. He helped colleagues from the Academy of Sciences pack the famous mosaic portrait of Peter the Great – the city's founder – by Lomonosov, and the original eighteenth-century street plans: 'It's hard to describe how I felt when they took the portrait off the wall. The workers removed it with enormous care and carried it down to the waiting car. I accompanied them in a state of dreadful agitation. Peter the Great had founded our Academy and I had looked after his picture with love and concern. Now I strongly believe I will never see it again.'

Knyazev took in the view along the Neva. The Admiralty spire gleamed in the sunlight. In the distance, past the bridge, he caught a glimpse of the Winter Palace. By the Vasilevsky Island ships were at their moorings and tall, powerful cranes stood at the Neva river bank. 'This is my city,' he suddenly exclaimed, 'my splendid city! So many have admired its beauty: Pushkin, Dostoevsky, Blok . . . Surely, we are not going to lose it to the enemy.' After his passionate outburst Knyazev kept drinking in Leningrad's unfolding panorama. At the end, he came to a decision: he would not leave the city under any circumstances. He was prepared to die there.

The introduction of rationing did not prompt an immediate panic. Consumer shops continued to display plentiful amounts of food. Although prices were too expensive for many Leningraders, the sight of foodstuffs was meant to be reassuring. As Elena Skrjabina put it: 'I think that all of these stores have a psychological rather than a practical use. When you see a shop window full of products, you can't believe this talk of imminent famine.' But she was still bothered, without being quite sure why. A neighbour tried to calm her fears: 'If something happens, you know you have hundreds of friends here in Leningrad. Your children will be quite safe. There is no reason to be pessimistic.' 'God willing,' Skrjabina said.

Yuri Ryabinkin's diary entry for 19 July shows a change in mood. It starts innocently enough. 'I'm reading *David Copperfield*. Played chess. Mum gave me some money, which I used to buy some soup and a plate of semolina at the Palace of Labour canteen. Then I came home. I learnt to checkmate with a bishop and a knight.' Ryabinkin is occupied with the everyday, yet knows that a war is raging. 'Aunt Tina turned up unexpectedly from Shlisselburg. She's been appointed head of a hospital. It was agreed that if anything happened to Mum, she will take me and Ira.' His world is still intact, but fears are beginning to take hold of his mind. 'They say we're going to study this winter. I don't put much faith in that. To be alive is the most you can expect nowadays.' He finishes: 'Yes . . . it's probably the most difficult, the most dangerous war we've experienced. Victory's going to cost us dear.'

Towards the end of July the first German plane flew over the city. It was on a reconnaissance mission and no bombs were dropped. Over the following days, other single German aeroplanes appeared. Again, there was no bombing. On 29 July Georgi Knyazev wrote: 'Once again, German planes have been seen, but they have not bombed Leningrad.' The nervous citizens speculated and feared for the future – did the Germans intend a major attack from the air? In early August Elena Skrjabina remembered a visit from a neighbour's husband. He was armed to the teeth and 'feels terribly important and proud of his rank as an officer of the active army'. He assured her authoritatively that no danger threatened Leningrad: 'The anti-aircraft defence is so tremendous that not one aeroplane will be allowed through.' After recording this conversation Skrjabina wrote simply, 'Can this be?'

But in reality the city's air defence was in poor shape. Bomber and fighter airfields to the west of Leningrad had already been overrun by the enemy. What remained gave little reason for confidence. Evgeny Moniushko remembered seeing a group of Russian planes pass overhead while he was occupied with trench digging: 'Flying over us at low altitude, one of them suddenly broke apart in mid-air, with one of its wings separating from the fuselage. The plane and its wing fell to the ground almost simultaneously and an explosion ripped through the air. To reassure themselves, some of the people around me claimed that the plane was German, but I knew it was one of ours.'

The training of civil defence workers to meet the German threat was hurried and superficial. Fire-fighting equipment was of the simplest kind: helmets, axes, crowbars, an occasional extinguisher, buckets and sand. The burden of firewatch duty mostly fell on Leningrad's women. While they worked conscientiously to sandbag houses and public buildings, they remained well aware of the absurdity of official regulations. When a civil defence instructor told one girl, 'You are standing on the roof. Here is the sand. If an incendiary bomb drops through the roof . . .', she replied sarcastically, 'And if it is an explosive bomb?'

The growing number of German reconnaissance flights made everyone jittery. Although there were no actual attacks, numerous alerts began to sound in the city. In late July and August Leningraders frequently mention them in their diaries: there were sometimes as many as four alerts a day and, on one particular day, twelve. The warnings were played over the radio loudspeakers in Leningraders' apartments and were accompanied by a cacophony of sirens and factory whistles. Between the warning and the all-clear, the radio would ominously broadcast the ticking of a metronome, to remind people that they should not leave the bomb shelter and return to their homes.

Spurred on by the resumption of the German offensive on the River Luga, on 10 August the city authorities at last set in motion plans to evacuate some 400,000 women and children from the city. Sporadic, piecemeal evacuations from Leningrad had occurred in July. The hapless children were sent west, to summer camps along the Luga river, at Tolmachevo and Gatchina. This was the worst possible place to put them. When German troops suddenly reached

Pskov, they had to be rapidly retrieved. Worried parents began to lose confidence in the city's evacuation policy. Elena Skrjabina caught the mood of fearful uncertainty: 'I hear about children at every turn. It seems to me that after such a terrible shock as war, concern for one's children is the most worrisome, the keenest anxiety – an anxiety that can lead to insanity.'

The new massed evacuation was to be compulsory for all children under fourteen. Mothers were petrified by this development. Whole families were summoned before special committees – appointed for each district of the city – and destinations assigned regardless of their wishes. One woman did not wish to subject her children to such an ordeal but was warned: 'You say you don't want them to leave Leningrad in an organised fashion; but if you wait, they'll be forced to flee the city on foot.' On 14 August Georgi Knyazev witnessed the distress involved: 'An agonising day . . . women are in a desperate state. Until the last few days they retained their self-control, but now their nerves are completely giving way.'

Dmitry Pavlov wrote the first Soviet account of the siege of Leningrad. While admitting some slowness in the evacuation procedure, and conceding that it was hard for mothers to be parted from their children, he added that 'before long feelings of alarm were replaced by relief, as they were transported into safety'. Such evasive official accounts fail to acknowledge the bureaucratic ineptitude which delayed the children's evacuation and the disorganisation which surrounded it. Those in charge also wished to conceal their decision to send so many small children away alone – it had been decided at the last minute that their mothers were still needed to work in the city. Elena Kochina witnessed one awful mass separation: 'They're evacuating children! Like frightened little animals they filled the streets, moving towards the railway station – the demarcation line of their childhood: on the other side life without their parents would begin. The small children were driven away. Their little heads stuck out of the body of the vehicles like layers of golden brown mushrooms. Crazed parents ran after the trucks.'

One member of the city administration later confessed that they had got it badly wrong:

> It was with catastrophic lateness that we attempted to send women and children out of the city. We collected them – mostly children – put them on cars and lorries, and moved them six or seven miles out to a transit point at Rybatskoe. But our railroads were not able to handle the volume. The children waited three days, five days, a week, expecting to be sent on any minute, unable to communicate with their families, who had thought them long since gone. Most of them had no money and the food for their trip was eaten on the spot.

Eventually, convoys of trains began to move off. They carried trucks loaded with machinery – covered with pine branches – from Leningrad factories that were being evacuated. Then came some of the workers' families. Finally there was carriage after carriage full of children, their compartments stacked with hard plank beds and flimsy mattresses. Vera Inber caught sight of a group of them, huddled together, peering out of a window: 'There wasn't a smile among them,' she remembered. By 18 August thousands of children were heading towards the major rail centres at Novgorod and Mga. Rapidly approaching them from the opposite direction – fresh from their dramatic victory at Lake Ilmen – were Manstein's Panzers.

Blitzkrieg – the Germans' lightning war – sent bombers ahead of an advancing army to pulverise enemy communications and smash any possible resistance. The Russians did not even know Manstein was there, believing that the children were being evacuated along the last clear escape route. Maria Mostovskaya was involved in the evacuation of some of these children. She remembered everything that followed:

> Now we realise that we were travelling towards the Germans, but at the time nobody knew that. Why should we have? It was a good area, a remote area. I was entrusted with the job of getting the children to the Novgorod region. It happened like this. We had just arrived at our destination. The people of Demyansk turned out to welcome us. We worked out where everybody was going to stay – and there were several thousand to accommodate. But then an urgent order came through. We had to move the children on. Then we realised that the Germans were moving fast towards us. Just imagine! We had a lot of nursery-school children. They were all hungry and exhausted.

> Suddenly we heard the Germans were dropping paratroopers, trying to cut us off. We used military vehicles, anything we could get our hands on, and ferried the kids to another station, Lychkovo, about thirty miles from Demyansk.

Mikhail Maslov was one of the young evacuees. 'There was a complete breakdown in communication', he stated. 'We should never have been sent to Demyansk. The Nazis were approaching and we were now right in their path.' Nina Malakova added: 'We were just being offered tea when the director of the collective farm rushed up. I still remember his words: "Nazi paratroopers are ahead!" All of the children were gathered together – we were now to be moved to Lychkovo. This had to be done as quickly as possibly – the Germans were famed for their speed – but we were loaded on to a fleet of cars that seemed to belong to the tsarist era.'

Mostovskaya described the scene at Lychkovo station:

> It was a fine day, a lovely day. It was especially good weather. The children had started to board the train. They were dressed in their best, bright clothes. Then German planes appeared. They circled and came back towards us. It was dreadful. The poor, terrified kids were crying 'Mummy! Mummy! Mummy!' For the first time in my life I lied to a child. 'Don't be afraid,' I said. 'There's nothing to be afraid of! They're our planes!' And then the bombing started. The pilots were flying so low. They'd take a look, press a button, and a bomb would immediately explode. Later on, they claimed they hadn't known. What rubbish! They knew very well. They could see perfectly. They deliberately bombed our children.

Elena Parakova was sitting in one of the carriages. A girl on the berth above her was gazing out of the window. 'Look – a plane!' she had said innocently. 'It's dropping something – leaflets perhaps, or maybe toys.' Then she fell down on top of Parakova. The train was being raked with machine-gun fire. Then the bombs exploded. 'I will never forget the children's screams as our carriage started filling with smoke', said Veronika Kirilova. 'All around me were scattered toys.' Three-year-old Elena Simoneva clutched her doll, and pressed it tightly against her body. 'I just had one thought,' she remembered.

'When my mother said goodbye to me, she had told me: "Don't let go of your doll." '

Ivan Fedulov and a group of older boys were standing near the platform. They had been helping to load children's luggage on to the train. 'Suddenly, I heard a terrible cry,' Fedulov recalled. 'Someone was shouting, "Bombers, bombers!" A plane flew right over us – and along the length of the train – dropping bomb after bomb, with terrifying, methodical precision. There was a huge explosion, and when the smoke cleared carriages were scattered everywhere, as if they had been knocked off the track by a giant hand.' The shockwave was so great that when Fedulov looked up, he saw a row of tiny, dismembered arms hanging from the telegraph wire. One child's leg had been impaled upon the branch of a tree. Fedulov gathered a few scattered survivors and ran into a nearby potato field and tried to hide. Another group was following him. 'A plane circled, and came back,' Fedulov said. 'Then it began machine-gunning the fleeing children. It was flying so low that I could clearly see the pilot's face – totally impassive.'

Alexandra Arsenyeva was on the train with her young daughter:

> The Germans began bombing the coaches. We put the kids under the seats, with mattresses on top of them for protection, and then flung ourselves on top of the mattresses. When things quietened down a bit we managed to get out of the coach. The station was on fire. Bodies were strewn everywhere. It was absolutely horrifying. The chief of the evacuation train was sitting on a stump, clasping his head in his hands. He had lost his family, and he had no idea who was where. Every time we heard some kind of noise, we would get down into a ditch and lie on top of the children. I threw blankets over them. Later, when we stood up, the children went on pulling blankets over their heads.

Eventually, hours later, another train appeared. It was moving slowly, back towards Leningrad, packed with soldiers, many badly wounded. Arsenyeva ran after it. Unable to get on herself, she desperately flung her daughter aboard, yelling, 'Take her to Leningrad!' They were reunited ten days later. She found that her little girl had lost the power of speech.

Soon, news of the massacre reached Leningrad. In the face of the growing German menace, families refused to continue with the evacuation. Stories of children being sent in the direction of the enemy advance, and of the bombing and strafing of their trains, were simply too agonising to bear. The spread of what official sources still called 'hostile and provocative rumours' created panic among parents.

The wounded children needed to be brought back to Leningrad's hospitals and survivors of the German air attacks reunited with their families. The city authorities never openly acknowledged the evacuation fiasco. 'When I got back to Leningrad I was told I had dreamed it all,' Valentina Lazarova said. 'More than two thousand children had died at Lychkovo, and others were wandering around the countryside, distraught and lost, but the official version was that this had never happened.' It was desperate mothers who now took matters into their own hands.

Mikhail Maslov and other surviving children had spent the night in a hay barn and were then sent back to Leningrad on an army train. 'I remember the crowd of women at the railway station', he said, 'when we finally reached the city. One mother was reunited with her son – he was wounded and his clothes were in tatters – and she was clutching him in her arms, crying in sheer joy. But others were denied permission to go to Lychkovo and look for their children. I have never seen such anger – those mothers rioted in front of the local authorities.'

Lidiya Okhapkina told of her efforts to get her young son back.

> I had gone, with my baby daughter in my arms, to get some bread. In front of me stood a bespectacled woman, and she was saying she meant to get bread for two days because she was leaving to fetch her son. I asked her where he had been evacuated. She told me he had gone with nursery school No. 21 – I remember the exact number – which meant he had gone to precisely the place where they'd sent my own little boy. I hesitated, then asked if she could bring my own son back too. At first she refused. She said there was a real risk of the road being bombed – and did not want to be responsible for getting my son killed as well. I saw her point. But I had a baby daughter to care

> for and there was no one else I could send. So I begged her, implored her, finally bursting into tears. There was a moment's pause, then the woman began to cry herself. 'How old is your little boy?' she asked. Then she agreed to bring him back as well.

Okhapkina needed to get the necessary documentation. The next day, her daughter again in her arms, she joined a queue at the district Soviet: 'There were a lot of mothers there – all extremely agitated. Some were shouting, "Bring back our children! Better to have them back here with us, to die together, than have them killed God knows where." The official tried to explain that the authorities had wanted to do things in the best way possible, then hurriedly gave out the documents. I went straight to the woman's house, gave her the permit, all the bread I had, and a little money. She left the same day.'

Lidiya Okhapkina started waiting. Two weeks went by. She began to lose all hope of seeing her son again. 'Then, as I was looking out of the window one morning, I saw a woman and two boys standing outside. One I recognised immediately. I ran down and put my arms around him, then kissed and thanked the woman. She told me that the journey back had been very difficult. They had travelled a short while by train, but it was bombed and they had to run from the coaches. They'd covered the long distance mostly on foot, getting a few lifts on lorries along the way, and also on carts and horses.'

Many mothers shared Okhapkina's desperate anxiety. The Germans were now severing Leningrad's road and rail links with terrifying speed. The last rail connection with the rest of the country was through the junction at Mga. On 25 August the Mga road was cut and the evacuation suddenly called off. Thousands of children, already in transit, were waiting at this town for their connecting trains. They were left abruptly stranded.

Vladimir Gankevich was on the last train to get through. It had left Leningrad early that morning, full of children, and was supposed to pick up more. They approached a small station and began to slow. Suddenly a little boy called Volodya shouted out in delight: 'Look at the balloons! Look, so many!' Gankevich looked. He saw in amazement that the sky was full of parachutes: German paratroopers were landing on the meadow by the railway track. He heard the thump of anti-aircraft guns and watched the Germans beginning to form up at the far end of the field. The train quickly picked up speed and raced through the station, without stopping. Gankevich was just able to catch its name – Mga.

No more children would leave Leningrad. We will never know exactly how many died in the dreadful journey out of the city, or the number eventually reunited with their families. One last bureaucratic mishap piled further agony on the suffering parents. In the rush to move things forward, many of the small children on the last trains out had not been issued with the proper papers. Instead, their names were written on their hands with indelible ink. It turned out not to be indelible. When it rubbed off, these infants had no form of identification at all.

On 25 August Georgi Knyazev noted in his diary: 'The information we are being given is totally inadequate. Why – suddenly – is there such a monstrous military threat from the south? From where does the enemy get such terrible strength?' He bemoaned the authorities' hopeless disorganisation. As the Germans encircled the city, more than two and a half million civilians were left trapped inside it, including around half a million young children. Elena Skrjabina wrote simply: 'Leningrad is surrounded. We are caught in a mousetrap.'

By the last week of August, anxiety over food was mounting. Hearing that the evacuation from the city had been called off, Leningraders began hoarding provisions. Elena Skrjabina recorded the worsening situation. She wanted to get some supplies in for her family. But the whole city was smitten with a 'fever' to get food. Everything was disappearing: 'You might accidentally overhear that in the Petrograd section of town they are distributing something or other. So you run there, and after that, to Narva Gate – and then on to Vasilevsky Island. You buy up everything you can get your hands on. But there isn't really anything substantial or nourishing. The stores are virtually empty. Everywhere there are enormous queues.' On 28 August she wrote, 'In queues from morning to night.' The Germans had dropped leaflets on the city. It was unnecessary to stockpile food, they said – the city would soon be in their hands anyway. On 30 August all Leningrad's commercial stores closed.

Desperate citizens now drove out to the surrounding countryside. There, although the Germans were close, they scavenged potatoes, vegetables, anything left by the fleeing rural population. It was rumoured that the supply of food within Leningrad would last less than a month.

At this time of deepening crisis, chief administrator Zhdanov distributed posters throughout the city. 'Comrade Leningraders! Dear friends! Our beloved city is in imminent danger of attack by German fascist troops. The Red Army is valiantly defending the approaches, but the enemy has not abandoned his despicable, predatory plan.' Elena Kochina glimpsed one of them one morning as she was taking her baby daughter to the paediatric clinic for milk: 'I saw a poster on the wall of a building – "Comrade Leningraders! Dear friends!" – I didn't read any further. I only pressed my baby girl closer to myself. I'm terrified for her.'

On 1 September the composer Dmitry Shostakovich spoke on Radio Leningrad. 'Just an hour ago,' he said, 'I completed the score of my second large symphonic work.' He had been working on the composition since July. If he completed the third and fourth parts he would name it the Seventh Symphony. 'Why do I tell you about this? I tell you this so that those who are now listening to me shall know that the life of our city is going on normally.' Shostakovich was a native Leningrader who cared deeply for his city and his broadcast genuinely moved people. 'It is extraordinary to think a symphony is being composed in such conditions,' Vera Inber wrote.

The piece of paper on which Shostakovich drafted his radio address is preserved at St Petersburg's Blockade Museum. On the reverse side are the notes of the studio director for the next day's transmissions. The topics to be covered included the construction of barricades, house defence and fighting with Molotov cocktails. He had scribbled at the bottom of the page: 'Especially emphasise, in all broadcasts, that the battle is nearing the closest approaches of the city; over us hangs deadly danger.' Leningrad's system of barricades was badly planned and shoddy. They were only a few feet high.

Occasionally, a tram was turned over and filled with sand, and some wooden pillboxes were built. For the most part, these emplacements were not manned or equipped with weapons.

The situation in the city was so desperate that even antique guns from the cruiser *Aurora* – which had been made into a monument for its role in the Bolshevik Revolution of 1917 – were sent to the front line and installed on the Pulkovo Heights, overlooking Leningrad. Voroshilov and Zhdanov declared: 'Let us all arise together. Armed with iron discipline and Bolshevik-style organisation, we will courageously meet the enemy and inflict on him a devastating defeat.' To achieve this, housewives and children were asked to throw stones or boiling water on the Germans if they entered the city.

Many felt that fighting should be left to the soldiers and that the leadership had no business asking citizens for further sacrifice. News had leaked out that the authorities were laying mines and explosives under factories, buildings and bridges. This was bitterly resented by the city's population, still seething over the bungled evacuation policy. The leadership was supposed to prevent damage, not cause it, people said. The mines placed them in serious danger, and the destruction of factories would deprive them of any chance of livelihood. One worker said forthrightly: 'And what are we supposed to do after the factories have been blown up? We can't be without factories – we have to work in order to eat. We will not blow them up.' By early September the civilian population lost its few remaining vestiges of confidence in the authorities.

On 7 September Yuri Ryabinkin responded with wonderfully black humour to Voroshilov's military efforts by drawing up a 'defence plan' of his own. He set it out in his diary, marked: 'Top Secret – plan for the defeat of the German armies surrounding Leningrad'. It was to be executed jointly by himself and the city's commander-in-chief. It begins with terse, sarcastic instructions, mimicking the tone of the authorities: 'Act in this way. Mine the whole of Leningrad. Create total panic in the city. Send all the people out into the forest, so that Leningrad is empty. Withdraw our troops. No one must understand what our commander-in-chief has in mind. The Germans will enter the city. Unexpectedly, like lightning, we will go over to a general offensive.' Then Ryabinkin returns to grim reality: 'So much for my dream fantasy. There is of course no one who could undertake a general offensive.'

Something else struck him. 'Today is the 129th anniversary of the Battle of Borodino,' he remarked. This great battle, fought between Napoleon's invading French army and the Russians in 1812, had ended inconclusively, but Napoleon had subsequently been forced to retreat. Ryabinkin felt the contrast with his present plight keenly, noting: 'Then the foreign invaders received a firm rebuff.' In September 1941, German armies were encircling the city and Soviet forces seemed utterly unable to stop them.

The Germans now subjected Leningrad to a ferocious air and artillery bombardment. They concentrated on specific targets: food storage areas, then water pumping and purification plants, electricity power stations and key factories. In the wake of the Badaev fire Vera Inber confided to her diary: 'This is Leningrad's central larder – the heart and stomach of the city. And the sinister heavy smoke that hangs about in layers is burning sugar, flour and butter.' On 11 September the bread ration was reduced to 500 grams a day for factory workers, 300 for office workers and 250 for dependants. Five days later the city authorities cut off the domestic telephone system. Inber got a shock that morning. The phone rang: 'A fresh young voice said, "The telephone is disconnected until the end of the war." I tried to raise a protest, but knew in my heart it was useless. In a few minutes we were cut off from everyone and everything in the city.'

People were thrown back on to their own resources. Reassuring contact with friends and relatives in different parts of the city vanished. Leningrad's air defence gave little protection; its barrage balloons hung forlornly in the air. 'They might as well be soap bubbles,' Elena Skrjabina said, as the German Heinkels and Dorniers flew at will over all parts of the city. Once again, people's terrible anxiety found an outlet – a belief that enemy agents were assisting the Germans. They were dubbed the 'rocket men': suspected saboteurs, who signalled to enemy planes the location of their targets by means of brightly coloured rockets and flares. Tanya Ryabinina described one such 'sighting':

> Two saboteurs were apprehended just a few steps away from our house. They had been hiding in a boarded-up kiosk. We owed our first bomb to them. They had signalled with beautiful green rockets, which we had stupidly admired on the first night of the bombing. They spent a couple of weeks in that kiosk, and during that time many bombs fell on the neighbourhood. I did not see them being flushed out. Apparently, they were caught with tracker dogs.

There is no evidence in either German or Soviet sources that these 'rocket men' ever existed. Those arrested as suspects were normally guilty of nothing more than carelessness in violating the black-out. Evgeny Moniushko provided a scientific explanation: 'At the beginning of September, strange lights appeared in the skies on two or three nights. It is possible that these were the distant flashes of the Aurora Borealis.' But many civilians, suffering the awful stress of the bombardment, and fearing for their future, clearly believed they were seeing something sinister.

An individual's suffering can easily be lost in a mass of statistics. During September 1941 Leningraders were subjected to twenty-three air raids, twelve of them at night, which dropped 987 high-explosive bombs and 15,100 incendiaries. The figures are terrifying, but it was the sometimes surreal images of war which seared people's lives. Elena Kochina recalled a bomb slamming into Bolshaya Street: 'Everything rocked, and the main entry door, right next to where I was standing with my daughter, fell off its hinges and flew upwards like a leaf. A sharp chill of fear ran through my body.' Lidiya Okhapkina was bathing her son. Suddenly the air-raid warning went. Before she had time to respond, a burning flare sailed through the window: 'The old carpet covering the window fell down. Window panes smashed to smithereens. It all happened in an instant. Outside I heard deafening explosions. My son was crying loudly. I grabbed him, bare and wet, and flung him on to the floor in the corridor. I pressed him to me and cursed the Germans – "Beasts, bastards!" When is this going to stop?'

Later Okhapkina went out to get bread. Half of the house opposite had been destroyed. She noticed its exposed walls, the variety of wall-papers, pink, blue and green, patterned flowers and stripes. 'And what was most strange, on one wall a big clock was hanging – and still going.'

Amid these horrors, the city was still warmed by the sun, and beautiful autumn weather continued. But it would not last. Within a month, temperatures would start to plummet. Signs began to appear in people's windows – 'Ready to barter for food'. All sorts of items were on offer: a pair of gold cufflinks, a full-length skirt of dark-blue woollen cloth, a sewing machine. Yuri Ryabinkin had been sent out by his mother to try and get some sunflower-seed oil. He'd lost the money – thirty roubles – and was very upset. 'Mum tells me this isn't the time to keep a diary,' Ryabinkin then wrote, 'but I shall carry on anyway.' Everything had changed for him. All his plans for the future – higher education, career – were dissolving. 'It's hard, agonisingly hard, to say goodbye to your dreams.' His diary remained a clear constant: 'If I don't re-read it maybe someone else will, and find out what kind of person I was.'

On 22 September, as Adolf Hitler was setting out his plans for eradicating Leningrad's entire civilian population, Georgi Knyazev ordered a hook to be installed in his ceiling. He had found a suitable piece of rope: 'If I should lose my beloved wife, see the devastation and utter defeat of my city and everything I care about, what would be the point of living on? It seems to me that the simplest way to end things is strangulation – not a beautiful end, but a reliable one.' The scientist was a courageous man. He believed in his people, and in his own resources, and he loved life. Nevertheless, the hook on the ceiling was there as a last resort. Knyazev knew that the city's food supplies were running out.

For each Leningrader, survival now depended upon a dwindling daily bread ration. The new allocation for dependants, 250 grams, was the equivalent of a small portion – about six thin slices – of a medium-sized loaf. This bread would soon be adulterated, as flour supplies drained away. Winter was fast approaching. Panic in the face of hunger, fear, and hunger-induced insanity could destroy people before death itself did. There were those who felt a kind of omnipotence, who believed that even after hunger had eaten away at them, it could not deprive them of willpower or undermine their values. But Knyazev looked bravely into the darkening glass of the human soul. He foresaw a borderline beyond which you were not yourself any more, no longer in control of your actions or behaviour. He resolved never to cross it.

The siege of Leningrad had begun. It was to be more than a life-or-death struggle. For the city's two-and-a-half million trapped inhabitants – faced with the total disintegration of their way of life – this was to be a fight for their very humanity.

4

The Noose

The Blockade Is Not Broken

On 11 September 1941 General Georgi Zhukov and a small group of military personnel flew with a fighter-plane escort from Moscow to Leningrad. The city was now surrounded, and as the Soviet commander and his staff crossed German lines near Lake Ladoga enemy planes gave chase. Flying low over the water, they managed to evade their pursuers and reach the safety of Leningrad's military airport. Zhukov was shaken by this narrow escape, but he now rehearsed the brief given to him by Stalin in a last, short meeting before his departure. Quickly dispensing with formalities, the Soviet supremo had scribbled a note ordering Voroshilov back to Moscow and passed it to Zhukov. Zhukov was ordered to present it on his arrival in Leningrad and then take command of the city.

That evening Zhukov and his chief of staff Lieutenant-General Mikhail Khozin arrived at Leningrad's Smolny Institute, the headquarters of the besieged city's administration, to learn that Voroshilov was presiding over a gathering of the Military Council. Zhukov asked to sit in on the meeting, and then, without a word of greeting, brusquely passed the front commander Stalin's note. Voroshilov read it silently, nodded and then quickly wrapped things up. Moments later, Zhukov transmitted a terse statement to Moscow: 'I have taken command. Report to the Supreme Commander-in-Chief that I expect to work more actively than my predecessor.'

The short, stocky Zhukov was fifteen years younger than Voroshilov, but already an ambitious and skilled military commander. In 1939, Voroshilov had begun the war against Finland with a series of wasteful frontal assaults on well-fortified positions; in the same year Zhukov had brilliantly defeated the Japanese at Khalkin-Gol, in the

Soviet Far East, by using his armour to outflank and smash the enemy. Initially, Zhukov brought a much needed drive and vigour to Leningrad's defence. In his brief meeting with Voroshilov, he made only one intervention, but an absolutely crucial one, countermanding the decision by Voroshilov and Zhdanov to scuttle the Baltic Fleet. To withstand the Germans, Leningrad needed its navy. Zhukov could see the bigger strategic picture, and was not infected by the mood of panic at the city's HQ. Veteran Nikolai Vasipov remembered the impact of that: 'Zhukov made a difference straight away. He demonstrated his resolve to us when he cancelled the order to sink the fleet.'

These ships were the pride of Leningrad but, unfortunately, responsibility for them had been held by Voroshilov, as North-West Front commander. In the early months of the war the fleet was based at the Estonian port of Tallinn. When the Germans broke into the city at the end of August 1941 its two battleships, two cruisers, eighteen destroyers and a host of smaller ships had been evacuated to Leningrad's naval base at Kronstadt. The evacuation proved catastrophic.

In the late 1930s, while Voroshilov trumpeted the Soviet Union's readiness to meet any military threat, its naval modernisation had ground to a halt. Russia's Naval Minister Admiral Nikolai Kuznetsov later asserted: 'Only a balanced naval force will secure maximum effect in war. If anybody had asked us what the Baltic Fleet needed, above all, we would have said without a moment's hesitation: minesweepers, sweeping gear and modern mines to fight the enemy. In actual fact things worked out differently . . .' When the war started the Baltic Fleet should have had over a hundred fast minesweepers. In reality, it possessed fewer than twenty. The Germans were well aware of this, and as they advanced into the Baltic they made widespread use of their minelayers to disable the Soviet navy.

In August 1941 the head of the North-West Front gave a nervous, knee-jerk response to the sudden German advance. 'The need for minesweepers was so desperate that we received an order to commandeer every vessel in Leningrad fit for duty,' Kuznetsov admitted. This was a desperate measure, for the navy needed fast modern minesweepers, and instead a flotilla of some twenty seagoing tugs was now despatched to their assistance – including a number of paddle-wheeled craft. The most unlikely vessel in this bizarre convoy was a luxury yacht that had formerly belonged to the last Tsar of Russia, Nicholas II. This museum piece was being employed against the combined might of the Kriegsmarine and Luftwaffe.

The Baltic Fleet offered a tempting target for a massed German air attack, for as Kuznetsov sadly remarked, 'our anti-aircraft guns were completely obsolescent'. However, the ships were not without protection – the Baltic Fleet could deploy its own air arm, consisting of some 600 aircraft. It was vital that these were at hand as the ships made their dangerous journey from Tallinn to Leningrad's nearby naval base at Kronstadt. Unbelievably, Voroshilov ordered the planes elsewhere.

On 25 August German forces were poised to break into Tallinn. Bringing up their artillery and mortars, they began shelling the Soviet ships crammed round the harbour jetties. The fleet should have been moved out as fast as possible, but there was a deadly delay. Kuznetsov was candid about the reason for it: 'It was the duty of the Commander-in-Chief of the North-Western Front to report on the situation and request the Soviet Supreme Command's permission to withdraw from Tallinn. But for some reason he hesitated to do so, when we could not afford to wait.' In desperation, Admiral Kuznetsov bypassed Voroshilov and appealed directly to Stalin. The evacuation order was given on 28 August.

At 11.18 that morning, just as German troops were breaking through to Tallinn's downtown business district, two Soviet destroyers led a first convoy of thirty-two ships out of the port. Two further convoys followed; then, at 2.52 p.m., the main Soviet battle fleet left the harbour. German reconnaissance planes flew overhead.

The line of ships stretched for more than fifteen miles. That afternoon there were sporadic German air attacks. Then, in the early evening, as the leading vessels kept close to the shoreline, they encountered a mass of mines, laid out across the Gulf of Finland. As they struggled to penetrate this barrier the Luftwaffe obliterated target after target. The transport ships, crowded with refugees, were the most vulnerable – and one, the *Virona*, went down with many of its passengers singing the Internationale. A commissar, watching the tragedy from a nearby minesweeper, exclaimed bitterly: 'Who would have thought that we would drown like blind cats in a puddle – where are our planes?'

Over fifty Soviet ships were lost – many to mines. On 30 August Stephan Kuznetsov, working in the harbour at Oranienbaum, west of Leningrad, heard the awful news. Kuznetsov – no relation of the Soviet Admiral – was deeply concerned. 'Tallinn has been abandoned,' he wrote in his diary. 'Many of our ships were sunk by the German air force on their way to Kronstadt. It is rumoured that in the waters of the Gulf of Finland more than 17,000 soldiers, sailors and refugees have drowned. I fear my father is one of them.' He concluded starkly: 'Death and destruction are coming.'

After the fiasco of the bungled evacuation Voroshilov and Zhdanov panicked and prepared to scuttle the remainder of the Baltic Fleet. They had signed the appropriate orders on 8 September, and all the ships that had managed to reach the safety of Kronstadt were then mined. The two men were hoping to block the coastal waters with the wrecks and therefore impede a German sea-borne assault. But such a threat was purely imaginary – for while the enemy had deployed their submarine fleet in the Gulf of Finland, the bulk of the Kriegsmarine had not even set sail. The Germans were intending to confine the remnants of the Baltic Fleet to port, not storm its harbours.

The plan to destroy the remainder of the fleet left Zhukov aghast. 'There are forty full battle complements on them,' he snorted, when he heard of this decision. 'Clear them of mines and bring them closer to the city – so they can fire on the enemy with their artillery.' He had immediately grasped the importance of using these ships – with their guns and marines – as part of a strengthened defence line. Saving the Baltic Fleet marked a real commitment to holding Leningrad against the Germans.

Zhukov later recalled this moment: 'I knew the city and its environs well because I had studied there some years before at a school for cavalry commanders. Much had changed since then, but I still had a good idea of the battle zone . . . Energetic and resolute action was called for. The strictest order and discipline had to be maintained. Troop control needed to be tightened. We were working to stabilise conditions in the blockaded city in a most complicated situation.' The reality was that Voroshilov had left Leningrad's fortifications in an utter mess.

Zhukov had to shore up the city's defences as fast as possible. Shortly after taking command he sent for Voroshilov's chief engineer, Boris Bychevsky. As Bychevsky laid out his papers and began to summarise the work undertaken to defend Leningrad, Zhukov was visibly unimpressed. Abruptly, he knocked Bychevsky's pile of plans off the table and then, turning to the large outline map hanging on the wall, suddenly asked him: 'What are our tanks doing in this area? There's something wrong here.' Bychevsky was startled: 'Those are actually tank mock-ups, Comrade Commander – wooden dummies. Fifty of them were made in the workshops of the Mariinsky Theatre.' Regaining a little composure, he added proudly: 'The Germans have bombed them twice.' Zhukov found this resort to scenery props hard to stomach. 'How long have you been playing these games?' he said sarcastically. 'You'd better watch out – the Germans will soon catch on to this little trick and start dropping wooden bombs on them.' As Bychevsky turned to leave, he heard Leningrad's new commander mutter incredulously: 'Why did they start fortifying so late?'

The military options available to Zhukov were extremely limited. To the west, a determined attack by the Germans had captured the key town of Uritsk and pushed through to the Gulf of Finland, leaving the battered Soviet Eighth Army cut off from the rest of the defenders in a narrow strip of land around Oranienbaum. Morale within this force had deteriorated alarmingly. Further south, the Forty-second Army was falling back from Pulkovo in disarray. Zhukov's deputy, Major-General Ivan Fedyuninsky, found the army's commander sitting with his head in his hands in a state of shock, unable to report where his troops were. To the east, the Forty-fifth Army was retreating from Pushkin – threatened by German forces on either side of it. Somehow, Zhukov had to stabilise a defence line. There could be no further retreat.

Stephan Kuznetsov was one of the Red Army soldiers trapped on the edge of the Oranienbaum pocket. On 15 September he wrote in his diary: 'All day artillery shelling has been going on. Our aircraft are destroyed in the sky above us. This morning it was announced that the enemy had occupied Strelna [to the east of Oranienbaum, on the Gulf of Finland]. This news is most disturbing and our soldiers are totally depressed.' Semyon Putyakov had been pulled back to a makeshift defence line on the outskirts of Leningrad, where the Germans were bombing his unit with impunity. 'The situation our army is in – all along the front line – is appalling,' he wrote gloomily. 'Three bombs exploded in our vicinity today – one high explosive, two firebombs. They say the Germans already have a 5th column operating within the city. Their intelligence system is so much better than ours. There is a terrible threat to all of us besieged in Leningrad.' It was too much to contemplate. 'I have lice,' Putyakov suddenly concluded.

Zhukov worked fast to remedy the situation. He immediately divided Leningrad into six defensive sectors. Trenches were hurriedly dug, strongpoints created and anti-tank guns distributed to hastily drawn-up reserve battalions. Crucially, Zhukov provided his defences with proper artillery support – ordering the big guns of the Baltic Fleet to strike hard at the German positions. The ships that Voroshilov and Zhdanov had wanted to scuttle mustered no fewer than 338 large guns – which could be fired from its warships, or moved inland to coastal batteries. Every one of them was now put to use.

On 16 September 1941 Zhukov issued military order number 419, which made a series of trenchant criticisms of the system of covering fire put in place by the hapless Voroshilov. Zhukov was unable to contain his exasperation with his predecessor. Unsurprisingly, Voroshilov's measures had proved totally insufficient: there was no co-ordination between the fleet's artillery and air force, nor any liaison with the gun batteries deployed along the rest of the front. Reconnaissance planes – vital to pinpoint the positions of German troops and gun batteries – had been sent into the air without any fighter escorts, making them easy targets for the Luftwaffe. The new concentration of firepower made a vital difference. In the week following Zhukov's deployments, just one of these naval batteries – a

356mm gun capable of firing a 1,500-pound shell – was able to knock out thirty-five German tanks, twelve artillery installations, a battalion of infantry and a troop and ammunition train.

Having made these arrangements, Zhukov issued a draconian order to Soviet troops defending Leningrad, stating that any soldier or officer found withdrawing from the defence line – which ran through the outlying towns of Ligovo, Pulkovo and Kolpino – would be shot immediately. Zhukov was nervous – much of Ligovo was already in German hands, and the Wehrmacht had moved up so quickly that the town's telephone service had not even been disconnected. On the evening of 17 September the foreman of Leningrad's Kirov Works received a most surprising call. A strange voice said in halting Russian: 'Leningrad? Very good! This is Ligovo calling. We shall come tomorrow to visit the Winter Palace and the Hermitage.'

This was a stylish piece of enemy bravura. In actual fact, the Germans were consolidating their lines and had already made the decision to besiege the city rather than undertake a full-scale assault on it. They were intending a static war of attrition, and tank formations were no longer necessary to implement this brutal plan. On 15 September their Panzer divisions were sent south, to join the preparations for Hitler's last great offensive of 1941 – Operation Typhoon – which would attempt to storm Moscow. In contrast, on 18 September German infantry could already be seen digging into siege positions around Leningrad.

But Zhukov's arrogance now revealed itself. He had promised Stalin he would save Leningrad from capture, and, carried away by the momentum of his actions, was reluctant to believe the mounting evidence that the enemy was in fact settling down to a protracted siege. Over three days, from 18 to 21 September, his head of intelligence Brigade Commander Yevstigneyev picked up the movement of a mass of German motorised troops, heading west – away from Leningrad to Pskov. It looked like a major regrouping. At Gatchina partisans saw the Germans loading their tanks on to railway flatcars, to be transported away from Leningrad, but Zhukov refused to accept these reports. 'Provocation,' he retorted. 'Find out who is behind it.'

On 23 September Moscow confirmed that Army Group North's chief tank formation – the Fourth Panzer Group – had indeed left the Leningrad Front. Two days later Yevstigneyev put together another report. The Germans had now mobilised local residents to build permanent trenches and dug-outs for their soldiers. And at Peterhof they were chopping down pine and spruce groves for their command posts, installing stoves and moving in beds and furniture. They were clearly getting ready to winter on the outskirts of Leningrad, and maintain a blockade of the city. But Zhukov remained unwilling to accept such a possibility. 'All my orders about active defence and local attacks remain in force,' he said.

Zhukov deserves great credit for properly organising Leningrad's defences, but he was now making a disastrous miscalculation. Erroneously believing that the Germans still intended to capture the city, he pushed his soldiers into a series of wasteful assaults against the enemy.

On 18 September he ordered the troops in the Oranienbaum pocket to attack the Germans – believing that this would hinder a further advance on Leningrad from the west. This was an impossible order to fulfil: the Soviet Eighth Army was woefully under-strength and had virtually no ammunition. The exhausted troops were clinging on to a narrow, forty-mile stretch of land running from the Voronka river to Peterhof, and were surviving only because of the concentrated artillery fire from the nearby ships of the Baltic Fleet. But when their commander refused to obey this suicidal command Zhukov sacked him and ordered his replacement to launch the assault instead. The attack went in on 25 September, when there was already strong evidence that the Germans had halted their offensive, and achieved nothing beyond losing thousands of lives. The enemy were too well dug in. Lieutenant-General Mikhail Dukhanov commanded one of these badly depleted divisions and witnessed the futile action. 'I could not approve of these measures then, and I cannot now,' he wrote later.

'Zhukov became an increasingly cruel and pitiless commander,' Nikolai Vasipov said. On 25 September another over-ambitious operation was launched – to reinforce the isolated Soviet garrison of

Oreshek, the island fortress off the shore of Shlisselburg, on Lake Ladoga. This would make sense if the Germans were continuing to move towards Leningrad from the east, but, once again, they had already dug in and gone over to the defensive.

Nikolai Vavin commanded the marine brigade despatched to Oreshek. 'This would always have been a difficult military task – whatever the circumstances,' he recalled.

> But for some reason our force was sent across Lake Ladoga, towards the fortress, at 3.00 p.m. – in broad daylight. Our guys just didn't have a chance. The Germans quickly spotted us from the air – and it became a mass execution. The first rows of boats were completely wiped out: the enemy's planes first bombed and then machine-gunned us. It was impossible to swim to safety – our marines could not jettison their heavy coats and boots in time – and men were drowning all around me. Out of my own landing group of 200 men, only 14 reached the shoreline.

Mikhail Neishtadt, radio operator at Leningrad's Smolny Institute, said of Zhukov: 'He was a big theoretician and strategist – but he never seemed to care about human losses. He continued to order offensive after offensive against the enemy, regardless of the cost in lives. On a number of occasions local commanders were pleading with him that they were barely clinging on, that they desperately needed more troops and ammunition and that to try and launch an assault in such conditions was madness. But Zhukov would not listen. I can still remember his chilling response: he would simply repeat "I said attack!"'

Neishtadt recalled a particularly disturbing incident:

> Something important had come up and Zhukov told us to put him through to Moscow immediately. Well, we did it – but suddenly, just as the conversation had begun, the radio connection went down. The fault had nothing to do with us – the other line was working fine – but Zhukov drew his pistol from its holder, and advanced towards us in a most threatening manner, yelling 'What's going on?' He seemed to feel that we were somehow responsible for this state of affairs. It was an ugly situation, but fortunately for us the connection was quickly restored. But I was shocked by Zhukov's reaction – he

showed himself as a bully, accustomed to intimidating others, regardless of whether they were at fault or not.

The most calamitous of Zhukov's measures was a decision to launch a series of massed attacks on the Germans from a tiny foothold on the eastern bank of the Neva river, known as the Nevsky bridgehead. This place became a killing ground – and one that over the course of the siege claimed hundreds of thousands of Soviet lives. As Red Army soldiers laconically put it, 'If you have not seen the Nevsky bridgehead, you have not seen the real face of war.'

Zhukov later claimed that the Nevsky bridgehead was vital for the city's survival, but engineering chief Boris Bychevsky was less enthusiastic: 'It soon became the bloodiest place on the entire Leningrad front.' The initial plan to create a bridgehead did indeed arise out of sound military thinking, for the course of the Neva dictated the way the city should be defended. The river ran from the Gulf of Finland through the heart of Leningrad, and then south-east, before changing direction and cutting back northwards towards Lake Ladoga. It thus formed a triangular promontory, jutting out as a bulwark against the advancing enemy. To the west of the Neva's tip, the Soviet forces still held a narrow defence corridor beyond the river, running through the small towns of Ligovo, Pulkovo and Kolpino. To the east of it, the speed of the enemy's flanking advance had taken Leningrad's defenders by surprise, and by early September the Germans had established themselves on the far bank. It was vital that they did not get across the river.

Zhukov spotted the danger straight away. Both sides were looking for crossing points, but these were difficult to find: the river was wide, fast flowing – and its banks were steep. But there was one small stretch of water, close to the Ivanova rapids and the village of Nevskaya Dubrovka, where the slope was far more gradual, and on the other side of the river there were good roads, running to Shlisselburg, and then on to Finland. On 12 September Zhukov sent a reconnaissance force to this key point. A week later, he ordered a night-time landing on the far bank of the Neva. The defence of the Nevsky bridgehead had begun.

Zhukov had assembled a scratch force of NKVD border guards, a brigade of marines and a regular infantry division to take the bridgehead. Mikhail Pavlov, a colonel in the 1st NKVD Border Guards, described the initial assault:

> The preparations were terribly rushed. Our unit was force-marched nearly 60 kilometres, to the village of Nevskaya Dubrovka, where we halted to pick up supplies and equipment. Our orders were to cross the Neva – but to our astonishment we found there were no boats! So we had to make rafts, each one taking a group of eight men, and piled high with ammunition. It was dark, but as we approached the river German flare rockets suddenly lit up the sky and then their artillery opened up. It was absolute carnage. Because of the lack of supply boats, each raft was carrying double the regulation load of ammunition and mountains of grenades. As we approached the far bank the enemy found his range and the water was rocked by explosions – our ammunition was blowing up all around us. Our guys on the rafts were sitting ducks – we lost an entire battalion during the crossing.

Pavlov's own raft was hit and he was thrown into the icy water. The current was exceptionally strong but eventually he managed to reach the far bank. He joined other scattered survivors, helped set up a food and ammunition depot and dug in.

Pavlov and his fellows were occupying a tiny stretch of land, little more than a mile wide and half a mile deep. Conditions were chaotic, with no orderly landings possible and Soviet units all mixed together, trying to improvise a defence right under the noses of the enemy – the Germans were only 600 yards away. On one occasion, Pavlov remembered running up from his trench to man a machine gun after the Red Army soldiers there had been killed. There was still plenty of ammunition – and he carried on firing for a while. Then a completely unknown commander wandered over to him and asked him who he was. Pavlov identified himself, and the officer looked at him for a moment and then said: 'You seem to know how to fight, so come and help me defend my command post – I'm down to my last two soldiers!' For the next three days – until further reinforcements arrived – there Pavlov stayed.

Zhukov had believed that attacking from this foothold might throw the Germans off balance, and initially this was a good decision – however costly in lives. The presence of this small Soviet force discouraged the enemy from launching a probing attack of their own, trying to get across the river in the opposite direction and moving closer to Leningrad. And it also offered a much bigger opportunity, to catch Field Marshal von Leeb off guard and break the German blockade of the city. But, to stand a chance of achieving this, the landing across the Neva needed to be exploited quickly – and the bridgehead widened.

The opportunity was there, for the speed of the Germans' flanking drive east of Leningrad, towards Shlisselburg, had left their forces vulnerable to a rapid and well-organised counter-attack. Between the Nevsky bridgehead and the nearest Soviet army, the Fifty-fourth, they held only a narrow corridor of land, some seven to nine miles wide. But here Zhukov was badly let down by the Fifty-fourth Army's commander, Marshal Grigory Kulik, who reacted to the situation slowly and with insufficient strength. Kulik seemed unable to comprehend the desperate situation Leningrad was in. He first claimed it was impossible for him to launch an offensive in the near future. Zhukov was rightly angry at this response, for while the welfare of his army was indeed the commander's responsibility, at stake was the salvation of a city of several million inhabitants. On 20 September, after the Nevsky bridgehead was established, Zhukov complained about the Fifty-fourth Army's inactivity to Stalin – who intervened straight away, telling Kulik he wanted immediate action: 'In the next two days, the 21st and the 22nd, you must breach the enemy's front and join up with the Leningraders or it will be too late. You have delayed too long. Now you must make up for lost time. If not, the Germans will turn every village into a fortress and you will never be able to reach the city.'

But the idea of a concerted attack just didn't work. Prodded by Stalin, Kulik did eventually release an army detachment, but after advancing for about four miles these troops were completely surrounded by the Germans and wiped out. On the other side of the enemy corridor, the force on the Nevsky bridgehead – trapped by devastating German artillery fire – was unable to advance at all. By 26 September it was clear that the first attempt to break the German blockade had been a complete failure.

All chance of surprising the enemy was now lost. And once the Germans had dug in, reinforced their position around the small Soviet enclave and brought up their heavy artillery the Nevsky bridgehead was a death trap. But Zhukov did not evacuate the battered force holding the bridgehead; instead he pushed more troops in to join them. Fresh Red Army divisions and brigades were crammed on to this tiny piece of land – and then designated the Neva Operational Group.

The capacity of these hapless soldiers to perform any meaningful military operation was virtually non-existent. The casualty rate was horrific. The notional strength of a Red Army division was around 12,000–13,000 men, although in practice they were often sent into combat at half that strength. But within weeks the 86th Division, one of the contingent ordered to reinforce the bridgehead, had been reduced to a mere 176 soldiers, the 265th was down to 180 and the 20th NKVD Division was no larger than a platoon. The Baltic Fleet's 4th Marine Brigade disappeared completely.

Many of the 4th Marine Brigade had been young cadets – just seventeen or eighteen years old – with only a few months' training under their belts. As none of them survived to tell their story, their presence is fleetingly glimpsed through scattered personal belongings recently excavated from the Nevsky bridgehead: a bloodstained party card, an embossed silver spoon, a hand-painted icon. One of the cadets was given a simple gift by his fellows – a roughly engraved water flask. Etched on its surface were the words: 'To Viktor Krovlin, on his eighteenth birthday – 29 September 1941'. Beneath them, fashioned with the same sharp implement – probably a field knife – was a crude sketch of the Nevsky bridgehead, marking out the hamlet of Moskovskaya Dubrovka, a temporary rope pontoon bridge that had been erected over the Neva and the bridgehead itself. Within a day of Krovlin receiving his present, the pontoon bridge had been destroyed by enemy fire. Within a month, the entire brigade had been wiped out.

One survivor of the Neva Operational Group later wrote: 'It was a complete violation of military doctrine to put such a large concentration of troops in such a small area.' The Germans were able to direct their artillery fire on the troop assembly points and the river crossing – and then pulverise the small scrap of land the soldiers grimly nicknamed the 'Nevsky piatachok' (the *piatachok* was a five-kopeck coin), where enemy fire was so accurate they had to move around crawling or bent double. It has been estimated that on 28 September alone – the day before Krovlin received his birthday present – the Germans bombarded the bridgehead with more than 8,600 bombs and shells. The battered Soviet force had little artillery support and even less aerial protection, and it was being systematically blasted to pieces.

This was a flat, marshy area offering Red Army troops scant natural cover. Colonel Leonid Yakovlev, commander of the 169th Artillery Regiment, admitted: 'The German bombing and shelling was devastating. They used flare rockets to light up our positions and dropped incendiaries to destroy the wooden buildings holding our ammunition and supplies. The Neva was literally boiling from the force of their fire. And sadly our answer was laughable – we were crippled by a chronic shortage of ammunition. On one occasion we only got off one or two shells, which had no effect on the enemy whatsoever.'

Mikhail Khalfin – deputy commander of the 339th Mortar Platoon – described the unique hell of the crossing:

> Time seemed to stand still. Our preparations took place during the constant din of German air raids, artillery and mortar shelling. The ground was trembling and shuddering as if it were alive. There was the roar and wailing of sirens from enemy Junkers, dive-bombing our position. Everything became hopelessly muddled in the dark. I could hear the scream of bombs, the cracking of machine-gun fire from the far bank – and the terrible cries of our wounded. Suddenly, a bomb exploded close to our assembly point, leaving us half buried in the earth. Soldiers around us hurriedly dug us out. And then came the command: 'To the boats! Forward!' We were desperately rowing across the Neva, using oars, wooden planks, rifle butts and even our bare hands – trying to get over as fast as possible, to avoid

a hit. And all to reach a dismal 500-metre strip of land, constantly erupting with explosions.

Of forty-six boats in this group of reinforcements, forty were destroyed in the crossing. Khalfin was one of the fortunate few who made it to the other side. 'Finally we reached the bank,' he remembered, 'and jumped straight out of our boat into a shallow communication trench. Suddenly, someone barked out instructions to us: "Drop all your kit. Fix bayonets!" The reason for this order quickly became apparent – we had to go straight into close-quarters fighting with a group of advancing German infantry.' Khalfin added despairingly: 'Most of us wanted to stop the enemy reaching Leningrad's outlying suburbs, and liberate our sacred land from the fascist swine – but what was the point of such senseless slaughter? Each one of us felt we would never return from this accursed spot.'

Zhukov was well aware of the heavy casualties the Neva Operational Group was suffering – and of the futility of their struggle. Senior Lieutenant Ilya Izenstadt, an NKVD operative in the 186th Division, had reported back to Leningrad Front's HQ the powerlessness of the beleaguered Soviet force:

> The German tactics were very effective. They brought intense artillery fire down on the places where our reinforcements were gathering – and subjected the crossing points to a devastating bombardment, day and night. They held a total battle initiative – and we could make no progress against them. Our own command system was crippled – we were unable to direct events in any meaningful way, and often completely lost contact with our troops. Those officers who supervised the crossing were almost invariably killed or wounded, and the Nazis quickly located our HQs and communication centres and put them out of action. Our losses were calamitous. We were unable to establish a proper pontoon bridge across the Neva and had to rely on makeshift crossing vessels that were often inadequate for the task. And on the far bank we could not provide our troops with any real protection from the enemy.

Red Army soldiers were being asked to endure a hopeless situation. Regimental Commissar Ivan Pankov made a powerful plea to front command: 'The majority of our troops are fighting bravely but people are literally crawling over the dead bodies of their comrades. Because our own artillery has failed in any way to disrupt the enemy's annihilating firing system, the heroic efforts of our soldiers are utterly wasted.'

Zhukov ordered them to hold their ground, regardless. On the HQ's situation maps, far removed from the harsh reality of front-line conditions, the enclave continued to look impressive, apparently tying down German forces which might otherwise be used for an offensive on Leningrad. It also seemed to offer a convenient jumping-off point for any future efforts to breach the enemy's blockade of the city. All this lent the decision an apparent logic. But it was a mirage, for the German position was simply too strong – and the bridgehead too small – to effect any meaningful breakthrough. Zhukov was deliberately turning a blind eye to the catastrophic situation on the bridgehead, and the needless suffering of the soldiers there, as more and more troops were fed into the hell-hole on the Neva. And the severe loss of life was draining the Red Army's capacity to launch any sort of successful offensive at all.

On 5 October Stalin rang Zhukov and asked about the situation in Leningrad. Belatedly, Zhukov acknowledged that the Germans had stopped their attacks and were now on the defensive. 'For the first time in many days we could tangibly feel that the front had fulfilled its mission and halted the Nazi offensive on Leningrad,' Zhukov later wrote, conveniently overlooking the fact that the Germans had decided to bring the offensive to a close, on their own initiative, more than two weeks earlier. Stalin now recalled Zhukov to Moscow to deal with a new crisis, the German offensive bearing down on the Russian capital. Leningrad party boss Andrei Zhdanov was left in overall charge of the city's military dispositions.

For all his effectiveness, Georgi Zhukov had bequeathed Leningrad a poisoned chalice. On his arrival, he had successfully organised the city's defence at a time of crisis and panic. But the piecemeal deployments he subsequently made were designed to prevent a German assault on Leningrad rather than break a blockade. Too many lives were then thrown away in wholly unnecessary counter-attacks. It was now vital to abandon the Nevsky bridgehead – and evacuate most of the Oranienbaum pocket as well – and instead concentrate Soviet troops and artillery further north, closer to Shlisselburg, where conditions for breaking the enemy's ring of encirclement were most favourable. But Zhdanov had neither the skill nor the experience to foresee this possibility.

From 8 September Leningrad was surrounded and cut off from the rest of Russia. Within a further ten days the siege lines had been drawn up – lines that would stay in place, with little variation, for the next sixteen months. To the south lay the forces of the Germans, to the north those of their allies the Finns. The proximity of the Germans was regularly announced, as enemy bombing and shelling became a part of everyday life, but inside the city people could sense the presence of something more deadly and cruel.

Thirteen-year-old Vladimir Zandt instinctively drew it. This young Leningrad artist was sketching in coloured crayon, and his first pictures show a series of sturdy preparations to confront the advancing enemy: the city's inhabitants gather by the radio speakers, listening for the latest news, while their troops march past, heading for the front; in the suburbs, line after line of anti-tank defences have been erected, and anti-aircraft balloons hang in the sky. The city appears calm and unflustered. Then there is a change. As the Germans begin to bomb the city Zandt sketches Leningrad's zoo on fire. One senses that this is a place he has visited and loves. Underneath is a stark exclamation: 'The elephant dies.' Something familiar, that he cares about, has been lost and the drawings are now different. 'Everyday life in a besieged city,' Zandt writes in a matter-of-fact fashion, but an almost tangible anxiety is permeating his impressions: the Nazis shell Labour Square, a tram stops in front of a dead body, loose cable hangs forlornly on the Nevsky Prospect. Each picture is enclosed by a noose.

The Wehrmacht was now digging in. Wilhelm Lubbeck's unit had reached Uritsk by the middle of September, and there they were ordered to halt and construct defensive positions. In the distance, they could see Soviet ships sailing out on the Gulf of Finland. During a break in the fighting, Lubbeck's staff sergeant decided to lead a small group on an excursion to the nearby tsarist palace at Peterhof. The palace and its grounds had remained largely undamaged and the men strolled down wood-panelled corridors and long, elegant halls, mostly empty of furnishings. Then in one room they found a piano. One of the soldiers pulled up a bench and began to play. As the sound of classical music began to echo around the chamber, and late-afternoon sunlight streamed through its large windows, the war seemed very far away. At the end of this brief recital the soldiers opened the piano and found several sheets of music inside, and folded them into their tunics as a souvenir of their visit. Within days – back on the front line repelling a Soviet counter-attack – the episode seemed almost surreal.

By October 1941, Lubbeck and his men were accommodated in freshly constructed dug-outs and bunkers, surrounded by a warren of trenches, observation posts and firing positions. Front-line positions were covered ditches, with slots for observation, and occasional bunkers – acting as defensive strongpoints. In the rear were the troops' living quarters: large bunkers with dirt floors, log walls and timber beams or tree trunks which were used for a roof, covered with a layer of soil for insulation. Inside were bunks, tables and wood-burning stoves where the soldiers could relax, sleep, eat hot meals, play cards, read mail and write letters home. A little further back were the heavy gun emplacements.

This was now a static war: on the front line, one of artillery barrages, sudden bursts of machine-gun fire and the constant threat of snipers; in the rear, one of supply and logistics – equipping and maintaining the besieging army. Behind the German army, their engineers had built a mass of interconnecting roads, supply and ammunition depots, feeding in to their forward positions. Everything was carefully organised and signposted. And then there were the roadside billboards. One crude but amusingly drawn placard depicted a German infantryman happily goose-stepping – with an obliging young woman in his clutches. The caption read: 'Important supply route – please treat it with the same love that you would show for your soldier's bride.' Another portrayed a man frantically scratching underneath his tight-fitting uniform. Next to it was written: 'Terribly serious warning! Whoever damages roads and log causeways by careless driving, breaking regulations, will be barred from any delousing.' The Wehrmacht was here to stay.

At Gatchina, south-west of Leningrad, Ritter von Leeb had set up his headquarters. Now that the front had stabilised, he was supervising the artillery bombardment of the city. Unlike the Soviet commander opposing him, he had not scattered his guns over the front; instead, he had concentrated them between the small towns of Uritsk and Volodarsky, between five and seven miles from the front line. There he had gathered no fewer than three artillery regiments, and from the rooftops of high buildings in Uritsk his spotters enjoyed superb views of Leningrad and were able to call down an unerring fire. This was normally done in careful, ordered sequence, starting at 10.00 a.m. and finishing at 7.00 p.m. The bombardment would begin with an intense barrage, followed by two hours' methodical shelling, then a pause, before the pattern was once again repeated. But on 17 September 1941, to herald the beginning of the siege, Leeb ordered a day and night shelling of the city; his army group diary recorded its duration precisely – it lasted a total of eighteen hours and thirty-three minutes. By the end of September 5,364 shells had been unleashed on Leningrad.

On 28 September Leeb received an order from army high command, stating that a capitulation of the city could not be accepted in any circumstances. It then reiterated:

> In order to eliminate Leningrad as a centre of Bolshevik resistance on the Baltic without sacrificing the lives of our soldiers, the city is not to be attacked by infantry. It is to be deprived of its life and defensive capability by crushing its air protection and fighter planes, and then systematically destroying its waterworks, food stores, and sources of light and power . . . Any move by the civilian population in the direction of the encircling troops is to be prevented – if necessary by force of arms.

Police General Walter Stahlecker's Einsatzgruppe A was now working closely with the German Eighteenth Army. 'As trench warfare began around Leningrad,' Stahlecker noted, 'we cleared a zone around our siege lines of all native inhabitants, and then apprehended those trying to return to the city from the surrounding countryside with food.' Stahlecker saw a chance to exploit the growing food shortage in Leningrad, recruiting informers for intelligence-gathering activities by offering bread to a few of these civilians. The remainder were interrogated and then shot.

On 11 October Colonel-General Georg von Küchler, the Eighteenth Army's commander, circulated the Reichenau Order among his troops – a brutal decree by a fellow Nazi general which set out the future conduct of German soldiers in the east. It declared: 'The most essential aim of our war against Jewish-Bolshevism is the complete destruction and elimination of the Asiatic influence from European culture. The soldier in the Eastern territories is not merely a fighter according to the rules of war; he is also the bearer of a ruthless national ideology. Combating the enemy is still not being taken seriously enough'. The order emphasised that 'Feeding native inhabitants from army kitchens is a misguided humanitarian act.'

But here lay a problem, and over the next month Leeb toured his front-line positions to consult with his officers. His overriding concern was what to do if conditions within Leningrad became so bad that its civilian population attempted a mass break-out towards German lines. On 24 October a discussion was held with divisional staff of the Eighteenth Army. It was reported that 'the troops fully understood that the millions of people trapped in Leningrad could not be fed by us' and that they would fire on those attempting to leave the city. It was doubted, however, if 'they would keep their nerve, and shoot again and again at women and children, and defenceless elderly men, in the case of repeated breakouts'. Chillingly, another solution would have to be found.

On 27 October Army Group North's war diary reported that 'the question of Leningrad, and especially of its civilian population, strongly preoccupies our commander'. It added that, out of concern for his men, he was considering laying minefields in front of the German lines 'to spare the troops having to fire at close range on civilians', before concluding in clinical fashion: 'Even if – as anticipated – a huge proportion of the civilian population will perish, it must not happen immediately under our soldiers' eyes.'

At the end of October Leeb toured his artillery units. He had now found a satisfactory solution to his dilemma, and the decision was recorded:

> The commanding general visited a number of firing positions of heavy and light artillery batteries. He viewed the winter lodgings and newly constructed gun emplacements and then discussed with commanders and battery leaders the use of artillery to prevent the Russian civilian population breaking out from Leningrad. According to Army Order 2737/Secret, such attempts are to be stopped – if necessary by force of arms. It is the task of the artillery to deal with such a situation, and as far away from our own lines as possible – preferably by opening fire on the civilians at an early stage [of their departure from the city] so that the infantry is spared the task of having to shoot the civilians themselves.

These orders were passed to all German artillery formations in front of Leningrad – and seemed to work in a satisfactory fashion. On 15 November the war diary noted: 'Some civilians who were trying to get close to our own lines were successfully hit by artillery fire.'

Wilhelm Lubbeck's unit were well aware of the starvation tactics employed by their high command. The German soldiers besieging Leningrad were generally well fed. Every night, an insulated kettle of hot soup was brought up to the front-line bunkers from the company field kitchen. It usually contained a generous ration of beef, or pork, and potatoes for the soldiers' dinner. They were also left small round loaves of bread – prepared in the large divisional bakery – and butter and cheese, for their breakfast the following morning. Frequently, the quartermaster also provided them with chocolate, a regular ration of small bottles of vodka, and a reasonably tasty artificial coffee, made from roasted grain. During periods of heavy combat, the troops were supplied with tinned goods – tuna, sardine or herring – which they could carry together with crackers or bread in the food bag on the side of their belts.

In contrast, the Russian soldiers and civilians opposite them were starving, and the German troops knew this. Once, there was a brief problem with the supply network – and for a few days the army cut back rations to half a loaf of bread a day. Lubbeck commented: 'Though only providing enough for us to survive, we knew it was far more than the amount supplied to the cut-off population of Leningrad.'

Some of the besieging troops remained troubled by the Wehrmacht's starvation policy, and by the thought of gunning down masses of desperate, unarmed civilians. 'The critical food shortage in Leningrad led to serious discussions among us,' Lubbeck continued. 'There was a real concern that the Russian authorities might decide to send the city's women and children across the lines to our side. It was not clear what would ensue in such a situation, but everyone agreed that mowing down a crowd of civilians with our weapons was inconceivable.'

Yet others on the front line accepted the situation with a callous black humour. One combatant – a private named Schütte – bored with the monotony of trench warfare, would infiltrate Red Army positions at night, armed with a submachine gun and a satchel containing a kilo of dynamite. Slipping past Soviet sentries, he would creep up to a bunker, and as he heaved the satchel inside would shout to the doomed Russians: 'Here's your bread!'

Schütte's 'bread deliveries' soon became famous within the army. 'He pulled off this feat at least a couple of times,' Lubbeck recalled. 'On the second occasion, I even heard the sound of the dynamite's explosion. What had begun as an unauthorised action soon won the approval of our superiors. On my and their recommendation, Schütte was later awarded one of Germany's highest military decorations, the Gold Cross.'

Lubbeck described how German soldiers in his regiment exploited the dire Russian food situation for sexual gratification. Putting a loaf of bread under their arm, these men would head for a certain area – a couple of miles behind the front – where they knew there were hungry Russian women or girls who would willingly exchange sexual favours for food. A story circulated about one particular soldier who responded to a woman's request for her 'payment' of a loaf by slicing off a small piece for her, and keeping the remainder for himself. Lubbeck disapproved of such barter, but observed: 'I knew of no one who was reprimanded or punished for engaging in this type of act.'

The growing contagion of sadism was seen most strongly in the German artillery units, as the testimony of its soldiers makes only too clear. Sergeant Fritz Keppe of the 2nd Battery of the 910th Artillery Regiment stated: 'For the bombardment of Leningrad our batteries received a special stock of ammunition, far beyond the average supplied to artillery units. It was almost an unlimited amount. And all our gun crews knew the purpose of these shells: to destroy the city and wipe out its civilian population. We therefore regarded the bulletins of our supreme command, which spoke of shelling "the military objectives of Leningrad", with ironic humour.' Corporal Bakker of the 1st Battery of the 768th Artillery Regiment had the same attitude: 'We knew that there were a lot of civilians in the city and that we were mostly firing on civilian targets. We would joke as we were shooting that we were saying "Hello Leningrad!"' Lieutenant Kruschke of the 126th Artillery Regiment added: 'Our soldiers, who were shooting at the city, would say, "Today we are feeding Leningrad again. They should be grateful to us – they have famine there, after all."'

The Wehrmacht had drawn up accurate grid maps of the city, pinpointing the targets for their artillery: firing points 89 and 99 were hospitals, no. 192 the palace for young pioneers, no. 708 the Institute for Maternal Care, no. 736 an infant school, no. 757 civilian apartments on Bolshaya Street.

And then there were the air raids. The Luftwaffe regularly hit apartment blocks, crowded with women and children. One damage report in October 1941 charted the wreckage at 74 Marat Street, which had been hit by two high-explosive bombs. Under the wreckage were found the bodies of three teenage girls and their thirty-five-year-old mother Tutina Zhukov. The body of sixty-year-old Vera Konenkova was found in the opposite wing of the house, where she had been blown from the window by the force of the explosion. One girl was still alive beneath the rubble: 'Vera Potekhina was found under the wreckage, screaming for help, and her father – being at the scene with the rescue team – began frantically pulling away the debris. As the obstacles began to be taken away, she saw him, and cried out: "Father – save me!" But when the last timbers were pulled away, the girl had died of a wound to the forehead.'

The Luftwaffe would soon move many of their planes south to support Operation Typhoon. Here the Germans had taken a calculated risk, transferring their armoured formations from Army Group North to support the great Moscow offensive. They were actually starting the siege with a numerically smaller force than that opposing them, trapped inside Leningrad and its hinterland. They knew that, over time, the defenders' rapidly diminishing food supplies would seriously weaken their capacity to launch any major attack. Until then, the Germans were relying on their army's professionalism – and its far more substantial supplies of food and ammunition – to get them out of trouble. 'The situation around Leningrad will remain tight until hunger becomes our main ally,' Hitler's chief of staff, Colonel-General Franz Halder, had said. But in the first months of the siege there remained a real risk that the Soviets might break out of the encirclement and link up with one of their neighbouring armies on the flanks of Army Group North.

Yet the morale of the defenders was waning, day by day, and the risk of such action dwindled along with it. 'This morning we watched three deserters being shot,' Joseph Finkelstein wrote on 1 October.

> The men had run away from the front – and their execution was intended as a warning to the rest of us. All three had blank stares on their faces. They undressed and stood in their underwear while a grave was dug, close by, but as they turned towards the firing squad, one brought his arms up and covered his eyes. His arms were forced down again. 'Shoot the traitors to the Motherland!' the officer commanded, and we saw blood spurt from the men's faces as they fell. But two of the bodies twitched and an NKVD man walked up and shot both in the head with a pistol.

'The situation with our food supplies is getting worse and worse,' Semyon Putyakov noted in his diary on 7 October. 'Our rations have been cut yet again.' Two days later he added: 'Our soldiers are all saying that, in contrast to us, the Nazis are feeding very well. If that is true we are in big trouble.' Putyakov was sceptical of the military communiqués, with their upbeat reports of vigorous Soviet resistance. 'Nothing is said in these reports about the food shortages we are suffering – instead, we hear that there are heroic deeds being performed by our troops all along the front line. But there is a strange lack of detail about where these so-called heroic deeds are actually happening. They are creating this myth about our fighting because they are frightened to tell us the real situation.'

Putyakov feared for Leningrad's civilians. On 27 October he saw groups of people coming out from the city, risking the perils of German artillery shelling to search for scraps of food in the outlying countryside. 'It's awful to see women and old men desperately digging the same patch of land for the tenth time, trying to find a few potatoes,' he wrote. The thought stayed with him. That night he confided to his diary: 'I got completely drunk.'

Stephan Kuznetsov was also worried about the deteriorating food situation. On 2 November he recorded: 'The temperature is really dropping now, and hunger is a constant presence among us. The food we are issued with is very poor. Today I saw some civilians crying by the roadside – they were so desperately hungry. They told me their babies are dying from malnutrition.' There was little Kuznetsov could do – the soldiers' rations were only a little better than those issued to civilians. 'There has been talk about a further reduction in rations,' he continued. 'We now receive only 300 grams of bread a day – and a so-called "soup" for lunch, that has the consistency of water.'

These men experienced a divide opening up between Red Army officers and the ordinary soldiers – and also felt the lack of any real, effective leadership. Kuznetsov wrote bitterly: 'A private here is treated like a beast of burden. I had no breakfast today – the officers stole it. That's starvation for you – everyone behaves like a dog!' Putyakov declared emphatically on 1 November: 'Our people and our army at Leningrad deserve a good military leader.' After Stalin's address to the nation, given on the anniversary of the revolution on

7 November, calling on the country to unite against the German invader, he added: 'This speech will do nothing. People here need actions not words.'

By November 1941, theft among those military units defending Leningrad was rampant. Kuznetsov awoke one morning to find that his 'comrades' had stolen his shaving razor and soap. His cigarettes disappeared shortly afterwards. Putyakov lost his belt. He was suspicious of everybody: 'We believe our officers have engineered a racket with the cooks in the canteen, so they can get more food. Our portions have definitely grown smaller.' In these straitened circumstances, Putyakov heard with amazement rumours that an offensive would be launched to break the siege. 'I don't believe it!' he wrote.

As winter set in, the Red Army guarding Leningrad was in a dismal state. Stephan Kuznetsov surveyed his fellow fighters: 'All our soldiers on the front line look like ghouls – emaciated because of the hunger and cold. They are in rags, filthy and very, very hungry.' Joseph Finkelstein's division heard reports of a mysterious enemy gun firing on Leningrad, apparently moving from one location to another in the city's suburbs. A group of soldiers claimed they had seen it in one of Leningrad's outlying parks, but the gun did not actually exist. 'Evidently,' Finkelstein wrote, 'these men have hallucinated because of starvation.'

But Zhdanov was now massing his forces for a new attempt to break the siege. And once again the fulcrum of this effort would be the Nevsky bridgehead. Zhdanov should never have been in charge of it, but no one else on the Military Council wanted the job of defending the city or organising the counter-attack. After Zhukov's departure for Moscow the post had fallen vacant. An undignified game of pass the parcel ensued, as everyone sought to avoid taking responsibility for Leningrad's fate.

When Zhukov had left Leningrad for Moscow on 7 October he had intended his deputy, Major-General Fedyuninsky, to be his successor. But Fedyuninsky was less than enthusiastic about taking command of the besieged city. He claimed that he lacked the appropriate army seniority for the job and, pointing the finger at others, said that Zhukov's chief of staff, Khozin, had greater command experience than him, and was thus a far better choice. The two men were of equal rank – Khozin had recently been promoted to major-general – and this argument smacked of desperation. Fedyuninsky realised that if placed in command he would be called upon to try and break the German blockade of the city. If he failed in this difficult and dangerous task, his own head might roll.

When Fedyuninsky's initial request to step down was declined he upped the ante, singing the praises of the unfortunate Khozin in an even more fulsome fashion, and once again declaring his eminent suitability for the job. Fedyuninsky cleverly developed his argument. He knew Khozin's skill well, he added, because previously he had served *under* him – a point to which he gave considerable emphasis – at battalion level, while Khozin had commanded a division. Dismayed at these goings on, Zhdanov then tried to recruit Marshal Voronov – who had arrived in the city to inspect the functioning of its armament industry.

Voronov seemed an ideal choice. He was a senior Red Army commander, a man of considerable prestige and experience, skilled in the use of artillery and a native Leningrader. Surely this was the time for him to step into the breach? In his memoirs, Voronov attempted to portray his arrival in the beleaguered city as a moment of destiny, when Leningrad's Military Council decided to pull together, united in a common cause: 'Never before in history had Leningrad been in such a dangerous position. The honour of our generation depended on our saving her.' In fact, they all were bickering and clawing like ferrets in a sack. Leningrad did not need a committee; it needed a commander. Yet when Zhdanov offered him the post, Voronov disappeared beneath a flurry of excuses. He would love the job, he reassured Zhdanov, but he was already deputy commissar of defence, and if he took on the Leningrad command as well Moscow might think he was trying to evade his responsibilities.

Faced with this unconvincing argument, Zhdanov turned to the hapless Khozin. Khozin also professed apparent enthusiasm for the Leningrad command, before adding that, as he had only recently taken over at the Fifty-fourth Army after the dismissal of Kulik, it would not be right for him to leave his men at such a time.

Reluctantly, he would have to decline Zhdanov's flattering invitation. Eventually, Moscow was called in to arbitrate.

In the meantime, Zhdanov – lacking in military qualifications and unable to see a viable alternative – decided to persist with the flawed strategy initiated by Zhukov. He fed more and more men into the Nevsky bridgehead and once again tried to cut through the German blockade of the city from this desperate and wholly unsuitable place. But, even after being strengthened, it remained impossible for this force to break out from the narrow strip of land along the Neva. Instead, its casualties rose and rose. Nurse Elena Svetkova crossed over to the Nevsky bridgehead in October 1941 and set up a small medical station to tend to the ever increasing numbers of wounded. 'We had a dug-out right by the river,' she recalled. 'Our equipment was absolutely basic: a portable oven, dry bandages, and spirits. There were now hundreds of wounded coming in every day – and there was simply no time for registration, or filling in forms. Sometimes I went out with a first-aid kit to the trenches, and then brought the wounded to our dug-out, carrying them on my back. I also had a sledge to pull heavily wounded soldiers. We needed to get these men back across the Neva for proper medical attention, but that proved virtually impossible.' Of those tended by Svetkova, only a handful could be carried across the river to safety. One of the fortunate few was a badly wounded young marine named Vladimir Putin. After the war, he became father to Russia's future president.

Svetkova remembered the build-up for the new offensive. 'Continuous reinforcements were pouring in – but what reinforcements: they were half-starved skeletons!' These unfortunates were unable to make any progress against the Germans. 'We were losing thousands of men a day,' Colonel Alexander Sokolov recalled. 'The trenches were full of the dead bodies of our soldiers. The enemy bombardment was overwhelming. In all my time on the bridgehead I remember only one brief period of daytime silence, when there was no shooting, bombing or shelling. It lasted a full ten minutes. The German fire was constant – and their positions were so close that during daylight nobody was ever able to stand at full height without being immediately picked off by a sniper.' Those men who did survive – faces and bodies blackened from the constant crouching in the earth – were left prostrate with exhaustion.

In an attempt to raise the morale of troops serving on the front, the Leningrad Military Council decided to send out groups of actors, musicians and dancers to perform for them. Tamara Pavlotskaya was one of a small theatre group sent out to the Nevsky bridgehead. 'I had visited our front-line soldiers a number of times,' she remembered,

> but never experienced conditions like this. The journey was incredibly dangerous. We were loaded into a military vehicle, which halted shortly before we reached the Neva, so that we could put on camouflage outfits. We were then given a small emergency ration, a few pieces of pearl barley, before being transported across the river at dusk. For the last stage of our journey, we all had to crawl on our hands and knees through the darkness. Remarkably, some sort of makeshift stage had been erected, right up by the Neva, where a small strip of land lay protected by a rising fold in the embankment, and there we hurriedly donned our costumes.

Pavlotskaya and her fellow actors were putting on a short musical comedy called *Bats*. This was normally very popular with soldiers, bringing forth guffaws of laughter and shouts of approval. On this occasion, there was no reaction at all. 'I have never seen such exhaustion,' Pavlotskaya continued.

> Before us, there was a sea of blackened faces. Some men had fallen fast asleep; others, whether out of fatigue or shell-shock, seemed absolutely numb – unable to respond to anything. Our comedy routine – with its singing, dancing and jokes – continued in absolute silence.
>
> Then something quite bizarre happened. As we struggled on with our performance, there was an odd, scuffling sound behind us, and then a startled goat appeared in our midst. Apparently, it had emerged from a nearby wood, and lost and disorientated, it climbed up on to the stage and just stood there. For a moment our actors froze – then we decided to carry on regardless. Remarkably, all around us, we felt our audience coming back to life, as if they were all emerging from some kind of terrible trance. There was a sudden

> transfusion of energy. Men began laughing, smiling, and nudging their fellows.
>
> For a few minutes the goat stayed rooted to the spot. Then it started to look around at us. Overcoming its bewilderment, the creature then wandered over to the lead singer, who was performing a short aria about unrequited love. The goat stopped and began to stare at her in a most doleful, sympathetic fashion. The soldiers were now watching transfixed. The goat turned towards them, and started to bleat in accompaniment to the song, its strange sounds rising to an extraordinary falsetto. As the impromptu duet reached its climax, there was a mighty roar of laughter, and the whole audience rose to its feet in delighted applause. I have never experienced anything so moving as that moment.

On 20 October the Neva Operational Group had been ordered to strike east, break through the German defences and join up with Khozin's Fifty-fourth Army. The recently arrived 115th Rifle Division and the 4th Marine Brigade were earmarked to head the offensive. More and more reinforcements had been pushed in – and although these men were weak with starvation, and in no real state to undertake an attack, on paper the dispositions looked impressive, with the force numbering 70,000 men supported by ninety-seven tanks – brought across the river on barges and rafts – and the artillery and aircraft of the Baltic Fleet, some of whose ships were now stationed on deep-water stretches of the Neva. Facing them were some 54,000 German infantry.

The enemy now occupied positions fortified in depth, flanked by swampy terrain, and protected by over 450 guns. The relentless German artillery fire proved decisive. The 4th Marine Brigade was annihilated, the 115th Division reduced to less than 200 men. After a week of fruitless fighting, the Neva Group was unable to expand its bridgehead and the offensive was called off.

Stalin, worried about the food situation in Leningrad, pressed Zhdanov to make another attempt. On 8 November he chided the city's Military Council: 'We are really concerned about your slowness. If, over the next few days, you do not break through [the German lines] you will have let down the citizens of Leningrad. You

Self-portrait of Elena Martilla – from the first winter of the Leningrad blockade. At the onset of the siege, this eighteen-year-old artist was told by her professor: 'Go out and start drawing what you see . . . We must preserve this for humanity. Future generations must be warned of the absolute horror of war.'

First casualties of the siege – in September 1941 the Germans began indiscriminate shelling of the city.

Marshal Kliment Voroshilov could strike a fine pose – but his defence of Leningrad was an utter calamity.

A Leningrad apartment during the siege. The radio transmitter dish in the upper-left-hand corner was never switched off – it was a lifeline for the city's inhabitants.

'Big piece of bread!' was all Alik could say. He was already crazed with hunger.

'The alert will soon be over' – the boy in the air-raid shelter looks like a wise old man.

'What are you doing to us?' The eyes of the youngest child are wide open in horror.

A Leningrader sits amid the wreckage of her home.

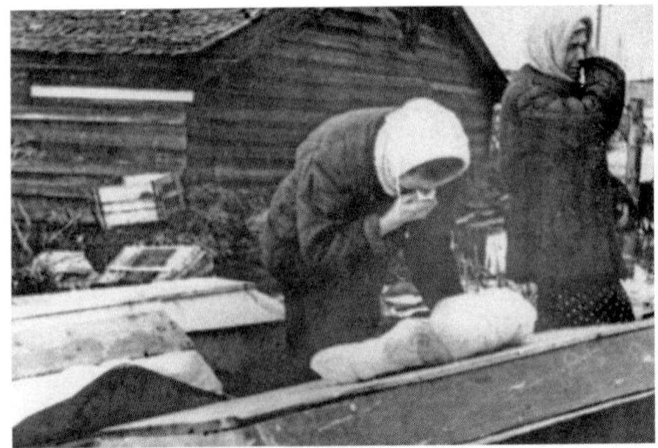

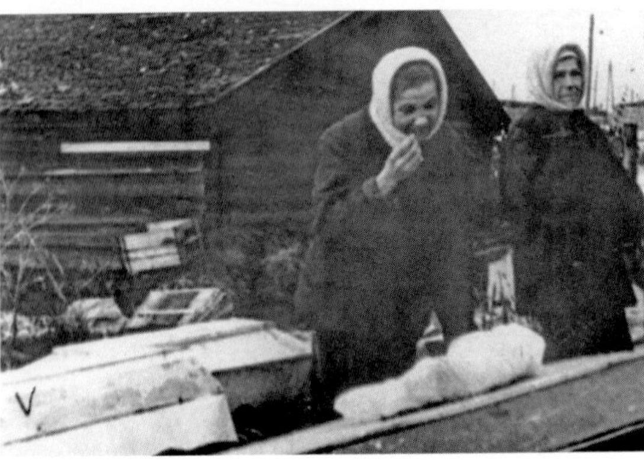

The agony of the siege: a mother buries her child.

'If we die, we die together.' A mother, weak with hunger, is going to perform a concert for wounded soldiers, and her child accompanies her.

'On duty': at the entrance to an apartment block a mother cradles her daughter and watches for incendiary bombs.

The Leningrad Madonna.

A devastated landscape – in the apartment block's entrance, two women huddle by a stove. Above frozen mounds of snow, searchlights criss-cross the sky.

Жиров никаких нет уже давно и сладости никакой
вместо сахара за Декабрь получили повидлой
за [illegible] нет ничего сейчас в городе
творится жуткая картина Свету нет
уже 2 месяца вода замерзла ходим к дворнику
уборная тоже неработает дров мало
суп варим в печке Керосину нет так что
из за супу и в комнате холодно сидим вечером
часов до 8 и 9 с лампадкой жгем воск
окна после бомбежек выбиты забиты фанерой
и днем темно на заводе тоже нет току
и очень холодно то [illegible] то посылают
за углем или пилить возить дрова
и других и на кладбище зарывать [illegible]
сейчас очень холодно кров уже не греет
t° – 28 - 30° в городе умирает очень
много народу по 20 тысяч в день
по всем улицам так и [illegible] покойников
(6)

A Leningrad siege diary and its teenage author. At the end of January 1942 Vasily Vladimirov wrote: 'They say the death toll has reached 20,000 a day. Everywhere in the streets you see people carrying dead bodies.'

Gathering water under the ice of the Neva – in January 1942 Leningrad's water supply finally failed. The city was without heat or light and temperatures were now dropping below –30 degrees Celsius.

'In the Public Library': in the coldest months of the blockade the city's inhabitants still came – dizzy with starvation sickness – to read and study.

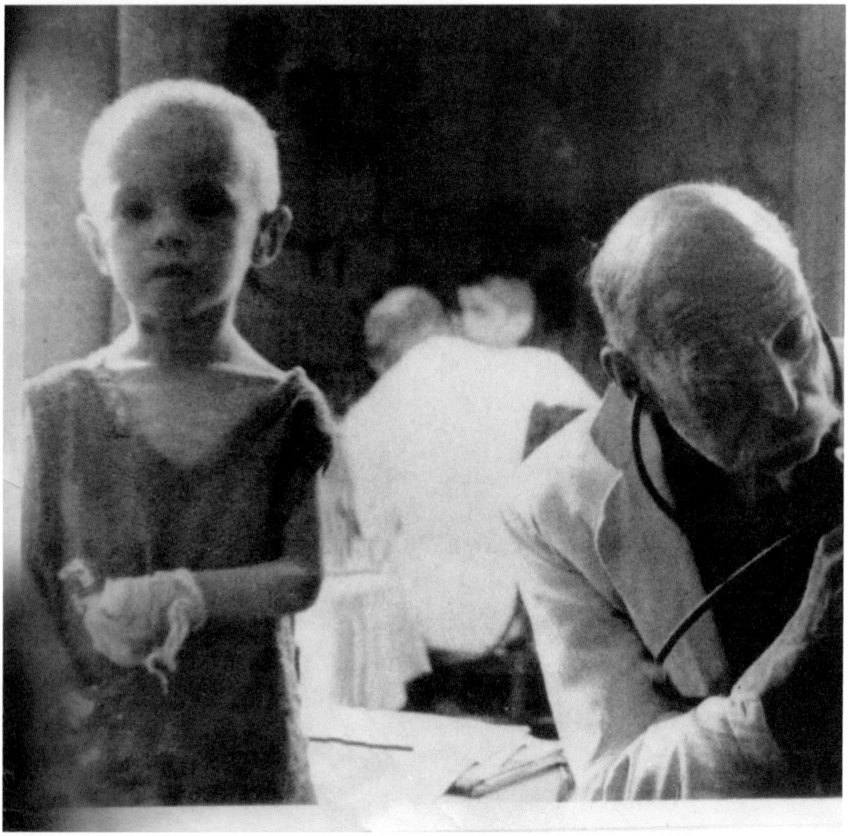

Scene from a Leningrad starvation hospital – the first of these "convalescent hospitals" opened in January 1942.

One February night Elena Martilla – desperately weak from starvation – realised that if she fell asleep she would die. To keep awake, she summoned all her remaining strength and painted this self-portrait. In the morning Martilla said in joyous affirmation: 'I did not die. I will not die. I will live.'

'I cannot count the riches of my soul.' Olga Berggolts' poetry – broadcast to Leningraders during the worst period of the siege – sustained people when all seemed hopeless.

Motorized sledges – manned by Red Army soldiers – fan out to protect the Road of Life.

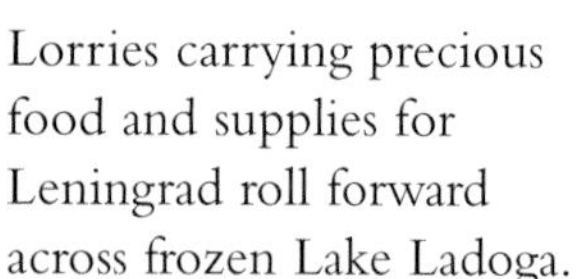

Lorries carrying precious food and supplies for Leningrad roll forward across frozen Lake Ladoga.

A driver takes a lorry-load of refugees across the Road of Life. His door is wide open so that he can jump for safety if the ice under the vehicle disintegrates.

Starving Leningraders called party boss Andrei Zhdanov a 'fat cat' and a 'pig'. He looks distinctly overweight as he visits frontline troops.

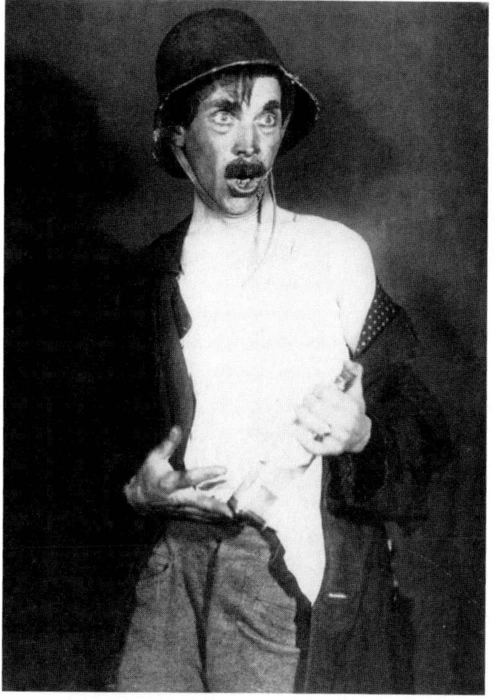

An emaciated actor from the Musical Comedy Theatre still transmits extraordinary energy to his audience.

On 27 March 1942 an army of Leningrad women moves into action and the great city clean-up begins. It is the turning-point of the blockade.

Lieutenant-General Govorov – the real hero of the siege – inspects an artillery position.

Tania Savicheva sways in a terrible trance, cradling a dying house plant which holds the memory of her lost family.

Karl Eliasberg conducts the Radio Committee Orchestra at the Philharmonic – probably for Shostakovich's Seventh Symphony on 9 August 1942.

Enthralled by the music - the audience pack Leningrad's Philharmonic Hall for the performance of Shostakovich's Seventh.

'We defended Lenin's city!' Propaganda posters showed Leningrad united against a hated foe.

27 January 1944 – the 872-day siege is finally over. With powerful yet restrained emotion a woman congratulates a Red Army soldier. That night, victory rockets are fired in celebration over Leningrad's Field of Mars.

An eternal flame burns in the Piskaryov Memorial Cemetery – mass graves lie on either side of the pathway: 'None is forgotten, and nothing is forgotten!'

are running out of time. Soon you will be without bread.'

Stalin was right to be worried. The only route available for supplies to get into Leningrad was a circuitous and dangerous one, first by rail link and then across the waters of Lake Ladoga, to the little port of Osinovets, and finally into the city. The Germans were already bombing all Soviet shipping on the lake, and now their forces were poised to capture the town of Tikhvin and break the rail connection. Once Tikhvin fell, the amount of food reaching Leningrad would dwindle to a tiny trickle. Something had to be done fast. But Zhdanov was attacking in the wrong place.

Attempts were made to put more Soviet tanks on the bridgehead. On the night of 14 November the last light tanks in the Leningrad reserve were brought across the Neva. By the morning the Germans had destroyed eight of them and disabled the remaining six, which had to be hulled down as stationary firing points. No support for an infantry attack existed any longer, and with floating ice on the river and a lack of a pontoon bridge, it was impossible to get any heavy armoured vehicles across. 'To talk about an offensive from the Nevsky bridgehead in such conditions borders on the senseless,' the Leningrad Front's tank commander, General Nikolai Bolotnikov, told Zhdanov.

Zhdanov persisted nonetheless. On 16 November Mikhail Neishtadt and four other signals specialists were sent from Leningrad's Smolny Institute to the bridgehead to set up a communications link. Zhdanov wanted to be in direct radio contact with his battered force. 'It was absolute hell there,' Neishtadt said simply. 'All our attempts to break the siege from this point failed. Our positions were being smashed to pieces by the enemy's artillery. If you somehow managed to stay alive it was a total fluke.'

Alexander Sokolov recalled the Germans mocking their predictable and utterly futile efforts. 'They watched our movements the whole time – and knew when and where we would go on to the attack. As we were starting to move forward they would taunt us, in broken Russian, through their loudspeakers, calling out, "It's time to assemble at your extermination points again – we will bury you on the banks of the Neva!" Then they trained all their guns on us, and unleashed a murderous barrage of fire.'

The devastating losses on the Nevsky bridgehead sapped the Red Army's strength, and robbed Leningrad of a fleeting chance to break the German ring round the city further north – near Shlisselburg – where conditions for a counter-attack were more favourable. When a military push was belatedly made from this spot, in late November, it was undermanned, poorly supplied and atrociously organised.

On 21 November Colonel Ivan Frolov and his 80th Rifle Division were shipped from the Oranienbaum pocket to Leningrad and then force-marched to the western shore of Lake Ladoga. En route, hundreds of the division's weakened, hungry soldiers died of exhaustion. They had received no supplies or ammunition, and many of the units had completely run out of bullets. But Zhdanov ordered them straight into an attack on a well-defended German position. Frolov, supported by the divisional commissar Konstantin Ivanov, refused to obey the order. He saw only too clearly that it would lead to yet another pointless massacre.

Frolov and Ivanov were dismissed from their posts, and on 26 November the attack went in. The unfortunate soldiers of the 80th Division were loaded on to trucks, driven to a position close to the German lines and told to launch a frontal assault on the enemy on a vast, open expanse of frozen lake, completely lacking in shelter and without being given any artillery or mortar support. At a distance of a little over a mile the German machine guns opened fire. The men were mown down in their thousands.

Zhdanov needed to find a scapegoat for this dismal failure. Following his personal intervention, Frolov and Ivanov were arrested on 2 December and on the same day they appeared before the military tribunal of the Leningrad Front. The two men were charged with 'cowardice and criminal negligence that resulted in the failure of the operation'. They were immediately found guilty and both were shot on 3 December. Zhdanov ensured that the trial was widely reported in the Leningrad press.

Stalin always wanted to hear regular reports about the situation in the besieged city, and once, when Zhdanov failed to keep him informed, had erupted: 'Do you imagine Leningrad is not really in the Soviet Union, but is somewhere out on an island in the Pacific Ocean?' Now Zhdanov was sending his master a stream of personal letters, blaming the failure to break the blockade on 'the weak performance of our infantry, and panic and cowardice among its officers, as a result of which hunger is now spreading'. 'Let us shoot Frolov and Ivanov,' Zhdanov had asked, and Stalin responded quickly: 'Shoot them – and tell the media.'

By December the Germans no longer feared a Soviet break-out from the city. The enemy's grip was tightening. On 13 December Hitler's chief of staff, Colonel-General Franz Halder, jotted down in his diary words of relief and grim satisfaction: 'The commander of the army group is inclined to the view – after the failure of all attempts by the enemy to break through our position along the Neva – that we may expect the compete starvation of Leningrad.'

Sometimes in war, strategic objectives take on a life of their own, exercising a strange magnetism which far exceeds their original purpose. The Nevsky bridgehead is one of them. It remains a bleak, depressing spot for a modern visitor, and its scarred landscape, criss-crossed with trenches, still yields the ghastly detritus of the fighting there. Yet this desolate place is the key to understanding why the siege of Leningrad went on for so long. Thousands upon thousands of Soviet soldiers fought and died here needlessly. Their pointless sacrifice crippled the Red Army's efforts to break the German blockade. The last chance to avoid Leningrad's tragedy had been squandered, and the noose inexorably closed around the city's throat.

5

Elena's Sketchbook

The Emerging Horror

On 2 October 1941 Elena Skrjabina recorded a new reduction of the bread ration in her diary. 'A few small slices – just enough for a sandwich,' she said. 'We have started dividing the bread equally among all. Everyone wants to use their portion in their own way. For instance, my mother tries to stretch her piece into three meals. I eat my entire portion right away, in the morning, with the coffee, so that I might have at least enough strength to stand in line or perhaps make some sort of trade. In the afternoons though, I become weak and have to lie down.'

At the beginning of October the bread ration for white-collar workers and their dependants had been brought down to 200 grams a day. In theory, this should have been supplemented by other foods; in practice, little else was available. The relationship between Leningrad's inhabitants and their dwindling bread supply was now a dominant factor in everyday life.

Because ingredients were so scarce, the proportion of flour used in a loaf made in the besieged city was constantly revised. In mid-September, oats that had formerly been reserved for horse fodder were added to the commercial bread recipe, as was malt. In October mouldy grain – retrieved from a ship that had been sunk in Lake Ladoga – was dried out and also added. By November, a standard Leningrad loaf also contained 'edible' cellulose, cottonseed oil cake, dust shaken out of flour sacks and floor sweepings. The bread was heavy and, when you took it in your hands, water dripped from it.

'The bread was now sticky and damp,' Elena Kochina recalled. 'It contained all kinds of junk – and only a little flour.' On one occasion, she returned with a particularly wet piece, and she and her husband then looked at it morosely. Despite their pangs of hunger they were, for a moment, reluctant to consume it: 'it lay on the table like a piece of clay.' Oilseed cake – previously used as cattle fodder – was particularly hard to digest; the 'edible' cellulose was not edible at all.

People began to scavenge for alternatives. They brought home the tough, dark-green outer leaves of cabbage that had previously been discarded. At night, dressed in dark clothes for fear of attracting enemy fire, they went to the outskirts of the city and dug up scraps of potatoes that lay rotting in the fields. They even gnawed at pine logs. In 1890 a young Norwegian, Knut Hamsun, had written a novel called *Hunger*. In it he described the crazed ingenuity of those beginning to suffer from starvation:

> I had to eat whatever came my way. I remember coming home and so wanting to eat! There was some firewood lying by the stove – one or two logs. So I took a log – it was pine, I recall – and began to gnaw. I was desperate to eat. I chewed and chewed away at that log, and the resin oozed out. That fragrance of resin gave me some sense of enjoyment that I was at least chewing something. I had to eat something.

Hamsun's work has been described as the only novel in world literature that has hunger as its main theme, and its powerful authenticity was based on the author's own experience of starvation. The book's hero is plunged into a bleak, isolated existence, which cannot be understood by the fortunate, well-fed people around him. But the hunger of the blockade was well understood by the Germans. They had researched its effect, and then enrolled it as the deadly ally of their blockading army. And as hunger's grip on the city became more cruel, Hamsun's observations no longer represented a source of solidarity or support. On 7 November 1941 Georgi Knyazev noted in his diary: 'A horrifying item has appeared in the newspapers. Knut Hamsun, that wonderful writer, has come to the conclusion that it is impossible for Norway to be an independent country and has been won over to the side of the Quislings: that is, towards complete collaboration with the Nazis.'

As the pangs of hunger grew, cats and dogs began to disappear from the city's streets. People scoured their own homes for additional sources of nourishment. One unlikely supplement was joiner's glue, scraped from furniture. Before the introduction of synthetic adhesives, this glue was based on animal proteins, and it included casein from fish residues. If one persisted with it, it could offer a source of nutrition, however paltry. Olga Grechina was given a recipe from a chance acquaintance on the street. The glue needed to be soaked for twenty-four hours and then boiled – during which time it gave off a foul odour of animal hooves – before being allowed to cool and thicken. A dash of vinegar or mustard would, apparently, make it palatable.

Faina Prusova had less luck with wallpaper paste. She wrote in her diary: 'On the advice of one elderly woman I boiled the wallpaper. But it made me feel so nauseous that I threw it out at once. Then I tried boiling a leather belt – the yard keeper suggested it – and got the same muddy, dirty water. Again, I poured it away immediately. At this point, I promised myself I would not eat any more muck – come what may!'

People were beginning to fear the approach of winter. On 17 October Olga Makarova wrote from the besieged city to her daughter Katya: 'It is already very cold here and it has started to snow.' The fact bothered her, and she returned to it. 'Surely the snow will not last long? – it is too early.' Makarova wondered what the food situation was like where her daughter lived, in Saratov. 'Do you have shortages?' she asked, a little plaintively. 'Do you have enough bread? It must be better than here.' It wasn't possible to say very much – letters out of the city were opened, and their contents carefully inspected, but Makarova did add sadly: 'I haven't eaten vegetables in such a long time.' She concluded briskly: 'I'm off to get some firewood. I hope this letter reaches you soon.'

On 21 October Georgi Knyazev recorded: 'Leningrad's food situation is worsening. There is little now that can be bought with money, so it has lost its value.' Almost every edible item was rationed, and most had disappeared from the shops altogether. 'People who have a lot of money no longer know what to do with it,' Knyazev went on. 'Some spend it on all kinds of trash – expensive perfumes and so on – others, who are more practical, buy up manufactured goods for the purpose of exchanging them when money completely loses its value.' The possibility of a return to a more primitive era, with a barter economy, stopped Knyazev short. 'Of all the trials awaiting us, hunger is the most terrifying. You have to train yourself to think as little as possible about the future.' Yet, moving along the street, Knyazev suddenly came across beds of earth, newly dug for next spring's flowers. He was deeply touched – and for a moment his apprehension lifted. 'Life triumphant!' he exulted.

At the beginning of the month, Yuri Ryabinkin had gambled at cards with his schoolfriends. His tally of roubles had kept mounting – until the total he had won, 400, seemed quite unreal. He hid the cash in a sweet tin. A few days later they all enjoyed a game of forfeits. Adolescent good humour was keeping fear at bay:

> Lopatin crawled up a whole flight of the spiral staircase on all fours; Finkelstein was then supposed to give Bron a piggy-back up it. I was instructed to catch a cat, and then kiss Ella. I did the first but refused the second, and my punishment was to have water poured down my neck. We had a lot of fun. We fastened a piece of paper to the cat, saying 'Supper – death to the cat!' then let it go. The terrified creature dashed off.

But those meagre slices of bread were now at the centre of everyone's lives. On 14 October Ryabinkin's sister went into hysterics – accusing him of getting more food than her. A few days later, Ryabinkin himself was suspecting a neighbour of hoarding food and not sharing it with anybody. On 25 October he wrote in his diary: 'A month ago I yearned for bread, butter and sausage; now, all I crave is bread.' On 29 October he drafted a longer piece. The staircase, which only weeks earlier had been the location of a joyful game, now represented a colossal obstacle to him. 'I can now hardly drag my feet, I'm so weak, and climbing the stairs is a tremendous feat for me,' he began. 'Mum says my face is starting to get puffy. All through lack of food . . . I must adjust to this hunger, but I can't. So what shall I do?' Schoolwork was a welcome distraction, but it was becoming harder and harder for him to study. 'I wanted to sit down and do some algebra,' he confessed, 'but instead of formulae, loaves of bread kept floating around in my head.' Ryabinkin had always been an energetic teenager, but a dull apathy was now setting in. He no longer took much trouble over his appearance. 'I'm none too fussy about myself now. I just rinse my face a bit in the mornings. I don't wash my hands with soap, don't bother to change my clothes. Our flat is freezing and dark.'

However, on 5 November, with the anniversary of the October Revolution approaching, Ryabinkin roused himself from his lethargy. He contemplated his future, writing with a sudden, savage maturity:

> How many people have lived before us, and how many have had to die? But it is good to die feeling and knowing you have achieved all your dreams from childhood and youth, good to die knowing that you have left successors to carry on your work. How difficult that is now. What is Hitler counting on? On building an empire, the very concept of which will be cursed by future generations. Because of his band of adventurers, millions upon millions of people are losing their lives.
>
> It's late now. The German artillery fire has died down for the moment. The candle's burning low. Hunger, cold, darkness, lice – the prospect of a crimson future wrapped in a dark shroud.

At the beginning of November ten-year-old Svetlana Magaeva was walking along a street by Leningrad's main university building with her mother. An old man came into view, already frail and walking extremely slowly. Her mother immediately recognised him: he was Professor Alexei Ukhtomsky, one of the Soviet Union's leading physiologists – years earlier, she had been one of his students. When the war started Ukhtomsky had refused to be evacuated, and, like many of Leningrad's academics, had resolutely determined to stay in the besieged city and continue with his research and writing. He was studying the after-effects of traumatic shock, but the distinguished professor was already suffering from the cold and lack of food. He chatted for a while with Magaeva's mother, then turned to

Magaeva herself, and pulled a small bundle out from his pocket and carefully unwrapped it. Inside was his ration of bread. Ukhtomsky took it and slowly and deliberately broke it in half. He looked at Magaeva and said firmly: 'Take it – the rest is ample for an old man like me.'

Magaeva was initially reluctant to accept Ukhtomsky's gift – he was an old man, after all, and he clearly needed it. But then a thought suddenly struck her: Ukhtomsky was moved to help her because she was a child, and denying his act of kindness would be churlish. So she took the bread, and in that moment something changed, although she struggled to make full sense of it. She had been brought up in the modern Soviet state as a communist and an atheist, but now, for the first time in her life, she was feeling the presence of something older and more primal. 'Bread is life,' she said to Ukhtomsky, in startled recognition. The old man was leaning on his stick. He smiled, bent and kissed her on the cheek, then slowly walked away. She still felt a little guilty, but resisted the impulse to run after him and return it. 'It was a strange sensation – but I felt that I had received some sort of blessing,' Magaeva said. 'We had shared bread together.'

'Conversation about food now took on a universal meaning and importance', Lidiya Ginzburg recalled. 'A discussion about how it's better not to salt millet when boiling it, because then it gets to be just right, became a consideration of life and death – the millet expands in your stomach, you see, and with the constriction of hunger that could be fatal. Reduced in its scope, "siege cuisine" nevertheless became enriched with tales of life's ups and downs, difficulties overcome and problems resolved. It subsumed every interest and passion.'

Evgeny Lyapin, a Leningrad mathematics professor able to keep tally of the city's diminishing supply of foodstuffs, spoke of the terrible science that underlay these desperate conversations:

> In normal conditions you'd imagine that a human being is something like a stove: while it's being fed firewood it stays alight; if there's no wood – and it's not getting any fuel – the stove goes out. In the same

> way, a human being is fed energy-building foods and he lives off this energy, he's active. But when there are too few calories coming in, then he uses what his body has stored up: fat, muscles. He uses all this up. When all this is burnt up – and any physicist knows the energy cycle – he dies.

But, as the horror of starvation took hold, survival in Leningrad was no longer just a simple mathematical equation. Lyapin was also aware of a sinister newcomer to the besieged city – an undercurrent of raw fear that left people struggling to carry on functioning at all. Everyday life was becoming darker and more frightening and some were literally sinking under the weight of the stress. When this happened, their bodies could no longer digest or metabolise the food that was left to them. 'Often during the siege', Lyapin explained, 'a person died when a small reserve of energy – in the simple, physical sense – remained in his organism. His "stove" could have gone on functioning – but he died nonetheless.'

German shelling was designed to spread this disabling terror. Having cut Leningrad off from its food supplies, the enemy now wished to break its will to resist. German gunners watched the city, pinpointed where people gathered to try and obtain food, and then struck swiftly. Vera Inber described the horror of being suddenly caught – above ground and vulnerable – in a sustained burst of artillery fire. She had just boarded tram no. 12 on Bolshoi Prospect:

> We had hardly started when the shelling began. Shells fell to the right and left of us. There was a roaring sound – the street was an inferno. The crashes reverberated as if we were at the bottom of a canyon. No one in the tram said a word. We were carried into the actual zone of fire. The most frightening part was to see people on the pavement running away from the very place we were approaching, getting nearer every moment. Suddenly the driver said: 'I'm not going any further – I'm terrified.' Everyone shouted at her: 'Don't stop! Keep going – we shall rush through it.' At first she obeyed, and we hurtled past one stop like a whirlwind. But at the next one – Sitnoy Market – a shell fell so close that the driver let go of the wheel and the tram came to a halt.'

> I can no longer remember how – but I managed to jump out, run across the street and into the baker's shop on the corner. At the very moment I entered the shop a shell hit our tram.

Inber took refuge in a bomb shelter underneath the shop. 'The shelter was damp, water dripped from above. All the time, people were moving about in search of a drier place. A child was crying . . . When things quietened down, we went out. Our tram stood there, smashed to pieces. It was petrifying. Someone pointed to it and said: "It's full of bodies." Everyone who had stayed in that tram was killed. Later, I learnt that the shelling had been deliberately aimed at Sitnoy Market – into the midst of the crowd of people gathering there.'

One November morning eighteen-year-old Elena Martilla was given a most unusual assignment. Martilla, a gifted young artist who had already exhibited at the age of eleven, had graduated from college with a brilliant career ahead of her – but then the war came, and everything began to fall apart. Along with many other teenagers she did hard manual labour, working on Leningrad's defences, and helping in the city's hospitals. But she could not let her talent just wither away, and so, at the end of October, she enrolled in Leningrad's last functioning art academy. Now her teacher, Professor Yan Shablovsky, had summoned her to his office.

As Martilla entered the cold, dark room she found Shablovsky unusually tired and despondent. The professor welcomed her, and then, after a short pause, spoke frankly, from the heart: 'Lena, things are getting very bad here. I don't expect to survive this. But someone must make a record of what is happening. Go out with a sketchbook and start drawing what you see. You are a portrait artist – so draw pictures of Leningrad's people under siege – honest pictures, showing how they are suffering in these diabolical circumstances.' Shablovsky gathered himself, and then, looking hard at Martilla, added: 'We must preserve this for humanity. Future generations must be warned of the absolute horror of war.'

It was already becoming very cold, with the daytime temperature dropping below freezing, so Elena devised a working method for her new task: when she saw something of interest, she would make a quick, rough sketch outdoors, and then fill in the details from memory as soon as she returned to her flat. One of her first subjects was a boy named Alik Malchik.

Martilla had found the young boy – about nine or ten years old – wandering the streets, in ragged clothes. He had a disturbed look in his eyes, and she immediately sensed that something awful had happened. At first, when she stopped and talked to him, he was only able to repeat one phrase, again and again: 'Big piece of bread, big piece of bread.' But slowly she was able to coax a story from him. He came from a village on Leningrad's outskirts and was one of large group of boys, all about the same age, who had been brought into the city to be taught an industrial trade. They had all lived in a dormitory close to one of the city's factory complexes. Then suddenly, soon after the outbreak of war, the factory and its workforce had been hastily evacuated, along with all its instructors. In the confusion, all the children had been left behind.

Initially there had been a certain novelty to their predicament. They had explored the whole building and scavenged for any remaining stores of food. But soon there was nothing left, the building was cold and unheated, and they realised they had been completely forgotten about. They had not been given ration cards and they were all desperately hungry, and as their villages were now occupied by the Germans there was nowhere else for them to go. Some of the boys formed gangs and roamed the streets, begging and stealing, but Alik had wandered off on his own. He was now going crazy with hunger and his contorted little face seemed scarcely human any more. Martilla was horrified, and also ashamed of her inability to help. 'What will become of him?' she asked in her diary.

Being out on Leningrad's streets was always dangerous, and when enemy artillery shelling began Martilla would take cover in the nearest bomb shelter. There she always found a mix of civilians, but on one occasion two young soldiers also joined the assembled throng. With the enemy remorselessly bombarding the city, there was something incongruous about the presence of these Red Army recruits. Martilla was struck by how very lost they looked, and others noticed too. 'You are supposed to be our guardians,' an old woman said sharply. Hearing this reprimand, the young soldiers tried to behave in a more assured way. But Martilla noticed the look in their eyes – that of startled animals, cornered by their prey.

On another occasion, in another shelter, the impromptu gathering included three old musicians. The German bombing raid seemed to be going on for ever, leaving people counting the explosions and hoping desperately that the deafening noise would end. As the shelter reverberated and shook, everyone inside it became more and more frightened. All of a sudden, one of the old men got out his violin and began to play. At first he was just tuning his instrument, trying out the sound, and then, abruptly, he conjured up the most beautiful melody. Martilla was utterly entranced, and she recaptured the moment for her diary: 'He is a really courageous person, and now I don't feel frightened either. There are explosions all around us, and he is playing the violin as if he is leading us to safety.' Everyone calmed down, and Martilla added: 'The terror was somehow less powerful – it had lost its grip on us. It was *outside* us now; and inside we had our music, and everyone felt its power. There was a most extraordinary sense of belonging.'

Martilla was always interested in the reactions of those around her and was drawn to the spontaneity of Leningrad's children. As she looked at passers-by, it struck her that most adults were responding to the stress of the siege by closing down, and becoming impassive and withdrawn, as if they were sleepwalking or in a trance. 'I felt people slipping away before my very eyes,' she wrote. 'There was a sort of narrowing of expression – a "blinkered" look – that no longer seemed to register very much.' But the faces of many of the children remained vivid and alert. Martilla felt they caught something deeply truthful about their shared experience. This truth was often harrowing – the profound sadness in the eyes of children who had lost their families and were now alone; and sometimes a look of absolute horror that seemed to say 'What are you doing to us?'

Yet on one occasion she witnessed something astonishing. The Germans had launched a particularly savage bombing raid. Everyone had taken shelter, nervous and jittery. Suddenly, the shelter's youngest occupant – a small boy – began an informed commentary on the din outside. He identified each plane by the sound it made – announcing whether it was a German bomber or one of the Soviet fighters defending the city. He also gauged the type of bomb being dropped – deciding whether it was an incendiary or explosive – and finally, and most remarkably, predicted how close it would fall. 'That's a Messerschmitt,' he would say, 'and that's one of ours. That will be a high-explosive bomb, but it's dropping further away from us.' He spoke in a completely calm fashion. Martilla's initial reaction was one of sadness and anger.

> It was as if that boy had aged fifty years in as many days – his face looked so old, and through this unnatural ageing I felt that he had been robbed of the innocence of childhood. It was horrifying to hear his natural curiosity welded to the ghastly machinery of war. But then I saw how his calmness was reassuring others. He told us that the alert would be over soon – and he was right! I looked more closely into his face – and saw an uncanny wisdom in it. What I glimpsed in that moment shook me: I realised that a little child could look like a wise old man. Amid the agony we were suffering, something extraordinary had briefly come to life.

But the hardship of the siege was unremitting. 'There was no way out,' Martilla said. The suffering was all too evident in people's faces, and already there were those who could no longer stand the mental strain.

'The oldest person in our seven-floor building was a woman called Kamilla,' Svetlana Magaeva recalled.

> By the end of the autumn she was so weak she had difficulty standing. Her neighbours took care of her, prepared food and burnt firewood and furniture in the stove to keep her warm, but Kamilla grew more and more enfeebled, until she was scarcely able to move at all. But one morning – shortly before she died – she had got out of bed, convinced there was food somewhere in her flat, and begun a frenzied search for it. Unable to find anything, she had taken her china dishes out of the cabinet and dropped them, one by one, on to

the floor. Then she got down on her hands and knees and started looking for bread crumbs amid the broken pieces.

As winter approached, the desolation of Leningrad's inhabitants was total – there was no help from anywhere. The policies of the city authorities, from whom tangible support and encouragement were desperately needed, focused only on preserving their own security.

Elena Martilla's walk to college took her along a place more badly bombed and shelled than the others. Its name was Tauride Street – an innocuous thoroughfare, and Martilla was surprised by the Nazis' determination to bombard it. Why had they hit one building after another, leaving only eight standing? A few streets away stood the Smolny Institute, a distinguished-looking building, with its white columns and golden dome. The Smolny, which housed the HQ of the city's administration, was now superbly camouflaged, and its gardens had been dug up. In wrecked, flattened Tauride Street stood the Tauride Palace, also possessing a dome adorned with gold and an ornamental garden. There was no trace of camouflage here – the building and its grounds had been left exactly as they were. With a shudder, Martilla realised that the city's regime was using the palace as a decoy, to draw enemy fire away from its own position – already well hidden. The deception had clearly worked – the Germans had targeted the wrong street. Hundreds of innocent civilians had died as a result of this cynical ploy.

The camouflaging of the Smolny had been done with astonishing speed and thoroughness. The city's chief architect, Nikolai Baranov, recalled that in early July 1941 Zhdanov had ordered several regiments of military engineers to be pulled out from the Leningrad Front – where they were desperately needed to work on the city's outer defence lines – to complete the project. The regime was mobilising hundreds of thousands of civilians – mostly women and teenagers – to work on these defences, eighteen hours a day, out in the open, with no real protection from German bombing and shelling. Now, vital specialist troops, who had the training to do the job quickly and effectively, were withdrawn from the front line so that they could better protect the city's government.

Baranov oversaw the operation. 'Our task was given total priority, and we were able to recruit decorators and painters from each of Leningrad's seventeen theatres. We also gathered a large workforce from all the city's textile factories to make special camouflage nets and tarpaulin. Fake items of scenery were also constructed – it was as if we were on a huge movie set. When we finished it all, I was called in to see Zhdanov. He was absolutely delighted.'

Lieutenant-General Alexander Sukhomlin was summoned to the Smolny for a military meeting in mid-July. 'I knew a lot about camouflage,' he later recalled, 'but nothing prepared me for this experience. An official car met me from the airport and took me to the city's HQ. I jumped out, ready to show my ID, then stopped and looked around in confusion. I had visited the Smolny before, but now I had no idea where I was. "Is this the Smolny?" I asked the driver in total bewilderment. He smiled a little, and then answered wearily: "Yes, this is the Smolny." What they had done to disguise the building was quite amazing.'

The regime showed rather less urgency in camouflaging the city's major landmarks: the Peter and Paul Fortress, the Admiralty Building and St Isaac's Cathedral – all of which were used by the Germans as orientation points for their air raids. Incredibly, they only commenced proper work on the first of these, the Peter and Paul Fortress, in late November 1941, over two months after the enemy had begun systematically bombing the city. Mikhail Boborov, an eighteen-year-old mountaineer, was one of the small team they employed. 'I do not understand why the authorities left it all so late,' Boborov said. 'When we started camouflaging the city's monuments in November the weather was already bitterly cold. The job should have been given to a large workforce, but there were only four of us – and one of our guys was over sixty years old. We were already weak from starvation, and we were being asked to do incredibly demanding physical work, yet they only issued us with the minimum bread ration, which had just been cut to a pitiful 125 grams a day.'

Boborov and his fellows slowly ascended the spire of the Peter and Paul Fortress. 'First, we used an inner staircase, carefully moving past the counter-weights of the spire's great clock,' Boborov continued.

'The steps were encrusted with pigeon shit, and above us we could hear the scuttling sounds of the few remaining birds, so weakened by hunger and cold that they could no longer fly. Then we clambered through a hatch on to the outside of the spire, and inched upwards, rung by rung, on a small exterior ladder. We were now about 120 metres above the city.'

Boborov looked around him. Despite the freezing temperature, he saw a scene of eerie beauty. 'It was an incredible view. I could see the city below me, engulfed in mounds of uncleared snow, and beyond it, the ships of the Baltic Fleet, at their moorings, encrusted with ice.' Boborov now had to get astride the carved stone angel and cross that adorned the top of the spire and somehow fix a rope and pully to it. 'I felt I had used up my last reserves of strength getting up there and for a few minutes I dangled on the wings of the angel, unable to haul myself any further. Then, with a last supreme effort, I pushed myself upwards, and my hands clasped the cross. I unfastened the ropes behind my back, and securely attached myself to the carving.' It was an astonishing achievement. City architect Nikolai Baranov wrote admiringly: 'To the best of my knowledge, such a climbing feat had only been performed once before, in the nineteenth century, and Boborov achieved it weakened from lack of food and in freezing cold weather. He risked his life, climbing a further 25 metres to the apex of the cross to fix a rope and trestle to it, so that vital camouflage materials could be hauled up.' But Boborov's ordeal was not yet over.

'I paused for a moment, only to hear suddenly the sound of our anti-aircraft guns opening up with their quick, staccato volleys of fire. I turned my head in alarm. Emerging from the clouds was a large formation of German bombers, flying low, and heading straight towards me.' The angel and cross atop the spire of the Peter and Paul Fortress was the sighting point in the enemy's flight path. Mikhail Boborov froze in horror. 'The planes were coming in so close I could clearly see the pilots' faces. Then they turned, banked over the city, and began dropping their bombs. The shockwave from the explosions knocked me off the cross, but fortunately, the knots of my climbing rope held firm and I swung round and round the spire, while all around me shell bursts erupted from our guns. It was a miracle that I stayed unharmed. When the raid ended, another of our climbers managed to haul me to safety.'

The city administration showed scant interest in Boborov's feat, and the small team was given no help whatsoever as it continued its vital task of camouflaging the fortress. 'We worked downwards from the spire, laying out the material,' Boborov remembered, 'but we were now desperately weak and our work proceeded with agonising slowness. Two of our team died of starvation before the task was completed. I survived – along with one of my fellows – only by eating the remaining pigeons trapped inside the spire. Those last few, bedraggled birds kept us alive.'

As temperatures dropped below freezing, the regime could at least have demonstrated a measure of consideration for those in its care by reducing the lengthy queues for bread, now forming up in the open and in the bitter cold. But while Leningrad's government thrived on an unnecessary and intrusive bureaucracy, the distribution of food remained poorly organised. In October 1941 the city's administration halved the number of bread stores open – reducing their number to thirty-four – but put no system of registration in place to match the number of ration-card holders for any given store with the quota of bread received from the bakeries. Instead, it seemed content to let the inhabitants acquire their bread anywhere they wished. The supply frequently ran out before everybody received their ration, and consequently queues began to form up well before 6.00 a.m. The city's leadership was somehow unable to devise a more efficient system, one that would relieve the necessity of having to stand in line, in sub-zero temperatures, for hours at a time.

In chilling contrast, much administrative time and energy was expended on monitoring the reactions of the population through a network of informers and secret police. By November, the mood within the city was becoming increasingly angry and demoralised, and war censors noted that letter writers were frankly describing the severity of the food situation. One message they intercepted stated: 'With each passing day life in Leningrad grows worse. People are beginning to swell up through hunger. Some are making "pancakes" out of mustard; powdered starch, which was formerly used as wallpaper paste, has disappeared from the shops.'

On 7 November, on the anniversary of the Bolshevik Revolution, a group of protesters gathered in Stachek Prospect, close to Leningrad's Kirov Factory. They were mostly children between the ages of ten and fourteen and they called for the opening of the city, so that starving women and children could leave. Printed leaflets were also handed out, calling on the factory workers to rise up and overthrow the regime. An army commissar named Kupovetsky ordered security guards to fire on the crowd, but the guards refused, at which point Kupovetsky began to fire at the assembled children himself. A German artillery attack commenced at this moment, forcing everyone to disperse, and shortly afterwards a Major Kalugin and three others were arrested for not carrying out the initial order. Eventually hundreds of women and children were rounded up for participating in this demonstration.

People began to speculate, out of sheer desperation, whether the situation might improve if the city were surrendered to the Germans. A sheet-metalworker named Bogdanov was overheard saying to his fellows in the city's Smirnov tram sheds that 'If the Germans take Leningrad, we shall have enough bread.' Anonymous letters began to be sent to front-line troops: 'Husbands and brothers, cease fighting and give yourselves up! You are suffering out there while we and our children are suffering here. We have no more strength, we are already collapsing from starvation. Surrender. We are sick of living in this hungry, blood-soaked country.' But the Germans would not have accepted the surrender of Leningrad, nor allowed its women and children free passage out of the city. Their position was now clear, and it was stated simply at a meeting of the besieging Eighteenth Army's HQ staff at Orsha on 13 November: 'Leningrad must starve to death. It is impossible for us to feed this city.'

As the siege progressed, Leningrad's radio station began to transmit to the German troops around the city, knowing that they were close enough to pick up the signal on their radio equipment. One of the radio staff was an Austrian communist named Fritz Fuchs.

Fuchs had fled from the Nazis when they entered his country, emigrating to the Soviet Union and settling in Leningrad. He now headed the radio's counter-propaganda department. He sent out a daily broadcast to the enemy – *Hier Spricht Leningrad* ('Leningrad Speaks'). In it, he tried to strike a balance between the rhetoric of defiance and a deeper, more problematic task: getting the Germans to consider what they were doing to the inhabitants of the besieged city. 'German soldier – have you really thought about the meaning of this war, and what you are inflicting on others, all the blood, all the suffering?' Fuchs began. 'You have marched triumphantly through half of Europe, and everywhere new cities have been waiting for you. You have always believed that you are the Master Race. But this is not tiny Belgium but vast Russia. You are now so close to Leningrad, German soldier, but you are never going to see the city.'

Fuchs was a courageous man, much loved by his fellow staff members. On one occasion, as he walked along a nearby street, a radio employee yelled out in friendly greeting, 'Fritz – what are you doing?' By now Fritz was no longer just a name; it was also abusive slang for the Wehrmacht troops stationed around the city. An old woman immediately rounded on the employee: 'How dare you swear at that young man. Show some respect for others!'

'German soldier, have you really thought about the meaning of this war?' Fuchs had asked, and in mid-November 1941 Radio Leningrad received a stark response to his question. One afternoon a most unusual delegation arrived at the radio offices: a body of political officers and militia, carrying a large hamper. Radio Leningrad's employees were trying to survive on their meagre bread ration and they now watched in amazement as a lavish picnic was set out in the broadcasting room. 'I could scarcely believe that such abundance still existed,' said one of them, Lazar Magrachev. 'A starched tablecloth was carefully laid out. A variety of sausages and cheeses appeared, along with a plentiful supply of bread and butter, biscuits and tea. This banquet was a reality – not some fantasy – but it was not intended for us. My first, involuntary reaction was to tighten my belt.'

The radio staff turned to one another. 'Where has it all come from?' Magrachev asked in bewilderment. 'No doubt the political department nicked the stuff from a hospital for the severely wounded,' one fellow responded. Then their guests arrived – two captured German officers. The head of the radio station led them into the recording studio and announced solemnly. 'Welcome to Radio Leningrad – please sit down and enjoy this little snack. Eat – with our compliments.' The Germans seemed most surprised by this offer – but after some initial hesitation they tucked into the food with relish. 'They gorged themselves,' Magrachev said. 'Then, suddenly, all the sound equipment was turned on. The authorities had clearly decided to record this little conversation with the enemy, and then broadcast it all over the city.'

The officers were asked to identify themselves, and then explain how they had been captured. The two men, both lieutenants, were named Ludwig Bismarck and Kurt Braun – and Bismarck spoke first: 'We were caught in front of our lines by one of your reconnaissance groups,' he said. 'We thought that we would be taken off and shot.' Bismarck was nervous, and anxious to appear conciliatory. 'This is not war, it is the devil's torture,' he added, revealing rather more than perhaps he had intended. 'Our soldiers are also suffering from the cold, and many are being killed by your artillery fire.'

But Braun, not so anxious to conciliate, then cut across him, speaking with calm deliberation: 'We know that everyone in Leningrad is dying of hunger. We have agents within the city, and they have reported to us that cannibalism has started to occur.' Magrachev always remembered the cruel smile playing across Braun's face as he continued: 'You will be destroyed. We have just captured Tikhvin, cutting your last supply route. Mass starvation within the city is now inevitable. You are all going to die.'

Magrachev felt an awful, inexorable power behind these words. There was an audible gasp from those around him, and the prisoners were hurriedly removed from the room. Whatever point had been intended by the banquet and the broadcast had failed. The remnants of the strange feast were then packed into boxes and carried out of the radio station. Their contents had been carefully inventoried, down to the last, half-eaten biscuit.

The glaring ineptitude of Soviet attempts to breach the blockade of Leningrad had encouraged the Germans to mount one last offensive operation before the onset of winter. In late October 1941 Army Group North prepared a small motorised assault group, which was detached from the main besieging force. Its destination was the railway station of Tikhvin, seventy-five miles east of Leningrad. Its task was to staunch the last trickle of foodstuffs reaching the city.

The Tikhvin military operation was devised with a simple, surgical precision. The advancing Germans would cut the only rail line from Moscow to Lake Ladoga, thus throttling Leningrad's last slender supply and evacuation route. This ran a perilous course from the port of Osinovets, still held by the city's defenders, across the waters of the lake to the Russian mainland. The Germans were already shelling and bombing everything that moved along it, and they realised that, with temperatures dropping, floating ice would soon impede the work of the Soviet supply flotilla. So now they prepared a deadly finesse. Once Tikhvin was seized, they knew that no more food supplies could reach the far shores of Lake Ladoga and Leningrad would be left with absolutely nothing. By early November German Panzers were closing in on their objective.

This was a small force, and weather conditions were deteriorating. The Red Army had no chance of matching its speed and fighting professionalism. German advance units broke into the town under cover of a snowstorm and the defenders simply ran off in panic. On 9 November a Wehrmacht communiqué proudly announced: 'Last night our tank and motorised infantry formations captured the important communications centre of Tikhvin, taking many prisoners. Much equipment was found abandoned, with the staff of the fleeing Fourth Soviet Army jettisoning vehicles and important military documents.'

This had not been, in any sense, a conventional military action. The Germans were well aware that they could not garrison Tikhvin indefinitely – the occupying force was far too small, and it was, after all, holding on to an isolated redoubt, over sixty miles east of their main front-line positions. It was a brutal spoiling raid. Its goal was simple: to accelerate mass starvation within besieged Leningrad. When Hitler heard the news he was jubilant: 'We are now deciding the fate of Europe for the next thousand years,' he declared. 'The city is firmly encircled and no one can free it. It is doomed to die of famine.'

Stalin was shown a transcript of Hitler's broadcast. He cabled Leningrad Front HQ and announced: 'Moscow is in a critical position and can provide no fresh reserves.' Leningrad was on its own.

The ghastly fruits of the Tikhvin operation quickly became apparent. Supply trains from Moscow now halted at the little station of Zaboroye, while masses of soldiers and civilians tried, in desperate haste, to construct a truck road to circumvent the enemy outpost. This was a near-impossible assignment. The new stretch of road would need to be more than 120 miles long, and pass through largely uninhabited regions and thick woodland. It would take weeks to build. On 13 November Leningrad's authorities reduced the ration for white-collar workers and their dependants to 150 grams of bread a day. On 20 November the ration was cut again, to 125 grams.

'The food situation is really bad,' Georgi Knyazev noted grimly on 12 November. 'From tomorrow the bread ration will be reduced again. The Germans want to starve us to death.' The same day, Elena Skrjabina dropped in on a friend. 'She treated me to her latest culinary creation,' Skrjabina recalled, 'jelly made from leather straps. This mess is beyond description – yellow and repugnant. As hungry as I was, I couldn't even swallow one spoonful – I choked. My friends were surprised at my disgust, for they eat it all the time. They say it is sold in great quantities at the marketplace.' She added: 'The markets are overloaded with beautiful things: quality materials – for suits and coats – costly dresses, furs. These are the only items that will buy bread and vegetable oil.'

Fourteen-year-old Dima Buchkin began to record some of the announcements posted at a gathering place known as Five Corners: 'I will exchange a cat for ten strips of glue,' one read. Another offered 'A silver samovar for three pieces of glue. And, forlornly: 'An old, covered lamp for one ration of bread.' 'An original Leningrad cuisine has developed,' Elena Kochina observed. 'We've learnt how to make gelatine out of joiner's glue. Many bring in soil that contains charred sugar from around the Badaev warehouses. They boil it, filter it, and make coffee.'

Vera Inber thought back to the burning of the Badaev warehouses: 'The future of Leningrad fills me with anxiety. The burning of the Badaev store was no joke: all those fats going up in smoke – the carbohydrates necessary to maintain life. Protein – meat – we hardly see it at all. Recently, a neighbour told me, "Yesterday, my daughter spent all day in the attic searching for the cat." I was prepared to be deeply touched by such love for animals, before he added: "We ate it."' The practice was now widespread. 'Caught and killed a cat,' ten-year-old Valeri Sukhov wrote in his diary. The next day he added: 'Ate fried cat – very tasty.'

There was now a sinister addition to the menu. 'Reliable sources – those who have contacts with the city's militia – tell us that a lot of sausage has appeared at the marketplace,' Skrjabina remarked. 'These reports warn us it is made of human flesh. The possibility scarcely bears thinking about – people at the end of their tether are apparently capable of anything.' She no longer let her son wander far from home.

The temperature was now dropping to −20 degrees Celsius. People who went out in the morning would fail to come back at night. Somewhere on their journey they would stop, unable to go on, and simply freeze in the street. Lev Pevzner recalled one such moment:

> That November I was walking back from work, and at a certain place, by the Haymarket Square, I just felt that I could go no further. I came to a section of iron railing, surrounding a small garden, and I paused and leant against it. It was so very cold. But strangely I felt good standing there, really, really good.
>
> A lady came up to me and said, 'Are you okay?' I replied, 'Yes, yes, I feel fine.' But she persisted, asking, 'Why don't you keep going?' I just kept repeating, 'I can't go on.' Then she shook me, saying, 'Get up, please get up.' She helped me get to my feet, and accompanied me all the way back to my house, making sure I got up to the second

floor and waiting there until my mother let me in. That woman saved my life.

But gradually, as death from starvation grew commonplace on Leningrad's streets, people started to become inured to it. On 15 November Elena Skrjabina noted in her diary: 'Today, as I made my way along the street, a man was walking ahead of me. He could hardly put one foot in front of the other. Passing him, I reluctantly turned my gaze to his blue, cadaverous face. I thought to myself that he would surely die soon. After several steps, I turned around and stopped to watch him. He sat down on a hydrant, his eyes rolled back, and then he slowly slipped to the ground. When I finally reached him, he was already dead.' Skrjabina was writing with a clinical detachment that would have been inconceivable to her even weeks earlier. She was struck by this:

> People are so weak from hunger that they are completely indifferent to death. They die as if they are falling asleep. Those half-dead people who are still around do not even pay any attention to them. Death has become an everyday phenomenon and people are used to it. They are apathetic, knowing that such a fate awaits everyone, if not today then tomorrow. When you leave the house in the morning, you come upon corpses lying in the street. They lie there for a long time, since there is no one to take them away.

On the morning of 16 November Georgi Knyazev got up and tried to wash and put some clean clothes on. He was unsuccessful. His efforts were interrupted by a series of air raids, followed by prolonged artillery shelling. So Knyazev resorted to a different routine, hanging rags across his window, to stop the glass flying all over the place, carefully taking the lamp and standing it in the corner of the room, and placing the mantelpiece clock right up against the wall. In the middle of the room he put a box filled with sand, and a bucket, to douse any incendiary bombs that might fall. All around him was scattered debris. Some of his neighbours – whose own accommodation had been wrecked – were now reduced to camping out in the yard. 'The flat is beginning to look like a barn,' Knyazev wrote glumly.

By the middle of November city architect Nikolai Baranov recorded: 'The supply situation in Leningrad has become truly catastrophic. Trams have stopped, water is no longer supplied to households, and the coal and oil for the city's power stations have run out.' He held the governing regime responsible for the mess they were all in. 'So much was lost in the Badaev fire,' he lamented. 'All our supplies were stored there. It was such an incredibly short-sighted decision to concentrate all our foodstuffs in one place.'

On 25 November Baranov was suddenly summoned to the Smolny, for party leader Andrei Zhdanov had woken up to the fact that in sub-zero temperatures people desperately needed firewood. 'We must get 2,000 cubic metres of it,' he said decisively. Baranov was taken aback. 'How do you intend to find such a large amount?' he asked. Much had already been scavenged, or burnt by German incendiary bombs. Zhdanov did not seem to know where to start. Eventually they agreed to demolish a large municipal fairground on the fringes of the city. Its wooden rides now stood empty and neglected.

Everyday life was contracting rapidly. Lazar Magrachev regularly announced air-raid precautions over Leningrad's radio. Back in September 1941, when the broadcasts began, the instructions given to him by the city authorities had been quite detailed: 'Citizens – be prepared in case of air-raid attack. Before going to bed check you have a black-out in place and that there are no lights on anywhere. Put out food and clothing – close to the bed – for the air-raid shelter. Make sure you have matches and candles. Be careful, stay calm and don't panic.'

Now this list was steadily diminishing. 'First, they crossed out the black-out warning – it became pointless, as there was no longer any electricity for the lights,' said Magrachev. 'Then the reference to candles and matches was removed – as these items were no longer available in the city's shops or stores. And placing one's clothing by the bed was also a redundant idea – as there was no longer any heating, and when people went to bed they wore all they could, to protect themselves from the cold. As for putting out food . . .' Leningrad's regime had so little to offer. By late November

Magrachev's radio announcement had shrunk to the point of absurdity. Nevertheless, he was still told to make it. He simply said: 'Citizens – be careful, stay calm and don't panic.'

The day after the bread ration was cut to 125 grams Vera Inber remembered an extraordinary interlude. She had just retreated to an air-raid shelter when one of its occupants began reminiscing about his work in the 'old days', before the Bolshevik Revolution. He had been a pastry cook in a sweet factory and had once helped make a remarkable piece of confectionery called the Chocolate Gospel, which was sent all the way to the Paris Exhibition. Lovingly, he recounted every detail of this wondrous creation. The Chocolate Gospel had won the competition, and a prize worth 25,000 roubles, but the strangest thing, the cook concluded, was that the Paris judges believed that it was formed with pure cream butter, when in fact it was made with margarine. The power of food was now so great that his audience listened spellbound, completely oblivious to the sounds of bombing outside.

Sixteen-year-old Valia Chepko whiled away her time by drafting a 'Menu for after starvation'. Her expectations were modest. The first course would be a soup – either potato, cabbage or mushroom. The main dish would consist of rice or oatmeal – and mincemeat or sausage. Then she stopped. The thought of food was tormenting her too much. A couple of days later she crossed out her jottings, writing bleakly underneath them: 'I no longer have such dreams. I will not ever live to see this.'

Yuri Ryabinkin was also struggling to hold back his despair. His mother's legs had swollen up and become as hard as stone and his own face continued to puff up. He would stand for hours in queues without getting any food and then argue with his mother and sister on his return. 'Our nerves are in shreds,' he noted gloomily. 'It's been a very long time since I heard a calm word from Mother. Whenever the subject of food crops up in conversation, there's cursing, shouting or hysterics. The reason . . . hunger, and the ever-present fear of shelling and bombing.'

On 24 November Ryabinkin wrote: 'How endlessly time drags on. How monotonous everything is. All my thoughts are occupied with food and the desire to escape the throes of hunger, cold and fear . . . Outside Leningrad the Germans hold the initiative. I think they must have advanced still nearer, as their shells are now exploding in our street, right outside our house. This morning I stood in queues from half-past six. Those endless lines of hungry people will be imprinted in my memory for ever. I spent a whole four hours standing in line, yet I didn't get anything. And now I have to queue up again.'

Two days later, Elena Skrjabina recorded a most welcome surprise: 'Unexpectedly, a completely strange Red Army soldier knocked on the door and gave us a pail of sauerkraut, which he carried with great caution. This is certainly an event!' But then she reported the current rumour that as a many as 3,000 people were dying each day. 'I don't think this is an exaggeration,' she declared. 'The city is literally flooded with corpses . . . Sometimes you come across large sledges on which corpses are piled high and covered over with a canvas. It is all too clear that this is not firewood – bare, blue legs protrude from underneath.'

The horror had a strange, formless quality. 'Today we saw a corpse on a small sleigh,' Vera Inber wrote in her diary on 1 December. 'There was no coffin. It was wrapped in a white shroud, and the knees were clearly discernible; the sheet was bound tightly round.' It seemed a return to a far older era. 'A biblical, ancient Egyptian burial,' she added. 'The shape was clear enough, but one couldn't tell whether it was a man or a woman. It had become merely a body belonging to the earth.'

Elena Martilla was finding walking around the city more and more difficult. 'I went to the art college today,' she wrote,

> but there were no lessons – instead, we just tried to warm ourselves in the administrator's office. They gave us some kind of soufflé, but I dread to think what it was made of – you could chew it, but it was impossible to swallow. Getting home was really hard. I would stop, and want to rest, but I knew it was too dangerous to sit down – if I did, I might never get up. So I devised a system, whereby I would put a tiny piece of bread in my mouth and suck it until I got to one of my 'stopping points'. Then I would allow myself to swallow it, before placing another small piece in my mouth, and moving on.

As Martilla walked along the Neva, on a path made between shoulder-high mounds of snow, she came across a small, huddled figure standing by a corner, absolutely still. At first she thought it must be an old woman, for the face was deathly pale and haggard, and the eyes tired and drawn. But when she drew close she realised with a start that it was a fellow student, Zoya. Zoya had stopped attending college weeks earlier – now it was quite terrifying to look at her. Her mother had suddenly died, and she had lost all will to keep going. Martilla tried to encourage her, but it was like talking to a statue. 'I will always remember her face,' she wrote, 'and can easily sketch it from memory. It was as if her features had suddenly turned to stone. She stood there, petrified – surrounded by a desert of ice.'

'Death reigns in Leningrad,' Elena Skrjabina had written, as the November days shortened. Yet the besieged city could still surprise, and amaze. To her astonishment, Vera Kostrovitskaya glimpsed, through the windows of a neighbouring apartment, a group of musicians huddled in their overcoats, on wooden cots, surrounded by gleaming wind instruments. At first she thought she was hallucinating. But every day they played, as if to spite the bombing, hunger and relentless cold. 'Usually the clarinet would begin, establishing the melody, then it would be repeated by the first two trumpets, and then the trombone and flute joined in,' Kostrovitskaya wrote. 'The drummer, when he was free, filled the role of conductor . . . During these hours, it seemed that one need only to gather one's strength, endure a week or two, and all would be like it was before the war.'

Electricity was cut off, pipes froze, the bread ration fell to 125 grams – yet they continued to play. 'But the more the city became shrouded in silence, the weaker became the sounds of their music. First the bass fell silent, then the flute could no longer be heard, and, as if paralysed by the cold, the tempo of the clarinet and trumpets became slower.'

It was the beginning of December 1941. 'Through the icy scab of the windows, criss-crossed with paper strips, there came some cautious sounds. But it was no longer a whole march or a song: a lone trumpet uncertainly drew out a piece of the melody and broke off; sometimes they lost the rhythm and mistakenly hit the cymbal. Then it all died down.' The trumpeter was now terribly thin, and mostly just lay on his back. The others could barely move at all. But every so often the trumpeter sat up, and brought the instrument to his lips. 'It was the only thing that he could give to his comrades in place of heat, fire and bread,' Kostrovitskaya wrote, moved by his courage. She was struck by one detail: 'A lonely teapot stood frozen to the table.'

In their defence lines around the city, Red Army soldiers were also suffering dreadful hardships, but they were becoming more and more worried about the fate of Leningrad's inhabitants. Semyon Putyakov and his fellow fighters were hearing awful rumours, that profiteers and speculators were stopping vital foodstuffs reaching ordinary people, and that the city authorities were doing little to stop them. 'There are particular people to blame for the extent of this terrible starvation,' he wrote in his diary on 1 December, 'but for some reason they are not being rounded up or apprehended. They are living as well as they did in peaceful times,' he added, 'and even better – for their capital is accumulating.'

Joseph Finkelstein had been given leave from his unit and made a brief visit to his family. He wrote dejectedly: 'People are dropping like flies because of starvation – food is the sole topic of conversation. My brother was forced to sell the family piano, our dining-room furniture and our father's fur coat to raise a few roubles. These things have been part of my life since I was a child. A prosperous-looking black-marketeer came round to buy our stuff, trying on the fur hat in front of our mirror. I resisted a strong urge to punch him in the face.'

The city authorities were becoming belatedly concerned. Yet still their bureaucratic jargon distanced them from the surrounding reality. An NKVD report of 3 December noted in dislocated fashion: 'Because of the reduction in the bread ration there has been a significant expansion of negative attitudes. These take the form of complaints about starvation and malnutrition-related illness.' The report continued: 'Criminal elements have taken advantage of current difficulties with the food supply by expanding their activities. In November 98 people were arrested for speculation: 63 have been tried and 10 have been shot.'

On 5 December Putyakov was sent into Leningrad on military business. He was shocked by what he saw: 'The streets have an unpleasant, almost sinister aspect. The tramlines are broken, and wire and cable hang loose. There is smashed, jagged glass in the windows; destroyed buildings all around us. Evidence of drastic food shortage strikes you immediately. You see the most terrifying things. There is still life here, but it is not normal life.'

The war censors were rigorously confiscating any letters that specified what these 'terrifying things' might actually be. The following extract was attached to an NKVD report: 'I witnessed a scene in the street where a cab driver's horse collapsed from exhaustion. People ran up to it with hatchets and knives. They hacked off pieces of the horse and carried them home. This was horrible. They looked like executioners.'

Yet early in December Elena Kochina recorded a remarkable act of kindness. She had joined a crowd following a cart laden with boxes. They contained macaroni. Eventually the cart stopped at a store, but there was already a huge queue. 'It went around the corner like a long tapeworm,' Kochina wrote. 'The line had been there from the previous evening.' The store manager began slowly letting people in while Kochina stood and gazed on sadly. 'I don't know what was written on my face,' she continued, 'but suddenly an old woman, close to the head of the queue, asked me softly: "When is your turn?"' Kochina explained that she wasn't even in the queue. And she added – surprising herself – that she had a small child at home and didn't know how she was going to feed her. The woman stayed silent. But when the last batch was let in to the store she suddenly exclaimed loudly: 'Why aren't you paying attention! You were standing in front of me, after all,' and pushed Kochina towards the door. She was the last person to be let in – the old woman stayed out on the street. Kochina got her precious macaroni, and her hands were trembling with excitement as she took hold of it. 'I was so stunned,' she remembered, 'I couldn't believe what had happened was real.'

For still the human spirit – the instinct to reach out and support others – survived within Leningrad. Some countered the prevailing mood of despondency, reacting to the crisis with remarkable resilience. Svetlana Magaeva's mother was now braving the icy winter conditions, searching apartment buildings in her neighbourhood for children who had lost their families to starvation, and were now helpless and on their own. She and a group of fellow teachers carried on their grim task, weak with hunger. They witnessed ghastly sights – entering rooms, and finding people lying dead in their beds – but carried on regardless. Whenever they found a child on its own they ensured it was taken to safety.

Elena Martilla was deeply moved by the consideration shown to her aunt Dora. When Dora was too ill to go in to work, her colleagues, desperately weak with hunger themselves, tramped across the frozen streets to bring ration cards to her and make sure she was properly cared for. Martilla felt a sudden surge of pride for the city that was suffering so much. 'Only Leningraders would do that,' she wrote appreciatively.

Martilla now looked through her growing collection of sketches and paintings. Amid the catalogue of death and devastation she began to see flashes of something else. It was hard to define it. She had witnessed people showing remarkable stoicism and fortitude in adversity, but this felt like something different. In one sketch, she had drawn a woman pulling a musical instrument on her sledge, traversing the frozen landscape of the city. Although weak with hunger, she was going to join a small concert recital in one of Leningrad's hospitals. Martilla had admired her courage, but now, as she returned to the drawing, a particular detail struck her. The woman's young child was making the journey with her.

Martilla held this particular sketch in front of her. The woman was carrying a small case under her arm, which must have contained her musical score. With her free hand she was tugging at the sledge. But it was heavy – her instrument was a double bass – and the little child was attempting to help her, pushing from behind. Martilla guessed that they were now the only survivors of their family, and with so little strength left they were struggling to negotiate the snowdrifts.

Nevertheless, they were going to this concert to try to help others. As Martilla looked at that woman and her child she felt the presence of something alarmingly fragile yet powerful and transformative. Their laborious journey was performed as an act of love. 'If they are going to die,' she wrote, 'they will die together.'

Martilla thought about her experiences working as a volunteer at a children's hospital, on Vasilevsky Island. As starvation had set in, more and more were brought in, desperately malnourished. There was so little that could be done for them. 'We would look into their eyes,' Martilla said, 'and it was heart-rending to see the pain they had suffered. They would say to us: "I am alone – I will die." And they would die, very, very quickly. We carried their corpses down to the basement and laid them next to each other, as though we were stacking little logs. Most of the workers in the hospital were women – the majority of the men were serving at the front – and we would turn to each other in our helpless grief, and say, again and again: "We have to try to protect them. We have to try to protect the children." It became our oath.'

Martilla turned to another picture, which she had entitled *On Duty*. She had sketched a woman stationed at the entrance to an apartment block, ready to extinguish any falling incendiary bombs. Every apartment had someone on duty – for people were divided into teams and normally worked two-hour shifts at the entrance – but this woman stood upright, calm and dignified, holding her sleeping child. And now, as Martilla looked at her, she felt the same defiant message: 'If we die, we die together.'

Martilla was strongly drawn to this picture, although she was not entirely sure why. So she began to experiment with it. First she moved the two figures around, and then she began to make changes to them. Over the next few days the changes became more and more pronounced. Martilla had been brought up a communist, but now – to her surprise – she found herself, quite spontaneously, adopting religious imagery. She gave the woman a cowl, and then played around with the backdrop, finally turning it into the shape of a halo. 'I have created a Madonna,' she said in delighted wonderment, 'a Leningrad Madonna.'

But Martilla was quick to hide her drawing. Conditions in the city were growing more and more dangerous. It was becoming harder to trust people. And she felt the approach of something, intangible yet profoundly menacing. Young children seemed able to see it. They looked over her shoulder, towards a point in the near distance. There was nothing there to look at, but their little faces were convulsed with dread.

6

The Abortionist

The Onset of Mass Starvation

THROUGHOUT THE MONTH of December 1941 Axel Reichardt, a senior researcher at Leningrad's Zoological Institute, continued to work on his great survey, *The Fauna of the Soviet Union*. Reichardt was an expert on beetles – the walls of his office were piled high with collection boxes – and he was totally immersed in his field of study. But now he was growing weaker and weaker from starvation. Nevertheless, he remained determined to finish his work.

During the 1930s Reichardt had published a host of erudite articles on the respective families of darkling and leaf beetles, and a widely praised monograph on the lesser cabbage moth. It is hard to see these activities as subversive, or representing a serious threat to the communist state, but in July 1938 the NKVD had arrested him. Could they possibly have suspected that his contribution to the first edition of *A List of Noxious Insects of the USSR*, published in 1932, represented a veiled attack on the regime? Or perhaps they simply disliked his Germanic name. A number of other zoologists with 'suspicious'-sounding names – including Lindberg, Richter and Stegman – had also been apprehended, and the NKVD seemed to believe they were all involved in some sort of conspiracy. But in 1939 Reichardt had been released and allowed to continue with his research.

Reichardt was fifty years old when the siege began, a dedicated academic who found it difficult to engage with others. His manner was aloof and abrupt, and his skill and sense of fulfilment lay in the gathering and classifying of information about the insect world. He was determined to carry on with this, regardless of what was happening around him. His daily routine now alternated between firewatch duties on the Zoological Institute's roof, transporting its most precious collections to the safety of the basement and continuing with his writing.

But food was running out, and the Germans were now targeting Leningrad's scientific institutions with artillery fire. The menace of the siege was becoming an inconvenience to Reichardt. It was necessary to acknowledge its existence, but he tried as much as possible to push it to the margins of his life. He found a satisfactory way of doing this.

Reichardt was a methodical worker. He liked to use a series of notebooks, drafting his preliminary observations in pencil and making his final commentary in Indian ink, but all would be written in the same neat, even handwriting. When his writing was interrupted, he used a square bracket to state briefly what was happening, and then returned to his discourse. On one occasion Reichardt momentarily paused to insert: '[5 p.m. – the building is shaking after a near miss from an artillery shell]', before resuming his exploration of the skeletal structure of the leaf beetle. On 16 December 1941 he wrote briefly of his project: '[If I do not die from starvation I will accomplish it]'. Shortly after this, he was found by a colleague, lying dead on a mattress in his office. His face was terribly swollen, but still clean shaven. He was wearing a white shirt and tie. He had remained immaculately dressed until the very end.

It was no longer possible to bracket out the corrosive effects of the siege, or its malign harm to people within the city. Before the war, Elena Kochina and her husband Dima had a strong, loving relationship. She had recounted in her diary a vignette from their marriage, which took place only a few days before the German invasion. It was suffused with an idyllic quality that seemed totally remote from their present suffering: 'Dima is on vacation. All day he's busy with our daughter: he bathes her, dresses her, feeds her. His well-groomed, sensitive designer's hands manage all this with amazing skill. His hair blazes in the sun like a red flame, lighting up his happy face.'

In September 1941 Dima had moved jobs, deciding to work as a lathe operator in a factory, so that he could get more food for his family. He would bring Elena his lunch, a small meat patty and a spoonful of mashed potato, while he tried to make do on a little soup. But in October something changed. 'Our reserves of bread are quickly diminishing,' Kochina confided to her diary. 'It must be Dima who is eating them.' By late November she was hiding bread and millet so her husband wouldn't devour it. 'Every day, when I leave the house, I hide it in a new place: in the chimney, under the bed, under the mattress. But he finds it anyway.'

In December Dima roused himself, suddenly becoming energetic. He would leave the house to scavenge, and on one occasion he found a crust of bread close to a store, but a boy tore it out of his hands. Dima was enraged. He grabbed the boy by his collar and began to shake him, until the boy's head wobbled on his thin neck like a rag doll's. He would have killed him if someone had not intervened. The following day he began to steal. He prepared for this with considerable cunning, sharpening the end of his walking cane, finding a bread store that was poorly lit, and then, at an opportune moment, spearing a piece of bread and hiding it under his coat. Recounting this escapade to his wife, he laughed convulsively, like a madman. Kochina looked at him with horror. The disintegration of her husband's moral values seemed to have an ominous meaning for the whole blockaded city. On 28 December 1941 she wrote the following blood-stilling description of the struggle to survive: 'Some seek to save their lives at any price: they steal ration cards, they tear bread out of the hands of passers-by, eating it under a hail of blows, they even kidnap children. They roam the streets, mad from hunger and the fear of death. Countless tragedies are taking place every day, dissolving into the silence of the city . . . Meanwhile, the Germans look at Leningrad with cold curiosity.'

In December 1941 the German besieging army used its reconnaissance and a network of spies to produce a situation report on conditions within the city:

> The people of Leningrad have become so habituated to our artillery bombardment that hardly anyone goes to the shelters any more, and casualties have therefore greatly increased. The number of deaths from starvation is now rising dramatically. For instance, on 17

> December, an informer on Stachek Street, between the Narva Gate and the city limits, saw six people collapse through hunger, lying where they fell, unable to move, over a distance of only five kilometres. These cases are now so frequent that people no longer go to the assistance of others. Because of the general exhaustion of the civilian population, very few are able to provide effective help.

It is hard to comprehend the mentality that lay behind such clinical cruelty. A meeting of the Wehrmacht's Eighteenth Army staff at Orsha on 13 November had repeated the injunction that details of mass starvation were to be kept from the troops, lest support for what was being done should falter. The injunction was futile – most of these soldiers knew anyway. Lazar Magrachev thought back to the abortive radio interview with the two captured German lieutenants, Bismarck and Braun. At one point, the interrogator had asked Bismarck: 'Are you a descendant of Germany's nineteenth-century chancellor?' Bismarck had looked aghast. 'No, not all – and my politics are completely different. I am a social democrat.' Magrachev could not help laughing. It was remarkable how many German prisoners brought into Leningrad immediately jettisoned their Nazi beliefs and underwent a sudden political conversion. Of course, they were trying to save their own skins. But Magrachev knew that some at least were also ashamed of what they were doing.

Finding some sort of distraction from the horror became all important. One theatre in Leningrad had stayed open that winter – the Musical Comedy Theatre – and its performances gave people a much needed respite. Georgi Maximov, the theatre's director, had noticed something interesting about siege psychology: 'In the first months of the war our attendances dropped sharply. But after 8 September, when the city was surrounded, they rose again, and continued to rise – despite the shelling and the bombing.' Cut off from the rest of the country, people needed an outlet that provided them with some form of escape. 'The theatre became an island of joy in a sea of grief,' actress Evgenia Mezheritskaya said. 'The front of the building might look like a military base, for the square was filled with camouflaged lorries, armoured cars and even light tanks. But inside, soldiers and civilians could, however briefly, forget about their worries.'

Sometimes there were seven or eight air-raid alerts during a performance. The audience would be led to the bomb shelter under the nearby Philharmonic Hall while the actors went to their posts, still in their costumes, to watch out for incendiaries. From 20 November these actors, who toured the front during the day as well as giving performances every evening, only received the minimum bread ration of 125 grams. They grew weaker and weaker. 'Every day things were getting worse and worse,' actor Nikolai Rudashevsky recalled. 'By December many of us were finding it hard to even walk to the theatre. So some of us moved into the basement of the Philharmonic Hall, close by, and laid out our blankets and few meagre possessions there. Each small space was separated by a flimsy curtain.'

But they were inspired to keep on somehow with their punishing schedule. Another of the actors, Yuri Panteleyev, remembered appearing before the marines of the Baltic Fleet. 'We had almost finished the show when one of the sailors reported that the Nazis were about to shell the area. It was decided to continue nonetheless, so we speeded things up, the singing became very loud and the men in the hall were roaring with excitement. The spontaneous applause and cries of "Bravo!" drowned out the noise of the bombardment. Threatened with death, the audience came totally alive. That evening we truly understood the power of performing to others.'

Amid the constant danger came moments of wonderful humour. Rudashevsky remembered one performance that December:

> We were putting on a comedy and my character, who was supposed to be heavily drunk, had collapsed behind some bushes. Someone then blundered into me, and I had to shout out: 'Who the hell stamped on my foot?' But as I yelled my lines an air-raid alert sounded. Everyone went down to the bomb shelter, but my feet and legs were so swollen I could hardly move – so I stayed where I was. After a few minutes we restarted – I began to shout out my lines again – and exactly the same thing happened, another air raid started. When we reassembled, a loud voice bellowed from the audience: 'Let's skip that phrase!'

The dedication shown by these actors was astounding. Tamara Salnikova recalled a performance of *The Three Musketeers* given on 7 December:

> It had been snowing all day. I was walking to the theatre from the Petrograd side of the city, towards the Neva. But I was finding it really difficult to keep going – it was bitterly cold, and I was already dizzy with starvation. As I crossed the Kirov Bridge artillery shelling started. I tried to take cover, along with several other women, and we rushed to the snow mounds on either side of the bridge, and flung ourselves face downwards. But suddenly, one of the women cried out, then began to crawl, leaving a trail of blood behind her. The shelling was still going on, but I followed her, and tried to haul her away from the bridge. Fortunately, at the Field of Mars, a militia unit appeared and they carried her off to hospital.

Exhausted by this, Salnikova eventually managed to reach the theatre. She was bloody and bedraggled: 'I went to the dressing room. The temperature inside was well below zero. I changed into my costume, and as there was a little electricity running I tried to melt my frozen make-up container on a small lamp. Then the hairdresser got to work and I did my vocal exercises. Unfortunately, my character was supposed to appear for the first act in a low-cut blouse! While I waited, I huddled on the sofa, wearing a large coat, trying to warm myself up.'

Salnikova made it through to the interval, which offered her something of a reprieve, for in the second act – mercifully – she had a warmer outfit. Suddenly, she heard agitated voices in the corridor outside:

> I looked out, to see that one of our best actors – Sasha Abramov – had collapsed. He had been standing next to the hot-water tank, trying to warm himself up, and drinking a little tea. His cup lay shattered beside him. Sasha died during the intermission. At that time, thousands were dying of starvation, but the loss of my colleague, lying there, still in his musketeer's costume, left me absolutely stunned. The stage director spoke to us, and tried to rally us. He told us that we needed to go on – for the audience's sake – but I felt lost in a fog of disbelief.

Now there were only two musketeers. Someone helped Salnikova change and got her out on to the stage, but as the curtain lifted she stayed rooted to the spot, unable to utter a sound: 'I was supposed to sing and dance – but nothing happened. I couldn't find my voice, and my feet simply refused to move. Then as I looked out at the full audience, waiting expectantly, I recalled the exhortation of our stage director: "It is the duty of us – as artists – to continue." The power of his words awoke something in me, and somehow, my duet happened after all.'

It was, nevertheless, becoming increasingly difficult to continue. As the temperature in the theatre dropped well below zero, barrels of water – on stage as a fire precaution – became rocks of ice. The musicians were finding it difficult to remain in the orchestra pit – the brass section was virtually frozen to its instruments and the ballet dancers – particularly vulnerable to the cold – almost flew on to the stage and off it again. 'Death was carrying off more and more of our people,' Maximov remembered. 'The future of the entire theatre troupe was in jeopardy. We were losing our strength to perform.'

One day the theatre was visited by Dmitry Pavlov, who was in charge of the city's food supply. 'He was really moved,' Maximov recalled. 'Under these dire conditions, he was expecting us to put on no more than a brief rendition. He was stunned when we delivered a whole performance.' Pavlov later recalled his visit: 'A fantastic picture rises before the eyes. It is December. Outside, the temperature is −25 degrees Celsius. The theatre is unheated. An operetta begins. The artists wear only light costumes; their faces are pinched and pale, but smiling. The ballerinas are so thin it seemed they must break in two. Between the acts many performers would faint . . . At the end of the performance the public rose. Too weak to applaud, they signified their gratitude by standing, silently and reverently, for several minutes.'

Pavlov rightly paid tribute to a triumph of human willpower, acknowledging the sheer pleasure that this theatre troupe had given their audience. People laughed who had forgotten how. But he and Maximov had a confrontation after the performance. 'How do you expect my actors to carry on when they are only permitted the minimum bread ration?' the director had asked him angrily.

The most astonishing acts of human willpower were demonstrated at Leningrad's Plant Genetics Institute. The Institute held a remarkable seed collection, with thousands of different samples of wheat, rye, corn and rice – gathered from all over the world. Now its starving employees were guarding the precious collection against marauding rats, storing them in metal cases and keeping them under constant surveillance. They were frightened that desperate citizens might hear about the samples, and break in and steal them. But they were even more worried about themselves. Could they continue to withstand the temptation?

Keeping watch over a source of food while suffering such cruel hunger seemed an impossible task. But they persisted. They divided the precious collection into sixteen different locked rooms, and as an additional precaution no one was allowed into them on their own. They thought to themselves: humanity seems to be destroying itself, but some day it will need those seeds. And when it seemed impossible to go on, they made a pledge to each other: 'With the world engulfed by the flames of war, we will keep this collection for the future of all people.'

A huge effort was made to protect the Institute's potato crop. The samples had been amassed by the Institute's director, Nikolai Vavilov, in an attempt to find a cure for potato blight. But in 1940 Vavilov had been arrested by the Soviet authorities on trumped-up charges, and the man who wanted to combat world famine was now dying of malnutrition in an NKVD prison in Saratov. His remaining employees decided to protect the potatoes nonetheless. If nothing else, they would honour Vavilov's memory, and preserve the crop as a symbol of his work.

While most of Vavilov's collection was in seed form, the potatoes represented a particular temptation, for they were an easily edible food. The scientist had gathered blight-resistant potato seeds from Chile, and they had subsequently been planted out, shortly before the German invasion began. The only way to preserve them was to harvest the crop and then store and freeze it. The crop was hastily transferred to the safety of the Institute's basement. Now, as staff kept watch over it in the icy cold, they realised that they faced a very real prospect of starving to death in a room full of food.

The cruel German science of mass starvation predicted a steady degeneration of human behaviour. But in the besieged city people reacted to hunger in different ways. One December day Zoya Taratynova was carrying a delivery of bread to a hospital. The cart was heavy, and she moved slowly, struggling with her load. A crowd began to gather around her – haggard, unkempt and desperate looking. Everyone in it was starving. Taratynova felt the atmosphere grow increasingly menacing. Suddenly, one of the wheels stuck in a tram track and the cart lurched sideways. Loaves of bread scattered all over the street.

Zoya Taratynova was a frail, fourteen-year-old girl. A few days earlier she had witnessed a frenzied mob hacking an old starving horse to pieces, as it lay helpless on the ground. Now she was absolutely terrified. The mass of people advancing on her scarcely looked human any more. But she turned to them, and pleaded: 'Please don't take the bread – it's for the hospital.' There was a pause, and a slight, almost imperceptible shudder ran through the crowd. Then everyone stepped forward to help. They stacked the loaves back on the cart and pushed it out of the rut for her. 'They could smell the bread,' Taratynova said, 'and even touch it – but not a piece was taken.'

One simple act of kindness could have the most astonishing effect. Twelve-year-old Andrei Krukov lost his father, who collapsed and died from exhaustion after bringing back food for the family. Vulnerable and distraught, he could only look to the future with dread. Then, early one December morning, everything changed. There was a knock on the door and a full plate of buckwheat appeared. This gift lifted everyone's spirits. The donors were not relatives or even friends, just chance acquaintances. They had met the Krukovs in an air-raid shelter several weeks earlier. As the family of a distinguished Leningrad scientist, they were able to obtain a slightly higher food ration. Learning of Krukov's bereavement, they wanted to do something to help.

But in the dire circumstances of winter it was a struggle to keep even the smallest of hopes alive. 'The cold is cruel,' Elena Skrjabina wrote on 7 December. 'There is no more firewood. How will we be able to heat our apartments?' She went on to record an unpleasant incident. An elderly woman living with her had acquired a little bread, and had sliced it and placed it on the stove to make toast for herself. But others smelt its aroma. Sensing an opportunity, the daughter of one of her neighbours pushed her way into the room and stole it: 'The old woman's grief is hard to describe,' Skrjabina wrote. 'All day she lies on the kitchen table and groans endlessly, talking constantly of her lost bread. Probably, if someone very dear to her had died, she would not lament nearly so much.'

On 11 December fourteen-year-old Yuri Bodunov wrote to his aunt: 'I know it is bad if a person is defeated by the hardships on his path. But we now only get 125 grams of bread, and occasionally a little piece of herb cake. We have become very thin. The house we live in was recently hit by an artillery shell, and all our windows are broken and covered with cardboard. We huddle by the stove trying to keep warm. In the evening we have a little candlelight. I can only dream of a decent meal.' Hunger was torturing Yuri Ryabinkin. He scrawled in his diary with sudden vehemence: 'I can't stand any more of this.'

Leningrad's Hermitage Museum possessed only meagre remnants of its previous finery, but it was still continuing to function. Enterprising marines from the Baltic Fleet, stationed near by on the Neva, had rigged up cable from one of their submarine's generators to give the Hermitage a little electricity, although the power source fluctuated alarmingly. The Museum even managed to hold a number of small symposia. But Orientalist Alexander Boldyrev was becoming increasingly worried. 'The sudden cut in rations has made this the worst period of the siege so far,' he wrote in his diary on 9 December. 'The university canteen doesn't even have yeast soup any more.' On 15 December he expressed his fears more fully. A new calamity – the wood allocated to us by the housing management has been reduced to one square metre. And that has to last a month . . .' Boldyrev paused to record a particularly intense German artillery bombardment, one that had lasted over an hour. 'A dull glow hangs through the frosty haze over Vasilevsky Island,' he noted grimly. Then he returned to his theme: 'Day and night, a single thought gnaws at one's consciousness: our melting food stores. Yet there is no help for it – hunger creeps towards us as inexorably as a glacier. Powerless, immobilised, as in a frightful dream, you can only stand and watch the intervening distance diminish.'

By the end of the month the ravages of hunger had advanced. Boldyrev was seeing Hermitage staff dying all around him: 'The situation is frightening. Not one sign of improvement in the shops and canteens. The trams have disappeared completely. Power is cut off, both at home and at the Hermitage. They say that somewhere, help is trying to get through to us. It won't arrive soon, that much is clear. The year 1942 approaches – and it is rumoured that the number of deaths in the city has reached 20,000 a day.' Boldyrev noted an odd physical sensation. He had experienced it once before, while standing in front of the bathroom mirror. Now it happened again: 'I felt a sudden physical chill,' he wrote, 'as though standing before an open grave.'

But the growing horror could bring out hidden qualities in people. Olga Mikhailova of the Hermitage remembered: 'The blockade began to reveal things more and more clearly. You could straightaway see the good and bad sides of a person. Those who were greedy certainly grew worse, and tried to live at the expense of others. But goodness would flourish too.' Here there were surprises. One of Boldyrev's colleagues in the Oriental Department, Anna Shah, had seemed severe and reserved. But something latent within her now came to life. She would try to help the elderly curators, getting them hot tea, visiting them if they didn't come in for work, making sure they got their bread ration. Through her little acts of kindness some of the most vulnerable managed to stay alive.

By December 1941, when it became clear that the German blockade would not be broken, some of Leningrad's civic leaders were evacuated by plane. This fact quickly leaked out, and caused great bitterness among the city's inhabitants, for it reinforced people's sense that they had been abandoned to their fate. On 8 December Georgi

Knyazev was left fuming by the sudden disappearance of a leading member of the Leningrad Academy. 'That wretched Napalkova,' he railed, scarcely able to contain himself, 'who accused others of faint-heartedness and cowardice – yet when it came to the crunch and things got really bad and difficult, deserted us all and fled.' Knyazev was completely disillusioned. 'That's how those who go around talking about self-sacrifice, brave deeds and heroism fix themselves up,' he continued. 'Only a few days ago Napalkova was urging me to speak at a meeting, and to say a few words on our duty to sacrifice everything for our country.'

On 10 December the war censors intercepted a flood of angry comments in letters sent out of the city. 'They are evacuating people by plane, but in order to get a seat you have to have good connections', one wrote. 'We ordinary citizens are condemned to starve to death.' Another noted: 'Some are flying out – the bosses or those who can pull the strings. The rest of us walk around like drowsy flies, weak from hunger.' People drew one simple conclusion from this kind of behaviour. A worker in an industrial plant was overheard saying: 'If our leaders are flying out of the city, it means that the Germans have been reinforced and will not be driven back from Leningrad.'

One citizen contacted the military authorities with news of an astounding invention – a powder which, if dropped on German lines, would make their soldiers swell up and die. The recipient noted laconically that while the man had clearly lost his mind it was encouraging that he had done so 'in a patriotic fashion'. But Vera Inber recalled a woman on the street declaiming a loud prayer: 'Lord, hammer a way through for our soldiers.' There seemed scant prospect of the blockade being lifted in any other fashion.

Life in the besieged city was becoming a matter of hard moral choices. Yet these choices were clouded by numbing exhaustion and an instinctive, overriding drive for self-preservation, which mastered many. Vera Inber was a kind and conscientious person, who gave of herself to others. One evening, as she and her husband were running across Tolstoy Square, trying to find shelter from an air raid, they found an old woman who had slipped on a patch of ice by a baker's shop and could not get up. No one else was around. They heeded her cries, and set her up on her feet again. But then the women pleaded: 'My darlings, I have lost my bread-ration cards – what shall I do without them? Please, help me.' Something inside Inber snapped. She felt overwhelmed by a wave of fear and exhaustion. Suddenly, she was absolutely at the end of her tether. She answered abruptly: 'Look for yourself. We cannot.' Her husband said nothing. But he dropped Inber's arm, bent down and began to search. Eventually he found the cards. Through this gesture something vital was reaffirmed. Inber and her husband now disregarded the air raid, and walked the woman back to her nearby home. Only then did they take shelter.

The most agonising dilemma was whether to try, in a weakened condition, to help someone who had collapsed on the street. Significantly, it was one of the things the Germans were interested in finding out about, specifically asking their informers within the city to report on it. In their cruel calculations, it represented a barometer of the degree of humanity left within the city. Elena Skrjabina recounted a chilling encounter faced by one of the women in her apartment:

> Last night Ludmilla returned home really upset. It was already dark when she started back from work, and she was in a hurry, but suddenly a woman threw herself at her and clung on to her hand. At first, Ludmilla was totally bewildered. The woman explained in a hoarse voice that she was extremely weak and could go no further. She asked for help. Ludmilla said that she had barely enough strength to get home herself. But the woman persisted, hanging on like a leech.

A terrible tug-of-war ensued. 'Ludmilla tried desperately to free herself but somehow couldn't. The woman, grasping her hand, dragged her in the opposite direction to our apartment. Finally, Ludmilla tore herself away, tripping over snow banks. She started to run. When I opened the door for her, she was a ghastly sight – pale, her eyes full of terror, barely able to catch her breath.' And then, after the relief, there was the guilt. 'Talking about what had happened, Ludmilla repeated again and again, "She will die. I know it. She will die tonight." I felt the two conflicting emotions which fought within her: joy that she had escaped, that she was alive, and the horrifying thoughts about the woman she had left to her fate: a certain death on a freezing December night.'

It required a colossal effort to assist someone when weak and exhausted. Nine-year-old Valentina Grekova remembered one occasion in December 1941:

> My mother was carrying me past the Admiralty Building on a sledge. We were both feeble with hunger. But suddenly we saw a little boy clinging to a rail. He was collapsing with exhaustion, unable to go any further. I remember my mother saying: 'We have to help that boy!'
>
> Neither of us had much strength left. But my mother moved me from the sledge and put the little boy on it. Then we found out his address, and slowly made our way to his home. When we got there, a woman ran out, calling his name in relief and delight. It was Boris Pushkin – and it turned out that he was a descendant of the great poet Alexander Pushkin. For us that seemed a good omen – by rescuing the little boy, we had made the right moral choice.

But making the right moral choice was no straightforward matter. Tatyana Antonovna remembered her mother telling her about an awful incident when she returned from work at one of Leningrad's factories:

> She was walking through the snow, and bodies were lying, scattered about, everywhere. But one man was still alive. He cried out: 'Dear lady! Give me your hand, I am freezing to death here.' She bent over him and said, 'Forgive me. I have a daughter at home. I am very weak, and can hardly walk myself. I haven't the strength to help you – you will pull me over and I'll fall. Forgive me.' She turned away and walked on. She did not help him. When she arrived home she told me about it, and then she broke down and cried. 'I have committed a sin – a sin,' she kept saying. 'But what could I have done? I would have been left lying there myself.'

But a person's weakness could induce a different kind of reaction, as Igor Chaiko noted in his journal: 'Mass starvation has commenced within Leningrad. Many people are becoming indifferent to the suffering of others, and some are even turning into predators. When people fall down, others step over them, not looking back. You hear their pleas, for they have lost their strength and fallen, but are not yet dead. Then someone begins to strip the clothes off from this person, and steals their bread-ration tickets. The rest remain indifferent to their feeble cries for help.'

Temperatures were falling to −30 degrees Celsius. A colleague at the Institute where Chaiko worked related a harrowing story. On her way back home, she felt dizzy, and had struggled to keep on walking. On a bridge, she saw a woman lying on the snow, clearly dead. She was struck by her face, for the woman's eyes were wide open, and two pearls of tears had frozen on her cheeks. She paused, carried on a little, and then fell herself. She was unable to get up. A voice inside her said she had to, otherwise she would die. But she just lay there. People walked by, without offering to help. And suddenly she didn't feel cold any more. All seemed strangely serene. There was only one thought in her head now: 'Death has come.'

Then she heard a passing pedestrian talking about her and the other dead woman. In a tone of bland indifference this voice said: 'The first one is dead, but the second still seems alive.' She realised that she was just going to be left to die. And at this moment she had another thought, and it was a stubborn one: 'I refuse to believe no one will help me.' But no one did. She lay there for a while, and she felt tears welling up in her eyes. With a start, she remembered the other woman's face.

A little more time passed – and the thought still refused to go. Instead, it became louder and more insistent: 'Someone must help me get up!' She realised that two figures were bending over her. They were sailors from the Baltic Fleet, and one was saying to the other: 'She still has a very weak pulse.' She was lifted up, and they resuscitated her.

The mood of the city's population lay on a knife edge. On one side were the finest human qualities, stoic co-operation and heroic endurance. On the other lay the basest, cruellest indifference and the predator's instinct for survival, regardless of the cost to others.

Despairing of effective leadership from the city's government, people were now organising. 'Conditions around us were terrible, but we realised that there was a better chance of survival if we formed into groups,' Anatoly Molchanov said. 'We were not instructed to do this by anyone; we made the decision ourselves, quite spontaneously. We gathered together in a spirit of mutual support. We called ourselves "friendly collectives".'

Each collective – whether it was formed up of family, friends or neighbours – sought out a natural leader, someone who possessed a strong will, and could hold the group together. 'The role of the leader was crucial', Molchanov continued. 'They kept people's spirits up – it was vital not to lose hope. They watched for the tell-tale danger signs – devouring your bread all at once, not washing any more, lying down and just giving up – and instead, gave everyone a job to do. When there was no longer any water, someone would be sent out to collect some, boring a hole in one of Leningrad's frozen rivers, and pulling it out by bucket. When firewood for the stove was running low, someone would go out and forage for more.'

A wonderful spirit of co-operation began to grow. 'In our communal apartment we had fifteen people living with us,' Alexandra Shustova recalled. 'And we always shared what we had. If someone got hold of carpenter's glue, we made a jelly for everyone; if someone went outside the city, and found some frozen scraps of food, we would boil them. One of us got a piece of horse hide. We burnt off the hair, and made a soup out of it – a delicacy. The crucial thing was, we were doing it all together.'

Through the comradeship of these groups, a remarkable idea began to emerge, that the most important thing was not simply to try and survive, but to keep one's humanity intact. 'People who isolated themselves from others went down,' Molchanov added. 'And we saw many people in the city becoming scoundrels, always seeking to profit from the misfortunes of others. But something else was coming to life as well – a deeply felt wish to help each other in adversity.'

As New Year approached, the food situation within Leningrad should have improved a little. The German offensive against Moscow had been halted, Tikhvin had been recaptured by Soviet forces and – with the firming up of the ice on Lake Ladoga, allowing vehicles to move across it – supplies were starting to be brought into the city again. In recognition of this, on 25 December the city authorities had increased the minimum bread ration to 200 grams a day. But things were getting worse not better.

On 31 December Nikolai Gorshkov recorded a worrying deterioration in living conditions. 'We now have no electricity at all – not even a weak supply. And the water supply has also completely failed,' he noted in his diary. Tamara Grebennikova and her family had just received a particularly unpleasant shock. They had sold their last precious possession – a gold bracelet owned by Tamara's grandmother – on the black market, to get a little wine. As they saw in the New Year, they simply wanted to celebrate staying alive. The bottle was nicely packaged, but it was a fake – there was only sweetened water inside. 'The most depressing thought', Tamara remembered, 'was that it had been factory produced. There was clearly a well-organised profiteering racket running within the city.'

An NKVD report of 25 December stated that over the previous two and a half months 1,542 people had been arrested for speculation, and more than 192 tons of hoarded foodstuffs had been uncovered.

People were trying to keep hope alive, nonetheless. Elena Martilla remembered their humble but cheering New Year celebrations. Her mother had managed to obtain a little dried fish, which she made into a soup, adding a tiny amount of barley. 'What a treat!' Martilla wrote with considerable feeling. 'Our guests brought several bits of firewood, a little bread, a small piece of chocolate and a gramophone. We laid a table, read verses of poetry, sang a little. Us younger ones sat on the sofa huddled in blankets.' But Martilla was now fainting several times a day with starvation sickness.

Svetlana Magaeva was woken up by her mother just before midnight on 31 December. There was a fire burning in the small iron stove. A little dinner table had been placed close to the bed and on it were some scones made with coffee grounds, and two glasses of champagne. Svetlana's mother had been able to purchase these things with her unused ration cards, because from 27 December there had been no bread available at their food store. Despite this worrying development, Svetlana was entranced by the simple magic of the occasion. 'It was fantastic,' she said happily. They turned on the radio – and heard the voices of Leningrad's poets, congratulating the city's inhabitants on the New Year. Uplifted, Magaeva wondered if they might survive the blockade after all.

But a day later Vera Inber was struck by the number of coffins appearing on the streets. By the Anichkov Bridge she saw two women pulling a sledge with great difficulty. A third woman sat on it, holding a dead child in a blanket. Long trenches were being dug in the mortuary for mass burials. 'The workers there only dig separate graves if they are bribed with bread,' Inber reported sadly. She added: 'As I write these words I can hear a mouse, crazy with hunger, rummaging in the wastepaper basket into which we used to throw crumbs . . . She hasn't even the strength to rejoice that all the cats have been eaten.'

Inber was helping at one of the city's hospitals. 'Most of the people admitted here now die immediately, in Casualty,' she noted. She had heard rumours that a new Soviet offensive was being planned, but was sceptical, and also unusually pessimistic: 'It seems to me that unless the blockade is broken in the next ten days the city cannot hold out . . . Leningrad has had all it can take from this war.'

'I so passionately want to live,' Yuri Ryabinkin wrote in his diary on 3 January 1942. But he was now badly bloated and unable to get out of bed. 'I can hardly walk or do anything,' he added three days later. 'I scarcely have any strength left . . . time's dragging on, dragging on endlessly. Oh Lord, what's happening to me!' This was the last formal entry in Ryabinkin's diary – only a few incoherent sentences followed. One could be made out: 'I am hungry – I am dying.'

On 7 January Vera Inber attended a lecture on 'The illness of starvation'. 'The outward manifestation of starvation is seen in swelling,' the professor intoned. 'The skin is dry, deprived of sweat and fat; the specific facial expression is apathy.' Inber carried on working, reading and writing. One evening she picked up a scientific book on chlorophyll, the life substance of plants. She knew little about the subject, but as she started to turn its pages she found it strangely comforting. A phrase began to resonate with her: 'The plants unfold the immeasurable surface of their leaves . . .' Inber was struck by this image. All around her lay the frozen devastation of the city, yet this was a reminder of nature's life force. 'Immeasurable surface of their leaves', she repeated, almost like a mantra. 'The words evoke in me a swaying ocean of green foliage and light particles, flying towards us through the icy space of the universe.'

This heightened yet distorted perception, so powerfully and unwittingly described here, is commonly experienced by people subjected to advanced starvation. Inber had entered a state of altered cognition, where the world was observed acutely by someone increasingly detached from it. As death from hunger approached, its victims found themselves drawing away and letting go. Yet this hyper-cognition could also function as a survival mechanism. A person who sees the beauty and wonder of the smallest details around them will cling more determinedly to any hope of life.

On 6 January Stalin had ordered a new effort to break the German ring round Leningrad. But the German defences were simply too strong for the Red Army. The Soviet troops defending the city perimeter were too weak and exhausted to contribute at all. 'All my thoughts are about hunger,' Semyon Putyakov wrote in his diary. 'No one believes the report that we have started a general offensive. Today our guardsman on sentry duty collapsed – he was taken to hospital, barely alive. I can hardly move my body or carry anything. Our commanding officers are now stealing bread from each other.'

Putyakov was bitter about a lack of any real leadership, both within the army and in the city's government, and about the corrupt placemen he saw all around him. He viewed his officers with absolute contempt – 'they are animals masquerading as people,' he exclaimed angrily. And he held Leningrad's regime in equal disdain: 'Then there are those in the city who live the cosy life. It is revolting to look at them. They do not care at all about those who are starving.'

Those deaths were mounting rapidly, and Alexander Boldyrev was deeply shocked by what he was witnessing. On 8 January he wrote:

'The death rate is astronomical . . . I saw with my own eyes a caravan of sledges, loaded with coffins, boxes, or simply corpses in sacks, making its way to the cemetery. There I saw corpses left just as they were, dumped at the entrance, turning black in the snow. For some reason one of them sat, his legs spread wide, on a large box, wrapped in a multi-coloured floor cloth . . . Are we nearing the end? We are a city of the dead, shrouded in snow.'

An NKVD report of 12 January admitted that the bread ration – pitiful though it was – had not been fully provided to the city's inhabitants since 21 December. There was little point in raising the ration if people could not get hold of it. And there was now a definite problem of cannibalism within the city. Seventy-seven cases had been reported in total, forty-two of these in the first ten days of January. These incidents had been passed over to the military tribunal, and twenty-two people had already been shot. People were talking openly about it. A laboratory assistant named Frolova was overheard saying: 'A woman on the Mytninskaya cut off part of her dead son's body and made it into cutlets. Soviet power has reduced us to eating each other.'

People were becoming more and more frightened about the food distribution problems. The NKVD report continued: 'Over the last three days there have been instances in which citizens queuing for food have demanded the servers give them bread several days in advance. On a number of occasions they have met any refusal with force, seizing and distributing the bread to others.' Stealing someone else's bread was now on the increase. 'The number of thefts and murders where food was the motive has risen,' the report stated. Leningrad's regime was beginning to lose its grip on the city.

Leaflets were now being distributed calling for hunger demonstrations. One began: 'Citizens – it will soon be five months since we found ourselves in the iron grip of the siege. Our troops lack the strength to break it . . . Leningrad has become a place of death. People are dropping dead in the street. Our government has no compassion for the people. We will all starve to death unless we take liberation into our own hands.' Everyone was to come to Uritsky Square on 22 January at 10.00 a.m., where the demonstrators intended a march to the defence lines and an appeal to the Soviet soldiers stationed there, asking them 'to cease their pointless struggle'.

The NKVD report concluded bleakly: 'The mortality rate continues to rise.' The official number of deaths for the first ten days of January was given as 28,043, but was almost certainly very much higher. Deaths were no longer being registered, for there were simply too many of them. The administrative system had all but collapsed. In public, Leningrad's leaders steadfastly refused to acknowledge the gravity of the situation; in private, they were now extremely worried. On 13 January Mayor Peter Popkov made a radio broadcast attempting to reassure the city.

That morning Elena Skrjabina had been struck by the number of sledges she saw carrying corpses. 'Corpses line the streets, their bare feet protruding from the snow drifts,' she observed. The previous day she had brought her son into hospital. He was so weakened by hunger he could hardly move, and the trip had been a nightmare. There she found the hospital director's own son, healthy and rosy cheeked, munching a large plate of ham and cheese sandwiches. 'This is going on all around us,' Skrjabina wrote. 'Everyone who has power or is in a position to deal with foodstuffs abuses his privileged place to the utmost. It makes no difference to them that people are dying like flies.'

Early the same morning Elena Kochina had gone to the store and begun to queue. Her daughter was sick, and she wanted to get back and feed her as quickly as possible. Others were already in line. It had snowed during the night, and she saw a long trail of footprints ahead of her. But eventually she reached the counter. As she took her bread someone snatched it away. She turned and saw a man standing behind her, chewing. In that moment Kochina forgot about her exhaustion – her daughter's life was at stake – and in blind fury she grabbed the man by the throat. 'He fell to the ground – I fell with him. Lying on his back, he tried to cram the whole piece of bread into his mouth at once. With one hand I grabbed him by the nose, turning it aside. With the other I tried to tear the roll out of his mouth. The man resisted, but more and more weakly. Finally, I succeeded in retrieving everything he hadn't managed to swallow. People watched our struggle in silence.'

Georgi Knyazev, surveying the general mood in the city, wrote simply: 'People are living on their last hope . . . the weakened just keep on dying.'

On 13 January Mayor Popkov announced dramatically: 'The worst is behind us. Ahead lies the liberation of Leningrad and the rescue of its inhabitants from hunger and death.' Popkov knew that the offensive had in reality made little headway against strong German defensive positions. He sought to distract people by exaggerating its chances of success. He conceded that there was a problem with the distribution of food, but he blamed racketeers. 'We must take effective measures in the struggle with disorganisers of the food supply system,' he enjoined, 'to combat the thieves and marauders who resort to all sorts of tricks to loot food and to wax fat on people's sufferings. Thieves and speculators will be mercilessly punished . . .'

The main point of Popkov's speech was to give a eulogy of praise for Leningrad's leader Andrei Zhdanov, emphasising his concern for the plight of the ordinary citizen: 'The delivery of food into the city, under conditions of near total blockade, was successfully organised as a result of the great work carried out by the Leningrad party and Soviet organisations, under the leadership of Comrade Zhdanov, who worked tirelessly, day and night, to supervise measures properly for providing the city with food.' The words were hollow. Revealingly, Popkov found it necessary to stress yet again that 'The government is showing the greatest concern for Leningrad and has taken all steps to provide the city with the necessary food stocks.'

Popkov had just seen the secret NKVD report of 12 January, which quoted informers relaying a variety of extremely critical comments: 'The situation in Leningrad is hopeless. It is impossible to live on 200 grams of bread. So many people are dying of hunger. All cats and dogs have been eaten and now they are starting on people. Human meat is being sold in the markets, while in the cemeteries bodies pile up like carcasses, without coffins.' An academic, Krachkovsky, had retorted to a colleague: 'We should not fear the Germans, but the awful chaos that reigns over us.' And an engineer named Dukhon had complained to a fellow worker: 'At no time in history has a city of millions lived under siege for five months. Thousands are dying of hunger in Leningrad, but our leaders eat very well, and don't care about the population. I am sure that with the help of a small group of people we could achieve a reversal of this situation.'

It was almost certainly fear of the planned hunger demonstration that prompted Popkov's broadcast. 'Don't be afraid,' leaflets had exhorted. 'Our troops are our fathers, brothers and sons. They won't fire on us. Don't fear the NKVD, they are weak, it is not within their power to hold back a mass of hungry people. Let everyone who reads this appeal make ten copies and post them in letter boxes in neighbouring buildings. Distribute them quickly!'

Evgeny Moniushko's brother was a party organiser within the city, and therefore well informed about the realities of the situation. He acknowledged honestly the painful irony that 'The most difficult period for bread supply occurred soon after the first *increase* in bread rations, which occurred on 25 December 1941. During the first half of January 1942, for reasons unrelated to the lack of flour, but instead due to the reduced amount of fuel for baking and the interruption of the water supply, bread deliveries to stores were seriously disrupted. As a result, there were severe bread shortages. Long lines of people stood in the freezing cold, refusing to disperse, even after enemy shells exploded near by.'

Moniushko emphasised that it was the failure to distribute food effectively – not the activities of the racketeers – that had led to the acceleration of deaths within the city: 'This delay proved too much for some people to endure, and, as a consequence, the number of starvation victims began to increase noticeably during this period. More and more frequently in the streets, you began encountering people pulling sledges with the bodies of those that had died tied to them, mostly only wrapped in old rags. It was also quite common to see dead bodies lying in the streets.'

Much, much more could have been done by Leningrad's authorities. It was, as always, a case of too little, too late – and the stress of living on such meagre rations, and being unsure whether they would even materialise at all, was simply too much for many people. Nikolai Gorshkov was struck by a growing mood of desperation. 'On a street corner, some people began to gather – mostly teenagers – when it was evening and already dark,' he wrote on 15 January. 'They waited until a bread wagon approached, then attacked it, and stole its cases of loaves.'

Yet the city's regime was capable of remarkable care and foresight when stockpiling provisions for itself. Vasily Yershov was a lieutenant-colonel in charge of food distribution within Leningrad. On one occasion, while thousands were dying of starvation, Yershov was despatched to the airport to organise a food shipment, which had been specially brought in for the families of Communist Party officials. Dozens of trucks were commandeered to transport ten tons of rice, fifteen tons of white flour, over two tons of caviar, approximately five tons of butter, more than 200 smoked hams, thousand of cigarettes and 150 bottles of expensive wine, along with other luxury items. Yershov remembered delivering a substantial portion of this haul to Zhdanov's HQ at the Smolny.

The Smolny Institute had its own private eating area for top party officials. It was known as Canteen No. 12, and it provided a plentiful stream of bread, sugar, cutlets, small pies and other cooked dishes throughout the winter. Employees were strictly forbidden to take food out of this cafeteria, through fear that the bountiful supply would become known within the city. Yet this stipulation was not always followed.

One January day Igor Chaiko had been asked to report to the Smolny. He was left in a waiting room, and near by he could smell hot food being served. Then, a little while later, dirty dishes were brought out, and left on the table where Chaiko was waiting. He was astounded by what he saw: 'One plate – full of macaroni pasta and meat – had not even been touched. It was incredible to think that someone was that well fed. The dish had been left, and as there was no one else in the room, I rushed over and began to devour this most wonderful food, the kind of meal that you could only dream about.' But after eating for a while Chaiko was overcome by a feeling of revulsion: 'I felt ashamed that I could eat from the plate of someone whom I had absolutely no respect for, who was a scoundrel and a swindler, a dishonest upstart. I pushed the plate away. But I was so hungry. I pulled it back, and began to eat the meat again. Eventually, pride won – I left the remainder of the plate alone.'

It was vital for people's diet to be supplemented with additional sources of protein. But at this stage of the winter, with the bread supply now uncertain, the NKVD report had to concede, 'the population has received no other foodstuffs whatsoever'. These other foodstuffs were in the city, but they were being diverted elsewhere. Chaiko thought bitterly about Leningrad's leadership: 'They say chiefs will always be chiefs. They dine well every day – they have parties, to which prostitutes are invited, who are bribed with boxes of tinned food, bread and butter. Everyone in the neighbourhood of the Smolny knows this.'

Nadia Minina, a twenty-year-old defence worker in the city, found out where these gatherings took place:

> Remarkably, there was a little cinema in Sadovaya Street that kept running throughout the winter. It had been taken over by party functionaries. It was close to a militia office and it was always securely guarded. While the rest of the city was freezing, it had its own separate heating system running. Party officials would bring in food and wine, and watch films with their 'girlfriends'. I knew the receptionist, and after they had left, I would go in and pick up any scraps of food that had been left on the floor, and put them in my gas-mask container.

Leningrad's leadership was also running its own food racket, and Chaiko stumbled across proof of how it worked: 'Accidentally, our department came across a document where the city authorities asked for a special delivery of 160 tins of food to be airlifted in. They claimed it was to supply a group of specialist engineering workers. But there was no evidence that this so-called group ever actually existed.'

Meanwhile, conditions for ordinary people within the city continued to worsen. 'The agony of starvation was like a giant serpent,' said Nikolai Baranov, 'ever squeezing the city more strongly in its coils.' Alexander Boldyrev was wrestling with a problem of his own, how to bury his uncle. On 18 January he wrote: 'With the caretaker's help we shall put him on a sledge, without a coffin, and take him to Marat Street, where the dead lie in a huge pile. From there they are transported to a mass grave at Okhta. How many now are dying each day?' Boldyrev feared for the future. 'Hunger, the grim reaper, has joined forces with the cold and darkness. The dark corrodes the spirit, and from there it is not a huge step . . . Can this nightmare possibly go on for much longer?'

On the same day, Nikolai Baranov attended a remarkable meeting. As an architect, it was particularly painful for him to see the state Leningrad was now in: 'One of the most beautiful places in the world lies terribly wounded, burnt out, littered with snow and soot. It looks as if some evil force has put to sleep a city that only a little while earlier was lively, and sparkling with thousands of lights.' He and a number of his fellow architects decided to make a gesture of defiance, however small and insignificant, against the pitiless enemy shelling of their city. They would hold a gathering at the Astoria Hotel, and its theme would be 'A New Leningrad'. For some, even getting to the Astoria represented quite an achievement. One of Baranov's colleagues had become so weak he had to lie down for the duration of the meeting, unable to lift his head off a pillow. Another – who no longer cared what he looked like – sprouted a mass of hair, with his beard almost coming up to his eyes. But as they began to talk of their future work, and how they would rebuild the city, a wonderful animation swept the room. A sense of hope was rekindled.

But Baranov and his colleagues were faced with an implacable foe. The Wehrmacht had been considering making a poison-gas attack, one that would hit not only Soviet troop positions but the entire inner-city area: hundreds of thousands of casualties could be expected as a result. Army quartermaster Eduard Wagner had finished the required calculations by the end of December 1941, listing the precise amount of combat gas required. But Army Group North was unsure whether it had enough artillery and ammunition to carry out the plan effectively. Starvation remained its principal ally.

Towards the end of January 1942 a new situation report was produced by the besieging army:

> In December a majority of the population of Leningrad exhibited hunger swellings. Again and again, people would collapse in the street, and lie there dying. But it is in January that mass starvation is truly accelerating among Leningrad's inhabitants. In the evenings, corpses are carried on hand-pulled sledges from houses to the cemeteries, but because of the impossibility of digging up the frozen ground they are simply left there, in the snow. Recently, relatives of the deceased no longer seem able to make the effort of going to the cemetery, and unload the corpses along the way, along the side of the road.

The cruel, abstract calculation of hunger as a weapon of war continued:

> One of our informers undertook to count for us, one afternoon, passing sledges carrying corpses on one of Leningrad's main streets. He saw over a hundred of them in less than an hour. In many cases the corpses are now piled up in yards or fenced in squares. One pile of corpses in the yard of a destroyed apartment block was measured: it was two metres high and over twenty metres long. Bodies are no longer being taken out of apartments any more – but simply left in unheated rooms. In many air-raid shelters the dead are also left lying there. In the Alexandrovskaya Hospital there are about 1,200 corpses placed in unheated rooms, corridors and the yard outside.
>
> At the beginning of January the number of victims of starvation was being given as 2–3,000 a day. Now, towards the end of the month, the rumour is that at least 15,000 people a day are dying – and over the last three months over 200,000 people have died.
>
> This is not a particularly large number in relation to the overall population.
>
> It must be taken into account, however, that the number of dead will increase greatly with every passing week of the present conditions, as long as hunger and cold continue.
>
> The food rations saved and distributed to people are having no real effect.
>
> Children are now particularly vulnerable to starvation – and small children, for whom there is no food, can be expected to die quickly.

> Recently, a smallpox epidemic is said to have broken out, which is also claiming many children's lives.

On 20 January Elena Skrjabina went to the hospital to visit her son. He was listless and apathetic, and Skrjabina was beginning to fear that he would die. Returning home that evening, she wrenched herself away from her present worries and thought about the past. She realised how much she loved her native city: 'How often it has delighted me. How the St Isaac's Cupola, and the spire of the Peter and Paul Fortress, glow beneath the setting sun in late April and early May. I love Leningrad in the winter – the snowy cover over the Neva ice, gardens and parks sparkling with frost, the crisp air fragrant with winter apples. Tonight is also a marvellous winter evening: the same Neva, the same parks. But my heart is wrung by agonising grief, by the hopelessness of our situation, by not being able to believe in anyone or anything.' Skrjabina's cry of despair was only too understandable. It was the despair of someone caught in besieged Leningrad, trapped between the cruelty of the Germans and the callous indifference of the city's government.

Yet a remarkable humanity still survived within the city: 'By January 1942 all the men in our communal flat had died', Andrei Krukov remembered.

> But the women kept on going, saving everything they could for their children. We were living in such atrocious conditions that many in the city decided they were already dead, and became hysterical or were no longer able to cope. We tried to live – we were determined to hang on. We all had our responsibilities – I was twelve at the time, and I was responsible for trying to get bread, my aunt for finding fuel products. We moved into one room and lived as a family, playing chess, reading Pushkin out loud in the evenings. Once a man came to inspect our stove, and he was so weak with hunger he nearly passed out. We shared our meagre store of food with him, giving him a little scone made with coffee grain, and he revived. It was vital to keep helping others.

The siege had become a fight to stay human. Outside, in the communal yard, pieces of flesh were being cut off corpses. Krukov was warned that a neighbouring family had now become cannibals. He knew the family – and had played with their son before the war. People were changing in the most terrifying ways.

Nikolai Baranov recalled one horrifying example, the degeneration of a colleague at the Architectural Institute named Sergei: 'He was an arrogant man, always believing he was better than others. At this difficult time, a form of madness overtook him, which was perhaps a mercy, removing him from a full awareness of reality. But then, to save his own life, he stole his wife's ration card, and threw his wife and daughter out of the apartment. His daughter died. Sergei had become a predator. He had a friend named Kolya, whom he invited over to stay with him. This was solely to steal his food supply – and when this had been achieved, Kolya was also cast out and left to die.'

Faina Viktorovna had loved her work as a midwife before the siege. As conditions deteriorated, she found that women sought her help not to deliver babies but because they felt utterly unable to continue any pregnancies which had begun. In their desperation, these women brought gifts of food, which they could barely spare, and pressed it upon her to ensure they could obtain an abortion. Viktorovna found that her apartment was overflowing with eggs, sugar, sweets, even a pan of pea soup with pork in it.

Viktorovna, a previously kind and generous person, found herself unable to share these plentiful supplies. Instead, she became obsessed with hiding and preserving her store. The hiding places became more and more complex. She even dismantled her table and hid canned goods inside its legs. Opposite her lived a family of six. They were dying of starvation – but she gave them absolutely nothing. The children died, one after another. The fifteen-year-old girl was laid on a trunk in the entrance hall; the body of the youngest boy was clearly visible, put out on the window sill, so that his body would not rot. 'I have nothing, nothing at all,' Viktorovna would say. She became afraid of sleeping in her room, and would spend the nights at the apartment of a downstairs neighbour. By a chilling irony, having so excessively protected herself from the terror of starvation, Viktorovna succumbed to fumes from a blocked stove flue. After she died the concierge opened up her room – and found enough goods to fill a storehouse. They were shared out among everyone in the building – and in that moment of sharing it felt like a dark spell had been broken.

On 23 January the last water-pumping station in Leningrad stopped working. Nikolai Baranov remembered seeing large groups of people going down to the Neva, to break holes in the ice and to draw water out. The river embankment was covered with ash, to stop people slipping, but some simply didn't have the strength to climb down. Desperately afraid they would fall, they formed a human chain, clinging on to the person in front, and passing buckets along the line. Complete strangers helped each other, ensuring everyone got the precious water home.

A day later, on 24 January, the city authorities raised the bread ration again, to 400 grams for factory workers, 300 for office workers and 250 for dependants. Rumours of this increase had been circulating for days, and the news distracted people from making their planned hunger demonstrations. 'A day of bread-rationing psychosis,' Alexander Boldyrev wrote in his diary. 'Since the morning crowds have been gathering around bakeries. Desperation for bread is desperation for life.'

It was all a cynical diversion. Food-distribution problems were worsening drastically. Even as they made the announcement, Leningrad's leaders knew that in a matter of days bread would no longer be reaching the stores. When that happened, people would be left with absolutely nothing.

The most terrible period of the siege was about to begin.

7

One Black Beret

The Authorities Lose Control

On 28 January 1942 Nikolai Gorshkov penned a grim portrait of conditions in besieged Leningrad, with the roar of German artillery reverberating around him. 'The temperature is −27 degrees Celsius,' he began, 'with a continuous cold wind blowing from the north-east. The shelling has caused fires in the city, as have accidents with the cheap stoves in people's apartments, which have not been installed properly. Many of the high-rise buildings are in flames. The fire brigade no longer has the resources to put the fires out – there is simply not enough water.'

Leningrad was burning. 'Poor people,' Gorshkov continued, 'they have no hope of saving their living quarters. They desperately try and get their belongings outside – sometimes having to throw their possessions out of the windows. You see many things lying there, broken into pieces: wardrobes, beds, tables, sewing machines, even pianos.' Fourteen-year-old Vladimir Zandt was drawing scenes of Leningrad under siege during that harrowing January. He sketched a house torn apart by a shell, and a group of civilians, drawing water from the Neva, 'using their very last reserves of strength', but the most vivid composition was a building ablaze on the Ligovsky Prospect. Zandt's caption was stark: 'There is no one who can put it out.'

Houses were left burning for days. 'The enfeebled inhabitants could no longer look after their makeshift stoves,' Dmitry Likhachev recalled. 'Accidents were frequent, and if a fire broke out, then little could then be done, for every apartment was full of debilitated people, scarcely able to move.' Likhachev remembered one incident. An incendiary bomb had crashed through every floor of a new house on Suvorovsky Prospect, destroying the staircase. A fire then started downstairs, and it was impossible for people to get out. In desperation, they hurled themselves from upper-floor windows. 'It was better to be smashed to pieces than burnt to death,' Likhachev concluded grimly.

The increase in the bread ration had turned into a macabre joke. On 24 January, the day it was supposed to have come into effect, the bakeries stopped working for lack of water. The crisis energised people. 'Thousands of Leningraders who were in a condition to move emerged from their dens,' Elena Kochina wrote. 'Forming a living conveyor from the Neva to the bakery, they handed buckets of water to each other with hands numb with cold.' Some bread eventually got baked. But life in the city was close to total disintegration now. At 7.00 p.m. the following day Vera Inber added a despairing note to her diary: 'Our position is catastrophic . . . There is no water, and if the bakery stops, even for a single day, what happens?'

'Still no bread,' Inber wrote on 26 January. A day later, Kochina observed helplessly that the supply of food was now completely disrupted. Massive queues were forming up outside the stores. 'People are passing out,' Kochina went on, 'and sometimes they just die there.' Despite the months of starvation, there was still an instinctive willingness to rally round and try to help. Again, massive human chains – thousands strong – linked up from the Neva to the bakeries, passing the water, person to person. 'We lowered sledges, saucepans and milk churns from the upper floor of our apartment,' Ludmilla Anopova wrote. 'We made our way slowly to the Neva, across the snowdrifts, and scooped up freezing water from the ice holes. On all sides lay abandoned corpses. Some were clothed, others were covered in shrouds.' This time it was to no avail. As the day drew to a close, Elena Skrjabina confirmed the awful news: 'There is no bread – none of the bakeries have baked their quotas.'

Now Leningrad's inhabitants were being pushed to the very brink. 'I have to fight for my life now,' Alexander Boldyrev wrote on 27 January, 'for my very existence. There is nothing in the stores . . . I have to find water – but where? The River Fontanka is polluted. Perhaps we are entering our final days?' Touchingly, even at such an extreme, he continued grumpily: 'And I have run out of cigarettes.'

The awful crisis brought out the best and worst in people. At the beginning of January Lidiya Okhapkina had moved in with her children to an apartment near their own. It belonged to a woman she had recently become friends with – they had met in a bread queue and got on well together, and it seemed sensible to pool their resources. Yet Okhapkina had noticed something. While she would divide her bread into three portions – for morning, lunch and evening – her friend would devour everything at once. The two women had decided to take turns standing in the food queues, but as the disruption to the bread supply began, something shocking happened. Okhapkina returned one evening to find that her little bread reserve – which she kept in a small satchel, hanging above the sofa bed where she slept with her two children – had gone missing. She confronted her friend, but she denied taking it.

On 27 January it was her friend's turn to go to the bakery. No bread appeared that day, and people were panicking. When her friend returned, she claimed that she had lost Okhapkina's ration cards. Okhapkina was left stunned by this news. 'How are we going to share the bread out now?' she asked, still in a state of shock. 'We won't,' came the brutal reply. 'I've no intention of dying because of you.' Shaken and angered by this turn of events, Okhapkina took her children and they returned to her old flat. But now she had nothing left to feed her family with. 'I moved the children and my things back into the freezing room, narrow as a coffin. It was unbearably cold – hoarfrost was on the walls, and snow lay on the window sill. How can we live, I thought, in such cold, with barely any food at all?'

That evening Okhapkina was galvanised into activity. She searched upstairs in a disused room and found a couple of chairs, which she broke up for firewood. And she managed to gather a few scraps of coal, scraping them off the cellar floor. But that night she could not sleep. It was not possible to survive without food and Okhapkina became almost crazy with distress, as her fears for her children overwhelmed her. She had no idea what to do. Then suddenly, she got out of bed, and flung herself on to her knees. 'I had no icons,' Okhapkina related, 'and I didn't know any prayers. My children had never been christened, and I didn't believe in God. I would sometimes cry out: "Save us – God don't let us die," during an air raid. But that was it. Yet now I desperately wanted to appeal for help.'

Words began to tumble out. Fearful of waking her children, Okhapkina whispered: 'God, you can see how I'm suffering – how hungry my little children and I are. I can't go on any more. God, if we are to die, could we all die together?' She was utterly desperate. 'I can't live any more – the suffering is too much.' And then, amid all the distress, something came to her. She began to recite a simple formula: 'Have mercy, God, on my innocent children.'

Early the next morning, she was woken by a loud banging at the front door. A voice called out, asking if Lidiya Okhapkina lived there. It was a Red Army soldier, carrying a parcel from her husband, who was serving at the front. He was fighting hundreds of miles away – and Okhapkina had not heard news from him for months. But now he had sent his family a kilogram of semolina, a kilogram of rice and two packets of biscuits.

On 28 January, fires began to break out in several different parts of the city. And again, there was no bread. Nikolai Gorshkov feared for the future:

> Today, there was a complete lack of bread in the city. Queues of quite incredible size began to form around the bakeries at 3.00 a.m., three hours before they opened. There are now many cases in the factories with workers – who have not received bread for two days – no longer going to work, or coming to the factory and then refusing to work. The canteens are all running out of soup. The streets lie desolate, and then suddenly one finds these huge queues. What a bitter time Leningrad is passing through.

Productivity in Leningrad's factories had fallen almost to nothing. People were too exhausted to work effectively, and by the end of January their diary extracts presented a uniformly grim picture: 'There is now no electricity. Our boss said "Sit down and wait" – and at first we just sat there, for several hours every day, but the electricity never came on. So we went to work more and more rarely.'

And from a worker in the Izhora Factory: 'Everybody is now walking very slowly, and some can barely lift their legs. It is hard to imagine such debilitation. We are just sitting here starving.'

The long-suffering city was now sliding into its final death agonies. 'The situation is most ominous,' Gorshkov wrote with mounting concern, 'for parts of the city are in flames, and the fires are completely out of control, casting an eerie, frightful light. People are talking about a growing number of incidents, where, under the cover of darkness, gangs attack anyone seen carrying food. They are also speaking of a rise in cannibalism, and it is truly hard to record this.'

Leningrad's authorities, quite unable to remedy the situation, now froze in panic. 'The city was walking on a tightrope,' Igor Chaiko wrote. 'This time will be imprinted on my memory for ever. The death toll had reached a quite terrifying level. The last days of the month were when people should have received their new bread-ration tickets. But at the end of January these were not issued – instead, there was a delay – and that delay finished many people off.'

Seventeen-year-old Vasily Vladimirov started to keep a diary after the death of his brother Boris, on 15 January 1942. 'The situation in the city is terrible,' he began.

> There has been no electricity for over a month and now there is no water – our toilet no longer works. There is very little firewood. There is nothing to make soup out of, so we boil glue. My uncle brought some hides home, and we scraped them, took the shavings, and then boiled them. It is so cold in the room. We have run out of kerosene, so in the evenings, from 8.00–9.00 p.m. we burn a little wax. The window panes are broken from shelling and bombing and just covered with cardboard. Sometimes we scavenge for coal, or search for a little wood. It is dark even in the daytime – and so very, very cold.

He felt the dreadful suffering all around him. 'Some of us are sent to the cemeteries to try and dig graves,' he continued. 'It is −30 Celsius, and a lot of people, weakened by starvation, are freezing to death in the city. They say the death toll has reached 20,000 a day. Everywhere in the streets you see people carrying dead bodies.'

Vladimirov was aware of the cumulative effect of an utterly inadequate diet. 'There are no fats or sweet things. We had a little jam in December, but there has been nothing in January. When my brother Boris became thinner and thinner, we saw a doctor, and demanded additional nourishment for him – but we were only given a little bread. Boris was no longer able to digest it. He needed fats – but it was not possible to get any. In canteens, the soup is only water mixed with a little flour.'

On 27 January Vladimirov wrote: 'There is no bread in any of the shops.' The following day he noted despairingly: 'My mother stood in a queue from 5.00 a.m. to midnight, but still did not get any bread.' On 29 January the temperature reached −32 degrees Celsius. They were ready to get up even earlier in an attempt to find food, but now the hands on the alarm clock froze: 'Our soup has no flour – only glue and two spoons of rice,' Vladimirov recorded. 'And we have only two more portions left. Tea is boiled water with a little salt. We are running out of firewood. We will all die of starvation and cold.'

On 29 January nine-year-old Geri Rostov made a simple sketch. He drew a piece of bread being cut by a knife. Underneath it he wrote: 'Starvation – how hungry I am!' Yet, even in this dire situation, there were fleeting moments of hope. Vera Inber had noticed something remarkable. 'The look of the city has changed,' she wrote. 'All the fences have disappeared.' People were now desperately scavenging for firewood. But then Inber added, in surprise and delight: 'The beautiful, centuries-old birch and lime trees have been left alone.'

A secret NKVD report stated blandly: 'The increase in the bread ration from 24 January did not improve conditions for the city's inhabitants. As a result of difficulties with the food supply, the lack of water and electricity and insufficient firewood the mood of the population has deteriorated further.' Informers reported total disillusionment with the city's leadership. 'Mayor Popkov lies shamelessly about the situation in the city,' was one overheard comment. The war censor was intercepting more and more letters, noting the steady rise in 'negative' comments. One extract read simply: 'Leningrad has become a morgue – its streets are avenues of the dead. In every entrance way to every house there lies a pile of corpses. Rows of corpses line the streets. They are stacked up in hospitals. The factories are all frozen. We inhabit a dead city – without light, water or transport.'

A thorough system of state censorship vetted all letters despatched from blockaded Leningrad. But the process of vetting was no longer deemed sufficient. From 25 January to 15 February 1942 – the most critical period of the siege – all postal links between the city and the front were deliberately cut, in order not to demoralise the defending troops.

As people stood in bread queues 700–800 deep, in the pitch dark of the early morning, the eating habits of the city's leaders became a regular topic of conversation. One person was overheard saying: 'Our rulers of course are full. They are sitting there, stuffed, at the Smolny. They get not only bread, but proper lunch and dinner. They don't care about us, about the starving people.' And an employee at one of the bakeries, named Silin, was reported as stating: 'The bureaucrats from the district party committee ran away when they saw the lines at the bread stores. They sit in warmth and light and stuff themselves, and do not see how people are suffering and dying. And when they see the food lines, they flee and start looking for the guilty little people. The little people aren't guilty – it is the bureaucrats who have created this mess. Zhdanov sits there and who knows what he thinks.'

In the secret copy addressed to Leningrad's leader, this last sentence was underlined by Andrei Zhdanov himself, showing his sensitivity to what was being said about him. He also marked, for punitive action, the name of a book-keeper at the Musical Comedy Theatre who was overheard remarking: 'The people are starving, but they bring Zhdanov cocoa in bed.'

Rather than take urgent action to improve the food situation, Leningrad's regime now devoted its resources to hunting down a 'counter-revolutionary organisation' that was 'seeking to exploit the food situation for anti-Soviet ends'. On 29 January the NKVD reported triumphantly that 'the insurrectionary group has been liquidated'. The 'insurrectionaries' were in fact staff at a medical clinic, their ringleader a doctor who had circulated the latest statistics on illness and death rates within the city. Their crime was to accuse the city's leaders 'of failing to take timely measures to store food within the city'.

'I am terribly thin,' Alexander Boldyrev had written on 31 January. 'My legs won't obey me – they shake continuously. They seem not to belong to me . . . Tomorrow we shall be without bread again. For the past few days, they have been loading the sledges with two or three corpses at a time.'

People were now dying like flies. Eighteen-year-old Alexandra Ivanova was the strongest in her family, and she had gone out to get bread for everyone else. But now there was no bread to bring home. On 31 January her father died, followed in quick succession by her three nephews, aged three, five and seven. 'They were so wizened by hunger they looked like little dried cockroaches,' Ivanova recalled. On 4 February her aunt died as well. She was now the only survivor, and as she was too weak to move the corpses on her own, they all had to be left in the room. Eventually Ivanova found someone to help her. 'We ran a conveyor system to the cemetery, using a couple of sledges,' she remembered. Coffins could no longer be obtained in the city – all she could do was to carefully wrap her father in a large shirt.

'Corpses, corpses, corpses,' wrote Igor Chaiko, 'left in the snow hills, along the city's streets and lanes, wrapped in blankets, curtains and shifts. Many of the dead are adorned with brightly coloured cloth around their heads, so that the vehicles which circle the city to pick up bodies will see them against the snow. The workers who gather them call their job "collecting colours".' Chaiko noticed that many people's human feelings had hardened and blunted, but that others still preserved a precious spark of dignity and compassion. He saw it most strongly in grief-stricken mothers, carrying their dead children to the mortuary. They lovingly held the little swathed bodies in their arms, walking mile after mile in the bitter cold.

The hunger was now agonising. 'We could see people's bones through their skin,' Tamara Zaitseva recalled, 'as they searched the city, scavenging for scraps of food. At home, we started eating our books – mother soaked the pages in water, and we swallowed the liquid. Father cut up his belt, and gave us a little piece each day. It tasted vile, but by chewing it we could briefly forget about starvation.' But across the yard from Zaitseva the little girl she used to play with had disappeared. Her mother and grandmother, maddened with hunger, had eaten her.

Under such duress, time seemed to grind to a complete halt. Matt Sundakov, a tiny child during the siege, recalled one fragmentary memory, which his mother confirmed had taken place at end of January 1942. It had a strange, dreamlike quality, with every motion laboriously drawn out. Beyond lay a vast, silent emptiness: 'My mother was sitting with me at our dining-room table. It was covered with an old oil cloth. There was nothing on the table except a few scattered crumbs of bread. Leaning forward, I began to carefully pick up those crumbs, using my right forefinger. Then, slowly, I started to drag them towards my hungry mouth.'

Sofia Buriakova had been visiting her brother every day. He had fallen very ill at the beginning of January and she would bring him a little food and make him tea. He responded to her simple acts of kindness, and his condition started to improve. Buriakova last saw him on 30 January. He was recovering, and was now able to get out of bed by himself. But, shortly before she left, he suddenly became anxious: 'Although I'm getting better, do please come tomorrow,' he entreated. Buriakova promised that she would. But on 31 January her son arrived unexpectedly – he had been given a few hours' leave from his military unit – and she did not have time to make the visit.

When Buriakova arrived at her brother's house the following morning she found his door locked. A neighbour told her that he had died the previous day. When Buriakova asked for the key to open the apartment she was informed that the caretaker had it, but no caretaker ever appeared. She was left shocked and bewildered, for her brother had been getting better. Then a horrifying suspicion formed in her mind: 'My brother had told me that he had entrusted to his neighbours the right to receive his ration cards . . . For that, I believe, they took his life . . . No doubt they were afraid that on entering I would see traces of a violent death.' Buriakova was unable to prove anything. Before she could return the neighbours took the body away in a hearse, and then told her coldly that she shouldn't come round any more. She had no idea where he was buried.

Yet in the stricken city there also remained people capable of performing remarkable acts of self-sacrifice. On 31 January Igor Chaiko lay in his apartment, desperately weakened from starvation and unable to get up. He owed his life to a friend who, sensing something was wrong, walked miles through the knee-deep snow, collapsing twice on his journey, to bring him a share of his meagre food store. Brave medical staff defied the horrific conditions, caring for the sick and malnourished, and searching apartments for children who had lost their parents. Here is an extract from one doctor's journal for 31 January: 'Having found the apartment, I entered without knocking. The room was dark, the walls covered with frost, puddles of water on the floor. Lying across some chairs was the corpse of a fourteen-year-old boy. In a cot was a second corpse, that of a tiny infant. On the bed lay a woman – also dead. By her side was a teenage girl, compulsively rubbing the dead woman's chest with a towel.'

Any kind of provision for the sick was now collapsing. On 4 February Mikhail Nosyrev wrote a long entry in his diary:

> February has begun – the sixth month of the siege. Everywhere people are dying; cold and hunger are paralysing the will to live. There are no means of transport or communication and such conveniences as light, water, electricity and gas have passed into the realm of legend. If you stay on the streets for a couple of hours you come across dozens of dead people, lying, solitary in the snow, and cartloads of corpses. The prices for foodstuffs on the black market are astronomical, and people are eating the most appalling filth, from joiner's-glue jelly to cuts from the soft parts of corpses. The emaciated inhabitants of the city, driven by utter despair, are turning into savages. Life has become a kind of nightmare – from which it is impossible to wake.

Nosyrev still tried to do the right thing. Near Fontanka Street he found a man lying on the ground, not yet dead. He went over to try and help, but did not have the strength to lift him up. No one else seemed willing to help, but he persisted. Eventually he recruited a passer-by, pulling an empty sledge, and together they sat the man up, and asked him where he lived. His tongue had swollen up, and it was difficult to make sense of the few words he was able to utter. But eventually something coherent emerged: he needed to attend a nearby office. With considerable difficulty, Nosyrev and his companion dragged him there.

At the office, some government employees were warming themselves by a large fire. They claimed not to recognise the man and, showing not the slightest pity for his condition, kicked up a row and threw everybody out. Nosyrev was left deeply angry. They put the fellow back on the sledge, for he was unable to stand on his own two feet, but what were they to do with him? Other passers-by, struck by Nosyrev's efforts, also offered their help, and one gave directions to the nearest hospital. Nosyrev was running out of strength, but he was determined not to abandon the man. He harnessed himself to the front of the sledge, his helper pushed from behind, and together they made their way to the hospital gates.

Nosyrev opened the gate, and then stopped, aghast. Straight in front of him was a huge pile of corpses, half clad, eyes open, frozen in a strange variety of positions, the bodies blackened from the cold. Behind it was another pile. The yard was overflowing with dead bodies. Pushing their way through these ghastly heaps, they got inside the hospital and made their way up to Casualty. The staff showed no interest whatsoever. Nosyrev left the fellow on a bench in the hospital corridor.

That evening he put a final comment in his diary, its concluding word written in block capitals: 'For the first time in my life, I have truly realised the meaning of the word HORROR.'

Yet the astounding, heroic perseverance of people like Nosyrev was keeping the city alive. Vera Rogova remembered crossing one of Leningrad's bridges, and seeing a man ahead of her walking increasingly slowly. When he got to the far side of the bridge he started to sink in the snow, then lay full length. Rogova realised that he was dying. She had a tiny piece of sugar in her pocket, and without thinking, she went up and put it in the stranger's mouth. Someone walking past reprimanded her: 'Why are you wasting your sugar – can't you see it's no use to him now?' The man did indeed die five minutes later. But Rogova looked up, and then said simply: 'I do not want him to die abandoned.'

Theatre producer Alexander Dymov surveyed the scene around him. 'We lead a primitive life,' he wrote, 'without water, without light, without warmth. Hundreds of people, carrying pitchers or kettles, queue despondently at a tap in a laundry some three blocks from their homes. They stand there for hours.' But he was not willing to succumb to despair. One evening, as a distraction from the gnawing pangs of hunger, he drafted a letter of complaint to his stomach, humorously mimicking the strictures of censorship within the Soviet state:

> Much respected citizen editor, Comrade Stomach! I am weak and feeble. I have great difficulty even dragging my feet and my face has long got out of the habit of smiling. I have been hungry for a long time but I am fighting, fighting not to fall down, for death quickly tramples the fallen. So far I am hanging on, and even continuing to write. And I have not yet stopped thinking, or reading books. You, citizen editor, prevent me from doing all this. Every moment I am conscious of your power, of your oppression, your interference in my internal affairs . . . I refuse to think of nothing but gorging myself. I want to dream of the future, a beautiful future, not being stuffed to the brim with potatoes, bread and sunflower oil. You need to understand that I want to stay a human being . . . Abdicate your role of dictator. Go about your modest business conscientiously – after all, at the moment you haven't that much work to do. Accept my sincere respects, your obedient servant, A. Dymov.

Georgi Knyazev was struck by a new phrase entering everyday conversation, as once unimaginable horror now filled the everyday and formed part of casual exchange. Everyone knew it was now almost impossible to secure individual burial for someone; in most cases, bodies were being buried in trenches or craters, blown out of the ground with explosives. So people would say to each other, with black humour: 'Look out – watch yourself, or you'll be fit only for the trenches.'

Knyazev wrote: 'I am alive because I have thoughts and plans for the future.' He wanted to continue his research, to teach a new course at university, and this had become an article of faith for him. When no bread appeared once again on 3 February, he declared resolutely: 'Let us escape from our present-day nightmare,' and defiantly resumed his study of the ancient Hittite culture of Asia Minor.

While they waited for supplies of food and fuel to be resumed, some, searching for a sense of purpose and meaning, turned to their remaining books – and to one book in particular. 'Whoever had energy enough to read,' Lidiya Ginzburg remembered, 'used to read *War and Peace* in besieged Leningrad.' Effectively abandoned by their own government, people found solace in Tolstoy's novel, which was set during another period of foreign invasion. They were searching for guidance, and also for an affirmation of basic human principles. 'Tolstoy had said the last word about courage, about people doing their bit in a people's war,' Ginzburg continued. 'And no one doubted the adequacy of Tolstoy's response to life. The reader would say to himself: "Right – now I've got the proper feeling about this. So then, this is how it should be."' Others were no longer able to read easily – their books had already been burnt for fuel.

The extraordinary courage evoked in Tolstoy's novel was soon needed. Early in February 1942, the month's ration cards were belatedly issued, and some bread started to appear again in the shops. But for some, after an entire week without food, it was now too late.

On 4 February a colleague of Nikolai Gorshkov made a visit to the local militia office. Twelve women were being held there, all charged with cannibalism. They openly admitted what they had done: 'One woman, utterly worn out and desperate, said that when her husband fainted, through exhaustion and lack of food, she hacked off part of his leg to make a soup to feed herself and her children. Another said that she cut off part of a dead body lying in the street – but she was followed and caught. These women are crying: they know they will soon be executed.'

Elena Taranukhina remembered the courtyard at the back of her apartment filling with corpses. She noticed with horror that the bodies of two women by the entrance had had their breasts hacked off. There was a tangible menace closing in around her. One morning she felt that something was horribly wrong, and abandoning her place in the food queue hurried home. She returned just in time. Her mother, delirious with cold and hunger, had put her baby daughter in a bathtub. Only there was no water in it. She kept repeating: 'What a fatty child, what a fatty child.' Her mother died two days later. Taranukhina tried to carry her to the mortuary but ran out of strength. She appealed to a man stumbling by, but he said: 'I will only help you if you give me some bread.' She had none – and was forced to leave the body in the street.

Sometimes neighbours sounded the alert. Maria Ivanovna, a housing administrator, was asked to visit one family after the mother began acting strangely. She remembered there had been many children, but now found only two. 'The rest have died,' the mother said, but there were no burial registration forms. Ivanovna found meat cooking on the stove. She was told it was mutton, but she lifted the lid of the pot and started to ladle up the soup. Suddenly, she uncovered a human hand.

The madness of unspeakable hunger was sweeping the city, and alongside it something more calculated and cold-blooded. 'There were villains who killed people to get their flesh and sell it,' Dmitry Likhachev acknowledged. A variety of chilling ruses were used to lure the unsuspecting victim into the murderer's lair. A place on Zelenaya Street was selling potatoes, and the purchaser would be asked to look under the settee where they were kept. When he bent down he was hit on the back of the head with an axe. One of the staff at the Academy of Sciences went to an address near the Sitnoy market, where she had heard things could be bartered for meat. She never returned. She had looked comparatively healthy, and was almost certainly killed and eaten. Army food supply officer Vasily Yershov confirmed that organised bands of cannibals were now working within Leningrad. One, comprised of medical workers and several doctors, had even infiltrated a hospital. A gang of twenty cannibals was waylaying and killing military couriers coming into the city.

For two weeks in February the authorities were in danger of

completely losing control. They had become increasingly frightened of any gathering of the city's inhabitants. On 9 February Alexander Boldyrev wrote angrily: 'Yesterday and today, mounted police dispersed people who were selling goods and chattels on the street.' He added: 'The police belong to that category of Leningrad citizens who receive more bread than anyone else – 500 grams. And it shows.' Yet the danger of protests against the city's government had lessened – people simply didn't have the strength to fight against the regime.

The real menace was from the growing wave of food-related crimes. The theft of food and ration cards, along with robberies at shops and bakeries, continued to mount. And while there had been only nine arrests for cannibalism over the first ten days of December, by the first ten days of February the figure had climbed to 311.

On 10 February Boldyrev saw a dead man propped up against a box near the House of Scholars. He must have stopped to rest there, and then been unable to get up. His skin was now a strange yellow colour. Boldyrev remarked: 'He showed only one sign of having attracted the attention of passers-by – his pockets had been turned inside out. Obviously this was an attempt to find his ration cards.'

Cannibalism was no longer at the fringes of people's lives; now its threat was ever present. 'It had become dangerous to make a journey through the city,' Elena Martilla said, 'and it was becoming increasingly difficult to trust others.' Tamara Grebennikova saw the body of a fifteen-year-old girl stowed under the stairwell of an apartment block. Bits of her body had been cut away. Looking at her, Grebennikova knew she had been killed for food. She was now terrified that the same thing would happen to her.

One day in early February Anna Nikitina's elder sister went to queue for bread. She never returned – and the following day her mother decided to go to the local militia office and report her as missing. Trying to hold back her mounting anxiety, she carried with her an item of clothing – her lost daughter's black beret – as a source of comfort, and to maintain some sort of connection with her.

When she arrived, the NKVD seemed unsurprised by what she had to relate. They asked her to register her daughter's details, and gave her a form to fill in. Then, in a brutal display of candour, they pointed to an adjoining storeroom, whose wooden shelves were stacked with crates. 'Go on through,' she was told. 'Take a look for yourself.' Nikitina's mother plucked up the courage to ask what was in them. 'Children's clothes,' was the chilling reply. 'You are welcome to search through them. They are all arranged district by district. If you find your daughter's underwear, remember the number of the crate. Then we can tell you where they killed her – and ate her.' Niktina's mother sat down, suddenly and violently. For a while, she just stayed there. She couldn't bear to look in the room, and eventually she went back home, clutching the black beret. Then the whole family got down on its knees and prayed.

The next day she returned to the militia office and with extraordinary bravery and determination began to search through the room's ghastly contents. She did not find her daughter's clothes, but the man on duty wanted to be helpful. 'Come back after our next clothes delivery,' he said. 'You'll be sure to find them then. The Petrograd side of the city is overrun with cannibals.'

It was an open secret that cannibalism was now rampant within besieged Leningrad. 'Mutilated corpses were all around us,' Vera Rogova said. 'And children would tell you that they were no longer allowed out of their apartments on their own.' Early one morning, at around 6.00, Rogova was leaving the apartment of a friend. She was in a hurry and she took a short cut, following a different route from the one she normally took. The quickest way to get to the nearby square lay through a long corridor, passing through an adjacent building. But Rogova normally avoided it – it ran at semi-basement level, and was dark and dilapidated, and something about it made her feel uneasy. But on this occasion she was short of time, and she overrode her fear.

As she walked along the corridor she felt a sense of dread. Suddenly, a door swung open and a man looked out. He was hairy and unkempt – and there was something about him that made Rogova shudder. He no longer seemed human; he looked like a beast. And then she saw he was carrying an axe. She started to run. The man immediately gave chase. He possessed an uncanny strength – and she could hear his echoing footfalls drawing closer and closer. For a moment Rogova felt a paralysing helplessness: the corridor seemed to go on for ever, and she felt trapped in a giant web, unable to break free. Then she found a sudden surge of energy and catapulted herself out on to the street, straight into a passing group of soldiers.

Two of the patrol took hold of her. 'A man is hunting me with an axe,' Rogova blurted out. But the others were already inside the building. Shots ran out. Minutes later, they returned. 'When we saw the look of terror on your face, we understood,' one said simply.

The evil Rogova had confronted was now entwined around the city. But she had refused to succumb to it. Amid the horror, others in Leningrad felt the same way. Eight-year-old Nina Pechanova had watched the members of her family die, and after her mother passed away at the beginning of February she was the only survivor. 'For three days I clung to my mother's corpse,' she remembered. 'I was terrified of leaving the apartment – I was so scared of cannibals.' Then she ventured out carrying ration tickets and got some bread. On her way home she was robbed. Two people stopped her in the street. 'Give us your bread, little girl,' they told her, 'or we will eat you.' Pechanova dropped the bread and ran home.

The time passed in a kind of trance. Once more, Pechanova clung to her mother's corpse in a delirium of hunger. But on the following day, showing remarkable courage, she gathered up the ration cards and returned to the store, and this time she safely brought her bread home. 'I decided that I was going to fight for my life,' Pechanova said, with quiet dignity.

An incredible spirit of resilience had sprung forth. On 15 February Vasily Vladimirov wrote a single, striking sentence in his diary: 'We want to stay alive.'

8

The Road of Life

Keeping Hope Alive

THE TRAGEDY THAT occurred in Leningrad in late January and early February 1942 could have been averted. By the beginning of December 1941 an ice road had been constructed across the frozen Lake Ladoga. It brought food into the stricken city and allowed a chance of evacuating the most vulnerable of Leningrad's inhabitants. Because it was the city's only link with the rest of mainland Russia, it held a powerful symbolic importance and it was later given the name the 'Road of Life'. But the food was not reaching ordinary citizens, and the planned evacuation was delayed by nearly two months. Hundreds of thousands of lives were lost as a result.

Constructing the ice road was a colossal Soviet achievement. It was built in atrocious conditions, over cracks and fissures on the lake's surface, and through frequent snowstorms, under almost constant German artillery fire and air attack. It ran from rail and loading depots on the Soviet shore of the lake, across a twenty-mile stretch of ice – parallel to the German siege positions – then on to the small port of Osinovets, on Ladoga's western shore, still held by Leningrad's defenders. From this transit point the precious cargo was unloaded and carried by rail and truck into the stricken city.

Initially the ice road was plagued with difficulties. Stretches of the route were extremely hazardous – 157 lorries were lost on the first crossing. Many drivers kept their doors open, so that they could quickly jump to safety if the vehicle started to sink. To avoid the sudden gaps which opened in the ice vehicles drove with their head-lights on – although this made them a target for the Luftwaffe's bombers. But by the end of December 1941 over 4,000 lorries and trucks were bringing more than 700 tons of food and supplies into

Leningrad every day. A month later the figure had risen to over 2,000 tons.

At the beginning of February 1942 Vera Rogova was a traffic guide on the ice road. 'There were six lines of traffic – three in each direction – long, continuous columns, one following after another,' she remembered. 'The ice kept moving, so our job was to clear away rocks and blockages, and, if necessary, switch lorries from one line to another. Our traffic guides were normally stationed at 500-metre intervals along the road, and it was difficult and dangerous work. Out on the flat, open expanse of the lake it was bitterly cold, with temperatures dropping to below −40 degrees Celsius, and there was nowhere to take cover from German attack. We did what we could – putting medical units along the road, to help the wounded, or anyone suffering from frostbite, and setting up anti-aircraft guns to provide some sort of protection. But conditions were terrible.'

However, motivating the 30,000-strong workforce was never a problem. 'We all took a military oath,' Rogova said, 'but it was not really necessary. Everyone felt the urgency of the situation – we all knew that Leningrad was starving to death. There was supposed to be a distance of six metres from one lorry to the next, as a precaution against German bombing attacks, but the drivers never kept to it – instead, they drove almost bumper to bumper. They were trying to get as much food into the city as possible.'

Ivan Krylov worked as a loader on the eastern shore of Lake Ladoga, at the starting point of the ice road. 'We were stacking the lorries and trucks with food and ammunition,' he recalled, 'and labouring night and day to do so. It was exhausting work, shifting the large sacks of flour and sugar, and loading heavy ammunition cases. The Germans constantly tried to bomb our supply columns, and there were often seven or eight air raids a day. Usually, we just kept on working through them – moving the cargo, regardless of the explosions around us. There simply wasn't time to halt and take shelter.' But Krylov also emphasised the extraordinary spirit of self-sacrifice: 'We had all heard about the reduction of the food ration within Leningrad – and that people were trying to live on 125 grams

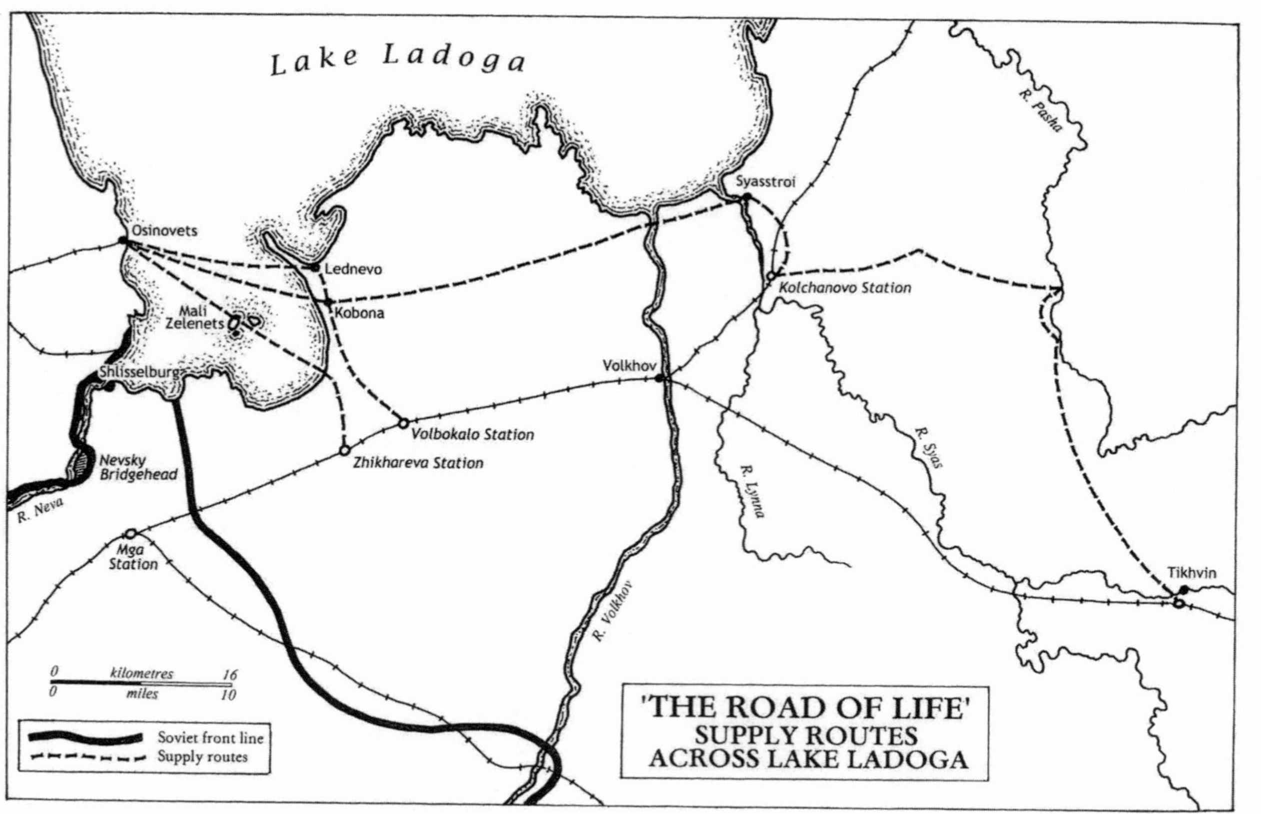

Lake Ladoga
Osinovets
Lednevo
Kobona
Mali Zelenets
Shlisselburg
Nevsky Bridgehead
R. Neva
Mga Station
Volbokalo Station
Zhikhareva Station
Volkhov
R. Volkhov
Syasstroi
Kolchanovo Station
R. Pasha
R. Syas
R. Lynna
Tikhvin
0 kilometres 16
0 miles 10
Soviet front line
Supply routes
'THE ROAD OF LIFE'
SUPPLY ROUTES
ACROSS LAKE LADOGA

of bread a day. So we kept on going. We really felt that the ice road would save people's lives.'

It should have done. The enemy put the supply route under air and artillery attack, but were unable to halt the flow of traffic. Every measure was anticipated. Soviet air pilots flew overhead, protecting the convoys. 'There was a fear that the Germans might send troops out over the ice, so marine brigade commander Nikolai Vavin was put in charge of a specialist force to guard the precious cargo. 'There was a danger that the enemy would try to capture the ice road by a direct infantry assault,' Vavin acknowledged. 'So we assembled groups of motorised sledges – each sledge carrying three or four Red Army soldiers – and they fanned out over the ice, keeping watch against any German incursions. It was vital to stop the ice road being disrupted.'

Yet these heroic efforts were frittered away. By 10 February 1942, when deliveries across the ice road had reached 3,000 tons a day, Leningrad still remained in the grip of a starvation epidemic. The city's inhabitants quickly deduced why the food wasn't reaching them – their leaders were stockpiling it. A high-school teacher named Makarova lamented: 'Only under a barbaric government such as ours could this situation occur, where people are reduced to cannibalism while those in the Smolny eat their fill.' A concierge called Yegerov warned: 'The population have reached their limit. In the queues they curse the leaders of our city. They say that Popkov sits in the Smolny – replete – choosing not to see what is going on around him.'

A director at the Lenfilm studios, Mikhail Tsekhanovsky, observed: 'I am astonished that there has not been a general uprising of the starving. The only reason can be people's sheer physical weakness. They have completely lost faith in Soviet power. The Red Army defenders of the city are utterly exhausted. With the beginning of the warm weather the Germans could walk into the city, and take it without loss.' A chief engineer at an industrial plant complained: 'I am sick of the hypocrisy of our leaders. They announce that they are increasing our rations, but there is no improvement whatsoever. Instead, the situation worsens, and tens of thousands of people are dying of hunger. It would be better if our country became a German colony.'

It would not have been better for Russia to have become a German colony, but letters sent out from the city showed the overwhelming mood of cynicism and despair: 'Our leaders gorge themselves while at least 7,000 people a day die of starvation,' one correspondent wrote. 'They pretend not to see what is happening under their noses. Corpses lie scattered about the streets; they don't even make an effort to clear them away . . . The total darkness in which we live causes morale to sink lower with each day that passes. Like the doomed, we no longer react to anything – we await death as a release from this nightmare reality.'

Yet even now some of Leningrad's inhabitants refused to give up hope. Instead, they took refuge in grim yet self-sustaining humour. On 12 February the NKVD reported – in all seriousness – that there were now widespread rumours that Mayor Popkov had been arrested on charges of sabotage. They had misunderstood comments relayed to them by their network of informers. A housewife was overheard saying: 'Popkov and the other leaders of Leningrad only take care of themselves; they never think about us.' A textile worker named Vladimirovich fashioned this widely held belief into sardonic humour – and the joke spread: 'Mayor Popkov has proved to be a saboteur. He was caught in the act of sabotaging Leningrad's food supply, and has now been found guilty of causing the deaths of most of the city's inhabitants.'

On 6 December 1941, with the ice now thick enough to support regular convoys of traffic, an evacuation plan had been drawn up to get the most vulnerable inhabitants out of the city. It was known as Order 447, and it envisaged that from 10 December there should be a mass evacuation of civilians across 'the Lake Ladoga motor road', and that by 20 December at least 5,000 civilians a day should be moved, with the figure then increasing still further. But this crucial measure was never put into effect. After a conversation with Stalin, Zhdanov discouraged it. The policy of mass evacuation was jettisoned, and over the next six weeks only a paltry few thousand crossed the lake to safety.

After a long delay, a revised plan was drawn up on 22 January 1942. The first evacuation convoy finally left the city on 2 February. Why, in such appalling circumstances, was Order 447 not put into effect immediately?

The Red Army was now counter-attacking – recapturing the vital rail junction of Tikhvin and, further south, pushing back the exhausted Wehrmacht forces. Overjoyed by these successes, Stalin's high command was flooded by a heady wave of optimism. It decided to prepare another major offensive for the new year – one which would repulse Army Group North and break the siege of Leningrad. In theory, this was a good decision – as long as the counter-attack was properly prepared and executed. But it was followed by a very bad one. For, once the new military offensive had been agreed upon, Stalin and Zhdanov decided that a mass evacuation would convey the wrong political message – that there was not the will to defend Leningrad – and so the plans were cancelled.

All now rested on the January counter-offensive. A number of armies were recruited under the command of General Meretskov, intended to push westwards to relieve the besieged city. 'People still say that Meretskov's units will be in Leningrad by 10 January,' Vera Inber wrote cautiously. 'Well, if not the 10th, the 15th or the 20th – as long as they are there!' But these hopes were soon dashed. Lacking effective artillery preparation and air support, the Soviet forces impaled themselves on a series of well-defended German strong-points.

On 21 January, in increasing desperation, Leningrad's military command sent several companies of tanks from the city's Kirov Works across the ice road to support the hard-pressed attackers. This was a desperado's throw of the dice, for no one had any idea whether the ice would withstand the weight. The tank turrets were removed – to be reassembled on the far shore – and, cautiously, the vehicles moved out over the lake. Remarkably, they crossed without mishap. But these reinforcements proved insufficient – the counter-offensive was stuck fast. So, after a six-week delay, the evacuation plans for the city were reinstated.

Journalist Pavel Luknitsky made one of the first journeys with the evacuees. Those running supplies westwards, across Lake Ladoga and into the city, had shown real concern for the plight of Leningrad's starving; in the transport convoys moving in the opposite direction, from the city to the eastern shore of the lake, corruption and mismanagement were rampant. These latter arrangements were of course organised by the city authorities – and it showed.

The official who accompanied Luknitsky across the lake took all of his relatives with him, and had every intention of returning to the city with goods for the black market. Trucks, buses and cars crawled, halted and broke down, and were abandoned, leaving the route littered with disabled vehicles. There was no food or shelter for those making the journey. Even starving people near to death had to pay for their fare in bread. 'We all fought to get supplies into Leningrad,' Vera Rogova remembered. 'But those travelling out of the city had to bribe their way across the ice road. It was impossible to survive if you were not able to offer food or goods in payment. Those unable to do so simply perished.'

Evacuation on foot was not permitted, although some tried – bribing the guards along the way with a little food or tobacco. When they reached Lake Ladoga many of these groups were arrested by NKVD patrols. Others attempted to walk across the frozen lake. 'These poor people were absolutely desperate,' Rogova said. German reconnaissance planes had noticed their movements. The Luftwaffe could have bombed them. Instead, they dropped clusters of mines along their route, which would explode when touched. They were disguised as cans of food.

A fleet of motor vehicles carried people to the lake. Leningrad's privileged elite travelled in heated buses, fitted with stoves, with tin chimneys protruding through the roofs. The majority made the journey on open trucks, with some left clinging to the outsides of the vehicle's gasoline tanks. It usually took an hour and a half to cross Lake Ladoga, but the whole journey lasted at least thirteen hours. In Luknitsky's truck, a three-year-old girl had died before they reached the lake's eastern shore, and other deaths soon followed. The government official travelling with Luknitsky seemed oblivious to the suffering. 'During the blockade I never went hungry,' he said smugly.

On 11 February Elena Skrjabina began her evacuation. It started late – they had to wait for more than three hours for the family of one of Leningrad's hospital directors. 'Finally a robust, glowing woman appeared, elegantly and warmly dressed,' she recalled. 'With her were two well-fed girls, about twelve or thirteen years of age, and another little girl with a governess.' One of Skrjabina's sons, seriously weakened by starvation, had to be left at an infirmary at a staging post along their route. Several hours later, the wife of the hospital director unpacked fried chicken, meat pies, chocolate and condensed milk, and began sharing it with her daughters. Nothing was offered to their fellow passengers. At the sight of all this food, Skrjabina's other son fainted.

On the evacuation route, the starving met the people who had flourished at their expense. Elena Kochina travelled out of the city with the son of a high-ranking food-supply official. 'During the blockade we ate better than before the war,' he bragged to Kochina's husband. 'We had everything.' His girlfriend also worked in the supply department: 'We ate whole boxes of butter and chocolate,' she added. 'Of course, I didn't see any of that before the war.' Kochina felt a rising surge of anger. Their sheer tactlessness was extraordinary, since they were telling this to the very people they had robbed. But then she looked round at the other passengers: 'They listened with indifference, evidently finding it all very natural.'

Kochina's husband asked the young man a final question. 'So, if things are so great for you in food supply – why do you want to be evacuated?' The answer was frank. 'I'm bored in Leningrad. There isn't anybody around to have a laugh with and I can't go out dancing any more. I'm going to join my mother in Sochi – she's a dietary physician in a sanatorium.' Kochina's husband smiled. 'Well, things won't be too bad for you there either,' he said with bitter sarcasm.

Most evacuees scarcely had the strength to move. 'We would see sick, emaciated mothers, wrapped in blankets, clinging to their babies and small children,' recalled Olga Melnikova, a medical worker on the ice road. 'These people looked horrific. Their children were so tiny, so wizened – we called them the "aged little people". Just before dawn, when the drivers reached Lake Ladoga, they would accelerate to get across the ice road as fast as possible. The women were packed on to the open sides of the truck, and they no longer had the strength to cling tightly to their offspring.' What followed was utterly harrowing. 'Just imagine what happened when the trucks hit a bump,' Melnikova said. 'The mothers, jolted by the sudden impact, could not keep hold of their children. Their precious bundles flew out of their hands and down on to the ice. The drivers would not stop – but the poor little children were killed on impact anyway. We would find clusters of corpses out on the frozen lake, still swaddled in shawls. We would carefully unwrap them, and find babies, eight months to a year old, and little girls and boys. But we were never able to identify who they were.'

No heated transport was provided for the majority of evacuees. Sometimes a lorry would break down on the ice, and its occupants would be forced to wait in the freezing cold for hours. 'We would try and get the children into a medical tent,' Melnikova remembered. 'You would take them by the hand and feel no more than a thin layer of skin stretched over it. You could have counted every single bone underneath. We gave them bits of rusk and some sweetened tea. And if a child was in a very bad condition we had to inject them with camphor to keep their hearts going. 'These children entered the tents dull and listless, hardly able to move. They seemed to have no strength left, and no will to live. But once they were offered a little food and warmth their eyes returned to life. 'When the driver came back to say the lorry was ready, what a fight they put up,' Melnikova said. 'It was heartbreaking – they resisted so ferociously. They didn't want to leave the warm tent. Someone had looked after them for a while.'

The evacuation had come too late for many of Leningrad's citizens. 'Hunger has changed the appearance of everyone,' Elena Skrjabina wrote. The godmother of her younger son had naively believed that the city's leaders would take care of them, and that no one would go seriously hungry. She was now swollen up, and her once beautiful face had turned into a transparent mask. 'Everyone is now blue-black, bloodless,' Skrjabina continued, looking at the evacuees around her. Many would not survive the journey. On the eastern side of Lake Ladoga they were loaded on to trains, and at every stop orderlies would pound on compartment doors with hammers. 'Do you have any dead?' they would yell. 'Hand them over to us!'

Dmitry Likhachev revealed the real name given to the ice road. 'It was never the "Road of Life" – the sugary term used by later writers,' he said. 'It was always known as the "Road of Death". The Germans shelled it, snow blocked it, and lorries often sank through holes. A story reached us of a woman who had lost her mind. She had been forced to travel in the second lorry of a convoy, with her children in the first. Right before her eyes, the vehicle ahead of her sank under the ice. Her lorry quickly went round the hole in which her children were struggling underwater, and roared on without stopping.' So much more should have been done to help. Instead, robbery and corruption were rife. The weak had their possessions stolen and were pushed under the ice. 'How many people died of starvation, were killed, froze or vanished without trace on that road?' Likhachev remarked angrily. 'God alone knows!'

And still these efforts failed to lessen the starvation catastrophe engulfing the city. Towards the end of February 1942, a German army situation report noted with grim satisfaction:

> The ice road across Lake Ladoga is now being used to evacuate some of Leningrad's inhabitants. The number of evacuees is insignificant compared to those still dying within the city. The drastic reduction in Leningrad's population continues unabated. Estimates of the daily death rate vary, but they are always in excess of 8,000, and often significantly more. Causes of death are hunger, exhaustion, heart failure and intestinal disease.

By the third week in February more bread was at last getting to the shops. Fearful of the breakdown of law and order in parts of Leningrad, the regime now disgorged some of its hoard of food. On 18 February Vasily Vladimirov wrote in his diary: 'Sausage has appeared in a few of the shops. There is a rumour that more meat will become available.' Some good-quality frozen beef and mutton did indeed make a surprising appearance in the city. By releasing these food products the city authorities hoped to assuage the mood of discontent. But previously loyal party workers were disillusioned by their callous, calculated self-interest. On 23 February the NKVD reported comments made by the head of one of Leningrad's industrial plants: 'The authorities announced that we had substantial reserves of food – but in practice they could not even lay in stores of dried roach, which we used to use to stoke up ovens. I have been in the party a long time, and used to carry out its directives in good faith, but now I realise that I have been lying to the people.'

Writer Ivan Gruzdev put things more bluntly: 'Leningrad's leaders are appallingly incompetent. They are responsible for a massive number of deaths from starvation. Ordinary people loathe Popkov, and many women on the streets say they would like to shoot him dead personally.' Artist Anna Ostroumova wrote scathingly about the food-supply system: 'In bakeries and co-operatives they cheat the unfortunate inhabitants; in soup kitchens and children's centres they simply steal. The same thing goes on, I think, at the highest level of food distribution. What happened to the 200 cars of food, brought in as a gift to Leningrad from the collective-farm workers? On many occasions we have received gifts of food from various districts – but what do we actually see of it all? Everything gets lost in the "apparatus".'

Yet a true Road of Life was indeed being built in besieged Leningrad. It was not the ice road over Lake Ladoga, and it did not transport supplies or ammunition. It brought to life inner resources within people. 'We used this phrase about someone who had discovered the will to survive,' Anatoly Molchanov remarked. 'It was said of these people "they have found the road of life". And this road, this will to survive, was often unearthed in the darkest circumstances, when all hope seemed extinguished.'

Svetlana Magaeva's mother fell seriously ill in January 1942, and her daughter – also weak with starvation – was taken to a children's home. The children there were between eight and ten years old. They had all witnessed unspeakable horrors, and many had lost their entire families. They lay on their beds, feeble and emaciated. Then, at the beginning of February, a young teacher named Olga Symanovskaya walked into the room. Most people dressed in drab colours, but Symanovskaya wore a striking white beret. She walked over to the windows, and pulled the heavy black-out curtains to the sides, flooding the room with light. Then she said in a loud, commanding voice: 'Come, let's all sit up and do our morning exercises.' The children looked at her in astonishment – they thought she was completely mad.

The exercises Symanovskaya was hoping to introduce were mental rather than physical. She wanted the children to recite some lines that she had written: 'We have survived the month of January – and we will survive the month of February. When the month of March arrives, we will sing songs of happiness and joy!' She repeated this again and again: But the children had already come to a decision: 'If she wants to do these morning exercises, she can do them on her own.' They watched her in silence.

Undaunted by this response, Symanovskaya spent time with each child, chatting to them and offering words of encouragement. The next morning she returned. She could see that several of the children's beds were now empty – their occupants had died during the night. But once again she repeated her recitation. And once again, she was met with complete silence. This little ritual continued day after day. But over time the children began to look forward to Symanovskaya's visits. They liked her cheerfulness, the fact that when she chatted to them they stopped thinking about hunger and death. One morning, a number of them attempted the recitation, but their voices faltered, and the exercise petered out.

Then Symanovskaya no longer came to the home. The children learnt that after one of her visits she had fallen very badly, and was now unable to stand up or move. Suddenly, they realised how weak she must have been, and how much of her remaining strength she had tried to give to them. The next morning, every person capable of sitting up and speaking recited the morning exercises. They chanted them every day, and taught them to every new child entering the home.

Mikhail Chernorutsky, a doctor practising during the siege, noticed that the mental state of those suffering from starvation affected chances of recovery. He studied people suffering from clinical dystrophy – a disorder caused by defective nutrition – and observed:

> We saw quite a few cases in which, all other conditions being equal, a weakening of the will to live, depression and giving up one's daily routine considerably hastened the course of the disease and led to a sharp deterioration in the general state of the patient. Conversely, firm and purposeful self-belief, cheerfulness, optimism and an organised pattern of life and work – even if such an outlook seemed entirely contrary to actual events – sustained the weak body and apparently gave it new strength.

Valentina Burakova, a district nurse, agreed: 'I found in my work that it was not only nutrition that was conducive to survival, but also morale.'

It was vital to stick to some sort of routine. 'During the worst period of the blockade my dinner consisted of boiling water with no more than 50 grams of inedible bread soaked in it,' said Evgeny Lyapin. 'Yet I always ate it from a plate, with a spoon. You might think I'm talking nonsense – at this stage of starvation, what did it matter? But you had to build up some sort of daily rhythm that resembled the life of a normal person. I knew this from my own experience, and was also told it by doctors who saw many people within the city.'

Faina Prusova had developed her own theory, one she nicknamed 'don't keep lying down all the time'. Her daughter, a medical student, protested: 'When you're lying down you use less energy, so you need less food.' From a scientific point of view, this observation was correct, but something else was coming into play. 'It's paradoxical,' Prusova would reply, 'but I believe that those who move about and keep working will live.' She encouraged her family to make an effort, to wash every day, try and keep the flat clean, and put a fresh cloth on the table. In February 1942 her daughter no longer had the strength to go to the Medical Institute. But Prusova said to her: 'You must continue with your studies – you must! If you stop going there, you'll die.' This response was purely instinctive and made little sense from a rational point of view – her daughter was utterly exhausted. Yet the heartfelt sincerity of the appeal touched her, and she kept on studying.

Maintaining cheerfulness in besieged Leningrad was no easy task. But psychiatrists practising within the city were reaching towards a concept that some of its inhabitants had already glimpsed in practice: a remarkable human spirit can manifest under the most extreme conditions. People stayed alive because they were sustained by feelings of devotion, whether towards their city, a loved one or a child.

Within Magaeva's children's home, the story of one little girl – Tanya Utkina – was a revelation to its occupants. Tanya looked like an Egyptian mummy: she had the face of an old woman, and her arms and legs were as thin as spaghetti noodles. 'Nobody thought she would survive,' Magaeva admitted. 'In fact, we expected her to die at any moment. She was just a skeleton, thin skin over bones, and when the doctors tried to inject glucose, there was no muscle left, and they were unable to find her veins. She had continuous diarrhoea – and no medical intervention seemed to work.'

But then, little by little, something started to happen. The diarrhoea stopped, and Tanya began to digest her food. 'To our astonishment, we saw her sitting up in bed,' Magaeva said. 'After a little while – although her legs were still like matchsticks – she managed to stand, and then, wobbling, she started to walk. All the children and adults in the home gathered to watch. Tanya smiled at us as she took one step after another, and joked that she should be charging each of us a fee for her demonstration. We felt as if we were witnessing a miracle.'

Tanya Utkina had a simple yet powerful reason to live. All her family had died, except her baby sister Sophie. Sophie was evacuated, but Tanya, already desperately ill, was too weak to travel with her. On the brink of death she told herself: 'I must live so that I can care for Sophie.' That thought alone may have saved her – the doctors could give no medical explanation for her recovery.

A desire to help others motivated people to survive. It began to create a sense of community, the 'human brotherhood' celebrated by Leningrad poet Olga Berggolts in her radio broadcasts over the city. Berggolts' poetry arose out of a strongly felt compassion for the suffering of those around her, and was formed in a spirit of defiance against a cruel enemy. It was read to the city as an act of love, and it touched Leningrad's inhabitants deeply. It took them away from the unremitting hardship of the siege, however briefly, and gave a vision of something greater in its place. 'Her voice united us,' Alexei Pavlovsky said. 'She invoked the courage of Leningrad, a courage that could counter the deaths of hundreds of thousands of our citizens.'

On 26 January 1942 the collapse of the electricity system forced Leningrad's Musical Comedy Theatre to close. 'Now, nothing was left open,' Berggolts remembered. 'And many of the city's inhabitants did not even have the strength to read at home. I think that never before and never in the future will people listen to poetry as Leningrad did that winter – hungry, swollen and hardly living.'

Berggolts could communicate her ideas simply and powerfully. Galina Ozerova remembered how her verses were 'so clear they just stuck in your mind – their rhythm lodged itself inside you'. Colleagues at Radio Leningrad admired her skill, and appreciated her kindness and concern for others. When Lazar Magrachev heard that his father had been robbed returning from a bread queue, and his ration card stolen, it was Berggolts who found him a replacement. But on 29 January her husband Nikolai died of starvation. Berggolts pulled his body to the Piskaryov Cemetery on a child's sledge, and wondered how she could carry on without him.

Somehow, she found a way. In the dark days of February 1942 her poetry sustained Leningrad's inhabitants. 'We listened to her every day,' Elena Martilla said. 'It was a light for us at the end of a long, dark tunnel.' Berggolts spoke from the heart, and created a powerful, intimate rapport with her audience. 'I will talk to you during the artillery fire,' she said, 'lit by its glow . . . What can the enemy do – destroy, kill, that's it . . . but I can love. It is not possible to count the treasures of my soul. I will love and I will live.' 'There was a remarkable nobility about those verses,' Maia Babich recalled. 'They really shook us out of our instinctive, animal drive only for food.'

When it no longer seemed possible to go on, some uncovered an extraordinary, unexpected resilience. At the beginning of February Elena Martilla was fainting six or seven times a day, and she hardly had any strength left. She could walk only with the help of a cane and, although just eighteen years old, she now looked like an old woman. When she went out on to the streets, she encountered more dead bodies than people left alive. 'I was really afraid I was going to die,' she remembered.

One night she felt an overwhelming urge to lie down. It was a dangerous urge, and Martilla sensed that if she succumbed to it she would not get up again. There was a saying among people in besieged Leningrad: 'Don't go to bed – it's dangerous!' If you had a sort of 'animal instinct' that you were dying, you must not go to sleep. You had to try and resist it. Martilla wanted to resist, but she was feeling desperately tired. A bitter despondency swept over her. Everything seemed hopeless: she would die young, not fighting for some noble cause, but in her own bed, a useless, worthless death. She started to cry. But then her mood changed. She became angry, and the anger galvanised her. 'If I am going to die,' she thought, 'let me die with dignity, as an artist, with a brush in my hand.'

Martilla realised she would have to find a subject to engage her interest powerfully. She decided to paint a self-portrait. There was little light in the room – the kerosene lamp was weak – but she took out paper, blue paint and a brush and, looking at herself in a mirror, started to paint what she could see. The room grew colder and darker, and Martilla's brushstrokes became more hesitant. Inexorably, everything was slowing down. She could not find the strength to go on, and she paused, motionless, in the freezing silence. Then a last, defiant thought entered her head. 'Maybe people will realise Leningraders do not give up that easily.' Making a supreme effort, she began to paint again.

Looking up from her picture, Martilla saw a faint glimmer of light through a gap in the curtain. Morning was approaching – a morning she had thought she would not live to see. 'I felt a wonderful joy and serenity,' she remembered. 'And then I said out loud: "I did not die. I will not die. I will live." As I repeated this, I felt a surge of strength, as if some force was permeating every cell of my being.' Martilla knew something had fundamentally changed. Each day, she felt a growing power and certainty within her, a conviction that she would survive. A week later, she painted another self-portrait. 'In the first I looked at myself through the eyes of death,' Martilla said. 'Now I wanted to celebrate being alive.'

In the blockaded city, others understood what Martilla had gazed upon. Alexandra Ivanova saw all six members of her family die in quick succession, and the corpse of her three-year-old nephew was so wizened he scarcely looked human any more. She felt the futility of trying to stay alive. But looking at the bodies of those she had loved, something extraordinary happened. The sense of hopelessness vanished, and in its place came a sudden self-belief. 'My life is valuable,' she said to herself, in astonished recognition. 'I can help others.'

The horror of the siege warped human relations, but in the midst of starvation the family bond stayed strong, and many mothers gave all they could to their children. Sometimes, simple words of encouragement held enormous power. Twelve-year-old Andrei Krukov adored classical music, and had always wanted to be a violinist, but this dream now seemed lost for ever. But one morning his mother praised his musical skill, and then asked him not to stop practising. She knew that children in besieged Leningrad were sometimes allowed to give short music recitals to hospital patients or front-line troops, and would be rewarded with a little bread. 'If I don't survive this,' she said with loving concern, 'I want you to have something to fall back on.'

Food rations were measured exactly, but at the border between life and death hidden resources within the body were released, resources that medical science could not easily determine. Leningrad doctor Mikhail Chernorutsky called the variations in this state *vita minima*, 'life at the limit'. He said frankly: 'Something else is coming into play, something that we don't understand.'

In a Leningrad hospital five-year-old Peter Tsvetkov was dying. His breathing was extremely irregular and he could no longer eat anything. His mother, beside herself with despair, tried to find extra nourishment for him nevertheless. She sold her winter coat on the black market, and got him a little bread, butter and sugar. She spread the butter and sugar on top of a piece of white bread and tried to feed him. But he was so wasted that he lacked the strength to chew. Yet he could feel his mother's presence. Making a huge effort, he ran his tongue along the top of the bread, and began to suck. He wanted to respond to her – and this tiny movement was enough. The taste of butter and sugar awoke something. He began to recover.

Thousands were dying every day, but beleaguered Leningrad had somehow stayed alive. 'That winter, death looked straight into our eyes,' Berggolts told her fellow Leningraders, 'and stared long, without faltering. It wanted to hypnotise us, like a boa constrictor hypnotises its intended victim, stripping him of his will and subjugating him. But those who sent us so much death miscalculated. They underestimated our voracious hunger for life.'

9

The Symphony

Finding the Will to Survive

One morning in late February 1942 Lidiya Okhapkina walked down to the Neva river, following the tramped-out path through the snowdrifts. She was struck by how much the city had changed. Familiar houses had been reduced to ruins. Many had broken windows, dark holes reminiscent of eye sockets; others were missing parts of their structure, with people living in what was still left standing. A five-storey building on one street corner was on fire, and a passer-by told her that recently installed stoves – known as *burzhuikas* – had caused it, and that the house had been burning for three days. Odd bits of furniture, beds, broken cupboards, lay piled up outside. There was no wind, and blue flames crawled unhurriedly around the windows, as if caressing its frames and sills.

The Nevsky Prospect, Leningrad's most famous thoroughfare, was almost deserted, and lay under a thick blanket of snow. Its houses were all damaged, and the few remaining windows were boarded up. Trams and trolley buses stood motionless, covered with snow. 'The city has been injured, terribly injured, like a man badly wounded in battle,' Okhapkina thought. 'It is living such a difficult life. But Leningrad is still alive – it is refusing to die. People have clung on to hope and have not lost their determination. A time has to come – sooner or later – when this nightmare, this horror, will come to an end.'

Elena Martilla also surveyed the scene around her. 'On Leningrad's frozen streets,' she wrote, 'gripped by a severe frost, death has reaped an immense harvest.' She was struck by the terrifying silence, 'as if you have been lowered deep into a well, the shaft filled with earth, and everyone has gone far away.' And yet there remained the pulse of the metronome, ticking through speakers on street corners, and from the transmitter dishes in people's homes. Martilla listened to its sound – distant, weak, but living, 'like the pulse of a patient fighting for life in the silence of a hospital ward. The sound reverberates in the hearts of those awaiting a miracle – recovery.'

Red Army soldier Sergei Milyaev paid a visit to his family in Leningrad. 'The city of death greeted me and took leave of me with corpses, darkness, dirt and silence, sinister silence,' he wrote. Yet he was struck by the faces of some of the people in the streets, 'frowning, emaciated, yet firmly courageous'. Milyaev heard horrific stories, and said sadly: 'Much of what has happened here is deeply shocking. But a titanic fight for life is taking place. I feel the heroic, gasping breaths of this great city.'

Leningrad's steadfast courage would now be tested even further. On 18 February 1942 Nikolai Gorshkov recorded a most alarming development: 'There are a lot of diseases appearing within the city – many related to the digestive system, causing chronic diarrhoea – and these are finishing off its already exhausted inhabitants. Cases of typhus are also occurring, because of the absence of water and steam baths, and the impossibility of keeping clean.' Typhus had broken out at a children's home on Mozhaisky Street, and another case had been reported at one of Leningrad's hospitals. Gorshkov believed the city authorities were culpable: 'In January they at least gave out 250 grams of soap to each person. But in February there has been nothing. They say the factories haven't made enough. Today quarantine will be imposed on the city, in an attempt to prevent infection spreading.'

There was still a chance of containing the spread of typhus, but Leningrad was already facing a dysentery epidemic. At the beginning of March Nadia Makarova sent an anguished letter to her sister, describing its onset within the city:

> It is very hard to write, but I need to tell you the whole truth, and let you know how things really are. After two weeks of sickness and diarrhoea our dear and beloved mother died. Her illness was horrendous. We have a most dangerous epidemic in Leningrad – a form of

> 'starvation diarrhoea' – and everyone is dying like flies. Three days before mother died I lost little Misha and Fedya. I now have only two of my children left, but both are suffering terribly, and their fate will surely be the same as the others. They are very weak and ill, and we have nothing to help them with.
>
> The situation was hard enough before this disease came. For five months we have been living like beggars. My feet are swollen like barrels and I have awful kidney problems. I have become an old woman. And Misha and Fedya died so terribly – if you could see what we are going through here your hair would stand on end.

The combination of starvation and dysentery was fatal, and the death toll now rose higher and higher. By early March Anna Ostroumova reckoned it had reached between 20,000 and 25,000 people a day, and quite understandably she found the figure totally overwhelming. 'A headlong, irrepressible rush to destruction,' she wrote vividly. 'Some horrible, violent whirlwind has landed on earth, and everything has become mixed up in it and started to spin. Leningraders are choking in its black smoke, fire and snowstorm.' Olga Freidenberg put it more simply: 'It was a flood of death that no one could handle.'

Leningrad's inhabitants had faced air raids, artillery bombardment and starvation, and this new danger was almost too much to bear. 'Dear Aunt Natasha,' a young boy named Slavik wrote, 'This is a salute from Leningrad. I have lived through so much in this war. The bombings, hunger, all the filth – and now we have epidemics too.' Yet an outbreak of dysentery, although deeply frightening, was almost inevitable – for, after the breakdown of the city's sewage system at the end of January, human waste was simply flung into streets and courtyards, and the river water had become contaminated.

People were no longer able to withstand the onslaught. 'Before she became ill, starvation had already broken mother's strength,' Nadia Makarova wrote. 'Things have been so terrible for us. There has been shelling every day, we are without water, light and firewood, and we are constantly hungry. What a good life we are leading!' Nine-year-old Valentina Grekova lived on Labour Square, near St Isaac's Cathedral, where enemy shelling and bombing was particularly intense. 'It was wearing us down,' she said. 'We all expected to be killed by German artillery – we even nicknamed our square the "Labour of Death" – but it was dysentery that finished off my father.' Many others were struck down with him. On 2 March Dmitry Likhachev's own father died, and as he took the body to the mortuary he was overtaken by a procession of vehicles carrying corpses, piled high, with some stacked upright:

> I recall one lorry that was loaded with bodies frozen into fantastic positions. They had been petrified, it seemed, in mid-speech, mid-shout, mid-grimace, mid-leap. Hands were raised, eyes open. I remember the body of a woman: naked, brown, thin, upright . . . The lorry was going at speed, leaving her hair streaming in the wind, and behind her, the other bodies were bouncing and jumping as they went over the potholes in the road. It looked as if she was making a speech – calling out to them, waving her arms – a ghastly, defiled corpse with open, glassy eyes.

It was now almost impossible to find a coffin, or arrange a decent burial. On 9 March Nikolai Gorshkov wrote: 'Heaps and heaps of bodies are piling up every day outside the mortuaries. They are digging fresh mass graves with excavators.' Nadia Makarova wanted to lay her mother to rest with some semblance of dignity:

> We were unable to bury her separately, but had to lay her in a mass grave, and there were at least 3,000 bodies in it already. Everybody seems to be doing this now – you can't get a coffin anywhere. Those willing to dig separate graves are charging more than a kilo of bread for them. We just didn't possess that amount of food. We gave what little we could simply so that mother could be put next to Fedya and Masha, in the same corner of one vast trench, full of corpses.

Mortuary staff no longer showed any respect for the dead – there were simply too many of them. When Ivan Yakushin's uncle died, his father did manage an improvised coffin, using a couple of boxes, and he carried it to the mortuary on a sledge. The workers were warming themselves by a fire, and they told him that they had no intention of digging a separate grave. Abruptly, they pulled the body out of its fragile casing, slung it on to a large pile of corpses, and then thanked him for bringing in more firewood.

Sofia Buriakova had been forced to bury her father in a large communal pit, leaving him covered only by a sheet. As she walked away, she felt he was staring at her in silent reproach. She saw rows of bodies in each trench, hundreds in every line. The workers carried new arrivals in on stretchers, walking over the dead that had been placed there earlier. 'Having grown numb from this work,' she observed angrily, 'the gravediggers have lost all sense of human decency.' At the entrance Buriakova had been greeted by a corpse, propped upright, with a cigarette jammed in its mouth. A frozen arm, encrusted with ice, was pointing the way to the mass graves.

The city had become a living nightmare, and Nadia Makarova found herself bursting into tears all the time. 'I think all my children will die,' she wrote in anguish. 'I am going crazy.' The dysentery outbreak accelerated the death rate, and also represented a psychological tipping point, when people, already stretched to the limits of human endurance, were simply unable to take any more. Once again, there was a surge of cannibalism within the city.

Twelve-year-old Valentina Rothmann had volunteered to help remove bodies from abandoned apartments. She was uncovering more and more of them, and to her horror she found many had their buttocks cut away. Seeing one row of disfigured corpses, Rothmann felt that she was witnessing a grotesque harvest. She could not help shuddering – for she knew that remaining bits of flesh were being torn off and sold on Leningrad's black market.

Rothmann's young group of helpers lacked the strength to carry the growing number of dead out of the buildings. In desperation, they began tipping corpses from upper-storey windows, but the bodies disintegrated on impact with the mounds of snow and ice below. Rothmann, weakened by starvation, had to scrape up the mangled remains and load them on to a cart.

The dead were engulfing the city, their bodies hacked and dismembered by the crazed living. 'This is what the end of winter brought us,' Viktor Kozlov said. 'Decomposing bodies lay in the streets. Severed legs were found with all the meat cut off them. Bits of human bodies were uncovered in bins; the corpses of women with their breasts cut off were dragged up from basements. The dead met the half-dead, for some people were injuring themselves in their desperation for food, even cutting off and eating their own buttocks.' It seemed as if Leningrad's last hellish moments were at hand. Seven-year-old Natalia Stroganova remembered taking a walk with her father. Corpses were being dragged out of buildings, and ahead of them was a big sledge, piled high with bodies, loosely tied with rope. Heads, arms and legs dangled from its sides. 'You needed to see this,' her father said starkly.

The threat of infectious disease had been anticipated by the Germans. As early as 7 October 1941, when Hitler stated that the capitulation of Leningrad should not be accepted, his justification was the 'extremely high risk of epidemics, which are expected within the city'. On 4 November the German high command also emphasised the likelihood of epidemics breaking out in Leningrad, making clear that its policy of blockading and starving the city's inhabitants removed the risk 'of any disease being transmitted to German troops or occupied territories to the rear'.

Army Group North now watched for signs of disease, knowing that its effect on a population already weakened by starvation would be catastrophic. On 18 February 1942 the first outbreak of smallpox was carefully recorded. Its intelligence was accurate, for on the same day Nikolai Gorshkov had also noted its deadly arrival within the city.

Hitler began commenting, in private conversation, on the extent of cannibalism in Leningrad. News had reached him that the death toll in the city now exceeded one million. The Wehrmacht believed Leningrad's total collapse was imminent. At the beginning of March 1942 Radio Berlin interviewed a deserting Red Army officer, who painted a horrific picture of conditions inside the Nazi blockade. 'I come to you straight from Leningrad,' Soviet Lieutenant Sokolovsky announced to his German audience. 'The city is on its last legs. Putrefied corpses are now its main source of food. The remaining inhabitants eat meat aspic made out of glue and human flesh.'

All hinged on whether the diseases could be contained. 'Spring was approaching,' said Evgeny Moniushko, 'and with it, the threat of a wholesale epidemic hung over the city. There were many corpses under the snow, and the drifts had masses of human waste poured on them – all would become a source of infection once they had melted. And once that happened, the city would die.' Vera Inber wrote: 'At this moment, with the approach of spring, the fate of Leningrad is being decided. One is left breathless with horror at the thought of typhus or dysentery sweeping unchecked through the city. Who would have the strength to survive it?'

On 8 March – a traditional holiday – Leningrad's female population was ordered out on the streets by the nervous city authorities, and told to begin a massive clean-up operation. 'Today is Women's Day,' Vasily Vladimirov wrote in his diary, 'and to celebrate it Mother has been out clearing the snow, joined by masses of other housewives.' This was just a beginning. By 15 March over 100,000 tottering inhabitants, mostly women, were doing several hours of street cleaning a day, and the number continued to rise.

This was an astonishing mass effort. One journalist reported: 'Everybody was turning out – there were housewives, schoolchildren, professors, doctors, musicians, old men and women. One would appear with a broom, another with a crowbar, a third with a child's sledge. Many hardly had the strength to drag their legs, yet five people would harness themselves to one tiny sledge, and pull and pull, trying to clear the mountains of accumulated waste.' Leningrad poet Nikolai Tikhonov wrote: 'It was a stupendous feat, performed by people worn down by months of starvation. The Augean Stables were child's play in comparison.'

'We had to liberate our streets from millions of cubic feet of frozen dirt and refuse,' Kyra Petrovskaya remembered. 'All around me were women and children. They moved slowly, for they were malnourished and weak – and I couldn't visualise how the city could be cleaned by such an enfeebled workforce. But then there is strength in numbers. There were tens of thousands of people like us, chopping, digging, scarping, clearing tiny patches in the overall chaos of snow and ice.'

Elena Martilla felt that a decisive moment had arrived: 'We were all surrounded by these huge, frozen piles of waste. Whole buildings were enclosed by dirty snow mounds, some reaching as high as the second storey. And now, anyone who was able to walk or even crawl got outside and began working, using sledges, barrels, bits of wood, and whatever else came to hand.' Martilla and some other teenage girls attempted to clear a courtyard of ice-encrusted refuse. They had not been issued with shovels or pickaxes; all they had for this task were some strips of plywood. Unsurprisingly, they were unable to make much progress. 'At the beginning, many people were unenthusiastic,' Martilla said. 'We were all so weak, it seemed we could accomplish very little. And the authorities were cruel and heartless. They arrested one old woman who collapsed through sheer exhaustion, because she did not return to the clean-up post the following day.'

The starving deeply resented well-fed city officials ordering them to do hard manual labour. Lidiya Tager, director of a ballet school, was married to the head of provisions for the entire Leningrad Front. During the terrible winter she had appeared at the school in a succession of expensive new dresses, shoes and hats. Vera Kostrovitskaya, one of the ballet teachers, started counting them: she saw at least four different fur coats, twenty dresses and innumerable items of expensive jewellery. While ballet students were dying of starvation, Tager was blatantly profiteering, selling or exchanging food that rightfully belonged to the city's inhabitants to acquire luxury items. Chubby-cheeked, with a glowing, rosy complexion, she now ordered her emaciated, hollow-faced charges to get down to work. When some appeared a little reluctant, she threatened them with the loss of their bread-ration cards. 'Hypocrites, sluggards!' she railed, before grabbing a shovel and vigorously miming the actions of digging and throwing. Then she stood there and watched as everyone laboured for hours.

Leningrad's leadership was unhappy with the initial results. On 26 March it announced sternly: 'Up to now the clean-up campaign has been completely unsatisfactory. The snow and dirt have been removed from less than half of the city's houses. Some streets are still impassable to pedestrian and vehicle traffic because of piles of heaped-up ice. Hundreds of neglected garbage pits have become a real source of infection . . .'

Dmitry Likhachev remarked pointedly: 'Most of the city's inhabitants had begun to clean the streets and clear the refuse with bodies so weakened they could barely grip a spade, let alone wield it.' He had just returned from a visit to the Smolny, noticing that the headquarters of Leningrad's government was completely covered in camouflage netting and that people inside it appeared extremely well fed. He was received by an official who looked plump and healthy, whereas Likhachev had found it difficult even to climb the stairs. The aroma of cooked food was everywhere. 'The whole place smelled like a dining room,' he said in disgust.

However, the popular mood was beginning to change. The whole city was working, and as it did so it started to find sustenance in its shared undertaking. 'We had declared war on dirt,' Elena Martilla said proudly, 'and through this declaration, the isolated and inactive regained a sense of purpose.' In their midst were clusters of people who had never given up hope.

The staff of Leningrad's Public Library slowly but steadily shifted the large pile of refuse in the street outside their building. The library had stayed open even after it had lost its water supply, electricity and heating and the last of its reading rooms was forced to close. Readers congregated in the director's office, which was heated by a small stove and lit by a kerosene lamp. The staff continued searching for books in the library stacks with burning pieces of wood in their hands. They also did their best to answer people's queries, even finding a recipe for making candles in an eighteenth-century manuscript.

Elena Martilla had sketched the gaunt faces of those who congregated there, still ordering books when dizzy with starvation sickness. Popular topics for library searches included a study of just and unjust wars, the love of a Russian soldier for his regiment, the representation of Germans in nineteenth-century literature and scurvy and vitamin deficiency. Martilla added a dedication to the staff, 'for their unshakeable defiance in the cold days of the siege'. They had kept firewatch, repaired the roof when it was hit by artillery shelling and fought to preserve the city's wealth in books. 'People came to the library to read, even when weak from cold and exhaustion,' Faina Borovskaya recalled. 'Some died in their places, with a book propped up in front of them. We would carry the bodies outside, hoping that the lorries would take them away, but increasingly they were simply left in the snow.'

Outside Leningrad's Hermitage Museum the accumulated filth was also being tackled. The clearing contingent was headed by Pavel Gubchevsky, who had been given a complete discharge from army service because of a serious heart problem, and was now head of the Hermitage's museum guard. Some of the Hermitage's treasures had been evacuated, some moved to the ground floors or basement for safekeeping, some simply left where they were. The guards kept watch over a display area ten miles long, with 1,057 rooms in the Winter Place alone.

Gubchevsky recalled his workforce: 'It was composed mostly of ladies of fifty-five years of age or more, including some who were over seventy. By the spring of 1942 many had died and others were in hospital, and I could count on about thirty of them.' But these thirty elderly ladies stood guard over the buildings of the Hermitage, at the gates and doorways and in the rooms, round the clock. They removed debris after artillery shelling, and now, seizing crowbars, shovels and brooms, they advanced into the streets and began clearing the mounds of snow, ice and dirt. Leningrad's inhabitants watched their efforts in stunned astonishment – then more and more of them pitched in to help.

On 27 March Vera Inber wrote: 'The entire population of the city – everyone who is capable of holding a spade or crowbar – is cleaning the streets. The task is rather like having to put a soiled North Pole back in order: all is chaos – blocks of ice, frozen hummocks of rubbish, stalactites of sewage.' But an indomitable spirit was coming to life, and everyone was beginning to feel it. It was not disease which was sweeping the city, but a determination to survive.

Eleven-year-old Fima Ozerkin said forcefully: 'Nobody ordered us to clean our courtyard; we did it of our own free will. Have you noticed that the large snow mound has gone? That is because Tolya and I have cleared it up. And tomorrow we shall do some more clearing.'

Vera Inber was moved to see pieces of clean pavement reappearing on quaysides and bridges. After the long winter months of suffering, they seemed strangely beautiful. She noticed a woman, yellow-faced and badly swollen, wearing a smoke-blackened fur coat that hadn't been taken off all winter. The woman was leaning on a crowbar, gazing wonderingly at a scrap of asphalt that she had just cleaned. She paused for a moment. And then she went back to work. Elena Martilla believed that this collective effort was the turning point: 'As they worked, people passed on their strength to each other. And through this strength came an affirmation of our common cause. We would defy Hitler's cruel order that our city should be erased from the earth. It would stay habitable. We were proud to be called Leningraders.'

A new energy was surging through the city. An inoculation programme was introduced and more than 400 disinfecting points were set up. Vitamin C was extracted from pine needles, and a drink was manufactured to combat scurvy. At the beginning of April Leningrad's power generators were repaired. And on 15 April the trams started running again. Vera Pavlova was a nurse at one of the city's hospitals:

> There had been no water, no light, no electricity – and almost everyone had been suffering terribly from starvation diarrhoea. Many of our patients were on the verge of death. And then one morning we all heard the sound of a tram bell clanging. There was a gasp of astonishment, and then everyone who could move got over to the window, some crawling on their hands and knees. We all looked out. The tram that had stood immobile on the Bolshoi Prospect all winter was now sailing past us. If only you could have seen the joy there was in that room! People came back to life, shouting to each other in their happiness: 'Lads, it's victory, it's victory!'

All winter fourteen-year-old Vladimir Zandt had been drawing scenes from besieged Leningrad, enclosed by a noose. But now the noose was jettisoned. Instead, he coloured an expansive picture of the first trams running, and underneath it wrote: 'Despite all the losses, all the deaths, the city is coming alive again.' Corporal Falkenhorst, a captured German prisoner, said: 'I began to lose my faith in Hitler when I heard the sound of tramcars on Leningrad's streets, on the morning of 15 April 1942.'

Yet Soviet soldiers around the city were still suffering terribly. On the Nevsky bridgehead the battered Red Army force had clung on throughout the winter. Thousands of soldiers had been pushed on to this tiny scrap of land, on the eastern side of the Neva, as Zhdanov ordered them to make one pointless assault after another. Towards the end of April there were only forty or so left, and they were all badly wounded. They had no radio contact with army HQ.

'There was a grim camaraderie among us,' Alexander Sokolov recalled. 'We all knew each other's names. We sang, told jokes. We had been ordered to hold the bridgehead at all costs, but we had only a handful of men left to do it.' The Germans were intensifying their bombardment and preparing for a final assault. Sokolov was the strongest swimmer and it was agreed that he would try to cross the Neva and get a message to Zhdanov. It simply said: 'Help us!' On reaching the far bank Sokolov lost consciousness, but he was found by a passing patrol and taken to a military hospital. The NKVD interrogated him, found his message, and sent it to the Smolny. Zhdanov sent a message back. He instructed the tiny force to hold on – another major offensive would be launched from the bridgehead at the beginning of May. On 27 April the Germans overran their position.

On Leningrad's Field of Mars cabbages and potatoes were being planted. Vegetable gardens were springing up everywhere. And while they waited for them to grow, people ate weeds and wild grasses to satisfy their hunger for something green. 'Grass, grass, grass,' Igor Chaiko wrote. 'The whole city is eating different kinds of grass. At the garden fences children are calling out to each other, hauling grass through the rails, eating it as if they were rabbits. Children with skeletal figures and faces of old people. The winter has left the impression of a grave, a dark, horrible, enclosed space, out of which we have climbed, almost by accident. We are waking from a state of stupor, deep underground.'

When the spring thaw came, nine-year-old Veronika Nikandorova recalled going out to the edge of the city with her brother, to look for food. 'There was barbed wire around the fields, with red rag hanging from it, a warning that the area was mined,' she said. 'But we took the risk anyway – after the winter, we weighed so little that we didn't think we would detonate anything. So we climbed over the wire and began to walk across the minefield, carrying our little wicker baskets. My brother walked ahead of me, and when the heavy clay stuck to me, and I couldn't pull my feet out, he came back and helped me. We would see little pieces of cabbage, or some carrot left over from last year's harvest, and we picked up everything we could find. We took it home, washed it, and made a soup. My mother was in bed, in a bad way, so we took care of things.'

Others had no family left to help. Alexander Fadeev remembered meeting some of Leningrad's children at the end of April 1942. 'Their faces and eyes told me more than could be gathered from all the stories of the famine,' he wrote. The children that Fadeev saw had forgotten how to play, and kept to themselves. Often they were silent for hours on end. One lunchtime he visited an orphans' kindergarten, and saw a little girl putting bits of her bread aside. 'I want to remember my mummy,' she explained. 'We used to eat our bread together – she would always put a little piece aside for me. Now I want to do the same. I love her – and I want to remember her.'

In a torn child's notebook eleven-year-old Tanya Savicheva had recorded the death of each member of her family. On 13 May, at 7.30 a.m., when her mother passed away, she wrote: 'The Savichevs died. All died. Only Tanya remains.' Elena Martilla knew Tanya, and found out about the contents of her diary: 'She lived on Vasilevsky Island, very close to me,' she remembered. 'When Tanya lost everyone she became deranged with grief. She would clutch at a small house plant, which had only a few withered leaves left, and was almost dead. Somehow, it seemed to remind her of her family. She would stand by the stove, swaying from side to side, holding it close to her, in a terrible trance. She was trying to bring it back to life.'

Yet, amid the agony, hope was returning. Special dietary canteens were opening up in the city, to provide additional nourishment. The diary of kindergarten teacher Nina Zakharyina reflected a growing sense of optimism. On 6 May she recorded: 'My neighbour went outside the city and returned with a bouquet of dandelions. We boiled them – and then ate our fill.' They subsequently tried burdock root – again boiling it. 'Delicious,' Zakharyina exclaimed happily, 'not even bitter.' She was setting up a 'kitchen garden' in a box on her window sill, and queuing up for dill and lettuce seeds. On 10 May she wrote: 'You can feel the revival of the city. Trams now run regularly along the streets – and there are plenty of people in them.'

Dmitry Likhachev also made a 'kitchen garden'. 'We turned our dining-room table upside down, unscrewed the legs, then filled it with soil from the square outside. We put it by the window and planted our radishes. We ate the leaves as a salad, for the vitamins. People dug up dandelion roots, stripped off oak bark, ate grass porridge – what didn't they do! The starvation diarrhoea had struck so many people, but miraculously, there were no further epidemics.'

The German menace remained. On 24 May the enemy targeted Zakharyina's kindergarten. 'Two hours of artillery shelling,' she recorded. 'The children stayed huddled in the corridors.' The ice road had now been replaced by ferries running across the open waters of Lake Ladoga, and Vera Rogova was helping to evacuate Leningrad's orphans. Their boat was waiting at the jetty, clearly marked with the Red Cross, but one little girl was too terrified to board it. She clung fiercely to Rogova, calling out, 'Mother, mother!' It was heartbreaking. Eventually Rogova had to pull her away. 'I am not your mother,' she said firmly. The boat began to move across the lake, and then it disappeared from sight. Suddenly a swarm of

German planes appeared, and there was a loud explosion. Several hours later, Rogova saw rows of white children's bonnets drifting back towards the shoreline.

On 29 May Nina Zakharyina wrote: 'What beautiful colours nature has – spring green is all around us, trees are in bloom, everything is crystal clear and sharp. Then the artillery shelling begins again. How cruel it is – beauty, then death and mutilation.' But the following day she felt able to say emphatically: 'There is shelling every day, but it is spring nonetheless, and people are rousing themselves and becoming more joyful. You can see women sitting at open windows, or on park benches. Some have started knitting; others are using make-up again, and finding fashionable items of clothing – resilient Leningraders!'

At the beginning of June Vera Inber took an evening stroll through the city. 'The silver barrage balloons rose lightly in the pale, pink sky until they seemed to dissolve into it,' she remembered. 'The lime trees along the Botanical Gardens by the river have already begun to bloom, and their scent deadens the smell of decay from the rubbish, which is not yet completely cleared.' Suddenly, Inber wondered: 'Could it be true that happiness will return again – that mankind will wake up one morning and find that Hitler isn't there any more?'

Within Leningrad, life and death intertwined. On 23 June Igor Chaiko recorded starkly: 'At the university wall, at 1.00 p.m., a woman is dying. She is lying on her back, stretched out – her eyes wide open, staring at passers-by. Her feet are like two thin sticks. She has a red and white floral bag under her head, and her hand is clutching at its string. It is a bright, sunny day.' But Chaiko also remembered the rejuvenating power of nature, as the seasons changed, and spring turned into early summer:

> I didn't have much strength, but I wanted to live. I found hope in the warmth of the sun's rays. In the early morning, I would walk to Krestovsky Island, and gather dandelions and nettles to make a soup. And that is how I started my 'campaign for life'. I had to make a real effort to do this – it was hard to even bend, let alone dig. One day, when I reached the island, I saw a group of small boys sitting on a

> tree branch, like a flock of sparrows, hungrily devouring the leaves. I found some linden flowers and began to pull them up, and as I did so, I experienced something that I had never felt in a kitchen or restaurant. I felt a wave of nourishment rising up from the earth. And then, suddenly, I understood – the land was restoring us to life.

Alexandra Amosova had a similar realisation. 'We gathered sackfuls of grass and sorrel, and picked all kinds of herbs,' she recalled. 'There was sunshine, light, and somewhere in the sky a lark was singing. I had a strong urge to lie down on the ground and kiss it. I wanted to kiss the earth that was giving us everything; to kiss the earth that was willing to save us.'

For many, a 'campaign for life' began by celebrating Leningrad's unique cultural heritage. The performing arts had started to blossom again within the city. 'Listening to music gave the city's inhabitants a form of escape, and an opportunity to rise above hardship and suffering,' Viktor Orlovsky said. 'Even when the bread ration had been reduced to 125 grams, some would exchange their daily meal for a ticket to a classical concert.'

Galina Vishnevskaya attended an opera as the city started its astonishing recovery. The temperature was still close to freezing point: 'Leningraders, who had suffered a frightful famine and a bitter winter, sat there in their fur coats and caps,' Vishnevskaya remembered. 'As the artists sang, their breath steamed in the cold air. The thrill I felt was not simply the pleasure of the performance – it was pride in my resurrected people, in the great art which compelled those human shadows – the emaciated musicians, singers, the audience – to come together in that great opera house, beyond whose walls air-raid sirens wailed and shells exploded. Truly, man does not live by bread alone.'

As the weather grew warmer, more and more people came to these events. 'For the first time, I went to a concert at the Philharmonic,' Igor Chaiko wrote, 'and I enjoyed it mightily. The hall was completely full.' Galina Babinskaya rejoiced in the queues at newly opened cinemas and theatres, the jazz that was starting up in the gardens of the Young Pioneer Palace and the classical concerts being held at the Philharmonic Hall. She exclaimed joyfully: 'Those who have not spent the winter here, who have not endured what we have endured, cannot understand the happiness of Leningraders when they see the rebirth of their beloved city.'

It was extraordinary to witness so much taking place. 'Before the war, I hardly ever went to concerts at the Philharmonic, or enjoyed plays at the Kirov Theatre,' Pavel Gubchevsky confessed. 'I took them all for granted. What a fool I was! Now I understand the work that goes into making such performances. The theatre has to be warm and lit up, the musicians have to assemble, the ballet dancers have to come together, the public too – and there are a thousand other "have to's". I had never appreciated the wonder of what was around me – in fact, I had hardly even noticed it.'

In the harsh conditions of the siege, which isolated Leningrad's inhabitants and threw them on their own resources, culture became a lifeline. It deeply touched people, and by doing so became a powerful source of affirmation. On 28 July Peter Kotelnikov decided to visit an exhibition of paintings. 'I do not feel competent to judge their artistic merit,' he admitted. He just felt it was incredible they were there at all. 'We are besieged – and yet we organise exhibitions,' he enthused. 'This is amazing. I do not think ancient Troy or Carthage, or the cities besieged by Attila and Alaric, ever put on painting exhibitions.'

The performing arts occupied a special place in Leningrad's revival. 'There was a powerful energy flowing between artist and audience in the besieged city,' pianist Maria Yudina said, 'one that allowed them to rise above the day-to-day horror they all faced.' Nineteen-year-old Alexandra Ivanova, who saw her family die of dysentery, and briefly felt an utter despair, had not succumbed to it. Wanting to offer something to others, she was now conducting a forty-strong choir, and entertaining troops along the front. 'It meant far more to us than just singing,' Ivanova emphasised. 'It was the victory of the human spirit.'

For those that went on stage, and performed to others, the creative intention was all important. It needed to be a gift from the heart – for honesty and integrity had a genuine transforming power, and could lift morale; whereas lies and hypocrisy diminished it. Ballet director Lidiya Tager decided to put on a concert simply to gratify her vanity and look good in front of Leningrad's political elite. In April 1942 all her dancers had scurvy and their legs were too weak to perform the classics. But when told of their condition, she resorted to bullying, once again threatening to take away their food-ration cards, and the concert eventually took place.

Tager walked on stage to introduce the performance. Her hair was dyed red, and she was dressed up like a model. She spoke in an unnaturally loud voice, recounting her love for the children and telling everyone that all winter she had been saving lives. The general public was unable to hear this declaration of kindness – it had not been invited – and the audience consisted solely of representatives from the Smolny, the party organisations and the council of the arts. The concert commenced, with the starving dancers struggling to entertain the self-satisfied and well-fed.

'Yes, there was a "dying swan" and other such nonsense,' said Vera Kostrovitskaya angrily. She had to escort one of the boys on to the stage, and then lead him as he danced. He was perilously ill, but had been forced to perform, heavily made up – 'to make him look like a living person'. During the interval he collapsed into Kostrovitskaya's arms, vomiting up the small amounts of bread he had been given.

A Leningrad military hospital saw a rather different rendition from *Swan Lake*. Nine-year-old Allochka Ivanova was also weak from starvation – but she desperately wanted to do something to cheer up the wounded soldiers. A small show had been arranged and Allochka was given a chance to feature in it. Excitedly, she put on a white ballerina dress that her mother had made for her, and listened to the announcement being made in the hospital ward: 'A first grader will now perform the dance of the small swan,' the compère said. 'Unfortunately, we are unable to provide any music to accompany it.'

Allochka had seen *Swan Lake* as a small child and had always dreamed of being a ballerina. But she walked out into the middle of the room wearing a short dress and headband made from rolls of cotton used for bandages. She had white plimsolls on her feet and her legs looked like matchsticks. She was greeted with silence – the soldiers lay on their beds, indifferent to her arrival.

Allochka hummed the music to herself, and then she started to dance. The room was very, very cold. After a while she became dizzy, lost her balance and fell. She picked herself up, danced a little more, and then fell again. She got up slowly. The room was swaying in front of her eyes, but now the audience was behind her. Soldiers sat up, applauded and shouted out words of encouragement. As Allochka began to dance again, their cries became stronger and more insistent, carrying her forward. She was able to finish, and as the applause grew around her, Allochka passed out. Her mother carried her home on a sledge.

In March 1942 orchestral conductor Karl Eliasberg made a remarkable decision. He would perform Shostakovich's recently completed Seventh Symphony – which the composer had dedicated to his native Leningrad – in the besieged city.

Shostakovich had been evacuated from Leningrad in October 1941, and had finished his symphony at Kuibyshev at the end of December. Stalin, realising its enormous propaganda value, had given it his full backing, and on 5 March 1942 it was premiered by the Bolshoi Theatre Orchestra and broadcast all over the Soviet Union. There was huge demand for this work in the West, and a copy of Shostakovich's musical score made a remarkable journey, first being transported by plane to Teheran, then driven to Cairo, and finally flown on to New York. Eliasberg knew that a performance of the symphony in besieged Leningrad would generate colossal interest and moral support.

The Germans had deliberately isolated the city from the rest of Russia, creating a mood of despair and hopelessness. But they had underestimated Leningrad's will to resist. By choosing to perform the Seventh, Eliasberg threw down the gauntlet – the city's heroic struggle would now take place on a world stage.

But Karl Eliasberg was desperately short of musicians. The only orchestra left in the city was the Radio Committee's, and when the first rehearsal took place, on 30 March 1942, it lasted a mere twenty minutes – everyone was too weak to continue. Clarinettist Viktor Kozlov admitted: 'The wind instruments could not play properly; we simply hadn't got the strength to blow.' It was still very cold – pianist Alexander Kamensky tried to warm his hands up by placing two scorching bricks on both sides of the instrument to radiate some heat. Twenty-five musicians had assembled; eighty were needed. Eliasberg secured an improved food ration, set up a canteen for the orchestra and put out an appeal on the radio.

More musicians began to appear. Some had played for military bands in the army – they were nicknamed 'the crew': they would turn up at the rehearsal, play, and then return for duty at the front. Enthusiasm for Shostakovich's new symphony was muted. 'It was a very complex piece of work, and we were only rehearsing piecemeal,' Viktor Kozlov acknowledged. 'Most of us felt daunted by it. We might talk to the person next to us, but the topic of conversation was hunger and food – not music.'

Eliasberg was a hard taskmaster. He demanded absolute commitment, and was prepared to withdraw the food-ration cards of people who did not attend rehearsals. But he also understood that he could not create a symphony by threats and intimidation – he had to win his musicians' hearts. He pushed and cajoled the orchestra forward.

'Dear friends,' Eliasberg began. 'We are weak – but we must force ourselves to start work.' But when the first trumpeter's solo arrived, there was silence. 'I'm sorry, sir,' he said, 'I just don't have the strength in my lungs.' There was a pause, then Eliasberg replied, quietly but firmly, 'I think you do have the strength.' The trumpeter looked at him, picked up his instrument and began to play.

Eliasberg won the musicians over by his sheer dedication. He remained working on the score long after the others had left. He saw to it that everyone had copies of their parts, and then of the whole piece, and would work with individuals and small groups, ensuring that the playing got stronger. 'We performed the music in sections,' Ksenia Mattus remembered, 'slowly adding more and more of them.' In June the orchestra began rehearsing at the Philharmonic.

Outside, the White Nights had returned. On 21 June 1942, one day before the anniversary of the start of the war, a fourteen-year-old Leningrad schoolgirl wrote, 'I went to the cinema this evening – the film was passable, but I'm so frightened of my algebra exam I don't know what to do.' Her exams were safely negotiated. 'I went for a walk in the park with my friend,' she wrote a few days later. 'We met two very nice boys, cultured, polite, well dressed – well, you could not fault them.' Evgenia Shavrova was also making a conscious effort to turn away from the past. 'I am not going to write about that difficult winter,' she declared firmly. 'It is finished – and the memories are too painful and gloomy.' She joined a needlework group – and started to go to concerts.

Not everyone found it possible to move forward out of the darkness. On 22 June Georgi Knyazev was struggling to stay cheerful, even as signs of renewed hope burgeoned around him. 'Corn shoots have appeared in the vegetable gardens,' he began. 'I don't come across vehicles carrying corpses any more.' Then his tone changed. 'They probably don't take them at the time I go to work,' he mused. 'I see passers-by walking with such difficulty, some even supporting themselves against the walls of buildings.' During the winter months, Knyazev had simply focused on surviving without looking ahead – keeping going, one day at a time. Now his thoughts began to wander erratically. He was concerned about his wife – she seemed too thin – and he feared she was becoming ill. Yet he looked out of the window, and saw the bright sunshine, and little children playing in the sand. 'What's there to worry about?' he thought. 'I'm fighting and I'll keep fighting!'

For him, optimism was tempered by a profound sadness. Improved food rations gave those who had starved for months a renewed vitality – the opportunity to re-engage with life after a winter dulled by privation. And this is turn reconnected people to their feelings again. For some the experience was deeply painful. 'The more nature comes to life, the brighter the sun, the greener it gets, the more depressed I become,' Anna Likhacheva wrote. 'Spring has awakened frozen emotions and has cruelly reminded me of my private grief. I feel the death of my beloved son so intensely, it calls up such pain and despair, that I could cry day and night.'

The concert was scheduled for 9 August – a plucky gesture of defiance, for there was a renewed military threat against the city. The Germans had boasted they would capture the city on that date, and hold a victory party at the Astoria Hotel. 'We felt that we were fighting for our culture,' flautist Galina Yershova said. The Nazi war machine was rolling forward, and had ripped a large hole in Russia's southern front. That summer, Leningrad felt a special kinship with the port of Sevastopol – the home of the Black Sea Fleet – which was also under siege. But the Germans had deployed one of their best generals – Erich von Manstein – and a formidable artillery train against it, and were now on the brink of victory. 'There is great alarm in my heart,' Georgi Knyazev wrote on 28 June, 'for there is bitter fighting at Sevastopol.' The town fell a few days later.

The Wehrmacht had not taken Leningrad by famine; now they would launch a full-scale assault. The capture of Sevastopol had freed up additional troops and siege guns, which could now be transported north. 'Soon, the enemy will start another offensive against us,' Vera Inber wrote fearfully on 5 July. Her prediction proved correct.

On 12 July 1942 Hitler received Major-General Agustín Grandes at the Wolf's Lair. The Führer talked of the new order of fascism that would soon rule over Europe. Grandes was the commander of a division of Spanish volunteers – the Blue Division – which was fighting with Army Group North outside Leningrad. Hitler was in an ebullient mood, for he believed that victory against Russia was now within his grasp. At the beginning of August, in an operation code-named Northern Lights, the German high command brought up Manstein's victorious forces in readiness for a new onslaught. The Führer had become impatient – the destruction of Leningrad was taking too long. He wanted the city finished off.

Yet, as Tamara Korolkevich bought tickets for the concert, she deliberately put the Germans out of her mind. 'The event was unmissable,' she declared. 'This music had been dedicated to us, and to our city. Can you imagine the power of that?'

On the evening of 9 August 1942 the Philharmonic Hall blazed with light. 'I remember walking in with my oboe,' recalled Ksenia Mattus, 'feeling strangely happy for the first time since the blockade.' The hall was packed. 'We were stunned by the number that had turned out,' trombonist Mikhail Parfionov said. 'Some were in suits; some had come straight from the front. Most were haggard and emaciated. And we realised that these people were not just starving for food, but starving for music. We resolved to play the very best we could.'

Karl Eliasberg had been able to hold his first full rehearsal only three days earlier. But at 6.00 p.m. he spoke over the radio:

> Comrades – a great event in the cultural history of our city is about to take place. In a few minutes, you will hear for the first time the Seventh Symphony of our fellow citizen, Dmitry Shostakovich. He began his great composition in Leningrad, when the enemy – insane with hatred – first tried to break into our city. When the fascist swine were bombing and shelling us, everyone believed that the days of Leningrad were over. But this performance is proof of our spirit, courage, and readiness to resist!

As Eliasberg stepped out on to the stage, and turned to the orchestra, a strange, deep quietness fell on the hall. The conductor lifted his baton – and the symphony began. In the city's apartments and along the front-line trenches, civilians and soldiers gathered around their transmitter dishes relaying the radio broadcast of the concert. As the first movement built up to a powerful crescendo an artilleryman remembered: 'My unit were now listening to the symphony with their eyes closed. It seemed as if the cloudless sky above us had become a storm, bursting with music.'

Waves of emotion surged through the concert hall. In the first movement it was anger; in the second, sadness. As the symphony reached its conclusion, some members of the orchestra faltered – they were utterly exhausted. 'It was so loud and powerful that I thought I'd collapse,' Parfionov confessed. In a remarkable, spontaneous gesture, the entire audience rose to its feet, willing them to keep going.

At the finish there was silence. Someone at the back began clapping, and then there was a thunderous ovation. A little girl came up and presented Eliasberg with a bouquet of flowers. 'People just stood and cried,' Eliasberg recalled. 'They knew that this was not a passing episode but the beginning of something. We heard it in the music. The concert hall, the people in their apartments, the soldiers on the front – the whole city had found its humanity. And in that moment, we triumphed over the soulless Nazi war machine.'

10

Operation Spark

The Military Breakthrough

At the beginning of April 1942 the Leningrad Front received a new commander, Lieutenant-General Leonid Govorov. At first glance, Govorov was an unlikely leader, having neither the theatrical flamboyance of Voroshilov nor the brutal directness of Zhukov. He was taciturn, rarely smiled and had a quirky, disconcerting mannerism: after listening to reports, he would suddenly snarl the word 'Loafer!' When Leningrad's engineering chief Boris Bychevsky first heard this interjection he not unnaturally thought his competence was being called into question. 'You have no idea how difficult things are here!' he retorted angrily. But Govorov's response was quite involuntary. He had got accustomed to saying it as an officer in the tsarist army when dealing with its many lazy aristocrats and, although he was now a general fighting for the Bolshevik state, it had become an ingrained reflex action. He had never been able to shake off the habit.

Govorov's bark was worse than his bite. Underneath the diffident exterior, he was warm-hearted and caring, and he soon made an impact. Mikhail Neishtadt, the radio operator at the Leningrad Front HQ, was impressed by his humanity. 'In terms of leadership, Govorov was the complete opposite of a ruthless commander like Zhukov,' he observed. 'He was a cultured, intelligent man, always concerned to save his soldiers' lives.' The forty-five-year-old Govorov was also a brilliant artilleryman, possessing the skill to transform the military situation within the besieged city.

Govorov had become an artillery officer in 1917 and first served with the White Army during the Civil War, before switching sides and fighting for the Bolsheviks. In May 1920 he was awarded the prestigious Order of the Red Banner for holding the Crimean town of Kakhov against a large besieging force, and this engagement became a textbook model for the correct positioning of artillery in city defence. He subsequently rose to become the Soviet Union's leading theoretician in artillery tactics and his trademark use of concentrated fire from heavy gun emplacements broke the Mannerheim Line in the war with Finland, and proved vital in the defence of Moscow in December 1941.

Yet, quite remarkably, Govorov was not even a member of the Communist Party when he took over Leningrad's command, and only joined, belatedly, on 1 July 1942. His political loyalty had already come under scrutiny, and during the army purges in 1938 he had very nearly been arrested. But Voroshilov had intervened on Govorov's behalf – he was simply too good an artilleryman to lose.

Govorov's skills were sorely needed. At the beginning of April Stephan Kuznetsov could only describe the condition of Leningrad's soldiers as appalling. The defending force was ill fed and ravaged with dysentery – Kuznetsov himself had been down with starvation diarrhoea for the last three weeks. 'The army is in rags,' he wrote on 5 April, 'filthy and very, very hungry.' Stealing among the men was rife – and the commanding officers were held in contempt.

In contrast, the Germans remained confident. Army Group North also had a new leader, for Leeb had stepped down in January, to be replaced by Colonel-General Georg Küchler. And Küchler, a solid and methodical commander, was about to deliver a powerful blow against Leningrad. On 5 April, the Germans launched their biggest ever air raid on the city.

Past battles have a powerful resonance at times of war, and 5 April 1942 was the 700th anniversary of one of Russia's greatest successes – Alexander Nevsky's victory over the Teutonic Knights on Lake Peipus. In 1938 Sergei Eisenstein had celebrated Nevsky's achievement in a stirring film, and the battle on the frozen lake – with thousands of Red Army soldiers hired as extras – was its crowning moment. Since the site was relatively close to Leningrad, a battle commemoration had obvious propaganda value. The besieged city was too preoccupied with its mass cleaning effort to do very much.

'I have been asked to give some presentations on the "Battle on the Ice",' Alexander Boldyrev said rather wearily, 'although as an Orientalist it is hardly my area of expertise.' Ironically, it was not the Russians but the Germans who had given most thought to it. The Luftwaffe was planning a full-scale re-enactment – one in which it intended to reverse the original result.

Months of planning had gone into the operation. The Germans realised that heavy artillery fire from the Baltic Fleet was the key to Leningrad's defence. They also knew that, until the spring thaw, its ships were vulnerable, for the majority of them were locked in the iced-up estuary of the Neva. So they decided to launch a massive aerial bombardment, grimly codenamed Operation Ice Attack. Preparations were carried out with Teutonic thoroughness. One of the Baltic lakes was used as a training ground, and contours were drawn on the ice corresponding to the exact size and position of all the Soviet vessels. Spy planes reconnoitred the anti-aircraft defences. The Luftwaffe's assault would be delivered on the anniversary of Nevsky's triumph; its objective – to sink the entire fleet.

Soviet intelligence had picked up the German preparations, but Govorov had little time to react. He strengthened the anti-aircraft defences, placing small-calibre ack-ack batteries and machine guns around the ships to repulse attacks by enemy dive-bombers. On the evening of 4 April long-range enemy artillery began shelling Soviet gun emplacements and landing fields, and several hours later more than a hundred German bombers, with additional fighter support, took to the air and headed straight towards the ships.

Leningrad's night sky was suddenly lit by a colossal firefight. Teenage artist Vladimir Zandt took a considerable risk in getting up on to the roof of his house to sketch it. He saw the searchlights frantically swinging across the city, the shell bursts from anti-aircraft fire and then the German bombers diving towards their target, the beleaguered cruiser *Maxim Gorky*, trapped in the frozen ice of the Neva. The ship received a succession of hits. No fewer than fifty-six planes had breached the city's air defences, dropping a total of 230 bombs. On 5 April the Luftwaffe returned in force and inflicted substantial damage, putting a battleship, three cruisers and a destroyer out of action for months. Govorov had received a baptism of fire.

Küchler's attention was now diverted elsewhere. Stalin's high command had attempted to relieve the pressure on Leningrad by counter-attacking further south, at Lyuban, striking at the communication and supply lines of the besiegers, but these efforts ground to a halt, leaving the Soviet forces dangerously overextended. In the following months Küchler was able to surround and destroy the Second Shock Army of General Vlasov. Effective resistance by these battered troops ended on 25 June, and Vlasov was captured shortly afterwards. On 30 June a delighted Hitler promoted Küchler to field marshal.

In this difficult situation Govorov quickly found his feet. He believed that the low morale of his soldiers arose from an unnecessarily high casualty rate. He felt that too much was being asked of the infantry and that they were not being given adequate artillery protection and support. So he vetoed all attempts by Zhdanov to re-establish the Nevsky bridgehead, remarking bluntly: 'Nothing can be expected from that except a bloodbath.' Instead, he built up his artillery's striking capacity, setting up new observation posts and dramatically increasing ammunition stocks. As a result, the quota of shells available to battery commanders rose from 800 to 5,000 a month – and at last the Red Army gained some real firing power.

Govorov was also willing to help Karl Eliasberg. Hearing that the conductor urgently needed to recruit a larger orchestra, he offered his support, allowing Red Army musicians to join the rehearsals. And on 9 August 1942, several hours before the performance of Shostakovich's Seventh Symphony began, he ordered a barrage of shells to be fired at German gun emplacements. This was a most dramatic overture – Govorov had realised that lighting up the Philharmonic Hall for the concert would make it a target, and as a precaution he launched Operation Squall, blasting all the enemy's artillery positions. The Germans were unable to recover in time to disrupt the concert. Govorov understood that the symphony would lift the morale of the defenders and shake the enemy's confidence, so he set up radio transmitter dishes, ensuring that Red Army soldiers could easily listen to it, and also ordered the concert to be played on speakers pointing towards the German lines. But music alone would not save Leningrad.

Manstein was arriving with a formidable array of reinforcements, and the morale of his force, after the capture of Sevastopol, was sky-high. One of his soldiers, Gottlob Bidermann, said proudly: 'Extraordinary leadership skills, combined with personal bravery, instilled within the ranks the belief that we could accomplish almost anything.' Govorov would have to fight his way out of trouble.

On 27 August Manstein surveyed the city of Leningrad, which lay invitingly outstretched before him. He had been promoted to the rank of field marshal for his reduction of the stronghold of Sevastopol; now an even greater prize seemed within his grasp. 'One could pick out the big Kolpino works on the Neva [the Izhorsky Tractor Plant],' Manstein remembered, 'which was still turning out tanks. The Pulkovo [Marti] shipyards were also visible, and in the distance were the silhouettes of St Isaac's Cathedral, the pointed tower of the Admiralty, and the fortress of Peter and Paul.'

Manstein's plan was brutally simple. He intended to break the Soviet front-line position south of Leningrad, using massive artillery and air strikes, and then advance to the city's suburbs. He would swing a detachment eastwards, across the Neva, to encircle and destroy the Red Army forces between Leningrad and Lake Ladoga and to cut all supply routes. 'Thereafter', Manstein concluded briskly, 'it should be possible to bring about the rapid fall of the city.'

German heavy siege guns from Sevastopol were now arriving, and they began to pulverise Leningrad's southern defences. But Stalin's high command now made a wise decision. The obvious course of action was to go on to the defensive, and attempt to block Manstein's advance. But German strength on this sector of the front was greatest – and the Soviet forces would be decimated by the enemy's air and artillery power. So it decided to counter-attack instead, and threaten to break the German blockade of the city further east, along the shores of Lake Ladoga. Govorov would advance on a broad front across the Neva, between Nevskaya Dubrovka and Shlisselburg; the

Soviet troops on the other side of the German corridor would push forward and try and join him.

This was a bold plan, and all depended on its timing, for in order to divert Manstein from his assault on Leningrad the Red Army needed to advance quickly. Govorov's careful military preparations now paid off. On 27 August, as Manstein surveyed the city from the south, Govorov launched a two-hour artillery strike on German positions to the east, culminating in a bombardment by rocket missiles. As the enemy recoiled from the force of the onslaught, his troops moved on to the offensive. The Soviet forces on the other side of the enemy corridor did the same, and day by day they edged closer to each other. By the beginning of September only four miles separated them.

The German high command began to panic. On 4 September Hitler phoned Manstein and asked him to take command of the sector and retrieve the situation. 'Instead of the planned offensive against Leningrad,' Manstein recorded in frustration, 'we were faced with a battle south of Lake Ladoga.' The attack on the city was called off.

The month of September saw difficult fighting in the swamps and marshes to the south of the city. Although the Germans achieved some local successes, the real threat to Leningrad had now passed. Soviet soldiers had begun to show a new confidence when fighting the enemy.

Turning the tables on a cruel and vindictive persecutor is not just a matter of material resources. It also tests will and self-belief. Svetlana Magaeva remembered an incident at her Leningrad children's home that summer. A young teenager named Dennis Davidov had been brought into the house. He was polite and intelligent, but completely unassertive. With the horrors of war all around him, it was understandable that he hated confrontation and the use of force – but now he cowered at any sign of trouble, covering his face with his hands and saying: 'Please don't hurt me. Forgive me if I did something wrong.'

A group of boys began to pick on this unfortunate fellow. Their ringleader was named Leonid Smirnov. Smirnov was only nine, but the hardships of the previous winter had given him the wizened face of an old man. He was cold, sullen and hostile – and he enjoyed tormenting Davidov. Davidov's trousers were far too large around his waist, and he had to hold them up with one of his hands. Smirnov would punch or kick him, so that he would lose his grip and the trousers would drop to the floor, exposing long, thin legs that looked like toothpicks, and then all the boys would laugh.

A teacher tried to intervene to help. She told the children that Davidov was a descendant of the Dennis Davidov who had been a national hero during Napoleon's invasion of Russia in 1812. By saying this, she wanted the boys to respect Davidov, but her efforts backfired. They simply wondered how – with a brilliant military leader as an ancestor – the present Davidov could be so pathetic.

Then one day Davidov appeared totally different. He entered the room wearing a belt. It was a genuine leather belt – and such items of clothing were a rarity in Leningrad after the privations of the winter, when most had been cut into segments, boiled, and then chewed in an effort to keep hunger at bay. It emerged that Davidov had not eaten his daily portion of sugar cubes for many days, and when he had saved up enough, he had exchanged the sugar for the belt on the black market.

Magaeva and the other children talked about what had happened. They considered the actions of Davidov genuinely heroic, for he had been willing to risk his life to purchase the belt. Then Magaeva added: 'Smirnov stopped abusing Davidov – not because he had a change of heart, but because Davidov no longer appeared to be a weakling. Doing what he did to acquire that belt showed he valued the respect of his peers, and his worth in their eyes, above his portion of sugar. This was a powerful statement when, for so many months in the city, scraps of nourishment had meant the difference between life and death. His actions gave Davidov dignity, and no one ever tried to abuse him again.'

By the end of September 1942 the military situation around Leningrad had reached a stalemate. All attention was turning southwards, to the titanic battle at Stalingrad. The Germans had broken into the city, but the Red Army was defending it, street by street, and house by house.

Vera Inber became increasingly drawn to Stalin's namesake city on the Volga, feeling that its fate was somehow linked to Leningrad's. On 20 September she wrote: 'Ferocious fighting at Stalingrad.' Four days later: 'Fighting in the streets.' On 9 October, 'Stalingrad is still holding out.' The experience of war in the two cities was very different – Leningrad was facing a static siege, Stalingrad a full-scale battle – but the intensity of suffering they were enduring bound them together.

Everyone in Leningrad was gripped by the faraway struggle on the Volga, and followed its terrible progress through the communiqués. 'It shows in the expression on people's faces, in the trams, on the streets,' Vera Inber wrote. 'All the time we feel for Stalingrad.' When Inber heard that the Germans had thrown their whole military might against the workers' settlements there, she wrote starkly: 'Now everything will be decided at Stalingrad – the whole fate of the war.'

Leningrad's defenders were engaging the Germans in a series of artillery duels. In static warfare, the role of the big siege guns was all important and Govorov knew that previous Soviet attempts to cut the German ring around the city had failed because of poor artillery preparation. He wanted to batter the enemy's siege lines, and to do so he had to reduce the impressive striking power of the Wehrmacht's own artillery. Govorov wrote: 'The key to a breakthrough on the Leningrad Front lies in precise counter-battery fire directed against the enemy's gun emplacements.' His approach was simple: 'We must hit them before they hit us.'

To wrest the initiative from the Germans, Govorov needed an accurate picture of where their guns were situated. The sites were well camouflaged, and difficult to detect by aerial reconnaissance, so Govorov began to use a system of decoys, to draw the enemy's fire and through this reveal the location of their units.

On 30 October Senior Lieutenant Alexei Amelichev moved his 152mm artillery battery on to the Pulkovo Heights under the cover of darkness. 'At first light, I readied my gunners, and checked my map co-ordinates,' Amelichev recalled. Above him, a Soviet reconnaissance plane was circling. 'I wanted to provoke a strong German response,' he continued, 'so I decided to give their commander a wake-up call. We aimed at Army Group North's HQ at Gatchina, and the nearby airfield and railway station.' Amelichev's men let off a series of volleys, and then ran for cover. 'It was as if we had ripped open a hornet's nest,' he said.

Within minutes, sixteen different enemy batteries opened fire on Amelichev's hurriedly vacated gun position, raining down hundreds of shells, and a group of Junkers also appeared, dive-bombing it in relays. But in their rage the Germans had disclosed many of their artillery positions. This incident was well publicised by the Soviet authorities – all of Amelichev's unit were decorated for valour. Although this was incredibly dangerous work, Amelichev's defiant bravura appealed to Red Army soldiers, and soon others were following suit. The decoy system not only gained accurate intelligence of enemy deployments, it also raised the morale of the defenders.

Stalin's high command now asked Govorov to prepare detailed plans for breaking the German blockade of Leningrad. He was to have them ready for preliminary inspection on 22 November. On that day, wonderful news came through. The Red Army defenders had held out at Stalingrad, and now a massive Soviet counter-attack had torn apart the enemy's positions to the north and south of the city. 'A special announcement on the radio,' Vera Inber wrote. 'Our troops have switched over to the attack. We have advanced seventy kilometres and occupied Kalach.' The German army at Stalingrad was now surrounded. 'The turning point,' Inber added, simply yet powerfully. The night was incredibly beautiful, with the blue moonlight and white snow creating a luminous glow. And then the enemy's artillery opened up, with a sudden, angry burst of shelling. 'They are trying to take revenge,' she thought.

In October Manstein had hoped to regroup his forces, and then prepare for another assault on Leningrad. It would never take place. The Wehrmacht's brilliant commander was transferred to the southern front – and given the task of attempting to rescue the Germans trapped at Stalingrad. Hitler's war machine had now been thrown on to the defensive.

The atmosphere in besieged Leningrad was now very different. Pipelines had been laid under Lake Ladoga, allowing additional fuel and power to be transported into the city. People looked back at what they had endured. 'In December 1942 we often sat by our stove and had a smoke,' Igor Chaiko wrote. 'We would roll our rough tobacco, share the cigarettes, and talk about the hardship of the previous winter, and how much better things had become. December 1941 was unbearable. The bread ration had dwindled to an absolute minimum, and people were dying all around us. You would lose all your strength, all your ability to fight. The horror was unspeakable – in our small room, a year ago, twenty-eight people died.' The previous winter had indeed been unspeakable. Yet it had been endured. Leningrad had stayed alive and continued to fight.

In the winter of 1942 a light entertainment was put on in the Musical Comedy Theatre. It was a piece of fun about the Baltic Fleet, called *The Wide, Wide Sea*. Leningrad's inhabitants loved it. There were more than a hundred performances, but it was almost impossible to get tickets – it was always sold out. Red Air Force pilot Igor Kaberov saw its premiere. Everyone took their seats and began enjoying the show. But at the start of the second act the singing was interrupted by a sudden crescendo of bombing and shelling. The Germans had launched a simultaneous aerial and artillery strike against the district in which the theatre stood. The curtains quickly closed. But then the leading actor came to the front of the stage. 'What shall we do, comrades,' he said, 'take shelter or continue the performance?' There was a thunderous round of applause, and then the entire audience rose to its feet and roared: 'Continue!' Igor Kaberov wrote: 'I shall never forget this. I had seen much during this war, but I was astounded by the heroism of the actors and the half-starved people who filled the hall. "Continue the performance!" – what greater appreciation of a play is possible?'

After weeks of careful preparation, Govorov was ready to take the fight to the enemy. Over 4,500 Soviet guns and mortars had been massed on either side of the German corridor or 'bottleneck', as it was nicknamed, east of the city. Leningrad's forces would once again move forward on a broad front, between Nevskaya Dubrovka and

Shlisselburg. This time, they intended to keep going – join with the Soviet forces advancing from the opposite direction, and break the blockade. The plan was codenamed Operation Spark.

Every detail had been carefully rehearsed. A special training ground was constructed in one of Leningrad's suburbs, featuring mock-ups of enemy strongholds, dug-outs and trenches. Red Army soldiers practised quickly climbing ramparts formed of wood, peat, snow and ice, similar to those defended by the Germans on the steep eastern bank of the Neva. Firing ranges were set up to hone the accuracy of Soviet artillery. 'By the beginning of January all the musicians in our artillery orchestra knew their scores,' Govorov remarked, in an allusion to the performance of Shostakovich's Seventh, 'and we were ready to launch our own offensive.'

At 9.30 a.m. on 12 January 1943 Igor Kaberov felt the thunderous roar of Leningrad's guns shaking the earth around him. The bombardment lasted two hours and twenty minutes – and then the Red Army stormed forward. Soviet soldiers charged across the frozen ice of the Neva; Kaberov and his fellow pilots took to the sky to provide air cover.

Both sides knew what was at stake. The German order of the day stated: 'The city of Lenin is the source of the Bolshevik Revolution and the second capital of their state. The liberation of Leningrad is one of the most important goals of the Soviet regime – and success for them would equal their defence of Moscow and the battle for Stalingrad.' On the Soviet side, a sense of destiny was invoked. A delegation of workers travelled to the front line and solemnly presented the assembled troops with the Red Banner awarded to the city for its defeat of Iudenich – the White Army commander – in 1919. His forces had reached the outskirts of the city, but were then driven back by the determined defenders. Iudenich's army had been repulsed in weeks; the Germans had been besieging the city for sixteen months. But now Red Army soldiers swore on the banner that they would break the blockade – or die in the attempt.

The Germans were taken aback by the intensity of the assault. 'It was a nightmare,' a sergeant from the 227th Infantry Division later wrote. 'That morning the Russians opened up on us with guns of every imaginable calibre. The shells exploded precisely where our bunkers were located. Our company commander was killed and some of our front-line soldiers were overcome by panic. Rather than endure any more of the bombardment, they stepped out of their front-line trenches with their hands raised above their heads.'

The Soviet forces established two bridgeheads on the far side of the Neva, and brought tanks across – transporting them across the ice on reinforced wooden rails. The following day they began to move forward. But the Germans quickly regrouped, and then sent reinforcements in. The Red Army was advancing across difficult terrain – low-lying and swampy, dotted with clumps of trees and bushes – and the enemy held the crucial high ground, the Siniavino Heights. They put their troops and guns on this natural stronghold, and then bombarded the advancing Russians.

In the past, the Wehrmacht's war machine had destroyed one Soviet relief effort after another. Its well-drilled co-ordination was too much for its opponents, and Red Army forces had impaled themselves on a succession of well-defended fortifications. On the afternoon of 13 January an assault on Shlisselburg was beaten off, and withering enemy fire from the Siniavino Heights hindered any further progress. The Soviet forces advancing from the east were struggling to make headway against a German strongpoint – Workers' Settlement No. 8 – in which every building had been turned into a fortress. A crisis point had been reached.

Before the start of the operation, Georgi Zhukov – newly promoted to marshal of the Soviet Union – was brought in by Stalin's high command to oversee the operation's logistics and planning. Now he began meddling in affairs that were the responsibility of the Leningrad Front. He rang up Lieutenant-General Nikolai Simonyak, head of the advancing 136th Rifle Division, and asked him why he had failed to attack the Siniavino Heights. 'Because the approach to it is very difficult,' Simonyak answered. 'The ground is hard to cross and all the German guns are trained on the entry point. Our casualties would be enormous.' In previous offensives, the Red Army had frittered away its strength in frontal assaults against just such entrenched positions. Now Govorov wanted to avoid unnecessary loss of life and maintain the momentum of his attack. He instructed his officers to skirt the German stronghold and keep moving. But Zhukov had other ideas.

'Who are these cowards of yours who don't want to fight?' he shouted threateningly. 'Who needs to be ousted?' 'There are no cowards in my division,' Simonyak replied firmly. 'Wise guy,' snapped Zhukov in irritation. 'I order you to attack the Siniavino Heights immediately.' This was precisely what the Germans were expecting, and they knew such an assault would be suicidal for the Red Army. Still Simonyak refused to be intimidated. 'Comrade Marshal,' he said. 'My division is under the command of General Govorov. I take orders from him.' Zhukov slammed the phone down. No attack was made on the Siniavino Heights – and word of what had happened quickly spread throughout the army.

A new spirit was motivating Leningrad's commanders and soldiers. The Germans pulverised the road through the marshes below the heights, and believed they had rendered it impassable. 'It was like entering an inferno,' Red Army veteran Nikolai Vasipov remembered. 'The trees had been smashed into jagged splinters and the air was thick with smoke from the burning peat. The cries of the wounded echoed all around us. The enemy did not think we could survive in that hell-hole – but we kept pushing forward.'

On 15 January a Soviet ski brigade crossed the frozen Lake Ladoga, outflanked the German defences and broke into Shlisselburg from the east. Fierce fighting began inside the town. Army Group North's commander, Field Marshal Küchler, ordered its garrison to hold out to the last man.

The distance between the two advancing Soviet fronts was now barely half a mile, and General Govorov ordered his men to make a final breakthrough. The key to the German defence line was a redoubt at Workers' Settlement No. 5. The enemy thought it unassailable, but on the evening of 17 January Red Army assault groups began crawling through the ditches towards it. Around them, clumps of burning peat glowed eerily in the darkness. A savage battle erupted around the pillboxes. Infantry and tanks collided with each other in the semi-darkness. For two hours fierce fighting raged – and then, suddenly, the

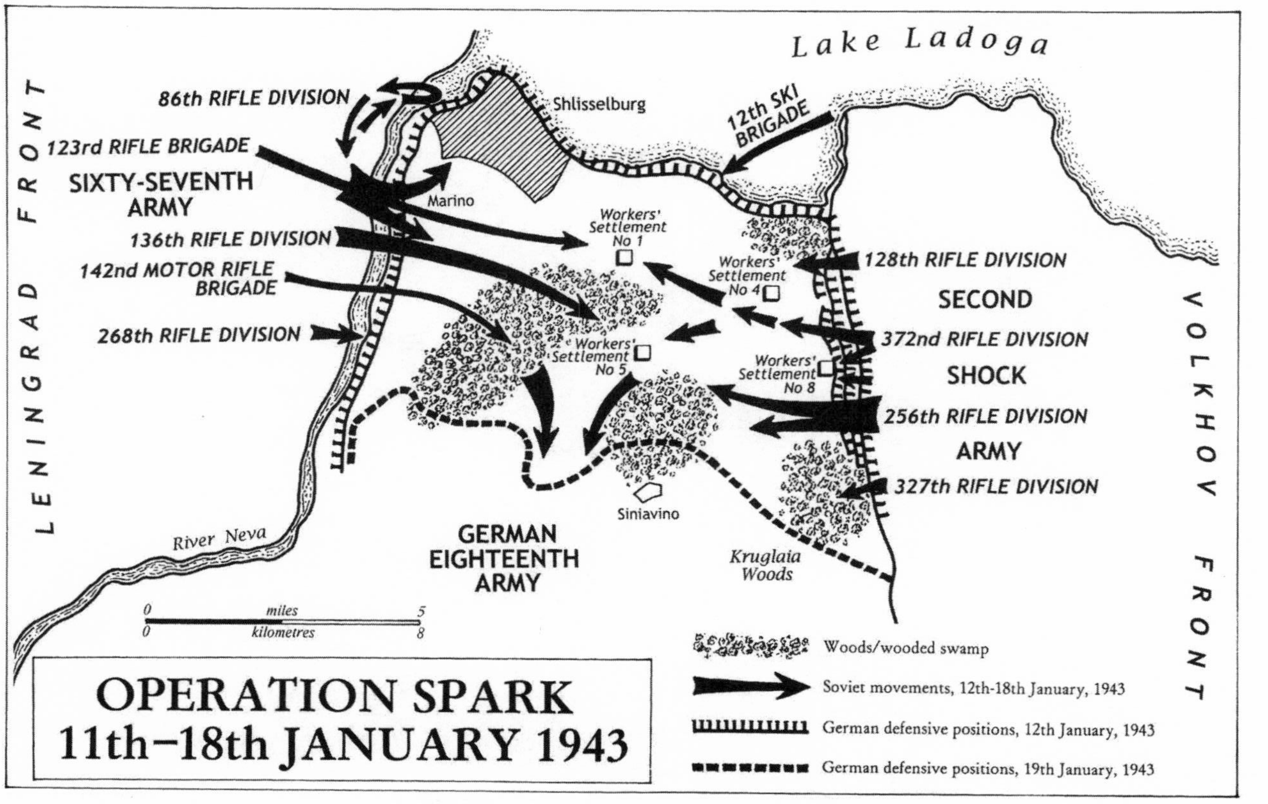
Lake Ladoga
LENINGRAD FRONT
VOLKHOV FRONT
86th RIFLE DIVISION
123rd RIFLE BRIGADE
SIXTY-SEVENTH ARMY
136th RIFLE DIVISION
142nd MOTOR RIFLE BRIGADE
268th RIFLE DIVISION
Shlisselburg
Marino
12th SKI BRIGADE
Workers' Settlement No 1
Workers' Settlement No 4
Workers' Settlement No 5
Workers' Settlement No 8
128th RIFLE DIVISION
SECOND
372nd RIFLE DIVISION
SHOCK
256th RIFLE DIVISION
ARMY
327th RIFLE DIVISION
Siniavino
Kruglaia Woods
River Neva
GERMAN EIGHTEENTH ARMY
0 miles 5
0 kilometres 8
Woods/wooded swamp
Soviet movements, 12th-18th January, 1943
German defensive positions, 12th January, 1943
German defensive positions, 19th January, 1943
OPERATION SPARK
11th–18th JANUARY 1943

Germans seemed to lose all will to continue. Their troops pulled back towards the Siniavino Heights. On the morning of 18 January Govorov's men made contact with the Soviet forces advancing from the east.

Leningrad had been holding its breath. On 16 January, when news came through that Shlisselburg had been recaptured by the Red Army, Vera Inber wrote: 'An extraordinary day. The entire city is waiting . . . any moment now!' On 17 January seven-year-old Lyalya Pritvits told her mother that the blockade would be broken the next day, without fail. Apparently, her kindergarten had been told this by the army unit with whom they maintained a friendly correspondence. 'They will break through the blockade, and bring us some ginger biscuits,' Pritvits said solemnly.

At 11.00 p.m. on 18 January a communiqué was read over the radio to the besieged city. It announced simply: 'The blockade of Leningrad has been broken.' Everyone went out on to the streets, and for one extraordinary night no passes were needed; music played, poems were composed and speeches were made. 'I don't think anyone was sleeping,' schoolgirl Evgenia Shavrova wrote happily. Vsevolod Vishnevsky, composer of the popular Leningrad musical, *The Wide, Wide Sea*, jotted a few words down in his diary: 'Seventeen months of blockade, of torment, of expectation – but we held out!'

Vishnevsky spoke for the whole city. 'This happiness, the happiness of liberated Leningrad, we will never forget,' said Olga Berggolts. 'The cursed circle is broken.'

11

Something Necessary

The Siege is Lifted

THE BLOCKADE WAS broken on 18 January 1943. A vital link now opened up with the rest of Russia – the 'mainland', as it had been known in the dark days of the siege. It was achieved by the bravery of Red Army soldiers, but it was a victory for the people of Leningrad. 'We have waited a long time for this day,' Olga Berggolts said. 'Yet we always believed it would come. We hoped for it even during Leningrad's blackest months – January and February of last year. We hoped for it when our friends and relatives died, and we ourselves, turned to stone by sorrow, buried them in the frozen ground, in mass, communal graves, lacking even the strength to relieve our hearts with tears. We will be victorious!'

Yet although the months of isolation had now ended, and the Germans had been pushed back to the Siniavino Heights, they had not been dislodged from the majority of their positions around Leningrad. Soviet forces were completely exhausted by Operation Spark, and further military actions in late January and February made little progress. Army Group North remained within striking distance of the city, and the siege continued.

It would take time and colossal effort to repulse the enemy fully. The Germans held an arc of fortifications running from Pulkovo, south-west of Leningrad, to the rail junction at Novgorod, which they nicknamed their 'Northern Rampart'. This defence line was a hundred miles long and four miles deep. Its approaches were heavily mined and covered with barbed-wire entanglements, and behind them were anti-tank ditches, bunkers and a warren of pill-boxes. Strongpoints and centres of resistance had been built at road junctions and gaps between stretches of forest. It would not be possible to breach this line without massive reinforcements.

Leningrad's defenders concentrated on protecting the narrow strip of land they had recently won: the lifeline that connected them to the rest of the country. In less than three weeks – defying frequent snowstorms and enemy bombs and shells – a parallel road and railway was constructed, twenty miles long, which ran over the Neva on a temporary, pile-supported bridge. Ivan Krylov was on the construction team: 'We were determined to get foodstuffs into the city as quickly as possible. The Nazis kept the whole route under constant surveillance. Our trains and lorries could only travel at night, and even then there was constant artillery shelling. But when things got bad, we thought of the women and children we were trying to reach.' On 6 February 1943 the first trainload of provisions arrived at Leningrad.

The route remained extremely vulnerable – it was only five miles wide and the enemy held the high ground above it. 'Everything with which we are supplied, every sack of flour, every tin of food, goes through this narrow corridor,' Vera Inber wrote. The bridge over the Neva was its most vulnerable point, and at 1.00 p.m. on 9 February the Germans sent in their bombers to destroy it. Igor Kaberov and six of his fellow fighters engaged them in a fierce aerial battle – and the bridge was left undamaged. Several days later, a member of Kaberov's air force unit received a letter from his family in Leningrad:

> We're alive! Your godfather has taken to his bed. Zoya and I are not well, but we can still move about. We have some coal and a little more bread now. What joy all of us felt when the blockade was broken! We live with one thought: that now things will be easier for us. The day will come when the siege will be lifted. We heard on the radio and read in the paper about your victory in the air. We are so proud of you.

But Stalin ensured that the celebrations were muted. The Soviet leader did not want the rest of the country to learn the extent of the tragedy suffered by Leningrad, or to ask how so many people had been left to starve to death. Olga Berggolts was invited to Moscow to broadcast her reflections on the siege. 'I am convinced that they know nothing about Leningrad here,' she wrote to her family. 'No one seems to have the remotest idea of what the city has gone through. They say that Leningraders are heroes, but they don't know what that heroism consisted of. They don't know that we starved, they don't know that people were dying of hunger. I couldn't really open my mouth on the radio, because they told me: "You can talk about anything, but no recollections of the starvation – none, none. On the courage, on the heroism of Leningraders, that's what we need – but not a word about hunger."' Red Army soldier Ilya Nemanov remembered the sudden arrest of one of the men in his unit. He had recently arrived from the Leningrad Front. 'He tried to describe the siege to us,' Nemanov recalled, 'but he mentioned the mass starvation. That wasn't something we were supposed to hear about.'

Major-General Fedyuninsky recalled a conversation with Stalin soon after the blockade of the city was lifted. He had told the Soviet leader how Leningrad had become a ghost of its former self. Corpses were left on the streets because there was no one to pick them up. 'The worst thing', Fedyuninsky said, 'was that someone dying of hunger would retain their consciousness through to the very end. It was as if they were watching the approach of their own death.' He concluded: 'The siege of Leningrad was one of the greatest tragedies in human history.' But Stalin was reluctant to engage with this. 'Death was cutting down not only Leningraders,' he replied. 'People were dying on the front line and in the occupied territories. I agree that death – and starvation – is appalling when there is no way out of a situation. But there was nothing more we could have done for the city. In the winter of 1941 Moscow itself was hanging by a thread. War and death are inseparable. Leningrad was not the only place to suffer from that swine Hitler.'

A defiant optimism was now taking root in the city nonetheless. On 3 March Igor Chaiko wrote: 'The second spring of the war is approaching. A thought is forming in fiery letters in my mind: I can overcome anything. The dangers of the last year and a half have not passed, and war and starvation have not yet ended. And there are the terrible memories of the things we endured – being so hungry that it almost drove you crazy. Yet spring is a symbol of life. The Germans are shelling us again, but the menace is shrinking in the sunlight.'

On 25 March Chaiko went to a violin recital at the Philharmonic Hall. The encore was briefly interrupted by the sound of anti-aircraft fire. The performer shuddered, and then carried on playing. On 16 April Vera Inber was taking a walk with a friend when German shelling began. Shrapnel started falling around them and they hurriedly took cover. 'A marvellous day, a spring wind, but not too strong,' Inber wrote, deliberately disregarding the enemy onslaught. 'I want to stay alive so much!'

Shortly afterwards, Inber visited the city's Botanical Gardens. One of its curators told her that the precious trees and shrubs had nearly been demolished by a Red Army tank unit. Pursued by German planes and desperately seeking cover, the tanks had accelerated into the gardens. Directly in their path were some of Leningrad's oldest trees, including a black poplar planted by Peter the Great. The curator rushed out to try and stop them, but was brusquely told to get out of the way. 'Can't you see there's a war on?' the infuriated officer yelled at him. But the curator stood his ground. 'Comrade Commander, these trees have been tended for two hundred years. You will ruin them in a few minutes.' There was a pause, and the two men looked at each other. Then the officer turned to his crew. 'Turn back,' he said, 'the position is unsuitable.'

Inna Bityugova was one of the many Leningrad children working on the city's allotments. As she helped cultivate a vegetable garden, she became more and more fascinated by what was happening around her. As the new shoots pushed up through the soil, she began to think about what made them grow, and what was infusing them with life. Bityugova bought a writing book. On its cover she drew the vegetables she was tending – the beetroots, turnips, radishes – with smiling, friendly faces, and little arms and legs. Then she began creating adventures for them.

In one story, a little green vegetable man ran into a large stone building. On a bed in one of the apartments a little girl was sitting. Her arms were as thin as sticks, her cheeks were hollow, her eyes were sad. She was too weak to move. The enemy had brought hunger to her. But the little green vegetable man was stronger than all the enemy armies put together. He had come to help the weak little girl. Her cheeks grew rosy, her arms round and her eyes shone again. She got up and began to walk. Then Bityugova became more ambitious. In a subsequent story, the vegetable man was surrounded by enemies who tried not to let him through. They dropped bombs and fired shells, but he was invincible. He ran into a dug-out where a soldier sat hunched over a map. The soldier had a long march ahead of him. But suddenly he realised that he was no longer lonely – Soviet children were thinking of him. The soldier ate the vegetable and felt a giant's strength pour into his veins. Courageously, he marched on to victory.

Bityugova's simple yet touching patriotism was inspired by the Red Army's military successes that summer. A major German offensive at Kursk had been decisively defeated. By 13 July 1943 the Red Army was advancing into the Ukraine and southern Russia. The enemy was in retreat.

Igor Chaiko noticed the reappearance of cats and dogs on Leningrad's streets. Cats were much in demand to combat the growing rat population, and cost up to 2,000 roubles to purchase. They were sent into the city by train. The first contingent had created a stir when they arrived at the Finland Station, for disturbed by German shelling during the journey they had broken out of their boxes and sought out more comfortable accommodation in the passenger compartments. Astonished loaders, waiting on the platform at Leningrad, had been greeted by a mass of feline faces peering curiously out of the windows.

At the end of July the Germans commenced a series of spite artillery attacks, firing in short, concentrated bursts and singling out civilian targets. The next few months saw the worst shelling of the war. New signs in blue and white paint started appearing on Leningrad's main streets: 'Citizens – in the event of an artillery bombardment, this side of the street is the more dangerous.' One Sunday afternoon they hit the tram stop at Sadovaya Street, where people congregated to visit the allotments outside the city. Bits of bodies lay in the road, mixed up with cans, shopping bags, spades and vegetables. A torn-off arm lay on the pavement with a cigarette in the fingers, still smoking. Around it were beetroots and carrots, swimming in a pool of blood.

But amid this carnage Leningrad's inhabitants kept a feeling of solidarity. 'We are all one family,' seventeen-year-old Zera Vorozheikina wrote, 'baptised by the monstrous blockade, united in our grief, our experience, our hopes and expectations.' A sense of destiny was emerging. 'We felt that the fate of the Motherland was in our hands,' wrote Viacheslav Kondratiev, 'and we conducted ourselves in accordance with that idea, feeling ourselves to be citizens in the full and authentic meaning of the word.'

On 9 September General Govorov began drawing up plans finally to smash the German siege. He would launch a two-pronged attack, from the Oranienbaum bridgehead and the Pulkovo Heights. It would be necessary to move large quantities of troops and guns into these areas. The offensive would be launched in the winter, when the ice was hard and his soldiers could move more easily.

The city authorities were fully aware of these preparations. While Govorov trained his soldiers in assault techniques, they decided to promote an 'official' version of the siege, in which the city successfully defied the enemy under their own heroic leadership. Their intention was ruthlessly to suppress any other interpretation, and they began tightening their censorship. Vsevolod Vishnevsky was told that his new play, *The Walls of Leningrad*, could not be performed – some of its characters were thought to be 'too negative'. 'The details are entirely authentic and taken from life,' Vishnevsky wrote in frustration. 'Much is being forgotten.' On 30 September, after a tip-off from an informer, an NKVD house search uncovered Mikhail Nosyrev's diary. The entries for February 1942 – which showed that one of the city's hospitals had been in a state of total collapse – were too candid for their taste, and Nosyrev was arrested and the diary confiscated. Other arrests soon followed.

That autumn the Soviet military build-up continued steadily. From 5 November 1943 troops, ammunition and supplies were shipped over to the Oranienbaum bridgehead and brought up behind the Pulkovo Heights. Under Govorov's careful supervision, a massive array of artillery was gathered to support the offensive: over 21,000 guns, more than 1,500 Katyusha rocket launchers and some 600 anti-aircraft guns. It was the biggest concentration of firepower ever assembled in the Soviet Union.

Army Group North's commander, Georg von Küchler, was aware of these preparations. He had already begun to prepare a fall-back position for his soldiers – a well-defended series of strongholds about 150 miles to his west, known as the Panther Line. Küchler knew that Hitler, who was reluctant to surrender any scrap of Russian territory, would only authorise a withdrawal from Leningrad in an absolute emergency. But on 21 September the commander had ordered that the entire civilian population between his army's present position and the Panther Line be evacuated. They would be force-marched hundreds of miles to the rear.

On 7 October an intelligence officer from the German Eighteenth Army submitted a report to Küchler's HQ:

> Many people are saying that they would prefer to be clubbed to death on the spot rather than take part in this evacuation. Even members of the population who are still pro-German rightly suspect that such a march will cause incredible misery and cause the loss of countless lives. Considering the state of people's clothing, the lack of food or proper transport and the expected weather the participants – particularly women and children – will soon be in an indescribable state.

Nevertheless, on 30 November Küchler stressed: 'The population of the occupied Russian zone east of the Panther Line must be evacuated as speedily as possible. All able-bodied men must be seized. No consideration will be given to preserving the unity of families. No horse-drawn transport will be provided. Proper execution of these orders is the duty of all commanders and officers and any failure to do so will be treated as an exceptionally grave offence.'

On 17 December Vera Inber's husband was chatting to one of his medical students, who was about to take an anatomy exam. 'Well, are you shaking with nerves?' he joked. 'Others are shaking today,' she answered. 'It's my turn tomorrow.' Within an hour, she was lying dead in the mortuary, having been killed outright by a German artillery shell. The funeral was held two days later. The head of the coffin was draped in muslin, and Inber wanted to throw it back, to see the young student's face, but was told in a whisper that the base of the skull was all that remained of it. 'Only a waxen, adolescent hand was showing through a heap of artificial roses and lilies,' Inber wrote. 'As we took leave of the dead girl, everyone kissed it.'

The sky was clear and beautiful, with a slight, long-awaited frost – essential for the start of the offensive. The Soviet assault force of a million and a quarter men now outnumbered the Germans by more than two to one. So many heavy guns and rocket launchers had been brought up that they averaged 320 guns for every mile of the front. More than a thousand freight cars with shells had been brought up. Some of the ammunition had been produced in Leningrad's factories. Each of these shells had a carefully stencilled inscription: 'For the blood of our workers', 'For our children's anguish' or 'For our murdered friends'.

Govorov wanted to overwhelm the Germans with his first assault. 'The fate of Leningrad hangs on the speed of our advance,' he warned his commanders. 'If we are held up, the city will be subjected to such a terrible shelling that it will be impossible to stand it – so many people will be killed, so many buildings demolished.' On 15 January 1944 Govorov ordered the bombardment from the Pulkovo Heights to commence. It would be the heaviest barrage of the war. Between 9.20 and 11.50 a.m. Soviet artillery launched more than half a million shells and rockets on to the German lines.

Pavel Luknitsky was reading when the windows in his room began to rattle violently, and then the whole building started to shake. He ran outside. Everyone was looking up at the sky. The sound of artillery seemed to fill the entire city, but no one heard any explosions. Then it suddenly dawned on people: 'Those are our guns,' someone cried. 'It's begun! It's begun!'

'Soon, soon we will be free,' Evgenia Shavrova wrote on 16 January. In just a few days, Govorov's troops took back the outlying towns of Pushkin, Pavlovsk, Ropsha and Peterhof and captured the heavy guns that had been bombarding Leningrad for so long. 'Peterhof Palace is damaged so badly that it will be beyond human efforts to restore it,' Vera Inber said sadly. Climbing over the wreckage, she looked at the remains of the great terrace and the avenue of fountains, descending towards the sea. The Samson Fountain and Grand Cascade lay in ruins before her.

The advance gathered pace, and this time the enemy was unable to halt it. On 22 January a communiqué said the Germans were retreating so fast that Soviet forces were struggling to keep up with them. At 8.00 p.m. on 27 January Govorov proudly announced: 'The city of Leningrad has been entirely liberated.' The 872-day siege was over.

That night, everyone congregated at the Field of Mars. Twenty-four victory salvoes were fired from 324 guns. Hundreds of military flares were launched into the air, their different colours cascading towards the happy onlookers. 'The whole sky was lit by a phosphorescent glow,' Vera Inber recalled, 'as if a meteor had just flown past us. First there was a plethora of crimson lights, and then gold stars would stream downwards, like ears of grain from some bounteous, invisible sack.' The searchlights from the Baltic Fleet shone on Leningrad's buildings. One illuminated the angel on the spire of the Peter and Paul Fortress with an arc of light so strong it seemed almost solid. Among the assembled crowd that winter night, it actually felt hot, and people unbuttoned their coats. 'I just can't comprehend that the siege is over,' Evgenia Shavrova said. 'It is impossible to describe my joy.'

The city's inhabitants contemplated a life free from constant exploding shells. 'How many artillery strikes have there been only recently, just this month, how many victims?' Shavrova thought. 'Our classmate Rita's father was killed, Lena's mother was wounded. A shell that landed in the courtyard of Nevsky No. 27 killed Sima Pavlova's mother and father.' By a sheer fluke, Sima had not been at home at the time. 'Children can now walk on the sunny side – "the most dangerous side" – of the Nevsky Prospect,' Olga Berggolts wrote. 'The children of our city can now walk peacefully on the sunny side! And they can live peacefully in rooms that look out on the sunny side. They can even sleep peacefully and soundly at night, knowing that they won't be killed.'

In this heady moment of triumph, Leningrad's regime put the finishing touches to its own history of the siege. Propaganda posters showed the city standing united against a hated foe. One, 'We defended Lenin's city', showed soldiers, sailors and workers gazing unflinchingly from a Leningrad skyline. There was something genuinely stirring about such images, and Georgi Knyazev remembered a party colleague observing: 'In fifty or a hundred years this poster will be a museum piece. Our descendants will bow their heads before it.'

Great leaders rally people at a time of crisis, and win over the dissident and the critic to the larger cause. Yet Leningrad's collective unity had arisen from a remorseless policy of repression. 'Even when there was no electric light, no water supply, no newspapers,' Dmitry Likhachev recalled, 'the authorities were still watching over us.' It is this aspect of Leningrad's story which has kept these events from being fully understood by the wider world until now, and which still bewilders and deters Western attempts to integrate Soviet heroism into the narrative of resistance to Nazism.

For, even as the horrors of the siege gripped the city, party secretary Andrei Zhdanov had hunted one political agitator for more than two years. The regime was exceptionally sensitive to any form of criticism, but the lengths it went to in this particular operation were truly astonishing.

On 24 December 1941 insurrectionary leaflets had been discovered on the pavement outside one of Leningrad's train stations. Some seventy were collected, written by hand on copying paper. On the morning of 9 January 1942 more leaflets were found at the station. The author used the nickname 'The Rebel'. 'Citizens,' he said, 'down with a regime that lets us die of starvation! We are being robbed by scoundrels who deceive us, who stockpile food and leave us to go hungry. Let us take action. Let us go to the district authorities and demand more bread. Down with our leaders!'

Zhdanov diverted considerable resources to tracking down the culprit – doing so at a time when Leningrad's food-distribution system was all but collapsing. The NKVD kept the station under surveillance and patrols were organised in the surrounding area. Transport staff were also put on the look-out and the handwriting of more than 18,000 railway workers analysed. These measures were unsuccessful. 'The Rebel' eluded capture.

Letters began to be sent directly to Zhdanov at the Smolny. On 30 September 1942 the war censors intercepted an anonymous document posted to the party secretary, complaining about the distribution of food. The handwriting was examined and compared to the leaflets – it was the work of 'The Rebel'. A second subversive letter was sent on 6 November in an envelope which had the brand name 'Secrets'. The war censor now intercepted every letter using this type of envelope and 1,023 letter-writers and their families were then interrogated by the NKVD. 'The Rebel' was not among them.

On 30 January 1943 two more letters were sent, one to Zhdanov and one to Mayor Popkov. The paper was now despatched to a laboratory for chemical analysis. It was established that the particular brand was sold only in the Smolninsky and Volodarsky districts of the city. In the aftermath of Operation Spark, construction workers were labouring round the clock, under constant German bombing and artillery fire, to build a railway across the Neva and into the city. Astoundingly, Zhdanov launched a bureaucratic offensive of his own. Deputies from local assemblies examined the handwriting of 13,000 citizens in the two districts in an effort to uncover the culprit. Police looked at a further 27,860 military registration documents. All firms in these localities were investigated, and handwriting samples taken from 5,732 employees. But, at the end of it all, the NKVD could only observe: 'These measures have still failed to yield any results.'

On 27 September 1943 there was a breakthrough. In further complaints about food rations, sent to both Zhdanov and Popkov, 'The Rebel' identified himself as a worker in the furnace room of a factory. His description was examined carefully. The type of industrial plant he referred to existed only in the Volodarsky district, and workers of every factory in the area were now put under observation. On 12 December 1943 a steel worker in Workshop no. 42

named Sergei Luzhkov aroused suspicion. Graphologists matched Luzhkov's handwriting with that of 'The Rebel' and he was arrested. The fifty-year-old factory worker made a full confession, admitting that he had written all the leaflets and letters himself. He had done so without the knowledge or assistance of anyone else. Luzhkov was then passed over to the Military Tribunal for sentencing.

'The Rebel' began complaining about the distribution of food to Zhdanov in September 1942. In the same month, the Hungarian Jenö Varga – one of Stalin's economic advisers – had visited Leningrad. 'I was allowed to fly in from Moscow,' Varga said.

> I was supposed to be giving a few lectures, but I wanted to find out about life in the city under siege. I took half a loaf of bread with me. But in Leningrad, where hundreds of thousands had died of hunger, where the nourishment of the population always bordered on starvation levels, and where many were still dying as a consequence of malnutrition, I was taken to a canteen at the Smolny where everything was 'normal'. There was a single restriction: at the noontime meal one was not allowed to eat *two portions of meat*. Everyone received additional packages of food for breakfast and supper. These were civilian party functionaries.

'When I returned to the Astoria,' Varga concluded, 'I gave the half-loaf of bread to the chambermaid – she was beside herself with happiness! Such was the chasm between the "privileged ones" and the ordinary people.'

Zhdanov wasted a vast amount of time and resources trying to track down and punish a legitimate critic. Under different leadership, complaints such as those of 'The Rebel' might have presented the city's authorities with an opportunity. They might have turned such complaints against the Germans, publicising their brutal starvation tactics, their refusal to accept the surrender of the city and the scale of suffering they were deliberately inflicting. By doing so, Leningrad's leadership could have united with its people. But, corrupt as it was, it was deeply frightened of taking this step.

Leningrad's authorities distrusted any process of emotional engagement with the tragedy befalling the city. Instead, they created a brittle notion of heroism, one that extolled stoic endurance but denied the desperate hardship that gave rise to it. Medals were awarded for courageous service – praising the qualities of 'utter selflessness and iron will'. *Leningrad Pravda* urged the city's inhabitants to bear the privations of the siege and carry on with their work. 'Under conditions of encirclement it is inevitable that deprivation and misfortune will affect the weak and give birth to depression among the timid,' the state-sanctioned newspaper announced. 'It is to Leningrad's honour that such people are few among us. But no matter how few they are, one must remember that provocateurs and enemy agents try to take advantage of our difficulties, by sowing doubts, disbelief and defeatism.'

Under this edict, the public expression of grief was represented as a crime against the state. But such grief lay at the heart of ordinary people's experience. In her memoirs, Olga Berggolts described the many blockade diaries she had read: 'Singed and icy, the triumphant Leningrad tragedy breathes from the many, many pages of these diaries, where a person writes with total candour about everyday cares, efforts, sorrows and joys. And, as a rule, the deeply personal is at the same time more universal, more general. History suddenly speaks with a simple, living human voice.'

During the spring of 1944 the retreating German army was ejected from one defence line after another. On 25 March a map of Leningrad was found among the belongings of a captured Wehrmacht artilleryman. The city was neatly divided into squares, and each 'military objective' was given a corresponding number. They were grouped under headings: schools, museums, hospitals, theatres and medical institutes.

Over the summer the Finnish army was also pushed back from its positions, and on 21 July 1944 the Soviet forces reached the prewar border between the two countries. Leonid Govorov – the real hero of Leningrad – was promoted to marshal of the Soviet Union in recognition of his achievement. On 9 July Evgenia Shavrova visited the family dacha where she had spent most of her childhood. It had been abandoned three years earlier, when the Finns advanced southwards towards Leningrad. 'The entire street was overgrown with tall weeds that reached above our heads,' Shavrova recalled.

> There was wild burdock, gigantic goose-foot, nettles, and some completely unknown plant that we had never seen before. Shutters banged in the wind, doors creaked, and something rustled mysteriously. There was no sound from anything living. Our dacha was half boarded up. The leg of a piano was sticking out of the door, and from the balcony of a neighbouring house, a couch was hanging . . . We didn't stay there long – it was sad and simply frightening in that desert of nettles. The whole way back on the train we couldn't talk.

In the autumn of 1944 German prisoners of war were brought into Leningrad to repair and rebuild the buildings they had bombed and shelled. The city was still half empty, and eleven-year-old Elena Kozhina recalled its strange, brooding atmosphere: 'There were so few people that their figures seemed to dissolve on the broad avenues. Even the monuments were nowhere in sight: they had either been taken down from their pedestals or surrounded by sandbags or wooden boards. There were many ruins, some still standing – carcasses of uninhabited houses – without roofs or floors. Cars and trolleys were rare. Squares and parks stood abandoned or partitioned for vegetable gardens. This silence, emptiness and immobility was the city's spirit – it seemed frozen somewhere between life and death.'

Kozhina remembered an extraordinary ritual that took place, every day, at the same hour of the evening. Columns of German prisoners were led along one of Leningrad's main thoroughfares:

> And as if by some invisible sign, people emerged from nowhere to watch. They stood silently at the pavement's edge, close to the prisoners, unable to tear their eyes away. All these people had survived the blockade . . . The Germans walked by, not looking at us. Their faces were exhausted and tense. Some looked straight ahead, some walked with their heads lowered, and a few tried speaking with each other, pretending that they were paying no attention to us.
>
> We all stood silently. There never was a single shout, curse or insult. Not a sign of anger or hatred. Nobody addressed them at all. We stood like a thin, immobile wall, and behind us stood the ghosts of our dead.

Kozhina felt that something very important was happening during those moments: 'Some difficult internal task was being completed, a task of silent necessity. But we could not break through to understanding what it was.'

The Germans kept walking. Kozhina knew all the slogans: 'Death to the child killers!' 'Stand up for the struggle against the dark fascist force, the cursed hordes.' And she knew that the struggle still went on, but far away: 'Bombs were raining down on German cities, and now it was Germans crouched in cold basements, like us two or three years ago. Now it was German children who could tell from the roar in the sky which planes were coming and what they were carrying.' But what Leningrad had suffered was more complex: 'Something had been displaced in us. They were no force, these prisoners, no cursed horde – just tired, ragged, undernourished people like ourselves. Were they enemies and killers? Yes. But we had no desire for revenge. So heavy was the burden, on each of us, of our unexpressed grief, so irreversible were our losses – so incomparable to anything else – that it was absurd to think of vengeance. What could we take from them, and how would it help us?'

A strange, half-suppressed sound came from the woman next to Kozhina. She wore an old worker's coat that reeked of diesel oil. Did she want to shout out all her pain and suffering? But the sob was choked back as quickly as it had begun:

> A feeling of inescapable duty held us there, on the pavement, watching them. And during our silent, mournful vigil, strange flashes of light and freedom would sometimes occur – as if we were not standing with our burdens, but slowly and laboriously ascending to some place where there is no hatred, death, homelessness, or despair. Where is this place? We did not know. But the feeling was there – that something was happening to us during these moments that we stood together, a half-step closer to something necessary.

What Leningrad endured, and emerged victorious over, transcended the fighting of the Second World War. The city's astonishing heroism stands on a grander, more timeless stage.

The Germans kept on walking. And Kozhina recalled: 'The Leningrad of the early, quiet autumn, the autumn of 1944, an empty and triumphant Leningrad, gazed at them and us through the bombed-out windows of condemned buildings. Above us the clear evening sky glowed, in all its serene vastness.'

Epilogue

'THE SIEGE OF Leningrad was fundamentally about heroism, but how do we define that heroism? All of us were victims.'

These are the words of blockade survivor Andrei Krukov. How many of the city's inhabitants died during the siege? The grim mounds at the Piskaryov Cemetery – marked simply by their year – remain frighteningly enigmatic. In the summer of 1943 journalist Alexander Werth visited Leningrad and spoke with Mayor Popkov. He asked him how many fatalities had occurred during the winter of 1941–2, but received no answer, except that 'a few hundred thousand was much as could be said for the present'. When Werth pressed his point, and asked what the present population of the city was, Popkov smiled and said, 'Is it really necessary for you to know?'

The city's authorities did eventually decide on a figure. It was announced that: 'During the blockade 632,253 citizens of Leningrad died.' Dmitry Likhachev said pointedly: 'Who made the reckoning – of those who slid beneath the ice, of those who were picked up in the streets and immediately taken to the mortuaries and mass graves? What about the inhabitants of the suburbs and city's surrounding villages, who fled into Leningrad? And all the others – the refugees without papers, who died without ration cards in the unheated accommodation allotted to them?'

Likhachev believed that the death rate was deliberately underestimated by a factor of between three and four. In August 1942 it was stated at a meeting of the city's governing council that on documentary evidence alone (taken from burial registrations) about 1,200,000 people had already died. The mortality rate reached its apogee in February and March 1942, even though the bread ration had been increased a little. It was at this time, Likhachev remembered, that a mouse died of starvation on his window sill.

The story of Leningrad's suffering has struggled hard to reach the light of day. Evidence of that struggle is found outside the city, on the far bank of the Neva, on the killing ground of the Nevsky bridgehead. The Red Army soldiers who fought here were astonishingly brave. 'Do not forget me!' Alexander Sokolov wrote to his son Slavic on 22 March 1942. 'I never stop thinking about you, even for a minute, during these difficult days of our "army life". We are defending our Motherland heroically.'

At the end of March 1942 all non-essential military personnel were evacuated from this shrinking stronghold. Nurse Olga Budnikova found leaving particularly painful – she had fallen in love with one of the divisional staff, Boris Agrachev. She gave Boris her small Browning pistol as a keepsake. 'It's good to kill Germans with,' she said. He looked at her – they both knew the situation was hopeless – and despair overwhelmed him. 'It's good to commit suicide with,' he responded bleakly.

The official version was that this bedraggled band of survivors was evacuated to safety in April 1942. But Olga was never able to trace Boris, and she always wondered what had happened to him. In fact, he and his comrades were overrun by the Germans. In 1991 battlefield archaeologists excavated their last command post – they found eleven bodies, and Agrachev's was one of them. The men had run out of ammunition and had tried to fend off the enemy with spades.

Fifty years after she had parted from a man she loved, Budnikova attended the deeply moving reburial ceremony. During it, she was handed a small wooden casket that had been found by Agrachev's side. In it was a hurriedly written note. It simply said: 'Olga – I am so sorry.'

It is hard to make sense of the sheer enormity of what happened, or to come to terms with it. For years, Elena Martilla was forced to hide her siege sketchbook from the NKVD. Even in the 1980s she was able to show only one or two pictures: she was told that her work was too 'psychological', too 'pessimistic'. Then, in 1991, she received an invitation from a leading gallery to exhibit all her work. The invitation came from Berlin.

For the first time in her life Martilla saw all her siege drawings – more than eighty of them – hung in three separate halls. And during the exhibition she came face to face with German veterans from the besieging army. 'No words were necessary,' Martilla said. 'I could see it in their eyes – I was at Leningrad.' She took a group of them round – they were asking questions, asking about conditions in the blockaded city, and then they all stopped. 'They just stood there, with tears in their eyes,' Martilla recalled. And then one of them stepped forward. 'I ask for your forgiveness,' he said. 'None of this was necessary, from a military point of view. We tried to destroy you, but we destroyed ourselves as human beings. On behalf of all of us, I ask for your forgiveness.' As he spoke, Martilla became acutely aware of a different siege memory – the callous indifference shown by Leningrad's leaders towards ordinary people's suffering. They would never ask for forgiveness. 'War is terrible,' she replied, 'but my quarrel is with fascism, not with the German people. And fascism exists in all of us.'

The light was dimming in Andrei Krukov's St Petersburg apartment. We had been talking about the performance of Shostakovich's Seventh Symphony in the besieged city. Krukov is a musicologist and the leading authority on the wartime concert. 'It was an incredible event,' he said, 'and conductor Karl Eliasberg made it happen, but I also want to pay tribute to Leningrad Front commander Leonid Govorov. A push was needed – an incentive to get it all going – and Govorov provided it, allowing soldiers from the army to join the orchestra. At a time of siege, this was a quite exceptional decision.'

We turned to Krukov's own experience. He was twelve years old when the blockade began. He showed me his keepsakes: the fragments of an incendiary bomb he had doused with sand, the embroidery his aunt had worked on to keep her mind off the bombing and shelling. And his diary – a little pocket book, with neat, pencilled entries. 'I started my diary on 19 September 1941,' Krukov said. 'I tried to write every day. I felt that something quite unbelievable was happening.' He added: 'The critical period for Leningrad was from the middle of December 1941 to the middle of March 1942. These three terrifying months should be separated from the rest. The city was dying before our eyes – it was sheer struggle for survival. We now know the most dreadful facts abut this time – and we need to know them. But we should not let them define our understanding of the siege.'

Then Krukov spoke about what many veterans call the 'spiritual experience' of the blockade. How he had received help from complete strangers and the remarkable spirit of mutual help and sacrifice that had sprung up in the midst of horror and depravity. And then he turned back to his diary. 'I felt that something exceptional was happening,' he said, 'something on a great scale, that would affect all of us. Many people kept diaries during the siege. You see, a lot of free time had appeared, and it was vital to keep living, spiritually, not to revert to being an animal.' He showed me a diary entry in January 1942. It read: 'We are all covered in soot, we are all hungry, we are all cold.'

We will never fully understand the horror of the siege of Leningrad – or how people found the will to survive. The heroism of the city's beleaguered inhabitants is so extraordinary it is difficult even to grasp. But Krukov looked up at me, gathered himself and spoke with simple conviction: 'We wanted to repel all that. The suffering was on an unimaginable scale – yet, astonishingly, Leningrad did not succumb. People somehow found the strength to reach out and help others, and by doing this, something mysterious yet deeply powerful came into being. We were fighting a battle to keep a human face, to stay human beings. And we won it.'

Notes

Introduction

The introduction draws on the contents of two St Petersburg museums, the Museum of the Blockade and 'The Muses Were Not Silent'. The German war cemetery is at Sologubovka, about forty miles south-east of the city. Michael Stephan and fellow German photographer Susanne Schleyer mounted an exhibition there, examining the Nazi invasion of Russia. For establishing the broader themes of the siege, I am grateful to blockade veterans Irina Skripachyova and Klara Taubert. Andrei Zhdanov, who presided over the defence of the city, died of heart failure in 1948; Peter Popkov, along with many other members of Leningrad's war-time government, was executed in 1950. For Stalin's post-war purge of the city's ruling elite and the distortions of subsequent Soviet propaganda – which saluted Leningrad's heroism but denied much of the suffering that gave rise to it – see Lisa Kirschenbaum, *The Legacy of the Siege of Leningrad, 1941–1995*. For two recent surveys of the city's astonishing history see Solomon Volkov, *St Petersburg: A Cultural History*, and Arthur and Elena George, *St Petersburg: the First Three Centuries*. The story of Vera Lyudyno's diary is found in the *St Petersburg Times* (27 January 2004), on the sixtieth anniversary of the lifting of the siege.

Chapter 1: 'An Almost Scientific Method'

Mikhail Neishtadt has kindly told me how news of the outbreak of war reached Leningrad. Background material for the chapter is from Richard Overy, *The Dictators: Hitler's Germany, Stalin's Russia*; Alan Clark, *Barbarossa*, and Werner Haupt, *Army Group North*, and the memoirs of Manstein and Raus. German veteran testimony is drawn from Robert Kershaw, *War without Garlands*, and Paul Carell, *Hilter's War on Russia*. Wilhelm Lubbeck's account is from *At Leningrad's Gates*; Max Simon's is found in Rupert Butler, *Hitler's Death's Head Division*. Evgeny Moniushko's description is in *From Leningrad to Hungary: Notes of a Red Army Soldier*. Of particular value are Wolfram Wette, *The Wehrmacht: History, Myth, Reality*, and Omer Bartov, *The Eastern Front, 1941–45: German Troops and the Barbarisation of Warfare*, and also Jürgen Förster, 'The German Military's Image in Russia', in Ljubica and Mark Erickson (eds), *Russia: War, Peace and Diplomacy*. Stahlecker's report is in Office of US Chief of Counsel for Prosecution of Axis Criminality, *Nazi Conspiracy and Aggression*, VII (Washington, 1947). The chapter follows a line of argument recently expressed by Jörg Ganzenmüller, *Besieged Leningrad, 1941–1944*. I am grateful to Roberto Muehlenkamp for his detailed compilation, 'The Siege of Leningrad in German Documents', which is found with accompanying translations on www.rodoh.us. The source for the broader military narrative is David M. Glantz, *The Siege of Leningrad*.

Chapter 2: 'The Biggest Bag of Shit in the Army'

Radio operator Mikhail Neishtadt recalled Stalin's concern about the situation in Leningrad in 'Stalin is on the Line', an interview in *Smena* (19 January 2005). General comments on Voroshilov are found in Khrushchev, *Khrushchev Remembers*, Sergo Beria, *Beria: Inside Stalin's Kremlin*, Felix Chuev and Albert Resis, *Molotov Remembers*, Otto Chaney, *Zhukov*, and Simon Sebag Montefiore, *Stalin: The Court of the Red Tsar*. Dmitry Volkogonov's perceptive and highly critical assessment of Voroshilov in Harold Shukman (ed.), *Stalin's Generals*, remains the main reference point, but important new information on his feud with Tukachevsky is found in Lennart Samuelson, *Plans for Stalin's War Machine*, and Yuri Dyakov and Tatyana Bushuyeva, *The Red Army and the Wehrmacht*. David R. Stone's 'Tukachevsky in Leningrad', *Europe-Asia Studies*, 1996, was also very helpful. Shostakovich's friendship with Tukachevsky is related in his memoirs, *Testimony*, ed. Solomon Volkov. Extracts from Lyubov Shaporina's remarkable diary are taken from Veronique Garros and Natalia Korenevskaya (eds), *Intimacy and Terror: Soviet Diaries of the 1930s*. For the Soviet–Finnish War see Carl van Dyke, *The Soviet Invasion of Finland, 1939–40*, and Alexander O. Chubaryan and Harold Shukman (eds), *Stalin and the Soviet–Finnish War*. Veteran Mikhail Lukinov's testimony is from

Artem Drabkin's 'I Remember' collection on the Russian Battlefield website. Nikolai Baryshnikov, in *Finland and the Leningrad Blockade, 1941–44*, has suggested that the country tacitly supported Hitler's starvation policy. Finland advanced to within twenty miles of Leningrad's outskirts, cutting the city's northern supply routes, but its troops then halted at its 1939 border, and did not undertake further military action. William Moskoff, in *The Bread of Affliction: The Food Supply in the USSR during World War Two*, is one of the few Western historians to draw attention to Anastas Mikoyan's sensational disclosure – made in 1977 – that Voroshilov and Zhdanov prevented trainloads of grain and other vital foodstuffs reaching the city. I am grateful to Mikoyan's son Stephan, who discussed his father's comments with me, and stressed their importance. Red Army war diaries are from Stanislav Bernev and Sergei Chernov (eds), *Blockade Diaries and Documents: NKVD Records, Diaries and Personal Documents from the Early Days of the Blockade*.

Chapter 3: The Butcher's Hook

This chapter introduces three of the most powerful diaries (Knyazev, Ryabinkin and Okhapkina) from Ales Adamovich and Daniil Granin's groundbreaking *A Book of the Blockade* – Georgi Knyazev and Lidiya Okhapkina survived the siege, but Yuri Ryabinkin almost certainly died of starvation in January 1942 – the published accounts of Vera Inber, Elena Skrjabina and Elena Kochina, and Lidiya Ginzburg's *Blockade Diary*. The 'official' account of the evacuation in Dmitry Pavlov's *Leningrad 1941: The Blockade* can be compared with eyewitness testimony from the survivors of the Lychkovo train massacre. The recollections of the adults – Mostovskaya and Arsenyeva – are from *A Book of the Blockade*. Those of the children (Maslov, Malakova, Parakova, Kirilova, Simoneva, Fedulov and Lazarova) are from interviews with me. On 18 August 1941 Fedulov – the oldest – was nine; Simoneva – the youngest – three years old. The full details of the massacre have only recently come to light. For broader context, see Lynn H. Nicholas, *Cruel World: The Children of Europe in the Nazi Web*. Background information for the chapter is drawn from Leon Goure, *The Siege of Leningrad*, and Harrison Salisbury, *The 900 Days*. The material from Joseph Finkelstein's 'The Great Battle Has Begun' can be found on Artem Drabkin's 'I Remember' collection.

Chapter 4: The Noose

A reappraisal of Zhukov's style of command is long overdue. St Petersburg historian Lev Lurye commented: 'Zhukov's plans continued to assume that the Germans would make an all-out assault on Leningrad, even when abundant evidence existed to the contrary. Soviet troops were dispersed all around the city – with tragic results. In January 1943 a successful breakthrough was achieved only because our forces were properly concentrated in one place.' The clear intelligence that from 18 September 1941 the Germans were digging in for a siege is set out in John Erickson, *The Road to Stalingrad*. For the botched evacuation of the Baltic Fleet, Admiral Nikolai Kuznetsov's *Memoirs of a Wartime Minister of the Navy* can now be supplemented by Arvo Vercamer's 'The Naval War in the Baltic, 1941–44', available from Jason Pipes' excellent Feldgrau website. Zhukov's reorganisation of the artillery defences is set out in a useful article on 'Heavy Artillery at Leningrad' on the Jagdmoroner Abteilung website. I am grateful to Marine Brigade commander Nikolai Vavin for details of Zhukov's attempts to reinforce Oreshek. The comments of veteran Nikolai Vasipov have kindly been provided by Phil Curme. Vladimir Zandt's pictures are on display in the Blockade Museum. German responses are from Wilhelm Lubbeck, *At Leningrad's Gates*, and material exhibited in the St Petersburg Museum of Artillery. All Wehrmacht documents are from Muehlenkamp, 'Siege of Leningrad'. For the bulk of the testimony in this chapter I am indebted to the Museum of the Nevsky Bridgehead in St Petersburg, and its associated veterans' association. Many of their accounts have been collected in Arkady Bely, *Life at War*. The musical performance is described in Zoya Gabrielyants (ed.), *The Musical Comedy Theatre during the Siege Years*. The diary extracts from Putyakov and Kuznetsov are in *Blockade Diaries and Documents: NKVD Records*; Finkelstein's are from 'The Great Battle Has Begun'. The story of Frolov and Ivanov is from an article by Sergei Glazerov, 'Why Breaking the Leningrad Blockade in November 1941 Failed', *Pravda* (1 March 2006). The conversation between Stalin and Zhdanov is from Simon Sebag Montefiore, *Stalin: The Court of the Red Tsar*. In July 1957 the Military Tribunal of the Supreme Soviet reviewed the case, and annulled the sentence passed by the Leningrad Front on 2 December 1941. Although Frolov and Ivanov were rehabilitated, the information was kept secret and the archives have only recently been declassified.

Chapter 5: Elena's Sketchbook

The shape of this chapter is informed by a series of interviews with Elena Martilla, who gave me unlimited access to her remarkable collection of siege sketches. Further information is from her catalogue *Leningrad Artist Elena Martilla* (St Petersburg, 2005) and from extracts printed in Cynthia Simmons and Nina Perlina, *Writing the Siege of Leningrad*. Olga Makarova's letter is from the St Petersburg Blockade Museum archive. Svetlana Magaeva has told me of her meeting with Ukhtomsky; it is also briefly described in her *Surviving the Blockade of Leningrad*. Lyapin's account is in Adamovich and Granin, *A Book of the Blockade*. For camouflaging the city, details are from Nikolai Baranov, *Silhouettes of the Siege: Notes of the City's Chief Architect*, and my interview with Mikhail Boborov. The material on Radio Leningrad is from Lazar Magrachev, *A Report from the Siege*. The accounts of Dima Buchkin, Valeri Sukhov and Valia Chapko are exhibited in the Blockade Museum; Vera Kostrovitskaya's is from Simmons and Perlina, *Writing the Siege of Leningrad*. Extracts from Lev Pevzner's 'Recollections of Life in Leningrad during the Siege' can be found on www.crees.ku.edu/documents. The 7 November demonstration is discussed by Richard Bidlack in two important articles: 'Survival Strategies in Leningrad during the First Year of the Soviet–German War', in Robert Thurston and Bernd Bronwetsch (eds), *The People's War: Responses to World War Two in the Soviet Union*, and 'The Political Mood in Leningrad during the First Year of the Soviet–German War', *Russian Review*, 59 (2000). The NKVD material has been published by Nikita Lomagin in *The Unknown Blockade*.

Chapter 6: The Abortionist

'A. N. Reichardt (1891–1942) – An Appreciation', by O. L. Kryzhanovsky, in *Beetles and Coleopterologists: Our Predecessors* on the St Petersburg Zoological Institute website www.zu.ru/coleoptera. The accounts of Zoya Taratynova, Andrei Krukov, Valentina Grekova, Anatoly Molchanov, Tamara Grebennikova and Nadia Minina are from interviews with me. The section on the Musical Comedy Theatre is from Gabrielyants (ed.), *The Musical Comedy Theatre during the Siege Years*. Yuri Bodunov's letter is from the Blockade Museum archive. Caroline Walton kindly found and translated sections of Alexander Boldyrev's diary. Siege veterans generously drew my attention to Igor Chaiko's diary, which is found in Viktor Frolov (ed.), *Works of the State Museum of History*, and to *By the Light of Half a Candle: The Diary of Nikolai Gorshkov*. Evgeny Moniushko's comments are in *From Leningrad to Hungary: Notes of a Red Army Soldier*. Vasily Yershov's recollections are discussed in Richard Bidlack's 'Survival Strategies in Leningrad'. All NKVD reports are from Nikita Lomagin, *The Unknown Blockade*. The experiences of Tatyana Antonovna and the terrible story of midwife Faina Viktorovna are found in Marina Loskutova (ed.), *The Memory of the Blockade: Original Research Compiled by the Centre for Oral History at the European University of St Petersburg*.

Chapter 7: One Black Beret

Dmitry Likhachev's frank account of the siege is from his memoir, *Reflections on the Russian Soul*. Vasily Vladimirov's diary is in the Blockade Museum archive. Material on the dwindling productivity of Leningrad's factories is from Jörg Ganzenmüller, *Besieged Leningrad*. Complaints about the regime hoarding food are found in the two articles of Richard Bidlack, already cited, and Nikita Lomagin, *The Unknown Blockade*. The testimonies of Alexandra Ivanovna, Tamara Zaitseva, Tamara Grebennikova, Nina Pechanova and Vera Rogova are from interviews with me. Sofia Buriakova's experience is in Simmons and Perlina, *Writing the Siege of Leningrad*. Alexander Dymov's dialogue with his stomach is from Adamovich and Granin's *A Book of the Blockade*. Maria Ivanovna's encounter with cannibalism was only included in the book's 2003 edition. Elena Taranukhina's experience is provided courtesy of the BBC's 'Witnessing War' archive. The extract from Mikhail Nosyrev's diary can be found on the composer's website: www.nosyrev.com. Anna Nikitina's testimony is from *The Memory of the Blockade*.

Chapter 8: The Road of Life

This chapter has benefited from the considerable help of Svetlana Magaeva, who discussed all the cases with me. Background information is found in her *Surviving the Blockade of Leningrad* and 'Physiological and Psychosomatic Prerequisites for Survival and Recovery', in John Barber and Andrei Dzeniskevich (eds), *Life and Death in Besieged Leningrad, 1941–44*. Elena

Martilla has shared the story of her remarkable self-portrait, and generously given me permission to use the picture. Additional detail is in Simmons and Perlina, *Writing the Siege of Leningrad*, and the catalogue *Leningrad Artist Elena Martilla*. The accounts of Vera Rogova, Ivan Krylov, Alexandra Ivanova and Anatoly Molchanov are from interviews with me. The NKVD reports are in Nikita Lomagin, *The Unknown Blockade*; Army Group North situation briefings from Roberto Muehlenkamp, 'The Siege of Leningrad in German Documents'. Pavel Luknitsky's account is in Harrison Salisbury's *The 900 Days*. The testimonies of Olga Melnikova, Evgeny Lyapin and Faina Prusova are from Adamovich and Granin, *A Book of the Blockade*; Anna Ostroumova's account is in Simmons and Perlina, *Writing the Siege of Leningrad*.

Chapter 9: The Symphony

My understanding of the performance of Shostakovich's Seventh Symphony has been greatly assisted by musicologist Professor Andrei Krukov, Olga Prut, director of the Museum 'The Muses Were Not Silent', and BBC Radio 3 presenter Stephen Johnson. All have generously given me material on Eliasberg and the Radio Committee Orchestra. Barbara Forrai of the Shostakovich Society and Caroline Walton have shared with me their memories of oboist Ksenia Mattus: Mattus' own recollections are in Simmons and Perlina, *Writing the Siege of Leningrad*. There is also an excellent article on the concert by Ed Vulliamy, 'Orchestral Manoeuvres in the Dark', *Observer* (25 November 2001). The accounts of Elena Martilla, Valentina Grekova, Vera Rogova, Alexandra Ivanova, Tamara Korelkevich and Galina Yershova are from interviews with me. Cory Doctorow has kindly shared the recollections of his grandmother, Valentina Rothmann. Svetlana Magaeva told me about Allochka Ivanova; a brief description is also found in her *Surviving the Blockade of Leningrad*. Nadia Makarova's letter and Vasily Vladimirov's diary are from the Blockade Museum's archive. The testimony of Lidiya Okhapkina, Sergei Milyaev, Vera Pavlova and Galina Babinskaya is from Adamovich and Granin, *A Book of the Blockade*; that of Anna Ostromouva, Sofia Buriakova, Vera Kostrovitskaya, Evgenia Shavrova and Anna Likhacheva from Simmons and Perlina, *Writing the Siege of Leningrad*. The extracts from Nina Zakharyina's diary are found in Lazar Magrachev's *A Report from the Siege*. Galina Vishnevskaya's account is from her autobiography, *A Russian Story*; Ivan Yakushin's from his *On the Roads of War*. Alexander Sokolov's experiences on the Nevsky bridgehead were relayed to me by his daughter, Tatyana Favorskaja. Material on Faina Borovskaya and the Leningrad Public Library was kindly made available by Barbara Forrai, who interviewed her; additional information is found in Simmons and Perlina, *Writing the Siege of Leningrad*. Veronika Nikandorova's journey across the minefield is from *The Memory of the Blockade*.

Chapter 10: Operation Spark

The encounter with Bychevsky is from Harrison Salisbury, *The 900 Days*. Govorov's essential humanity, emphasised by Mikhail Neishtadt in his interview 'Stalin is on the Line', is also recalled in A. Petrov, 'The Improvement of Leningrad's Defences during the Blockade', *Red Army Studies* (1984). Background material on Govorov is from St Petersburg's Blockade and Artillery Museums. Details on the air attack of 5 April are from Werner Haupt, *Army Group North*, and Nikolai Kislitsyn and Vasily Zubakov, *Leningrad Does Not Surrender*. Additional information on Manstein's offensive is from his memoir, *Lost Victories*, and Gottlob Bidermann, *In Deadly Combat*. Vera Inber intuitively sensed the crisis point at Stalingrad in mid-October 1942. Just how desperate that crisis really was is revealed in my book *Stalingrad: How the Red Army Triumphed*. Govorov's decoy system is from the Artillery Museum. For *The Wide, Wide Sea*: Igor Kaberov, *Swastika in the Gunsight*. Operation Spark is largely based on Kislitsyn and Zubakov, *Leningrad Does Not Surrender*, and the testimony of Nikolai Vasipov, kindly provided by Phil Curme. For Simonyak's exchange with Zhukov see Glantz, *Siege of Leningrad*. The request for ginger biscuits is from Vera Inber's *Leningrad Diary*. The Izhorsky Tractor Plant at Kolpino, viewed by Manstein on 27 August 1942, was situated on the River Izhora, a tributary of the Neva. It had been converted to tank production at the beginning of the war and in September 1941, with the German front line only a mile away, it was bravely defended by the 72nd Workers' Battalion – which mostly consisted of men recruited from the factory. There was no shipbuilding at Pulkovo – Manstein was glimpsing Leningrad's Marti shipyards, in the southern part of the city.

Chapter 11: Something Necessary

Material from Ivan Krylov is from his interview with me; Igor Kaberov's from *Swastika in the Gunsight*. Berggolts' account of her trip to Moscow is from Lisa Kirschenbaum, *The Legacy of the Siege of Leningrad*. Stalin's desire to suppress the truth of what happened at Leningrad is shown in Catherine Merridale, *Ivan's War*, and Dmitry Volkogonov, *Stalin*. Bityugova's stories are in Vera Inber's *Leningrad Diary*. The extracts from Evgenia Shavrova's diary are in Simmons and Perlina, *Writing the Siege of Leningrad*. Zhdanov's duel with 'The Rebel' is from Nikita Lomagin, *The Unknown Blockade*. Jenö Varga's notes on his wartime trip to Leningrad were published after his death by Gerhard Duda, *Economics and Politics in Moscow, 1921–1970*. The quotation from *Leningrad Pravda* is in Goure, *The Siege of Leningrad*. Elena Kozhina's deeply moving description is from her memoir, *Through the Burning Steppe*.

Epilogue

The Epilogue is based on my interviews with Andrei Krukov and Elena Martilla. Dmitry Likhachev's estimate of the number of deaths during the siege is from his memoir *Reflections on the Russian Soul*. Alexander Sokolov's letter was read to me by his daughter, Tatyana Favorskaja; for Olga Budnikova's testimony and information on the 1991 excavation I am grateful to the Museum of the Nevsky Bridgehead.

Bibliography

Russian and German titles have been given in their translated, English form. All individual articles are cited in the Notes.

Ales Adamovich and Daniil Granin, *A Book of the Blockade* (Moscow, 1983)

Nikolai Baranov, *Silhouettes of the Siege: Notes of the City's Chief Architect* (Leningrad, 1982)

John Barber and Andrei Dzeniskevich (eds), *Life and Death in Besieged Leningrad, 1941–44* (London, 2005)

Omer Bartov, *The Eastern Front, 1941–45: German Troops and the Barbarisation of Warfare* (Basingstoke, 2001)

Nikolai Baryshnikov, *Finland and the Leningrad Blockade, 1941–44* (Helsinki, 2003)

Arkady Bely, *Life at War* (St Petersburg, 2005)

Sergo Beria, *Beria: Inside Stalin's Kremlin* (London, 2001)

Stanislav Bernev and Sergei Chernov (eds), *Blockade Diaries and Documents: NKVD Records, Diaries and Personal Documents from the Early Days of the Blockade* (St Petersburg, 2004)

Gottlob Bidermann, *In Deadly Combat: A German Soldier's Memoir of the Eastern Front* (Laurence, 2000)

Rupert Butler, *Hitler's Death's Head Division* (Barnsley, 2004)

Paul Carell, *Hitler's War on Russia* (London, 1964)

Otto Preston Chaney, *Zhukov* (New York, 1974)

Alexander O. Chubaryan and Harold Shukman (eds), *Stalin and the Soviet–Finnish War, 1939–40* (London, 2002)

Felix Chuev and Albert Resis, *Molotov Remembers: Inside Kremlin Politics* (Chicago, 1993)

Alan Clark, *Barbarossa: The Russian German Conflict, 1941–1945* (London, 1965)

Gerhard Duda, *Economics and Politics in Moscow, 1921–1970* (Berlin, 1994)

Yuri Dyakov and Tatyana Bushuyeva, *The Red Army and the Wehrmacht* (New York, 1995)

Carl van Dyke, *The Soviet Invasion of Finland, 1939–40* (London, 1997)

John Erickson, *The Road to Stalingrad* (London, 1975)

Ljubica and Mark Erickson (eds), *Russia: War, Peace and Diplomacy: Essays in Honour of John Erickson* (London, 2004)

Viktor Frolov (ed.), *Works of the State Museum of History* (St Petersburg, 2002)

Zoya Gabrielyants (ed.), *The Musical Comedy Theatre during the Siege Years* (Leningrad, 1973)

Jörg Ganzenmüller, *Besieged Leningrad, 1941–1944* (Paderborn, 2005)

Veronique Garros and Natalia Korenevskaya (eds), *Intimacy and Terror: Soviet Diaries of the 1930s* (New York, 1996)

Arthur and Elena George, *St Petersburg: The First Three Centuries* (Stroud, 2004)

Lidiya Ginzburg, *Blockade Diary* (London, 1995)

David M. Glantz, *The Siege of Leningrad, 1941–1944: 900 Days of Terror* (London, 2001)

Nikolai Gorshkov, *By the Light of Half a Candle* (St Petersburg, 1993)

Leon Goure, *The Siege of Leningrad* (London, 1962)

Werner Haupt, *Army Group North: The Wehrmacht in Russia, 1941–1945* (Atglen, PA, 1997)

Vera Inber, *Leningrad Diary* (London, 1971)

Michael Jones, *Stalingrad: How the Red Army Triumphed* (Barnsley, 2007)

Igor Kaberov, *Swastika in the Gunsight: Memoirs of a Russian Fighter Pilot* (Stroud, 1999)

Robert Kershaw, *War without Garlands: Operation Barbarossa 1941–42* (Shepperton, 2000)

Nikita Khrushchev, *Khrushchev Remembers* (London, 1971)

Lisa Kirschenbaum, *The Legacy of the Siege of Leningrad, 1941–1995* (Cambridge, 2006)

Nikolai Kislitsyn and Vasily Zubakov, *Leningrad Does Not Surrender* (Moscow, 1989)

Elena Kochina, *Blockade Diary* (Ann Arbor, 1990)

Elena Kozhina, *Through the Burning Steppe* (New York, 2000)

Nikolai Kuznetsov, *Memoirs of a Wartime Minister of the Navy* (Moscow, 1990)

Dmitry S. Likhachev, *Reflections on the Russian Soul: A Memoir* (Plymouth, 1999)

W. Bruce Lincoln, *Sunlight at Midnight: St Petersburg and the Rise of Modern Russia* (New York, 2000)

Nikita Lomagin, *The Unknown Blockade* (St Petersburg, 2002)

Marina Loskutova (ed.), *The Memory of the Blockade: Original Research Compiled by the Centre for Oral History at the European University of St Petersburg* (Moscow, 2006)

Wilhelm Lubbeck, *At Leningrad's Gates* (Philadelphia, 2006)

Svetlana Magaeva and Albert Pleysier, *Surviving the Blockade of Leningrad* (Oxford, 2006)

Lazar Magrachev, *A Report from the Siege* (Leningrad, 1989)

Erich von Manstein, *Lost Victories* (London, 1958)

Elena Martilla, *Leningrad Artist* (St Petersburg, 2005)

Catherine Merridale, *Ivan's War: The Red Army 1939–45* (London, 2005)

Evgeny Moniushko, *From Leningrad to Hungary: Notes of a Red Army Soldier* (Oxford, 2005)

Simon Sebag Montefiore, *Stalin: The Court of the Red Tsar* (London, 2003)

William Moskoff, *The Bread of Affliction: The Food Supply in the USSR during World War Two* (Cambridge, 1990)

Steven H. Newton, *Retreat from Leningrad: Army Group North, 1944–1945* (Atglen, PA, 1995)

Lynn H. Nicholas, *Cruel World: The Children of Europe in the Nazi Web* (New York, 2005)

Richard Overy, *The Dictators: Hitler's Germany, Stalin's Russia* (London, 2004)

Dmitry Pavlov, *Leningrad 1941: The Blockade* (Chicago, 1965)

Erhard Raus, *Panzer Operations* (Cambridge, MA, 2003)

Harrison E. Salisbury, *The 900 Days: The Siege of Leningrad* (London, 1969)

Lennart Samuelson, *Plans for Stalin's War Machine* (London, 2000)

Harold Shukman (ed.), *Stalin's Generals* (London, 1993)

Cynthia Simmons and Nina Perlina, *Writing the Siege of Leningrad: Women's Diaries, Memoirs and Documentary Prose* (Pittsburgh, 2002)

Elena Skrjabina, *Siege and Survival: the Odyssey of a Leningrader* (New Brunswick, 1997)

Robert Thurston and Bernard Bonwetsch (eds), *The People's War: Responses to World War Two in the Soviet Union* (Chicago, 2000)

Sergei Varshavsky, *The Ordeal of the Hermitage: The Siege of Leningrad 1941–1944* (New York, 1985)

Galina Vishnevskaya, *A Russian Story* (New York, 1984)

Dmitry Volkogonov, *Stalin* (London, 1991)
Solomon Volkov (ed.), *Testimony: The Memoirs of Dmitry Shostakovich* (London, 1979)
Solomon Volkov, *St Petersburg: A Cultural History* (New York, 1995)
Kyra Petrovskaya Wayne, *Shurik* (New York, 2000)
Alexander Werth, *Leningrad* (London, 1944)
Wolfram Wette, *The Wehrmacht: History, Myth, Reality* (Cambridge, MA, 2006)
Ivan Yakushin, *On the Roads of War* (Barnsley, 2005)

Index